...leman 1759. Æt. 16. the Poem in the Author...

d who dwells above,
I & Love
...ristian Race revere,
...gan Nations fear,
...ts on high,
...Purity,
...n where to roll
...eviral a...

...spacious Ball
Of his to this Perfe...
The lofty Mountain
The lowly Shrubs, a...
Sprang forth...
In full ... from
... from
..., that
curious
sma...
form'd
...'d
dea...
left
hak...
the ...

...th of Mr Daniel Treadwell of Portsmouth
...Professor of the Mathematicks at New-York, a
...tleman whose many useful Accomplishments ren-
...s Loss universally lamented — taken from the ~~~~
New-Hampshire Gazette May 9. 1760 —
Written by a ~~young~~ Lady — Mrs Br—t

...pring returns, Nature in Bloom appears,
...ols refulgent Beams the Prospect chears,
...eather'd Choirs their artless Joy express,
...all Creation Nature's God confess
...Tree each Plant in blooming Youth revives,
...with their Verdure charm the ravish'd Eyes.
...thou o Strephon must no more survey,
...radiant Glories of the rising Day;
...d are those Eyes that these gay Prospects charm'd,
...d is that Heart which every Virtue warm'd,
..." Joy those sprightly Scenes beheld
..."...el'd:

O thou whom once my partial heart had...
...erfect as some bright seraph from above;
...nd strove with varied graces to adorn,
...e flattering image it had vow'd to love:
...e now is fled that sentiment and truth

The Lowells of Massachusetts

Also by Nina Sankovitch

Tolstoy and the Purple Chair: My Year of Magical Reading

Signed, Sealed, Delivered: Celebrating the Joys of Letter Writing

THE

LOWELLS

of

MASSACHUSETTS

An American Family

NINA SANKOVITCH

St. Martin's Press ☙ New York

www.stmartins.com

Library of Congress Cataloging-in-Publication Data

Names: Sankovitch, Nina, author.
Title: The Lowells of Massachusetts : an American family / Nina Sankovitch.
Description: New York : St. Martin's Press, 2017.
Identifiers: LCCN 2016046599 | ISBN 9781250069207 (hardcover) | ISBN 9781466878112 (e-book)
Subjects: LCSH: Lowell family. | Massachusetts—Biography. | Massachusetts—Genealogy.
Classification: LCC F63 .S27 2017 | DDC 929.20973—dc23
LC record available at https://lccn.loc.gov/2016046599

Our books may be purchased in bulk for promotional, educational, or business use. Please contact your local bookseller or the Macmillan Corporate and Premium Sales Department at 1-800-221-7945, extension 5442, or by e-mail at MacmillanSpecialMarkets@macmillan.com.

First Edition: April 2017

10 9 8 7 6 5 4 3 2 1

For Jack,
forever and in all situations

Contents

Contents

Part Six: Reinvention

Dramatis Personae:

The Lowell Family

Sixteenth Century–Seventeenth Century

- Percival Lowle (1571-1664) married Rebecca (1575-1645) in 1590s. They had eight children. Three of their children emigrated with them to the Massachusetts Bay Colony in 1639: John Lowle (1595-1647), Richard (1602–1682), and Joan (1609–1677).

  - John Lowle had five children with his wife, Mary, including a son named John Lowle (1629–1694).

    - John Lowle was married three times and had seventeen children. With his third wife, Naomi Sylvester, he had a child named Ebenezer Lowle (1675–1711).

Seventeenth Century–Eighteenth Century

- Ebenezer Lowle married Elizabeth Shailer (1675–1761). They had six children, one of whom was named John Lowle (1704–1767).

  - The Reverend John Lowle changed the spelling of the family name to *Lowell* and married twice, but had children only with his first wife, Sarah Champney: two boys, both of whom were named John Lowell. The first son died in infancy, but the second son, John—"the Old Judge"—(1743–1802) married three times.

Eighteenth Century–Nineteenth Century

- John "the Old Judge" Lowell
  - married Sarah Higginson (1745–1772) in 1767. They had three children: Anna—"Nancy"—Cabot (1768-1810), John "The Rebel" Lowell (1769-1840) and Sarah —"Sally"—Champney (1771-1851).

– married Susanna Cabot (1754–1777) in 1774. They had two children: Francis Cabot Lowell (1775–1817) and Susanna "Susan" (1775–1816).

– married Rebecca Russel Tyng (1747–1816) in 1778. They had four children: Rebecca Lowell (1779–1853), Charles Russell Lowell (1782–1861), Elizabeth Cutts Lowell (1783-1864), and Mary (1786-1789).

⊘ John "The Rebel" Lowell married Rebecca Amory (1771-1842) in 1793. They had five children: Rebecca—"Amory"—Amory (1794–1878), John Amory Lowell (1798-1881), Anna Cabot (1801-1802), Anna Cabot (1808-1894), and Sarah Champney (1810-1816).

⊘ Francis Cabot Lowell married Hannah Jackson (1776–1815) in 1798. They had four children: John Lowell, Jr. (1799–1836), Susan Cabot Lowell (1801-1827), Francis Cabot Lowell II (1803–1874), and Edward Jackson Lowell (1805-1830).

⊘ Rebecca Lowell married Samuel Gardner (1767–1843) in 1797. They had a son named John Lowell Gardner (1804–1884).

⊘ The Reverend Charles Russell Lowell married Harriet Brackett Spence (1783–1850) in 1806. They had six children: Charles ("Charlie") Russell Lowell (1807–1870), Rebecca—"Little Bec or Becca"—Russell Lowell (1809–1872), Mary Traill Spence Lowell (1810–1898), William Keith Spence Lowell (1813–1823), Robert Traill Spence Lowell (1816–1898), and James Russell Lowell (1819-1891).

⊘ Elizabeth Cutts Lowell married Warren Dutton (1774–1857) in 1806. They had two children: John Lowell Dutton (1807-1844) and James Russell Dutton (1810-1861), who later changed his name to James Dutton Russell.

Nineteenth Century–Twentieth Century

John Amory Lowell married Susan Cabot Lowell (1801-1827) in 1822. They had two children: Susan Cabot (1823–1868) and John (1824–1897). After Susan died, John married Elizabeth Cabot Putnam (1807–1881) in 1829. They had four children: Augustus Lowell (1830-1900), Elizabeth Rebecca (1832-1904), Ellen Bancroft (1837-1894), and Sara Putnam (1843-1899).

John Lowell Jr. married Georgina Amory (1806–1830) in 1825. They had two children: Georgina Lowell (1827–1830) and Anna Lowell (1829-1830).

John Lowell Gardner married Catherine Endicott Peabody (1808–1883) in 1826. They had a son: John Lowell Gardner II (1837–1898).

Charles "Charlie" Russell Lowell married Anna Cabot Jackson (1811–1874) in 1832. They had four children: Anna Lowell (1833-1906), Charles Russell Lowell (1835–1864), Harriet Lowell (1836-1920), and James Jackson Lowell (1837–1862).

Mary Traill Spence Lowell married Samuel Raymond Putnam (1797–1861) in 1832. They had four children: Alfred Putnam (1835-1855), Georgina Putnam (1835–1914), William Lowell Putnam (1840-1861) and Charles Lowell Putnam (1845-1847).

James Russell Lowell married Maria White (1821-1853) in 1844. They had four children: Blanche (1845-1847), Mabel Lowell (1847-1898), Rose (1849-1850), and Walter (1850-1852).

James Dutton Russell married Sarah Ellen Hooper (1816–1848) in 1835. They had four children, including Warren Dutton (1840-1862).

Augustus Lowell married Katherine Bigelow Lawrence (1832–1895) in 1854. They had seven children: Percival—"Percy"—Lowell (1855–1916), Abbott Lawrence Lowell (1856–1943), Katherine "Katie" Lowell (1858–1925), Elizabeth—"Bessie"—Lowell (1862-1935) and her twin, Roger Lowell (1862– 1863), May Lowell (May 1, 1870), and Amy Lowell (1874-1925).

Harriet Lowell married George Putnam in 1860. Eldest among their five children was William Lowell Putnam II (1861-1924).

John Lowell Gardner II married Isabella Stewart (1840-1924), founder of the Isabella Stewart Gardner Museum, in 1860.

Mabel Lowell married Edward Burnett (1849-1925) in 1872. They had five children, including James Russell Lowell Burnett (1873-1947), whose name was changed to James Russell Burnett Lowell at the request of his grandfather James Russell Lowell.

↩ Katherine—"Katie"—Lowell married Alfred Roosevelt (1856-1891) in 1882. They had three children: Elfrida (1883-1963), James Alfred (1885-1919), and Katharine (1887-1961). After Alfred died, Katie married Thomas J. Bowlker (1858-1917) in 1902.

↩ Bessie Lowell married William Lowell Putnam II in 1888. They had five children: George (1889-1960), Katharine (1890-1983), Roger (1893-1972), Harriet (1897-1900), and Augustus (1899-1947).

Through the broad Earth roams Opportunity

And knocks at every door of hut or hall

Until she finds the brave soul that she wants.

—JAMES RUSSELL LOWELL, "HAKONS LAY"

. . . that ye, always having all sufficiency in all things,

may abound to every good work . . .

—2 CORINTHIANS 9:8

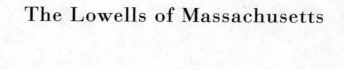

The Lowells of Massachusetts

Prelude
~ Writing a Family's History ~

On this stone, in this urn
I pour my heart, and watch it burn . . .
—AMY LOWELL, "BEFORE THE ALTAR"

In the summer of 1925, Ada Dwyer Russell built a bonfire in the back gardens of the Sevenels estate in Brookline, Massachusetts. Sevenels had been home to the Lowell family for over half a century, but now Amy Lowell was dead, and no one of her family would ever live here again. Amy had instructed Ada before she died: *Burn all my letters*. On this hot and humid summer day, Ada would finally undertake the task. Even from beyond the grave, Amy's will was too strong to ignore. Ada had been Amy's companion for over thirteen years and she would not go against Amy's wishes now.

Their black cat, Winky, came out to the garden with Ada. Winky ran ahead as Ada made her way down a graveled path to the barn. No horses anymore, just the old pony carts in the back, dusty and covered with cobwebs, skeletons of the past. So much had started and ended with a pony cart. In front of the carts, where the horses used to be, Amy's Pierce-Arrow automobile. The wooden slats of the stalls had been removed to make room for the majestic car. George, the chauffeur, who had been around longer than Ada, had taken care of the car as if it were his very own baby, washing it and drying it with the softest of old rags, waxing it in round motions, covering it with flannel, winter and summer, to keep the dust off. The Pierce-Arrow would have to be sold and the proceeds added to the estate. Ada had no need of a car now.

She walked past the barn and around back to where piles of branches were stacked. Apple wood, felled during the winter's hard snows and dry as bone. Ready to burn. Amy had told Ada many times about her father's apple trees, and her grandfather's, and her great-grandfather's. Apple trees and pear trees and peach trees, rising up in row after row. Their branches had grown gnarled and weak over the passing decades. Now they would serve as fuel, their last service to the family. Winky slunk beneath one of the stacks of wood, then shot out again, giving Ada pause. What could be in there? But she called out a warning—*Shoo! Shoo!*—and then leaned over, gathering branches in her arms. Back and forth she went, from the stacks by the barn to the patch of dirt behind the pines. A safe place to build a fire.

Ada returned to the house, pulling a small garden cart behind her. She loaded the cart up with bundles of letters and papers. More fuel for the fire. Back again, and now the fire could be kindled. The sun was high in the sky and hot, but Ada did not hesitate.

Winky grew tired of watching the flames. He began chasing the darting dragonflies that flew in and out of the shadows cast by the pines. But Ada worked on without pause, the sweat drawing on her brow, the heat against her fingers. Bundle after bundle after bundle of letters tossed in. The branches spread wide to contain the smoking ash. A nest of fire. Each new batch of papers hatched shooting flames of red and blue and gold, which died as quickly as they had flared. More branches were added, to deepen the bowl as ash accumulated, layer upon layer. With no breeze and the air heavy and damp, the letters and notes never tried to escape. They sank into their fiery end without a fight, just the flaming up and then the sizzle down.

Ada later wrote to one of Amy's oldest friends, "I wish to tell you . . . that all your letters to her were burned, unread. She wanted me to do that—clear out the drawers of her desk in her own room. . . . I burnt all mine and that was easy in one way, it was only hot . . . and I watched it all . . ."[1]

Flames fed, then tamed down to coals, then ash.

Did Ada ever pause to wonder? The one lingering question: an orange glaze of heat amid the blackened sticks of charred wood.

What remains?

I found the answer to that question when I set myself the task of researching the Lowell family of Massachusetts. A longtime fan of the poetry of Amy Lowell and James Russell Lowell (I've been copying their poems into notebooks since the second grade), I happily discovered that not all the letters and papers of Amy were burned to ashes that day in Brookline. And despite the family practice of burning personal papers, there is a wealth of family documents dating across three centuries in the vast holdings of Houghton Library at Harvard University and in the Harvard University Archives, the oldest institutional academic archive in the country; in the collections of the Massachusetts Historical Society, Boston; and in the Arthur and Elizabeth Schlesinger Library on the History of Women in America, Radcliffe Institute, Harvard University.

The stories of Percival Lowle (the spelling of the family name was changed to Lowell in the early 1720s) and the generations that followed him are contained in hundreds of boxes and folders, on microfiche cards, and in digital reproductions and shelved town records. I couldn't help feeling, as I did my research, that these stories wanted to be heard, that they had been waiting for me and would now make themselves known: deliberate sighs rising up from still-folded letters, stamped legal papers, fading photographs, fraying journals and diaries; insistent grumblings from parchment and vellum declarations, battered school notebooks, worn leather sketchbooks, gray-paged keepsake albums. A microfiche reader whirring to hopeful life spooled out page after page of sermons and speeches and poems; essays and letters unfurled eagerly in front of me, accompanied by announcements of births, marriages, and deaths. But it wasn't just in libraries or archives where the stories of the Lowell family were found. As I made my way along the winding paths of a Cambridge cemetery, gravestones made their plea for remembrance. On some, the chiseled names and dates were still sharp; on others, the incisions had dulled to shallow marks that I could barely decipher.

The history of the Lowell family came to life in all the stories I found. Testimony taken in 1652 in a court case in Newbury, Massachusetts, mentions a ship: the *Jonathan,* which sailed from England and landed in Boston in 1639. Percival Lowle, age sixty-eight at the time, was on that ship, along with his wife and children and business partners. Town records from Newbury, Massachusetts, yielded other insights: Percival Lowle bought into the town, purchasing land—"a house lot of at least four acres, with a suitable quantity of salt and fresh meadow"[2]—and was welcomed into the community. He joined the Newbury congregation, for in seventeenth-century New England, community and congregation were one. To be welcomed to one was to be welcomed to the other; duty owed to one was duty owed to the other. And the duty of each member of the congregation was to work hard—to exercise one's own personal gifts—for the good of the community and for the approval of God.

Percival, his children, and each succeeding generation of Lowells would incorporate that duty into the very fabric of who they were. The obligation to work hard, using individual abilities for community benefit, became integral to their definition of self and of family. And in working hard, the family fortunes rose. The Lowells aspired to work harder and achieve more. In the mid-eighteenth century, the Reverend John Lowell coined the Lowell Family motto, *Occasionem Cognosce,* a simple phrase that combined the family's twin values of ambition and duty. Seize the Opportunity. Do well, and make good.

To follow one line of the Lowell family tree, from Percival Lowle in the seventeenth century all the way through to the next-named Percival in the twentieth is to understand how individual ambition and community obligation, combined with ample opportunities seized, created a stunning legacy of productivity and creativity. From this one line of Lowells came ministers, lawyers, and manufacturers; poets and activists; a judge, an astronomer, a college president; Federalists, Unionists, and abolitionists; an anti-suffragist who became the first female delegate to an electoral college; a loyalist turned revolutionary; a horticulturalist grown from a lawyer.

One of the most famous of the Lowell descendants is Robert Lowell, winner of the National Book Award in 1960 and of the Pulitzer Prize for Poetry in 1947 and in 1974. Many books have been written about Robert Lowell while those family members who went before him have become largely unknown, their stories hidden away and forgotten even as the history they made remains relevant and vital to the American experience. It is time now for the stories of the Lowell forebears to come out of the shadows. In following their individual dreams and utilizing their individual strengths with all the might and determination they could summon, these Lowell men and women made history.

Part One

MIGRATION

And every grain I scatter free,

An hundred-fold shall yield,

Till waveth like a golden sea,

This dark and barren field.

—MARIA WHITE LOWELL,
"THE MAIDEN'S HARVEST"

1

1638–1639

We venture goods, and lives, ye know, and travel seas and land
To bring by traffic heaps of wealth and treasure to your land.
—POEM COMPOSED IN HONOR OF
QUEEN ELIZABETH'S 1574 VISIT TO BRISTOL, ENGLAND

Percival Lowle walked down to the docks on a cool day in late November. The sky overhead was blue, the light of the sun bright and warm. But to the west, heavy gray clouds were collecting over the horizon. Percival quickened his pace. He had business to attend to. He dodged among the crowds of dockworkers, sailors, merchants, and tradesmen, intent on his goal. He walked past vessels from faraway places, rocking against their lines like animals tethered before a fight. Every form and type of rigging, flag, and frame was on display; boats from all over the world. Languages as unintelligible as the cries of birds batted among the foreign crews, mingling with the reassuring authority of the King's English and the rich, crude dialects of the dockworkers. Above the cacophony of voices: the squawks of gulls, the clanking of lines, the chiming of Bristol's famous bells at midday.

Percival stopped for a moment and drew in a deep breath, taking in with pleasure all the odors that wafted about him, the smells from bales and hogsheads and packets, from barrels and boxes and billets. It was the heady perfume of the world he knew. He wished he could bottle it up, to hold on to always. Change was coming, and although he was an adapter, had always done what was necessary to keep his family secure, this change would wrench them from all that they knew. It was one thing to move from the small village of Portbury in Somersetshire to Bristol, which he had done with Rebecca when they were still young. But the choice facing him now would take them much farther away.

Everything Percival knew about the geography of the world, he had learned on the docks of Bristol. The ships and their cargoes read like a map. Portugal, with its sweet wine; Toledo and steel; Italy and olive oil; France and figs. He surveyed the map of his England through the goods carried in and sent on: woolen cloths from Leeds, grain from Norfolk, glassware from London, cheese from Cheshire, butter from Wales, soap and clay pipes from Bristol.

Today, Percival was in search of woad from East Anglia, the dried paste of its leaves rolled into hard balls and packed into boxes. Nothing dyed wool better than the woad, the blue as rich and deep as the ocean on a sunny day. Woad once had been such a valuable commodity that farmers plowed under their fields of grains to grow more and more of it. The queen herself had stepped in to avert a famine: England needs food, Elizabeth had ordered, and she'd set restrictions on where woad could be grown and how it could be processed. Turning the dried leaves into paste was a smelly affair—potash and urine the key ingredients—and the queen had prohibited its manufacture within range of her own residences.

Percival knew that woad paste had been used by the ancient Britons of the north to color their bodies before battle—Romans called the warriors "Picts," meaning "painted"—but now a mill in Coventry wanted the woad to dye their wool. A chuckle from the old merchant as he found the ship he searched for. Yes, woad was still used today, but for covering bodies in comfort, not in battle. And now he would do battle to get a good price, and sell it on for a profit. This is what Percival did, and he was good at it: finding something someone wanted, procuring it through a wrangling of proposals and counterproposals, selling it on. Profiting from need but also satisfying that need. A promise made and a delivery on that promise.

For centuries, Bristol had thrived on the promises of its port. Percival Lowle was up to his elbows in all of it and had been for the past forty years. Two of Percival's sons, John and Richard, had joined him at Percival Lowle & Co., Importers and Exporters. William Gerrish was another partner, a man who would one day be a son-in-law—but not just yet. Percival employed a clerk, Anthony Somerby. His son John had taken on an apprentice, Richard Dole. All good men, all engaged in the business of trade and in the prosperity of the port of Bristol.

Percival Lowle was not only a merchant but also a certified gentleman. The Lowle family's coat of arms had been royally registered by his father, Richard Lowle, with a claim connecting the Lowles of Somerset to the Louel on the battle rolls of William the Conqueror. Richard Lowle had paid a fee to the College of Heralds in 1591 to ensure his claim, and he received his coat of arms, few questions asked. The coffers of Elizabeth needed filling and the Lowles wanted to be gentlemen (the Latin word for a gentleman in the 1500s was *armigero*—that is, one who bears arms). The Lowle coat of arms featured a dark shield upon which a clenched fist held three blunt arrows pointing downward, one vertical and two crossed diagonally. The head of a stag floated above the shield, an arrowhead in blue between its antlers.

The sale of the family arms had been good business for the queen; for the Lowles, it was a calculable cost of doing business, like a tax or a duty. But now the calculations were getting more difficult. Under King James and then King Charles, the royal coffers were bottomless and in constant need of filling. There were always more taxes to be paid, more duties to be figured out, and new costs of doing business.

Percival concluded his transaction for woad. Delivery was secured through an exchange of papers, a shaking of hands. Then a mutual shaking of heads as the men discussed future prospects: Hard times were coming for everyone. Harvests had failed all over England. Last winter had been brutal and long, the spring wet and short, the summer a mix of drought and drenching rains. Crops couldn't grow and there was not enough wheat for all the bread needed by the people of England, nor barley or rye, not enough onions nor peas or beans; even the sheep out on the rough had trouble finding grass enough to feed upon.

Percival asked the trader if he had paid up the latest royal commission, the fifth one demanded this year. Of course he had paid, as Percival had paid the commissions demanded of him, and the duties and the taxes. What could be done about it? The royal agents seized goods if money wasn't paid, and there was little protection from a Parliament that was dissolved by the king with regularity. The last time Parliament had met was in 1629, almost ten years ago now. King Charles, loyal advisers at his side, ruled alone.

Percival took his time walking back up from the docks into the center of Bristol. He looked around as he strolled, taking in the sight of a town he had grown to know so well. Its churches and its taverns, its shops and marketplace squares. Bristol had been good to him. Here he had found prosperity. Prestige. Children had been born to him, and more children, and grandchildren. A steady routine of church on Sunday and work every other day. Percival turned and looked back over the water. The storm to the west was holding off. He continued his walk, past the narrow streets of small shops and miserable hovels— barely a window to a room, dirt floors, little air—and then on up to the rows of finer homes on the ridge. Up to his own house, plastered and timbered, tall and stately, with glazed windows and a finely carved heavy wooden door. A house both solid and secure.

Percival arrived winded, a sheen of perspiration across his brow despite the cool temperatures of the day. Rebecca, his wife of forty years, greeted him in the front hall, took his long cloak, and then draped over his shoulders a robe lined in fur. The hall was cold; she didn't want him to catch a chill. She took his arm and drew him into the parlor, where a fire had been lit. It was warm in there and she would bring him a pot of ale. She knew Percival was worried about the decision he faced for their family. But it might be time for change. Before they lost everything. Percival settled himself back into a deep chair lined with embroidered cushions and draped with a heavy Venetian rug. Tapestries hung on two walls, a hunting scene depicted on one and a mythological fantasy on the other. Books were piled up on the ornate table beside him, the books embossed and the table inlaid with bone and mother-of-pearl. The logs on the fire roasted away atop a handsome pair of andirons fashioned to look like hunting dogs, their iron heads resting on iron paws. Tonight he would eat a good dinner prepared by a cook, cleared by a housemaid. Perhaps they'd dine on fish, always plentiful in the port town, or maybe a bit of meat, freshly slaughtered sheep brought in for winter from the summer grazing. There would be cheese and apples at the end of the meal, and wine to drink throughout.

His sons would likely fancy a game of cards after dinner. Gleek, primero, maw, cent, and new cut. The names of the card games sounded like drugs, and for many, the playing of cards was an addiction. Queen Elizabeth herself had been known to bet heavily on spades and deuces. But the Lowle family stayed clear of gaming debts, preferring to play for fun, not money. Richard would bring out a bottle of Madeira; John might sit down to read, his father having given him the gift just days ago of the recently republished Chaucer's *Canterbury Tales*. Rebecca would sit beside him, and his daughter Joan, too, talking gossip and discussing news from town.

Just yesterday, Joan had seen a neighbor woman taken to the cuck stool and dunked in the river Frome. The ancient practice of scold cucking had been moribund for years, until the town governors revived it in 1621. The cuck stool was a commode or chamber pot—*cukken* meant "defecation"—attached to a large lever. The lever moved the stool out over the river and then dipped it into the water. Women who had been found by the local magistrate to be too strident or rude were ordered to take their place on the stool. One by one, they were whirled out over the water and repeatedly dunked, to the great amusement of the watching crowd.

But Joan did not laugh at what she saw. Public humiliation was no way to lead a woman to goodness. Only a sense of purpose and duty could do that. And in England today, duty and purpose were becoming lost. A renewal was necessary, but where to find it? The Puritans sought renewal in cleansing the Church of ritual; the king sought renewal in strengthening his Archbishop Laud to punish the heretics; the royal agents only sought money and more money. Joan was soon to be married and was eager to start a new life, away from the tensions of religious factions and economic uncertainties.

Percival sat before the fire and dozed. He wasn't sleeping well at night these days, despite the upstairs bed lined with heavy linens and thick rugs to keep him warm, and the sachets of lavender that Rebecca tucked below the ticking to induce sleep. When Guy Fawkes had tried to blow up Parliament in 1605, striking a blow for Catholics, many of Percival's neighbors had sought to protect themselves from Catholic evils by carving demon tracks into the floorboards of their bedrooms. But Percival was never one for either superstition or overreaction, and he had kept his floors unmarked. Only if his beloved Rebecca had pleaded for it might he have acquiesced. She took care of him, and he took care of her. She was no more superstitious than he was, and just as practical. A fine floor was for polishing, not for carving up.

Now in his seventh decade, Percival had survived so much, and Rebecca had been beside him for most of it. When the plague came through Bristol, as it often did, working its way briskly through the crowded lanes and hovels, dispensing death like daily bread, both he and his wife had been spared, and their family, too. Percival hadn't been bothered by the extra taxes collected then, for he understood that money was needed to cover the costs of housing plague victims and removing and burying the dead. He'd paid up and counted himself lucky.

He'd avoided consumption, which was a death sentence, and smallpox, and the other pox, the French one, called syphilis, untreatable and debilitating. He'd survived epidemics of typhus and measles; he'd endured bad colds and nasty infections. Percival and his Rebecca were living longer than most, royals included.

But not all his family had been so lucky. Percival and Rebecca had lost two children, Edward at age four and Gerard, only one year old. Both boys were buried in the churchyard of St. Mary's in Portbury, in the countryside. Before they'd been put in the ground, Rebecca had taken snippets of their hair. She'd carried these locks with her when they moved to Bristol. Percival bought her a box for the mementos, from a Spanish sailor; a tiny box, damascened wood inlaid with an intricate design of crosses. The sailor was a Catholic, but no one needed to know that. Rebecca hid the box with its treasure in a trunk of birthing blankets. Blankets used when her babies had been born and now used to protect what remained of them.

Merchants had always paid royal taxes, tolls, and tariffs, back through centuries of commerce. Under Queen Elizabeth, Percival and all the traders along the English coastlines had wrangled their way through a labyrinth of duties and rules that not only set how much it cost to bring and take things in and out of England but from where and to where things could be brought and taken. Monopolies were granted by royal charter but then could just as easily be taken away again; arbitrary limits were set on who could manufacture and trade what and where. Taxes and commissions and fees multiplied upon themselves like fleas. As monopolies changed and taxes rose, corruption—the paying of bribes and granting of accommodations, currying favor and then gaining it through gifts, privileges, and subservience—became an even more necessary cost of doing business.

Under James I, who came to the throne in 1603 after Elizabeth died, the burden of taxation had grown even heavier. Corruption evolved to new heights of ingenuity. Paying off the right sheriff or royal officer or even the king himself could release a merchant from a tax or duty, or even an employment obligation—it seemed as if everyone and everything had a price, and the prices were rising.

When James was first crowned, the town leaders of Bristol came up with a plan. They would take up a collection from the local merchants and use the moneys to purchase presents for the new king and his family. The idea was to create an early favoritism toward Bristol on the part of James I, to secure the so-called royal treatment for the ambitious port.[1]

The plan failed. James took the proffered gifts but did nothing to relieve the increasing burden of taxes, duties, and rents. He even revived the ancient—and long-defunct—custom of purveyance. Purveyance was based on the assumption that all towns should be happy and willing to host their king and queen at any time. The royal court could expect to be fed, lodged, and supplied with drink wherever they might travel throughout England. All costs of such hospitality would be covered by the local merchants—and those who refused to comply would have their entire stores of goods seized, and perhaps even face imprisonment.

The aldermen of Bristol sent a party to Parliament to protest the purveyances. Not only was its practice unfair, they argued, but it was clearly illegal as well, given that Parliament had never approved the imposition of purveyance. James gave the members of Parliament no chance to respond; he shut chambers down. Parliament was dissolved. Then he sent a crew of royal purveyors directly to Bristol. Barrel after barrel of claret and sack were seized and carried back to the king. When the queen visited Bath months later, the merchants of Bristol did not hesitate to supply what she needed; "6 tuns, 5 butts, 3 pipes and 50 hogsheads of wine," along with sugar, spices, pepper, and an assortment of groceries, were delivered without delay.[2]

Under James's rule, Bristol was denied any commerce with either Turkey or the Levant, countries that had always been good trading partners, and the right to make certain products was taken away. The starch factories, long prosperous in Bristol, were shuttered; the workers were dispersed and the fortunes of the owners were destroyed. Anticipating where trade might be allowed, or which products might be made and sold, became a guessing game. The only way to have some advantage in the game was to offer absurd bribes and elaborate gifts, and hope for the best.

Managing a business did not improve under King Charles, who ascended to the throne when James died in 1625. Like James, Charles dissolved Parliament when it came too close to curtailing his activities. Charles continued the practice of ever-increasing taxes, customs, duties, and rents to pay for the royal lifestyle, and he initiated a new tax, the payment of "ship money." These were funds collected for the support of the Royal Navy, purportedly to defend the Church and England against the threats of Catholicism and Spain. But was there a need for such defense, Percival wondered, when the new king was himself married to a Catholic and the Spanish threat had diminished?

Percival and his sons, his clerk Anthony, his partner William—every day they went over the accounts, tried to juggle the figures, to work out a way to keep the business going. And now the bad harvest. Percival had heard the rumors all summer—a good trader always stays abreast of the whispers from field and factory, from incoming sailors and outgoing captains—and the fall had proved the rumors true. There wouldn't be enough food to trade, and getting enough to eat would cost plenty. What crops were gathered would be requisitioned, most likely, by the ever more greedy king, his Catholic wife, and his grasping archbishop of Canterbury, William Laud, a menace to rational men and the scourge of the Puritans, who had hoped for so much, for so long. It was no wonder Puritans were leaving in droves.

Bristol had long been involved in the exploration of the New World, dating back to 1497, when Sebastian Cabot, working under contract to King Henry VII of France, sailed from Bristol to explore the coast of Newfoundland. In the years of the 1600s, Percival Lowle had witnessed the outfitting of ship after ship for the purpose of traveling to America. He might even have been one of the investors joining in to send local boy Martin Pring off on a journey of discovery in the year 1603. Pring was twenty-three years old when he set out for the Americas, but as confident and brash a sea captain as ever sailed. He went with one purpose: to locate and load up abundant supplies of sassafras, "a plant of soveriegne vertue for the French Poxe."[3] Syphilis was a problem, sassafras was a known cure (or palliative), and the man who could supply the cure could be sure of good fortune.

Leading a fleet of two small ships, the *Speedwell* and the *Explorer,* Pring crossed the Atlantic from Bristol and landed on the shores of Massachusetts Bay. He named the spot Whitson Bay in honor of one of his sponsors. Seventeen years later, this spot would be renamed Plymouth. Pring set off into the woods, searching for the sassafras that would make his fortune. He returned home six months later, his two boats laden to the gills with the golden green cargo.

In 1610 and then again in 1618, captains from Bristol set sail to establish a colony in Newfoundland. The first settlement failed and the second prospered. In 1632, yet another ship sailed from Bristol to Newfoundland, captained by Welshman Thomas James. He landed in the bay he would name for himself (and that would forever be known as James Bay) and claimed the land in the name of Charles I, while affixing the seal of the town of Bristol to a large tree on the shoreline of the bay.

But it was the journey of John Winthrop that drew the interest and lit the imagination of Percival Lowle. Winthrop was younger than Percival and better educated, and came from a wealthy and prestigious family. But like Percival, Winthrop had a family he worried about, a wife he loved, and ambitions for a better way of doing things. Winthrop was a Puritan: he believed the Church of England needed to be reformed, stripped of meaningless ritual and hierarchical corruption. A revived piety would renew England, and Winthrop placed his faith in his countrymen's desire for change and renewal.

As a devout Puritan, Winthrop and his family had found life unpleasant under King James. But under King Charles, their daily existence became intolerable. The religious reforms sought by Puritans that had seemed possible under James now became unlikely. Instead of limiting the rituals of the Church, Archbishop Laud instituted more lavish, and what the Puritans considered more Catholic, practices into the daily liturgy, as well as into the physical space of the churches. Elaborate stained glass replaced simple windows, and ornately carved rails were built, separating the altar from the congregation. Above all else, Laud was devoted to maintaining the Church of England's controlling hierarchy. He went on a campaign to silence the Puritans, driving them from positions of power within and outside of the Church.

Winthrop's identity as a Puritan cost him his post to the law courts in early 1629. Although he had been born into a wealthy family and had himself enjoyed financial security as a lawyer, the family fortunes were dwindling. Winthrop's two sons had to drop out of Cambridge University, for there was no money to pay their fees. When offered the opportunity to participate in the formation of the Massachusetts Bay Colony, Winthrop saw an answer to both his financial and spiritual concerns. In the summer of 1630, Winthrop left for Massachusetts, leading a fleet of four ships carrying over seven hundred emigrants. Before he left, he was named governor of the colony, and upon arrival at Boston, he proclaimed the new settlement to be a "City upon a Hill" that all the world would look to for inspiration.[4]

Percival followed Winthrop's journey with interest, seizing up the reports that came into Bristol on ships returning from the west. He knew men who had gone over to the New World with Winthrop and understood why they had left. The Puritans whom Winthrop led across the sea were not separatists from the Church of England; they did not want a new church, but a reformed church, with fresh and pure congregations of faith set within the belief system of the existing Protestant religion. They were practical and determined. Percival knew that with the help of the wealthy Englishmen who funded the enterprise, Winthrop's men and women had a good chance at making their fresh start stick.

Now Percival had a choice to make. Many of his fellow merchants had already left—not for religious reasons, but for economic ones. Artisans were also joining the exodus, along with farmers and even gentry. Anyone tired of the corruption of England looked to the New World for a more wholesome atmosphere in the secular as well as spiritual arenas. England was crooked and complicated; settlements in the Americas were bound to be more honest and simple, if only for their relative newness. And there would be opportunity in America: economic opportunity.

King Charles himself recognized the economic potential of the New World. He granted a Royal Charter to the Massachusetts Bay Colony as yet another way to fund his many exploits. New supplies of fur and fish and corn would bring in money for him. It was the same desire for return of profit that explained why wealthy backers, including some of Percival's friends from Bristol, had invested in the colony at Plymouth in 1620 and now in Winthrop's fledgling one in Massachusetts. Bristol money was laid down in the hopes that the Massachusetts Bay Colony would provide a wealth of trade, and not only for the king.

In the early months of 1639, King Charles sent out the call for all able-bodied men to join the fight against Scotland. The Church of Scotland had thrown out bishops appointed by Archbishop Laud and refused to conform to the Church of England's rituals, the English Book of Common Prayer, and the Church hierarchy favored by Laud. King Charles, goaded on by his archbishop, proposed to march on Scotland. To carry out his plans, he needed money and men.

For Percival, the call to arms was the final straw. There was no security for his family in England, with taxes and duties rising all the time, harvests failing, and now a war to be fought. For almost forty years, he had prospered on the promises of the port of Bristol. He had grown old and grown rich, but he was weary of the old trades. It was time for a new trade. It was time to follow the promise of a New World. For the first time in his long life, Percival Lowle was heading out to sea. He was going to America.

2

~ 1639 ~

The Mariner that on smooth waves doth glide,
Sings merrily, and steers his Barque with ease . . . ,
But suddenly a storm spoiles all the sport,
And makes him long for a more quiet port . . .
—ANNE BRADSTREET, *CONTEMPLATIONS*

Picking up, packing up, moving on. After making the decision to go to America, Percival was faced with even more choices. What to leave in England, what to take along. What would be needed in the New World, what would be nice to have, and what could be left behind. No matter how Percival and Rebecca parsed the list, the number of items needed to set up a home in the colony was prodigious. Cisterns, saltcellars, cups, dishes, pewter chargers and wooden trenchers, knives and spoons, a cupboard or two, chairs, perhaps a couch or daybed, lanterns, candlesticks, candles, chests filled with chinaware, linens, cushions, and rugs, noon marks and hourglasses, and books.

Utilitarian books like *Directions for Health, Both Natural and Artificial* (they would have to doctor themselves) and *The Academy of Compliments* (they would have to know how to make new friends), *The Whole Duty of Men* (a primer on piety), and, of course, books of pleasure, like the writings of the ancient Greeks and Romans. Devoted Puritans might have felt uneasy reading the old pagans, but Lowle had been schooled in Latin and Greek; he had no qualms about consulting the ancients for a bit of advice.

Lowle considered his scrutoire: to take it or to leave it behind? The writing desk closed up like a chest and held boxes for storing a supply of pens, ink, and paper. Lowle was a records keeper by trade, and habits indulged every day for a lifetime could not be given up. The scrutoire was packed up for the journey. Rebecca's trunk of birthing blankets and the tiny Spanish box of treasure had to come along. The graves at Portbury would be tended by the sexton of St. Mary's, but the relics of the children would be carried by their mother.

Food would also have to be brought on board; none would be provided by the ship's agent. Percival's group was a large one: wife, Rebecca; sons Richard and John, along with their wives and six children; daughter Joan and her new husband, John Oliver, married just weeks before; Percival's partner, William Gerrish; his clerk, Anthony Somerby, and Anthony's brother Henry; and Richard Dole, apprentice. A community of travelers, multigenerational and sharing bounds of blood and friendship. Eighteen souls needing sustenance on the nine-week journey over the sea: beef, bread, peas, beer, mustard, vinegar, dried cod, butter, cheese, pottage, and herbs and condiments like cloves, prunes, raisins, sugar, nutmeg, mace, and cinnamon. Lemons and limes to keep away scurvy; wormwood to fight seasickness, although nothing beat a queasy stomach like a tonic of sugar, gum-dragon, milk, cinnamon, and ginger.*

The *Jonathan* set sail for Boston on April 12, 1639. The Lowle family settled into their tiny quarters, narrow cabins belowdecks with hardly space in which to turn around. Other passengers included the Blanchards: Thomas Blanchard and his very pregnant wife, Agnes, their two children, and Agnes's mother, niece, and one nephew. There were few solo travelers on board, as the Massachusetts colony discouraged single men, and women rarely traveled alone. Nicholas Noyes was on his own for the journey but for him it was a return trip back to the town of Newbury in the Massachusetts Bay Colony, after a year's visit to England.

The first days' traveling was easy, with a steady, mild wind allowing smooth passage. But no journey could keep up such an easy pace. The *Jonathan* was an old ship, and creaky. She had made her first trip to America back in 1623 and suffered through years of the rough waters and tougher weather conditions of the Atlantic Ocean. Now as the winds picked up and waves began to swell, there were mishaps. Her long oars split; the topmast shivered, twisted, and cracked. The boat was slowed, repairs were made, and then the journey resumed.[1]

Days of good wind carried the ship out into busy lanes of traffic. All kinds of boats were on the move, French and Spanish and Dutch, carrying pilgrim types and merchant trade and pirates. Contact was made between boats, once assurances had been made as to friend or foe, and news was exchanged: an "Earth-quake in New-England," the "Birth of a Monster at Boston," "in the Massachusetts-Bay a mortality."[2] Fare-thee-well and the journey west began again.

Until the days of dead air. Not a breath of wind or whisper of a breeze. The ship was becalmed below a blank sky, the sea motionless as a grave. Percival

---

* Gum-dragon (or gum-draggant) is a kind of gum taken from the roots of the goat's thorn tree found in the Middle East.

and his group wandered on deck, gazing out over the quiet water. The silence and the stillness created uneasy feelings of claustrophobia. Would the ship remain forever stranded, with sky and water closing in, smothering sound, sight, life itself? Regret gripped at Percival then. Perhaps the decision to leave England had been precipitous. Perhaps they would never arrive in America, but would remain straddled forever between two places. No past and no future. Percival's son John joined him on deck and reassured him: *The decision was a good one.* John was the son of happy temperament, and his optimism had often been rewarded. Percival prayed rewards would come this time as well.

The wind stirred to life. The ship rocked, then rolled forward. They were back on course. The wind grew stronger. A storm came in, rain driving down like pellets, passengers scurrying below. Roars of thunder amplified across the water; lightning cracked. The ship became like a toy tossed between truculent children, wave to wave, up and down. Rain and wind and thunder and lightning. Waves up and down, up and down, in ever-deepening swells. Passengers clung to the frames of their cabins, braced against the too-close walls, and prayed. Percival found his strength again: a storm had come and the tempest— all movement and power and energy—was easier to battle than the becalming state of waiting. But he, too, was on his knees, praying.

Safe to port, safe to port. Keep my children safe.

Percival had read of shipwrecks, vessels torn by wind and broken in two by the hard crack of swelling waves, hidden rocks, a strike of lightning down the mast. Bodies tossed into the sea, floating up and down in the waves, then sinking into the depths, gone. Death without a marker, loss beyond repair.

The storm passed. The sea calmed. Clouds dispersed; the sun shone. Passengers came up on deck, Nicholas Noyes and the Blanchards and the Lowles. Rebecca led the women in prayer; the men laughed together. Thanks were offered in words and in smiles. The children gulped in fresh air and turned their pale faces to the warmth of the sun. Percival counted his party: everyone there. It was his duty to conduct them all safely to the New World, no matter the skills of the captain or the caprices of God. To count them and make sure.

Ice floes floated by, carried from the north by currents. The frozen islands were so huge that foxes loped along their sides and streams flowed down their frozen cliffs. Temperatures plunged: it was as cold as a January day in Bristol. Then as the ice continued southward and the vessel made its way westward, the temperatures rose. Blistering days of sun. Heat like Percival had never known.

The wind came up, wind enough to move the boat forward. Breeze enough to relieve the heat. Still food enough to eat, water to drink. The ship carried on its journey westward, always following the sun.

Creatures of the sea accompanied the ship, leaping and skimming across the water: "Two mighty Whales we now saw, the one spouted water through two great holes in her head in to the Air a great height and making a great noise huffing and blowing . . ."[3] An infinite number of dolphins, schools of flying fish, and the solitary swordfish, its long fin a blade slicing through waves. Fish was the only fresh food passengers had for the journey. Shark was not tasty but mackerel made an excellent meal; porpoise was generally inedible but for the liver, which, when boiled and sautéed in vinegar, became acceptable and nourishing. Flounder was the coveted catch. Fresh from the sea, fried up while warm, the white flaked flesh melted in the mouth, almost sweet to the taste.

Percival and his sons, along with Anthony Somerby and William Gerrish, passed the long hours of the early-summer evenings with their fellow passenger Nicholas Noyes. Daylight lasted long past supper on the open sea and the men sat together under the cobalt sky, talking until the stars came out. Noyes had lived in New England for four years and had much to share about the ways and means of life in the colony. He had been among the original party settling the village of Newbury up the coast from Boston, on the Quascacunquen River. He had responsibility for its name, having suggested it—Newbury—in honor of the town in England where his brother the Reverend James Noyes and his cousin, the Reverend Thomas Parker, had been preachers. Now they were preachers in a new Newbury, in a new world.

Noyes told the men about the beauty along the Quascacunquen River—as lovely as countryside in England and more exotic for its wildness—and he boasted of fields rich for planting, and the coastline and woods so abundant with food. The waters around Newbury were alive with striped bass, white perch, mackerel, cod, sturgeon, and salmon. In the shallows at low tide, a treasure in shellfish waited to be scooped up—oysters, clams, and soft-shell crabs. Farther out, lobsters as long as a man's arm were easy takings. The woods were filled with venison, wild turkeys, pigeon, geese, woodcock, ducks, snipe, quail, and grouse.

Richard, Percival's son of sour temperament, asked about the troubles in paradise. He had been following the scandal of Anne Hutchinson, reports sent from New World to Old. Hutchinson challenged local Puritan clergy on church doctrine. She claimed to know the true will and purpose of God, and said that salvation came through an inner experience of God's love—the Covenant of Grace—and had nothing to do with outward acts of goodness—the

Covenant of Good Works. While the Congregationalist clergy did hold that only Grace would grant a person salvation in the hereafter, they could not downplay the Covenant of Good Works. How else could they ensure that their flocks performed the tasks necessary to make the settlements flourish and grow? The Covenant of Grace would get the Puritans only so far. They needed hard work to succeed. Anne Hutchinson had to be silenced.

The General Court of Massachusetts, led by Governor Winthrop, accused Anne Hutchinson of heresy. She was ordered to recant her criticisms of local clergy and to stop proclaiming the supremacy of the Covenant of Grace. But Hutchinson refused to back down. She said that she received her inspiration directly from God. She warned the men of the court that they were cursing themselves and their posterity to damnation with their actions. In response, the court banned Hutchinson from the Massachusetts Bay Colony and excommunicated her from the Church. Hutchinson found refuge in Rhode Island, where, as Noyes explained it, all sorts of heretics were welcome.

Noyes went on to tell his fellow voyagers about a Newbury man who had been one of Hutchinson's followers. Richard Dummer was not banished or excommunicated, which was fortunate for Newbury, as Dummer ran the gristmill there, and he was sorely needed. As punishment for his association with Hutchinson, Dummer was disenfranchised—losing his right to participate in the affairs of the community—and he was ordered to disarm. He turned in his swords, guns, shot, and match.

Anthony Somerby wondered if that was punishment enough. He was a man for rules and standards and discipline, which had made him a good clerk to Percival but not always the most merciful of men. Accounting mattered to Somerby: the good to one side, and the bad to the other. He was going to the New World in pursuit of order and sense, and wanted reassurance that he would find it.

Noyes explained that hard work mattered more than a mistake of faith, and after all, the mistake had been corrected. Dummer worked hard at his mill and now agreed to be guided solely by the rules of the community: the secular rules promulgated by the selectmen and the spiritual rules laid down by the clergy. Rules that were based on a commonality of purpose, faith, and resolve. And of care: Noyes assured Somerby that no one in Newbury was allowed to profit at another's expense; those who suffered an economic failure or family sorrow or crisis of faith were helped; all the children were taken care of and educated. He proudly announced that Newbury was preparing to hire its first schoolteacher, making it one of the first communities in New England to have a functioning schoolhouse. Somerby took note.

Not all the talk was of politics and religion. The men must also have talked about love. Noyes could explain to them the duties and pleasures of New World relationships. In the eyes of the Puritans, sex was a gift from God to mankind. Within marriage, sex was not just for procreation but also to foster bonds of companionship. Outside of marriage? Frowned upon, and to minimize the chance of it occurring, the Puritans discouraged bachelorhood. All single men were assigned a family to live with if they had no family of their own, and directed to find a wife as soon as possible. As for thornbacks, the Puritan term for an unmarried woman, such women were required to live with family and never allowed to be on their own.

Religion, politics, love, sex. Life and death. The ship rolled on.

Agnes Blanchard died giving birth to a baby girl. Agnes was washed and then wrapped in a white cloth. Bullets were tied to her neck and legs to ensure a quick sinking. Her body was carried across the deck by her husband, aided by men who had barely known the woman. Mourning travelers stood with their heads bowed. The bundle was pushed gently through a porthole. A gun fired in tribute. Two weeks later, Agnes's baby died. The child was fussed over one last time, wrapped up like her mother in white cloth and bullets, and then carried like her across the deck. A smaller bundle, pushed also to the sea. Sent to join her mother, but by then the ship had journeyed so many leagues on. The prayed-for reunion would have to take place in heaven. *Please, God.*

Days passed and travelers became jagged with fatigue, anxious with the monotony of sea and sky. The ship grew increasingly intolerable, the cabins below foul-aired and filthy, the deck above confining despite the open sky. There was no escape from the roll of the ship, the splinters of its boards and the sprays of salt that came over the railings, parching already dried-out skin. The food stores had been reduced to hard bread and moldy lemons. Talk between passengers had dissipated; faith still sustained the travelers, but the prayers were silent now, and private covenants were made, promising oneself to hold on. To hold out. To survive.

Percival leaned against the walls of his cabin and tried to drum the thought from his brain: *Who else will pass from life before the journey ends?*

Agnes's mother died. Three generations, lost on one ship's journey. But she would not be bundled and sent into the sea. On the morning of her death, great flocks of birds appeared in the sky. Land was sighted. The body of the old woman would be kept on board, to be buried later in the Massachusetts Bay Colony, her only contribution to the New World.

Nine weeks they had been at sea.

The coast of Massachusetts grew closer; the hills of Boston rose higher. Closer, and the travelers could now see the rooflines of the town, jagged rows that spiraled up from the harbor. Closer: The marshy shoreline of the bay curved around the vessel *Jonathan*. Doors of houses could be seen opening, settlers curious to see the new arrivals. The boat drew still, threw anchor. A smaller boat would come out to take them into port. Safe to port.

Percival planted his feet on the solid ground of a new continent. Sea legs aside, the experience was jarring, a reorganizing of the senses as he struggled to recognize smells, sights, sounds—was there anything familiar to him here? The buildings looked English, plain and simple timber-framed structures with steep roofs. The paths that wound away from the harbor were narrow, like the streets and lanes of home. The wharves smelled of tar and fish, much as they did in Bristol.

But how much more there was that was strange, foreign, and startling. Wonderful. The breadth of open space, above and beyond; the abundance of light, everywhere. Everything new under the sun, in this New World.

Boston was not the stopping point for the Lowles. They had agreed to travel north with Nicholas Noyes to his hometown of Newbury. The Reverends Noyes and Parker were good, practical men, Nicholas assured Percival; all the settlers of their small village were dedicated and hardworking. There was faith and there was food: fish, fowl, beasts, grains, and fruits, the bounty of nature just waiting to be partaken and enjoyed. A promise of peace and prosperity that could not be ignored.

The party traveling to Newbury did not go by road. There were no roads adequate to carry the wagonloads of their collected goods and supplies. The byways of New England at the time were only paths, wider than the original Indian trails that they encompassed but still mere paths, and bumpy, rocky paths at that. Broken paths, for every few miles there was a stream or a river, a barrier of water to cross over. The General Court had demanded that access be provided for travelers, that fallen trees be placed as temporary bridges, or in wider spots, canoe ferries be made available. But for Percival and his family, the best way north was by sea.

Percival stood beside Rebecca as the small vessel scuttled its way north along the coastline. Nicholas Noyes pointed out existing settlements: Swampscott, Marblehead, Beverly, and Gloucester. Then the boat traveled around Cape Ann and into Ipswich Bay. High waves in the bay threw a mist of salty, cold water across their faces. Like a baptism, or benediction. A long, low scrub of sand and rock formed a barrier between ocean and land. It was called Plum Island. There the boat would wait for the rising of the tide. Then the travelers could move on, up into the Quascacunquen River, which would take them to Newbury.

The tide rose by daybreak. Percival woke from where he had slept, curved up against the family's bundles of belongings. He shook his wife and sons and daughter awake. They watched the sunrise over the Atlantic Ocean. None of them would ever again stand on a deck, looking back toward England. Their long journey was almost over. The captain pulled anchor and the fast current carried the boat up and into the curve of the Quascacunquen. Tawny sand bordered by pines gave way to long meadows of waving saw grass and hay. In the distance, low hills were covered in the summer-heavy greenery of maples, oaks, and fir. The shoreline was dotted with thick stands of cordgrass growing alongside yellow-dusted flowers, tall and spindly rods of gold. The high grasses and swaying strands of flowers obscured clusters of clover, but Percival knew it was there; the scent of it played across the water, welcoming him with its familiarity and sweetness.

The birds were all new to him. Large white birds with long, thin necks; bearded birds tinted gray and blue; small beige-and-white birds; sleek white gulls like he'd never seen before, with their bright orange bills. Dark brown birds that looked like stretched-out ducks; they dived down into the water as the boat veered by and then sprang up again, yards away. Long-necked birds hunted and pecked, searching for snails, crabs, and mussels amid the mud-flat grasses. Smaller birds swung overhead, their cries sounding like flutes and reeds playing on the wind.

Hidden by the grasses and the pines, Newbury came into view only from the river landing. Percival clambered onto the wooden platform and took his first look. Wide meadows, dotted with sheep and interspersed with small fields of corn and grass, made a tidy quilt of gold and green. In the middle of the quilt, a prim little village, dun houses set on an ordered grid around a large rectangular green. Less imposing than Boston, for this was just a small collection of settlers, but still to Percival and his weary travelers, a relief. But approbation had to come first.

All immigrants arriving in the Massachusetts Bay Colony had to be deemed worthy; any would-be settlers come to town had to be stamped as acceptable by the authorities—the selectmen—who governed the town for the good of the town. Only then would the community extend its invitation; only then would Noyes's promise be made good: Come partake with us, worship, and build. Flourish.

Walking up from the landing, Nicholas Noyes led the group toward the meetinghouse, center of village life. The meetinghouse was imposing not only for its rustic simplicity but for its unexpectedly pagan decoration: a row of wolves' heads, nailed one after another, across the top of the doorway. Fur matted with blood, jaws slack and revealing long rows of sharp teeth, tongues lolling and black. Nicholas had explained to them one night on board the *Jonathan* that wolves were the bane of the New England farmer. Good bounty was paid by the town elders for their eradication. Hanging the heads above the church doors was a sign: A bold strike had been made for an abundant land blessed by God.

The Reverends Parker and Noyes came together from the meetinghouse, descending in a single motion the step of the building. Percival knew their history. They were two men joined in their love of the Lord; they had lived together their whole lives, first in England and then here in the New World. Even when the Reverend Noyes married, it was the woman who came to live with the two men.

The Reverend Noyes appeared anxious now, and then excited: His brother had made it home again. The Reverend Parker stood back, quietly curious to see the prospective members of the Newbury flock. Percival nodded at both men, then spread his feet to stand firmly on the chosen ground of Newbury. His family drew forward, hands open before them and heads bowed. They waited to be accepted into the fold of the community. Approbation and approval, and a new land to call home.

3

1639–1665

We must delight in each other;
make others conditions our own;
rejoice together, mourn together . . .
—JOHN WINTHROP, "A MODELL OF CHRISTIAN CHARITY"

The family of Percival Lowle was welcomed into the community of Newbury. Percival, being a man of means, was required to buy the family's
shares in the town. In addition to the house lot, he purchased one hundred
acres of town land, salt marsh, and meadowland. The first task before him and
his sons was to build shelter, two or three homes to house the families of Percival and Rebecca, John and Mary, Richard and Margaret, Joan and John.

How to build? There were simply not enough carpenters, thatchers, and
sawyers to go around, and even though the General Court of Massachusetts
set daily wages at a prescribed rate, prices were steep for those builders who
could be found. And so all the Lowles, old Percival included, put their shoulders into the work of felling trees, planing lumber, gathering oyster and clams
shells for the binding lime, and then raising the roof. Some clapboard was
available, brought over from England along with casement windows and
moldings, but for the rest, all parts and pieces had to come from the land.

The Lowles were not on their own entirely. Newbury, like all the settlements
of Massachusetts, was a community founded on ideals of labor and benefit: Help
extended to one individual was good for the settlement at large. A chopping bee
might have been held, neighbors joining together to clear the land and make it
suitable for the settling of stakes, building of houses, sowing of gardens.

As Percival and his sons worked on their houses, they took no notice
of the long marshes in the distance turning into autumn gold, the ribbon of
red trees, the bolts of color on the hills beyond. All of their attention was focused
on work: on settling, on building. Percival reckoned it was one thing—and
hard enough—to move from one town in England to another, find a home,
start a business, make a place in society. But starting over again in New
England was starting from scratch. Percival thought of the harbor snails in

Bristol, small and sturdy, fiercely clinging to the rocks of the shoreline; like them, all he had was what he had carried on his back, from one world to another. From what he had, he would create whole new whorls of existence. Foundation and fireplace, beams and braces, walls and windows. A roof. A door. Built to last in this New World.

As in every house of the village, the fireplace of Percival's home was its center, the locus for meeting and talking, and for eating and sleeping. A lug pole, a solid branch of green wood, was hung over the width of the fireplace, and from it swung what the family needed to survive: tools, pots, and pans. Food was prepared in ovens set at each of its corners, bodies were warmed by its coals and all the rooms heated: kitchen to the right, parlor to the left, and two rooms behind.

Every room had more than just one function, just as every person in this New World had more than one purpose: mother, yes, but also midwife or farmer or apothecary. Father and also teacher, farmer, cobbler, or sawyer. Sons could become clerks; daughters could be weavers. There was no set definition for any one place, or any one person except for the one overriding purpose of the meetinghouse—to provide religious guidance so that every member of the village could become a light of religion, a light in the wilderness.

How unlike England this concept was, the idea of versatility and utility. In England, one's station in life, purpose and role and place, was set from birth. In New England, the more roles a man (or woman) could fulfill, the better for the community. The house, the home, was a further representation of that utility, serving all functions of shelter, storage, and foundation.

After the building of shelter, the sowing of gardens. Rebecca took the lead, planting an English garden. She had carried over the sea with her packets of seeds, and slips and roots wrapped in paper. Flowers that once grew in her Bristol courtyard were now pressed into the sandy Newbury soil, accompanied by hope and prayer; sweet William, foxglove, phlox, pinks, and pansies. Lilac bushes, as bare roots, were planted beside the doorway and the fat bulbs of lemon lilies went in below the windows. Rebecca had an abundance of lilac roots; she planted more beside the front gate, which had been firmly posted in the ground.

Squared beds were laid out in the garden, row after row prepared for vegetables. The rows would be separated by spindly berry bushes, and amid them, more flowers were sown. What optimism Rebecca showed in her hard work, to dig and plant in the dying cycle of fall. Her heart gripped with faith that in the spring, mourning bride and poppies would bloom beside the bushes, and sweet alyssum would spread across the rows, shedding fragrance over the new garden. She dreamed through the long, cold winter of all the vegetables she would plant in the year to come: pumpkins, green peas, turnips, carrots, and cucumbers. But not potatoes. Rebecca frowned on potatoes; they were forbidden fruit, a suspected aphrodisiac but, worse than that, a source of leprosy and syphilis, as well. Herbs would be planted in case of illness—ingredients Rebecca would need for tonics, salves, and poultices. She'd learned many cures in England, and taught them to her daughter Joan, and daughters-in-law, Mary and Margaret.

On this new soil, with new possibilities, she'd try the medicinal snips and seeds offered by neighbors. Basswood for swelling, buckthorn for purgative, currants for cough, bloodroot for wounds, gentian for the stomach, wormwood to stimulate lust and valerian to kill it, and southernwood as a love charm (young women wore it in their shoes). One old recipe recommended, "Take a quantity of southernwood and put it upon kindled coals to burn and being made into a powder mix it with the oyle of radishes and anoint a bald spot and you shall see great experiences."[1]

The purpose of the garden was not only to feed and to cure; it was also to beautify. In an environment that frowned upon outward displays of wealth or decoration, the garden was one place where color and abundance could run riot without risk of disapproval or sanction. Rebecca had dreams of the rising plants and flowers, splashes of color against the colorless buildings of New England. A rising of joy, uncensored by the meetinghouse and fed by rain and sun.

The family was required to spend all day Sunday at the meetinghouse, and Thursday evenings. The pews were hard, the air was damp and cold, and the sermons were long. No dozing allowed; the tithing man walked the rows with a long stick and rapped the sleeping awake with a hard knock. A look out the window: drifts of snow against brown houses huddled under a long, low gray sky. Never had Percival Lowle seen such long expanses of snow, blown into drifts that were taller than a man's head, and blowing out flat and hard across the meadows of long-buried grass. January, February, March. And still the snow fell. Only in April did the long melting begin. Percival thought of the blue clumps of scilla in his garden in Bristol: They would have been up by the early days of March. All he saw now when he left the meetinghouse were beds of brown mud amid puckers of graying snow.

Spring came. The proof of Noyes's promise: Come to New England and flourish. Plants grew faster here, flowers bigger, fruits sweeter—was it the longer growing cycles of sun and rain, the larger spaces for growing, or just that the desperate need for it all that made everything better? Gratitude deepened for products that came from one's own labor and prayers. And for the Lowles, it was their own labor. They had no servants in the New World. With three husbands and three wives, and more and more children, help was at hand, and at home.

Percival Lowle entered the meetinghouse on a May morning, his first May in the New World, and felt it was easy now to worship the Lord, who had brought him to this place. During the sermons of the long winter, when the meetinghouse was gripped with cold and the benches seemed harder for the frost beneath the boards and wind came through the clamshell-shellacked logs, his faith had wavered. And it had quavered again, with fear, when it was his turn at the rota of sentry duty. Joining a few other men outside the meetinghouse, Sundays and Thursdays, he guarded the worshippers behind their closed doors from the threat of Indians.

No Indians had ever attacked the heart of Newbury, and at least one Indian family lived in the town. Still, the sentries walked their path of duty outside while inside, parishioners sat, their bottoms sore on hard-bottomed benches, their attention whipped back to the sermon by a hard rap on the shoulder from the stick-wielding tithe man. *Focus on the good,* Percival told himself as he walked the line. *Join wholeheartedly into the community of faith and work.* As John Winthrop had counseled, "always having before our eyes our commission and community in the work . . . So shall we keep the unity of the spirit in the bond of peace. The Lord will be our God, and delight to dwell among us, as his own people and will command a blessing upon us in all our ways."[2]

There was no other choice available to Percival. It was the New England way, the Congregational credo: communal good works and individual responsibility operating together to further the word of God. One religion: Congregational. The town was congregation, and the congregation was town. One community, bound together through a voluntary social compact to do good, and held together by their common covenant, common values, and common way of living. A conformity of style, language, religion, and direction. The circumscribed, controlled, contained community was necessary in order for the village to survive and flourish. Percival understood this.

But understanding and adapting were two different things. Percival was used to a port town, where differences defined the community just as much as similarities did. It was a merchant town, yes, but also a town of factories and learning, of artisans and laborers, of priests and doctors and lawyers, fishmongers and whoremongers, taverns and tabernacles. Bristol thrived on a layering of different languages and classes and faiths, not a solid wall of one faith, one tongue, one class.

The town of Newbury, on the other hand, was homogenous by design. Strength lay in unity of purpose and of religion. Congregationalist Puritans, unlike the separatist Pilgrims of Plymouth Colony, did not want to create a new church; they wanted to reform the English Church, and one of the ways they sought to achieve reform was by eliminating church hierarchy and so-lidifying local control. Churches were formed through voluntary compacts—a covenant among a community—and a religious leader was chosen by the community to lead it. This organizing principle drew from the teachings of the first reformer of the English Church, John Wycliffe: All that was needed to found a church was "an authority received from God, and consequently power and knowledge imparted from God for the exercise of such ministry . . . where a man possesses these, although the bishop has not laid hands upon him according to his traditions, God has Himself appointed him."[3]

All governing power was to be held by the community of the congregation (hence, *Congregational*) and such power was absolute: "For God's Word to function freely, and for each member to feel an integral part of the church's operations, each congregation must be self-sufficient, containing within itself all the offices and powers necessary for self-regulation."[4]

Included in self-regulation was the right to exclude unwanted types from the community in order to keep the town cohesive both spiritually and politically. In Newbury, as in other New England towns, anyone not adhering to the dictates of the meetinghouse "shall have free liberty to keep away from us, and such as will come will be gone as fast as they can, the sooner the better."[5]

When a pair of traveling Socinians stopped by a Newbury inn, the women were allowed to enter the premises, and given food and drink. Socinians believed that man was born innocent and good, but Puritan Congregationalists did not: They believed man was born depraved and evil. As the pair of women waited for the arrival of their meal, they began to talk to the locals about their Socinian beliefs. Suddenly, the stomach of the one of the women gave a terrible rumbling, for she was very hungry. The people of Newbury took the noise to be a sign of the devil within her. They took her outside immediately, stripped her from the waist up, and whipped her.

Later that same year, a Newbury woman came naked to Sunday-morning services at the meetinghouse. Lydia Wardwell was bare from her head to her toes, an offering she made to prove that man is born good, innocent, and humble (again, contrary to Congregationalist beliefs). Lydia was arrested, forcibly reclothed, and dragged to the Regional Court, which had convened in a tavern. The court fined her and sentenced her to a public whipping. For the whipping of thirty lashes, she was stripped naked (deemed a sign of wickedness, not innocence) and tied to a rail outside the tavern.

In the Massachusetts Bay Colony, the Lowles were prohibited from celebrating Christmas, and there were no Lenten fasts or Easter mornings. There were few holidays from work, no excuses other than attendance at the meetinghouse on Sundays, the daylong services that were not a pleasure, but a duty, and

at Thursday sermons, held weekly to further instill Puritan values and preaching. The only holidays were those decreed colony-wide by the General Court
or locally by the town selectmen. These included Thanksgiving Days (sometimes held twice a year); Election Day, when freemen of the town came out to
vote—the day was honored with a special " 'lection cake" dense with fruit
and wine; and Training Days, when men gathered to practice military drills.
In 1639, Governor Winthrop had overseen a training day held in Boston,
where more than one thousand men gathered together to exercise their guns
on the Boston Common. All went well and, as Winthrop noted in his journal, there was "no drunkenness" at all.[6]

Sloth, greed, covetousness, drunkenness: These were sins that interrupted
the workflow of the village, and they could not be tolerated. Governor Winthrop
had warned the people of Massachusetts Bay Colony again and again that any
failure to live by the laws of God would result in the colony's destruction. If
the village became a place of impiety and immorality, then God himself
would swoop down to punish the colonists and all would be lost. John Mayo,
preacher of the Old North Church in Boston, advised New Englanders, "You
should shine as lights. We have little tyme and much work. You are called to
the knowledge of god to the work of Christ, the more weighty the work, the
more carefull you should be. God threatens those that do not watch. . . ."[7] The
rule to live by was hard work by each and just rewards for all. As John Winthrop counseled, "Be pleased, therefore . . . to help forward this work now in
hand; which if it prosper, you shall be the more glorious, howsoever your judgment is with the Lord, and your reward with God."[8]

For John Lowle, Percival's eldest son, the transition to the New World was
marked by the deaths of his youngest child and his English wife. The renewal
he sought by leaving the uncertainty of England was delayed; he gathered his
five children around him and promised them he would do what he could to
keep them safe. He met another English woman, born in Yarmouth but having arrived in Newbury with her family the year before the Lowles. Wedding
banns were published three times at the meetinghouse during Sunday services. Elizabeth Goodale was married to John Lowle during the last days of
1639, a winter wedding solemnized by the local magistrate and celebrated with
the drinking of sack posset, a concoction of curdled cream and spiced wine.

Elizabeth brought him three more children and good luck. John was
named constable of Newbury in 1641, and four years later, he was appointed
town commissioner, responsible for settling small disputes. Two years after
that, he became town clerk. John prospered as he rose in the village hierarchy.
He owned large holdings of land, scattered houses and barns, cattle and

chicken to fill the barns, and all sorts of "household stuffe" to fill his houses.[9] The Lowle family status was confirmed; their duty was fixed. Peacekeepers, upholders of morality and piety, landowners, and law abiders. Hard workers, with many benefits gained for all their labors.

The Lowles were no longer merchants, trading cargoes and treasures from far away for merchandise created closer to home. In Newbury, there were few goods to buy or trade; here, everything had to be grown and made on its own. Colonists, no matter their profession—governor or former merchant—tilled the land. There was a maltser in Newbury, and a doctor, along with one sea captain, one sailor, one dyer, one glover, three or four tanners, seven or eight shoemakers, two wheelwrights, two blacksmiths, four weavers, one cooper, one saddler, one sawyer, and two or three carpenters. But no matter what their trade, they were all farmers, as well. To provide for one's own family, and for the community. To serve self and to serve others, and above all, to serve God.

Percival purchased more and more acreage beyond the initial lots he had bought upon first arriving in Newbury. While in England, Percival had been given the benefits of a farm as part of his role as bailiff for Portbury. He once again put to use his skills at managing the growing and breeding of living things. He sold what he grew in the fields and raised in his barns, and ate what was grown in the house gardens. He settled into old age, soothing himself with herbs, reading his old English books for peace, and attending services at the meetinghouse for company. At end of day, he sat with Rebecca by the southern windows of their small house for the pleasure of the view: the calm village surrounding them, the low hills beyond. Dusk settled, the clicking of crickets surged, and always in the background, Percival heard the distant roiling of the river.

Anthony Somerby, Percival's clerk in Bristol, arrived in Newbury determined to make his own way. He remembered what Nicholas Noyes had told him on the sea voyage—that Newbury was ready to start its own school—and upon arrival in town, he asked for the job of teacher. In the fall of 1639, he was hired as one of the first schoolteachers in all of New England and given a brand-new schoolhouse in which to teach, along with acreage to build his home and his gardens, and extra property in marshland (which would provide additional income from the harvesting of grasses). In 1647, he would succeed John Lowle as town clerk, and for the next thirty-three years he kept meticulous records of the doings of Newbury.

Summers following springs, followed by falls and winters. In the last days of the year 1645, Rebecca Lowle died. She had been Percival's wife from the sixteenth century into the seventeenth, from the Old World to the New. Now she would be buried in the tiny burial ground set a distance along from the town green. A month into winter, there would have been a blanket of snow upon the ground, but the ground itself was not yet fully frozen. A fire burned over the hard earth; then men working together dug a grave, their sharpened flat-bladed shovels cutting through the hard crust of soil. The opening in the ground took shape.

The funeral procession left Percival's house, headed by the family and swelled with friends and townspeople and accompanied by the Reverend Parker and the Reverend Noyes. In Puritan burial services of the 1600s, no sermon was given, no prayers offered in the meetinghouse or at the grave site. Only the tolling of a bell marked the ending of a life. Then the gathered crowd waited while Rebecca was interred, the pile of turned earth returned to cover her coffin. A wolf stone was set over the mound of earth, a huge oblong slab laid flat to prevent wild animals from digging into the grave.

The crowd moved away, turning back to walk to town and to an agreed-upon meeting place. It was time now to drink together, one of the few times such partaking was allowed and advantage would be taken. Brandy, gin, wine. Libations for the mourners, a loosening of tongues and of memories. A cele-bration of certainty: God would provide for the faithful. But for Percival, a terrible leave-taking and a further severing of his connection to old England.

Shortly after Rebecca's death, the town of Newbury was moved upstream a mile or two for a better position on the Merrimack River and a greater abun-dance of tillable land. The first wharf was built, and then another, setting the course for Newbury's future as an important colonial port. A new town green was laid out, a triangle this time. John Lowle and his family were granted a lot at number 28 High Street, the most prestigious address upon which to build a new home. John built his family a spacious dwelling constructed of huge tim-bers and summer beams, and sided with English clapboard. Rows of sparkling mullion casement windows offered views of the Merrimack River to one side and Frog Pond to the other, and of the town green straight ahead.

Percival was granted a lot off the main street, in a field by the river. There he built a house for himself and Richard's family. Percival was given the bed in the large front room to the left, warmed by the central fireplace and facing the southern light. Richard, Percival's second-eldest son, was always ailing from some illness or another, but he had also prospered in Newbury, cultivat-ing orchards and meadowlands in Newbury itself and on Plum Island, and breeding cows, sheep, and pigs. The house he built with his father was rich with household goods, including a gold-leaf Bible and thick rugs, woven "wearing apparel" and painted "chamber pot and pint pot." When he died, he left his "great Bible" and "great pot" to his eldest son; to his youngest, he left the right "to live in the house & have a sixt of the part of the Apples yearly so

long as he lives a single man without a wife and no longer." To his old friend
and executor of the will, Anthony Somerby, Richard Lowle left "a booke called
Mr. Hooker's politic."[10]

There were grandchildren to keep Percival occupied and old friends to
visit with, fields and cattle to be managed. But with Rebecca gone, there was
also a hollow spot, an unfilled space of air around him and within him, as well.
When the crickets surged at dusk, marking an end to summer, he thought of
how the two of them had sat together, marveling at the new world around
them. How they had watched the sun fade down below the expanse of low
hills, and stayed together in their chairs, side by side, until the moon rose. Sitting alone now, Percival noted the passing of time. The settling of years in a
new place, a new world.

In 1647, Percival's son John died. Another procession, accompanied by many
mourners, for Newbury had grown and John's status with it. John would be
buried in the new burial ground closer to town. It was spring and the soil was
easy to break, the grave easily dug. John was laid to rest, and a wolf stone set
atop the newly filled grave. Percival remained in the enclosed yard while the
mourners returned to John's house for drinking and talking. Rebecca lay up
the road; their son John was here, forever settled now. Another absence to be
felt and mourned.

Percival took to walking out during the day, carrying a stout staff and
dressed in a colorful doublet over baggy leaden-colored trousers, a fancy wide-
brimmed hat pressed down on his head and a large cloak across his shoulders.
He did not wear a wig, contrary to the style back in England, not simply
because it would not have suited him but because the Reverend Noyes condemned the wearing of wigs in Newbury. His clothes also conformed to the
the Sumptuary Laws, rules devised by the General Court to keep colonists'
dress sober and simple. The use of lace, silver, or gold in clothing was forbidden by the laws; slashes in clothes were limited to "one slash in each sleeve and
another in the back." Other prohibitions included "silver girdles, hatbands,
belts, and all beaver hats," along with "immoderate great breeches, knots of
ribbon, broad shoulder bands . . . silk ruses, double ruffles and capes."[11]

The prohibitions were matched by varied punishments, but as the latter
half of the seventeenth century settled in, the rules against a bit of decoration
in dress were not enforced. When the wife of Nicholas Noyes was brought before the local court "for wearing a silk hood and scarfe," she argued that her
husband was of great worth to the community and that mattered more than
what adornment she might add to her clothing. The court agreed and she was
discharged from all sanctions.[12]

Town life was loosening up, opening up. Taverns, called ordinaries in the English fashion, proliferated throughout the colony. The tavern named the Good Woman featured on its sign the figure of a headless woman. Another, called the Salutation Inn, had a signboard with the image of two men shaking hands; it was commonly known as "the Two Palaverers." In Newbury, men of good repute were granted licenses to "keepe an ordinary and give intertainment such as neede."[13]

The local taverns and ordinaries were the alternative meeting place to the meetinghouse. While previously all news was passed during Thursday sermons, now it was afternoon get-togethers at the tavern that served as the passing point for information. Notices of town meetings, elections, wedding banns, and other events were posted at the tavern, where they were thoroughly discussed, dissected, and approved—or not. Heads that shook over a planned marriage in the local tavern set the tone for the entire town. Taverns were so much recognized as the center of town that almanacs of the day listed distances between towns as not from town to town but from tavern to tavern.

News from England came to Percival through his local tavern, kept by Tristram Coffin at the foot of Ferry Street, not far from Percival's home. Coffin's tavern was the place all travelers stopped and the arrival point for all the newspapers and pamphlets coming from Boston and beyond. Percival first heard of the Civil War that had broken out in England while at Coffin's ordinary. His hometown had played a prominent role in the fight between the Royalists, led by King Charles, and the Roundheads, led by Oliver Cromwell. Early on, Bristol sided with Cromwell and his Parliamentarians, and housed troops of Roundheads. In 1643, Royalist troops stormed into Bristol and drove out the Roundheads. The citizens of Bristol were punished with royal-sanctioned looting and pillaging, then hit with heavy fines and forced to house legions of royal soldiers. A year later, the plague returned to Bristol and the agonies multiplied. In 1645, when Cromwell's forces took the city back, they found a town decimated by hunger, illness, and poverty.

Percival felt a mixture of both relief and anguish. His family had been spared what would have certainly been a terrible siege, especially for a merchant family with goods to loot, stores to steal, and a house to requisition. How many of his old friends had died in the battles fought over Bristol? Many in the Bay Colony made plans to return to England to join in the battle for reformation of a decayed and corrupt government. When the forces of Cromwell vanquished the Royalists, executing Charles and instituting a government giving absolute power to Parliament and abolishing the monarchy, even more Puritan colonists planned to return to England. They were eager to join what they saw as a victory of the Puritan movement. They wanted to return home, where they might now be able to practice their religion freely. No need to stick it out in America; England was safe.

Percival Lowle had not been a Puritan in England, and although he prospered in Puritan New England, he was not ready to celebrate the rise of Cromwell. Cromwell had murdered a king and was now instituting a regime based on what Percival considered wild ideas. A Rump Parliament, ruled only by the House of Commons; dissolution of the House of Lords; no more king. These were radical ideas and their implementation promised instability and insecurity for England. Life under Cromwell would likely prove to be as uneasy and as fraught with uncertainty as it had been under King Charles.

Certainly the house Percival and Richard shared was not as substantial or luxurious as the Lowle home had been in Bristol. They had no servants here in New England, no coat of arms plastered on the front door. Other than the taverns, there were few entertainments in Newbury, no traveling theater or bear shows. There were no bookstores or fine shops (one had to travel all the way to Boston for those). Tobacco was hard to find and cards were frowned upon. And yet life in Newbury suited Percival Lowle. He had stability in his plain little village. He had security and he had certainty. Town and clergy saw to that. From the strict laws against public drunkenness (punishment was exacted in the form of paid fines and public humiliation: the wearing of a large red *D* around the neck) to laws regulating ownership and use of firearms, dangerous behavior was controlled, and threats from Indians and other outside forces were largely imagined—at least during Percival's lifetime, a period of peace in Newbury.

There were some controversies over religion, but nothing that touched Percival personally. In religion, as in politics, he was conservative. He sided with the Reverends Parker and Noyes, had faith in their shepherding of the community, and believed in heaven and hell—but spent little time worrying about either. He had most likely heard news of Margaret Jones of Charlestown, hanged for witchery in 1648, but the hysteria of the Salem witch trials lay decades away. The son of Nicholas Noyes, another Nicholas and a minister, would play a role in those trials. He condemned eight alleged witches—"firebrands of hell," as he called them—to death by hanging. But there would be no hangings in Newbury.[14]

The outbreaks of violence between Native Americans and colonists that occurred throughout New England rarely touched down in Newbury, and never during Percival's time living there. King Philip's War—"a sickening slaughter" that took the lives of 5 percent of the English population and 40 percent of the Native Americans[15] and laid to waste entire towns, including Narrangansett, Marlborough, Deerfield, and native settlements—began in 1675. It would prove to be "not only the most fatal war in all American history, but also one of the most merciless."[16] William Gerrish Jr. would be called to fight, along with a few dozen other Newbury men, including Daniel Somerby, nephew to Andrew. Daniel died of his wounds from the battle at Narragansett. Newbury itself was not threatened during those years, and, unlike other towns, even refused to build fortifications. The townspeople simply garrisoned a few of the houses, just in case, and appointed local men to patrol, much as they had in the early days after Percival's arrival, when men were assigned to stand guard over the meetinghouse on Sundays.

There was no plague in New England, as there had been in Bristol, and the diseases that did pass through Newbury were few and far between (the smallpox epidemic that laid waste to the town of Gloucester never came to Newbury). In fact, given the healthy living conditions, the abundance of fresh vegetables, meats, and fish, and the relative absence of disease, men and women of the colonies were living well into their sixties and beyond, decades longer than their English counterparts.

Percival had chosen this new life for himself, and for his family. It was a good choice, this community they had found. Life here was settled and satisfying. They had their duties, based on commitments made to community and to family. Richard, farmer and landowner, was too ill disposed most of the time to participate in town activities. But John, while alive, had been prominent in the town. Percival himself had become involved in local politics, joining in efforts to gain Plum Island as the sole property of Newbury (important for grazing rights) and offering testimony on small court matters. When Governor John Winthrop died in 1649, Percival wrote and delivered a ninety-eight-line elegy honoring the man who had led him to America. It concluded with these lines:

> Here you have Lowle's loyalty
> Pen'd with his slender skill,
> And with it no good poetry,
> Yet certainly good will.
> Read these few verses willingly,
> And view them not with Monus eye,
> Friendly correct what is amiss,
> Accept his love that did write this.[17]

The first poem written by a Lowell in America.

Joan, Percival's daughter, also found her place in the Newbury community. After her first husband died, she married Percival's friend and former partner

William Gerrish, "a man of great energy and much prominence, and filled many civic offices."[18] Together they had ten children. One would become a lawyer and a judge; one became a minister; one served as a colonel during the First Indian War (1675–1676); and one received a royal office as collector of His Majesty's customs.

The children of Percival's son John prospered. The eldest, John, moved to Boston and became a cooper; his younger brother Joseph followed him to Boston and also became a cooper; James went to Plymouth; Benjamin remained in Newbury, where he worked as a blacksmith. John's daughter Elizabeth stayed in Newbury and married Captain Phillip Nelson, who became the largest landowner in the town, holding more than three thousand acres along the Merrimack and all the way up to the village of Haverhill. After her father John's death, seventeen-year old Mary Lowle had petitioned the court to obtain her dowry, held in trust for her by her uncle Richard. She wanted to return to England and needed the funds to do so. Upon receiving her dowry, however, Mary changed her mind. She married a man by the name of Thomas Wyburn and moved to Boston.

Percival Lowle lived until the age of ninety-three. He died on January 8, 1664, and was buried in the cemetery north of the town green. Again, as for his wife, Rebecca, the ground of the graveyard was frozen, but a space was made for him, close to his son John. All night long, a fire blazed on the spot, warming the earth so that it could be broken and a grave dug. The next morning, mourners walked from their houses, wrapped in coats and shawls against the cold. Words were spoken over the grave, Percival's body interred, a wolf stone laid across the resting site.

There were few left who could remember Percival from the time of his arrival in Newbury, but the Reverend Parker did. He remembered seeing the old man and his family walking up from the river landing, tired from weeks of travel and yet light on their feet, the glow of expectation on their faces. He remembered Percival settling in, growing his garden, playing at politics, strolling through the lanes of his adopted town. Now so many old friends were gone, including the minister's closest friend through all his life, the Reverend James Noyes, who had died in 1656.

Parker left the group of mourners when they headed back to Richard Lowle's house "to steep their tough old hearts in wine and strong drink and indulge in an outbreak of jollity of remembrance."[19] He was still a man of strict comportment, and could not allow himself any indulgence, even of grief.

In time, a marker would be placed over Percival's grave, noting his birth in England and his death in Newbury. In 1686, Anthony Somerby would be laid beside him. Clerk in England, friend in Newbury, and now companion for eternity.

In 1658, Cromwell died and the Commonwealth he had governed in England fell apart. Charles II was restored to the throne. Charles took a good look at what the colonists over in America were up to and realized that for years they had been blithely ignoring the laws that required New England to import only goods carried in English ships and coming via or directly from England. The leaders of the Massachusetts Bay Colony sent a gift to placate the disgruntled monarch: "10 barrels of cranberries, 2 hogsheads of special good samp [cornmeal mush], and 3000 of codfish."[20] Charles accepted the gift but still demanded compliance with the Navigation Acts. In return, the leaders replied that, "the laws of England are bounded within the 4 seas and do not reach American . . . the subjects here are not represented in Parliament, so we have not looked on ourselves as impeded by them."[21]

In 1684, the charter of the Massachusetts Bay Colony was revoked, and in 1686 a new entity created: the Dominion of New England. Under King James II, Sir Edmund Andros was instituted as the royal governor. Town meetings were forbidden to be held more than once a year; all land and resources were redefined as belonging to the Crown; laws, taxes, and trade regulations were to be enforced on the colonists. The colonists were in an uproar against the Stuart monarchy. In 1689, William and Mary came to the throne, deposing James II. New Englanders celebrated by throwing Governor Andros in jail and effectively dissolving the Dominion; "wine barrels were breached in the street" and the colonists rejoiced.[22] In 1692, the Royal Province of Massachusetts Bay was established and New Englanders returned to building up their colony, trading and shipping as they wished, and largely ignoring strictures set by the Crown.

By the end of the seventeenth century, four generations of Lowles had lived in the New World. Percival's John begat a son John in England, and he begat nineteen children, including a son Ebenezer, born in Boston, Massachusetts, in 1675. And there were Elizabeths, Josephs, Marys, Jameses, Benjamins: the American Lowles.

American: The term had been used for decades, as when in 1655 the traveler Thomas Gage, a preacher from Kent, England, wrote of his journeys through America: "Thus my good reader, thou seest an American, through many dangers by sea and land, now safely arrived . . ."[23] The preacher Cotton Mather used the word in 1684 to describe not Native Americans, as had been common, but men and women born in America of English stock. The adjective had begun with a promise: Come to the New World and flourish. And the Lowles did.

Part Two

RELIGION

For God is our witness, how greatly we long after you all . . .
how affectionately desirous we are of you, being
willing to impart to you not the Gospel of God only,
but also our own Souls, because ye are dear unto us.

—REVEREND JOHN LOWELL,
*MINISTERS OF THE GOSPEL
TO BE CAUTIOUS OF GIVING OFFENCE*

4

1724–1738

By his grace, we are what we are.
—THE REVEREND JOHN LOWELL

Early on a fall morning in 1735, the Reverend John Lowell looked down at his infant son, swaddled in white linen and sleeping in a wooden crib. His name was John, like that his father and many other Lowle men before him, all the way back to John Lowle of Somerset in the sixteenth century.

Baby John and his mother, Sarah, rested in the back room of the house where Reverend Lowell lived in Newbury on Greenleaf Street, not far from the church where he was pastor. The house was modest, purchased with funds granted to the young couple when Lowell was first ordained, in 1726. Modest but comfortable, for the house had a large fireplace, always well supplied with wood, due to the kindness of the Reverend Lowell's congregation. The furniture was sturdy and plain but prettified with the laces that came into Newbury harbor almost every week. The larder was stocked with Indian tea and Caribbean sugar, again thanks to parishioners, and a bottle or two of local-made rum. With over sixty distilleries running day and night in Massachusetts, rum was the most popular of the colonial drinks, and although the Reverend Lowell preferred beer, he liked to have a variety of beverages to offer his visitors.

And he had many visitors, for Reverend Lowell was a popular preacher. In the nine years since he'd been ordained as the very first minister of the Third Parish Church of Newbury, his flock grew, the benches of his church ever more crowded with the faithful. A blessed congregation, a happy home, and now a new baby. Sarah and John had waited so long for this birth. The Reverend Lowell bowed his head in prayer. So much had been given to him, and he was grateful.

John hadn't grown up in Newbury. His grandfather John, son of the John who was Percival's son, had left Newbury and moved to Boston. There he became a cooper, a manufacturer of barrels and casks, butts and buckets, butter churns and hogsheads. He was a busy man, his work much in demand,

and he built up a profitable business. He married three times and fathered nineteen children: John, Mary, another John (after the first one died), Peter, Joseph, Patience, Elizabeth, Ruth, Phoebe, Margaret, Samuel, another Samuel, William, another Elizabeth, Ebenezer, another William, Mehitable, Benjamin, and Nathaniel.

Ebenezer, his fifteenth child, became a cordwainer, a man who dealt in finely wrought cordovan leather. In the early eighteenth century, newly prosperous Bostonians were eager for luxury goods. The coast of the Massachusetts colony was becoming the locus of trade in America: It was here that ships were built, sailors bred, goods gathered—lumber, fish, corn—and then packed up and sent out across the sea. Profits went up, fortunes slowly grew, and suddenly, earthly rewards for hard work and dedication became a possibility. Fine china, clothing, and other expensive goods, long forbidden under Puritan rule, were becoming both available and acceptable in Boston (it would take longer for luxury items to be accepted in the outlying towns).

Ebenezer Lowell saw an opportunity in offering the best in crafted leather. It was what his fellow Bostonians wanted and were willing to pay for. By fulfilling their needs and desires, he built his own little fortune. Promises made and promises delivered. He moved his family into a fine house somewhere off Cornhill Street or King Street, in the scramble of homes and workshops, baking houses and taverns, print shops and candle maker' shoes that flourished in Boston in the new century. He bought his wife a tea table to put in their home, as proof that he could afford not only the luxury of tea but the table upon which to serve it.

When Ebenezer died at the age of thirty-six in 1711, he left provision enough that his wife, Elizabeth, and their three living children—Ebenezer, Michael, and John—could live comfortably, and the boys could choose their own careers. While Ebenezer and Michael would become merchants, John wanted to follow a different path. He left the bustle of Boston for the quiet village of Cambridge and, at the age of thirteen, entered Harvard College. He was the first Lowell to attend the school, setting in motion a continuous line of Lowells at Harvard that would last for three hundred years. He was also the first to change the spelling of the family name from Lowle to Lowell. Like attendance at Harvard, this, too, would stick. It was the beginning of the Lowells of Massachusetts.

John graduated from Harvard with no grand vision of the long line of direct progeny that would follow in his footsteps across the Harvard Yard. He had more immediate concerns on his mind. After seven years of schooling, four as a college student and three spent preparing to be a Congregational minister, it was time to find his flock. It was time to return to Newbury.

The newly built Third Parish Church was a large and elegant structure, sixty feet in length and forty-five feet wide. The ceilings were high, the windows large, and the meeting room spacious. Atop the church, at the end fronting the Merrimack River, a slender steeple rose high into the sky. The pulpit, square and plain, stood at the other end of the church. The Reverend John Lowell, a fresh young pastor, enjoyed the view as he stood there: his congregants before him, the well-to-do of Newbury, seated on their hard pews; beyond the windows, the masts of ships traveling back and forth along the river, then out to sea, bringing the world to Newbury, and Newbury to the world.

The Third Parish Church of Newbury was a far cry from the meeting-house his great-great-grandfather Percival had trudged to in the long, cold winters following his arrival in New England. No more rotting wolf heads nailed across the entranceway, no more clamshell-basted walls. Religion in Newbury had changed since the days of old Percival, not only in its space but also in its practice. Anne Hutchinson's nightmare had come true: Divine control over every aspect of one's temporal and eternal existence had lost sway. Now there were colonists who believed that a man could save himself in the life hereafter through good works, and that he could determine the conditions of his present world, as well. The idea of being divinely chosen by God still offered promise, but hard work brought money, plain and simple—money that could buy comfort and even a bit of luxury. God had lost some power, while mankind gained new abilities: One's lot on earth could be improved, and heaven could wait.

The Peace of Utrecht in 1713 had ended the cycle of wars in Europe, settling differences between France and Spain on one side, and Great Britain, the Netherlands, and Portugal on the other. With the coming of peace, world trade expanded. Merchants, shipbuilders, fishermen, lumbermen, craftsman, and whalers up and down the coast of Massachusetts stepped up and moved in to do business. The town of Newbury rose to the forefront, constructing massive wharves beside large shipbuilding facilities, and sending its sailors, fishermen, and traders farther and farther out into the world. What they brought back were goods, and the money to purchase them.

Wigs, cosmetics, and perfumes, long disdained by the Puritan faithful, were now in demand. Elaborate linens and cloths sold well, along with lace-detailed pillows, gloves, and hats; books bound in rich, embossed leather; paintings in gold-leaf frames; and marble statues of pagan heroes. Ready-made clothes were imported, the first of their kind, including brightly colored silk jackets, greatcoats, Scotch bonnets, and blue milled shirts. From the Caribbean islands came sugar, molasses, and slaves.

For everything that came in, there was a market. Where there was no waiting market, one was created. Tea came from India, brought in by British importers. At first, the colonists didn't know what to do with it. They tried boiling the leaves for a long time, which made the taste of the resulting liquid bitter and harsh; they tried salting and buttering the boiled leaves and eating them, discarding the liquid altogether, but the greens' flavor and texture was unpalatable. Finally, following the advice of merchants from the east, New Englanders realized that tea leaves should be gently boiled and the resulting tawny liquid sipped while hot. Tea tasted even better when a bit of Caribbean sugar was added. The Lowells of Newbury were fond of their sugared tea, like all their neighbors, although they rarely went into the teahouses that had sprung up around town. It was their place to be at home, ready to receive visitors, not gadding about Newbury.

Slaves were another valued commodity in Newbury. Prosperous shipbuilders and merchants and lawyers built themselves grand houses up and down the High Street, and outfitted their homes with the latest in decor and furnishings. Slaves were needed to act as servants and to keep the houses clean. Not all colonists approved of the institution. Judge Samuel Sewall of Newbury published the first antislavery tract in 1700, a pamphlet entitled *The Selling of Joseph,* in which he proclaimed, "These Ethiopians, as black as the first Adam, the Brethren and sister of the last ADAM, and the offspring of GOD; They out to be treated with a Respect Agreeable."[1] Reverend Lowell agreed—"Is not Slavery . . . a terrible thing?"[2]—and would pass the lesson on: "The precepts of revealed law, golden rule of the gospel, are that we are not to sell our brethren, that we are to do as we would be done unto."[3]

Along with the rising population and the growing prosperity of Newbury had come a proliferation of ideas and of religions. The Congregationalist ideal of community was fracturing. A group of Anglicans petitioned the General Court that they be allowed to build a chapel in Newbury funded by themselves; they also asked for an exemption from paying Congregational Church dues. The Anglicans were granted the right to build their Queen Anne's Chapel in 1711 and relieved from any responsibility toward funding the meetinghouse. Already under the charter for Massachusetts that was signed by King William and Queen Mary in 1692, electoral rights were extended to all men of property, regardless of their religious affiliation. The Congregational Church had lost its position of primacy, financially and politically. New ways of doing things, of worshipping, working, and living, were spreading throughout the colonies.

When Christmas came to New England in the early 1700s, through the rituals of the Anglican Church, there were many old Puritans who saw it as the work of the devil. They advocated that Christmas be kept as a day of regular business, with schools in session, shops open, and trade going on as usual. The Reverend Lowell was a conservative in many ways, adhering to the ban on celebrating either Christmas or Easter as a special holiday. But he welcomed the growing importance and elaboration of sermons to mark other special events. Any opportunity to spread the word of God was to be welcomed, in Lowell's view; there was no danger in using the celebrations of daily life to remind parishioners of the importance of God, grace, and good works.

Weddings began to be held in churches, presided over not by a government official but by a minister. Funerals also moved from graveside to church, with sermons prepared and printed as elegant black-bordered reproductions that were meant to be keepsakes. Special gloves were distributed at funerals, and mourning rings were given as memorials of the dearly departed. The rings often contained a lock of hair of the dead person, along with an engraved inscriptions, such as "Death Unites Parted Hearts," "Death Conquers All," "Prepare for Death," and "Prepare to Follow Me."[4]

Steeples instead of wolf heads, rum rather than beer, fine clothes instead of plain, wigs rather than caps, fancy perfumes, Anglicans, Christmas, mourning rings of gold. The singular, community-centered world of the Puritans was disappearing and a new multilayered world was rising up in its place. The Reverend John Lowell faced a challenge in this new world of multiplicity and diversity: how to keep his community united and his ministry strong.

From the start, the Reverend Lowell ran his Third Parish of Newbury along the long-established rhythms of the Puritan faith, with only a few tweaks. He loved to sing and added to the usual Sunday schedule the singing of numerous hymns and psalms. The Sunday service began in the morning with a long prayer, followed by the singing of a psalm (or two), then a sermon that lasted up to two hours. A break allowed for lunch. Then all the congregants met together again. Another prayer, another hymn (or two or three), and another long sermon. A final benediction ended the day's service.

In his preaching, John Lowell was a man of tolerance and optimism. His sermons were about the promises that faith offered, rather than on the punishments that would be leveled on the unfaithful: "Make a Suitable acknowledgement of our Need of Him, to enable us to . . . succeed, and by ascribing the Praise and Glory of all our Success to Him." Lowell did not use the fear of hell to control his flock. Instead, he simply advised them to show a "courageous and unwearied Opposition to Satan" while assuring them that God made man strong enough to oppose evil and to embrace good. He was compassionate and congenial, a pastor with a welcoming smile and the promise of hope lilt-ing like a song behind his words. Word of his preaching and of his manner spread, and his congregation continued to grow, for here was a laudable man.[5]

As one of the youngest in a clan of Lowells that spread around Boston, John Lowell had become, as a child, adept at getting along with everyone, people of all types and inclinations. When he set off for Harvard at the age of thirteen, he was resolute in his determination to become a minister but was also open to learning from a variety of teachers. Education at Harvard had changed since the early days of its founding, when its main purpose had been the crafting of Congregational ministers. Under the presidency of John Leverett, who stepped to the helm of Harvard in 1708, the curriculum and tone of the institution adjusted to wider goals. Harvard students would now be educated for a vari-ety of callings beyond just that of minister. By the year 1711, President Lever-ett proudly noted that the college graduated not only ministers but also scholars, judges, physicians, soldiers, merchants, and even farmers. He called his graduates "Sons of Harvard." Previous presidents had always referred to them as "Sons of Prophets."[6]

Leverett instituted changes in the curriculum that broadened the focus of a Harvard education from religion to other modes of understanding the uni-verse, including science and philosophy. Man's abilities to observe and to rea-son had to be trained, Leverett believed, along with his ability for faith aligned with action. The Puritan ethos of individual qualities being put to use for the betterment of the community was still the overriding purpose of education at the college. But now the nature of the service owed to the community was ex-panded beyond the singular goal of leading the faithful, and the tools used to serve the community had increased beyond the single one of faith to include reason.

To many Puritan pastors, the changes at Harvard marked a turn toward worldliness and materialism; even worse, the changes furthered the spread of faithlessness throughout New England. Leading Puritan minister Cotton Mather railed against what he saw as the lack of piety throughout Massachu-setts and the laziness everywhere: "Idleness, alas, idleness increases in the town exceedingly; idleness of which there never came any goodness!"[7] He complained about beggars on the streets of Boston—not for the lack of char-ity shown to them but for their own failure to work, and therefore their failure to follow the lessons of the Bible and the rules of God.

Mather attacked Harvard for harboring corrupt influences. He demanded that the college's overseers conduct an investigation to root out immoral and irreligious activity on the campus. The investigators found students participating in activities that were troubling but hardly damning: reading works of popular Anglican preachers; frequently partaking of strong drink; spending too much time on Saturday evenings socializing rather than praying; and going into town on Sunday mornings to have breakfast. Leverett played down the findings but noted in his own diary that he had noticed an increase among the students in incidents of swearing, "riotous Actions," and card playing.[8]

John Lowell enjoyed college, probably due to many of the activities charged in the overseers' investigation and noted in Leverett's diary. But also because of the debates he engaged in with other students, about the same issues being raised by Mather and other leaders concerned about their colony. What was the nature of duty? What was the relationship between reason and faith, the line between goodness and evil? What was the purpose of good works, the nature of grace? To further expound on the issues of their day, Lowell and his friends founded America's very first student periodical, *The Telltale*. The purpose of *The Telltale* was to offer "Criticisms of the Conversation & Behaviour of Scholars to promote right reasoning & good manner." The founders also started a club, called the Spy Club, whose members met to discuss such questions as "whether it be fornication to lye with one's sweetheart (after contraction) before marriage."[9]

Lowell's curriculum while at college included Greek, Latin, Hebrew, Logic, Natural Philosophy, Divinity, Ethics, Geography, Mathematics, Astronomy, and Metaphysics. Like many students of his time, Lowell studied the writings of Erasmus and most likely quoted amply from the theologian's aphorisms in his schoolwork. He seemed to have taken to heart a favorite line from Erasmus: "I detest dissension because it goes both against the teachings of Christ and against a secret inclination of nature." Throughout his ministry, Lowell would seek to calm turbulence in his community and maintain peace as best he could.

Within just three years of John Lowell's arrival at the Third Parish Church of Newbury, his congregation had grown so much that the Third Parish building had to be enlarged. People came from all over Newbury and beyond to hear the Reverend Lowell's offer of hope and his promise of joy, both on earth and in heaven. Proof of that promise seemed to have come when in August 1735, baby John was born to Reverend Lowell and his wife, Sarah. The child they had waited for for so long.

Reverend Lowell rededicated himself to preaching but also to studying the books on his shelves, written by both ancient philosophers and more recent ones. In order to spread the good word and build faith and hope in his congregation, Lowell had to feed and foster such faith within himself: "If the blind lead the blind they shall both fall for into the ditch," Lowell often said, quoting the apostle Matthew. The role of a minister was to lead his flock not into a ditch but into the glory of heaven, forever and ever. Ministers, Lowell preached, "are the Lights of the World, and should therefore shine before men."[10]

To the west, in the village of Northampton, another preacher was also gathering more and more followers. Jonathan Edwards, a Yale graduate, drew his flock through dramatic explorations of good and evil. In his sermons, he presented goodness as the light granted to the soul through the beneficence of God; but evil was always lurking, Satan ever ready to lure the doubtful away from the light and into the dark. Edwards believed the only way to salvation— and the avoidance of evil—was through a return to the religious traditions of the Puritans. Good works made no difference to God. Grace, the road to salvation, was preordained and could only be demonstrated by living a pious life; when a person failed to live piously, eternal damnation was guaranteed. And hell was a terrible, terrible place:

> How dismal will it be, when you are under these racking torments, to know assuredly that you never, never shall be delivered from them . . . after you shall have endured these torments millions of ages . . . the smoke of your torment shall still ascend up forever and ever. . . . your bodies, which shall have been burning all this while in these glowing flames, shall not have been consumed, but will remain to roast through eternity . . .[11]

Like Reverend Lowell, Jonathan Edwards had studied Locke, Descartes, and Isaac Newton, and, like Lowell, he believed that the laws of nature discovered through empirical science were proof of God's care and love. But reason and science were not enough. Only a profound acceptance of God, demonstrated through every aspect of daily life, could save sinners from spending eternity in the burning embrace of hell: "there is a Savior provided, who is excellent and glorious; who has shed his precious blood for sinners, and is in every way sufficient to save them, who stands ready to receive them . . ."[12]

New England had changed since the early days of the Bay Colony. There was no longer one community and one congregation, but instead a myriad of towns, and within those towns, a swelling of unhappy divisions and factions. The strength of the Puritan model, while rigid and intolerant, had been its certainty and its stability. Now coherence was disintegrating and people, especially those isolated in poverty or bad fortune, felt uncertain and unprotected. They needed security in their lives and a sense of promise. They turned to preachers like Jonathan Edwards, who preached rules and order, and offered the hope of salvation. By 1735, his church in Northampton had become the largest one in Massachusetts west of Boston, with over six hundred members, including almost all the adults in town and also children. Even a few "Negroes" looking for salvation in the word of God had been converted to Jonathan Edwards's revivalism.[13]

Joseph Hawley, uncle to Jonathan Edwards, fell into a deep depression over the state of his soul in the spring of 1735. Edwards would later describe it as a "deep melancholy, a distemper that the family are very prone to."[14] Hawley was a successful merchant and store owner, prosperous and well thought of throughout Northampton. He had been elected town clerk for the past twenty-four years, and his health was good, his family life rich. But he had become convinced that he was not a man of grace; he was certain that it was not heaven that awaited him but hell. He heard his nephew preach about pre-ordained salvation for some people and eternal damnation for the rest, and he despaired that his depressed state was proof of his sinfulness; his nephew had said in a sermon, "God sometimes expresses his wrath towards wicked men in this world not only outwardly but also in the inward expressions of it on their consciences."[15]

On June 1, 1735, Hawley killed himself. Edwards was stunned by the death. He blamed Satan for Hawley's suicide and exhorted his followers to remain stalwart against evil thoughts, and to pray for God's help: " 'Tis surely owing thus to God, and not at all to ourselves, if we han't . . . destroyed our own lives."[16] The village of Northampton and the surrounding countryside of Hampshire County was hit with a wave of attempted suicides, men and women driven to despair by the certainty of their own damnation. The attempts, some of which were successful and all of which were well publicized through word of mouth, put a damper on Edwards's exhortations to revive piety. There were even those who blamed his sermons for the hysteria over damnation. The fires of reform were tamped down, but they did not go out; they smoldered, as dissatisfaction with the practice and purpose of religion simmered and unease over the future lingered.

In early May 1736, at just eight months old, baby John Lowell died. A burial, a wolf stone, a private sermon. "Blessed are the dead that die in the Lord . . . [for they] enter into the Joy of the Lord."[17] Such a small grave. But what a bottomless well of sorrow it called forth. The tides of joy had turned for the Reverend Lowell and he became mired in grief. The death of his child signified for a time the end of all happiness for him. It was the starting point of a period of strife that had nothing to do with the death, but somehow it all became linked: life and death, heaven and hell, salvation and damnation.

Set off by Jonathan Edwards's preaching and now spreading across congregations, the questions over the right way to live and to worship divided the faithful and the despairing, the conservatives and the reformers. But it wasn't only a matter of religious doctrine. It was a questioning of all that New England had become. It was an amalgamation of disputes over not only faith but also money and politics, materialism and power. Underlying all debates was the central question: What role did God have to play in any of it?

The Reverend Lowell looked around and saw that New England had become disjointed and disgruntled. No longer was there a cohesion between all people, joined by one mission and one church. Peace had been lost: peace of mind, peace of place, peace in the knowledge of where one fit in the community on earth, and in the certainty of spending the hereafter in heaven.

He dipped his quill in ink and sat for hours in his study, working on his sermons. Pipe in hand (for he loved his tobacco), he labored to create the sentences that would buttress the faith of his congregation; that would bring them the peace they so desperately needed. Surrounding him as he worked were his treasured volumes, lined up in his bookcases, a solacing chorus of reason that joined with his own deep faith in mankind: Descartes, Locke, Erasmus. Shakespeare. Chaucer. Overlooking him and guarding him as he labored were five figures: the busts of Plato, Pythagoras, Socrates, Seneca, and Cicero. Men of reason, discipline, optimism. Men of faith, a world of faith very different from his own, but still exemplary for one underlying belief: the power of man as proof of God.

John Lowell worked and wrote, and then prepared himself to preach. He rose to his square pulpit in the Third Parish Church and spoke. He lowered his head and prayed. For a strengthening within his congregation, and within himself. For faith amid chaos. For comfort in sorrow. He prayed for peace in his heart, and in the hearts of his parishioners.

5

1740–1754

... the grey minister, with face
Radiant, let loose his noble bass.
If Heaven it reached not, yet its toll
Waked all the echoes of the soul ...
—JAMES RUSSELL LOWELL, "CREDIDIMUS JOVEM REGNARE"

George Whitefield came to America from England with one purpose: to bring lost colonists back to the Lord. Back to *his* Lord, a punishing and exacting God but one who would grant mercy to those who truly repented. Whitefield was only twenty-five years old when he arrived in New England in 1740, but he was already a famous religious orator and the closest ally of the Wesley brothers, founders of the Methodist movement. Whitefield had pioneered the use of outdoor revivals to bring the faithful to the church; the open-air sermons that he gave throughout London, Gloucester, and towns in between drew crowds numbering in the tens of thousands. He would demonstrate his evangelism now in the colonies, using the emotional exhortations he had grown so good at to save souls in the New World.

Whitefield was a funny-looking man, with a squint in one eye and a somewhat stunted stature. His sermonizing was slow and unimaginative, hardly on par with the vivid imagery and rhetorical flourishes of Jonathan Edwards. And yet when Whitefield preached, his rich voice carried far over the gathered crowd, warm and deep and full, like a tuba of exhortation calling to his people. The power it exerted over his listeners was almost magical: "my hearing him preach gave me a heart wound; by God's blessing my old foundation was broken up, and I saw that my righteousness would not save me."[1]

"Poor miserable creatures!" Whitefield preached. "What is there in your tears? What in your prayers? What in your performances, to appease the wrath of an angry God? Away from the trees of the garden; come, ye guilty wretches, come as poor, lost, undone, and wretched creatures, and accept of a better righteousness than your own."[2] He asked his crowds for confession and repentance, his voice stern and steady. In response, scores of men and women went into fits; they fell down in droves, waves of penitents crying out wildly, begging for mercy.[3] Benjamin Franklin came out to see him when Whitefield passed through Philadelphia, and wondered at the effect he had on the town's population: "it seemed as if all the world were growing religious, so that one could not walk thro' the town in an evening without hearing psalms sung in different families in every street."[4]

Whitefield not only demanded confession and repentance from the crowds that came to hear him; he also asked for donations. Huge sums were collected to pay his way through the colonies, and to fund the orphanage that he'd founded in Georgia for the children of deceased English settlers. Franklin admitted that having gone to hear Whitefield preach, "I silently resolved he should get none [for collection] from me. I had in my pocket a handful of copper money, three or four silver dollars, and five pistoles in gold. As he proceeded, I began to soften, and concluded to give the copper; another stroke to his oratory determined me to give the silver; and he finished so admirably that I emptied my pocket wholly into the collector's dish, gold and all."[5]

It was in the Reverend Lowell's nature—a good nature—to initially find hope in the movement fed by Jonathan Edwards in Northampton and then furthered by Whitefield in his journey of revival meetings across America. He saw no threat in the return to a more rule-bound, hell-bound religion, only a kind of promise. He had seen for himself how placid and comfortable his prosperous Newbury congregation had become. Such placidity in his materially comfortable flock was leading to flaccidity in their spiritual muscle. Perhaps, Lowell thought, the new spark of ardent preaching could get their blood moving again and harden up the faith and resolve of his flock.

John Lowell would never threaten his congregation with hellfire and brimstone, but if another preacher did, perhaps his flock would pay attention. Lowell felt, as Jonathan Edwards later articulated when he defended the revivalists, that the revival's renewed focus on piety, with stricter observance of the Sabbath, closer attention to the Bible, and greater concern with eternal salvation, was a good thing: Such commitment to faith was the work of God. And so the Reverend Lowell extended an invitation to George Whitefield to come to Newbury to preach at the Third Parish Church.

Whitefield welcomed the invitation, but there were other villages and towns to visit first. Throughout the fall of 1740, he traveled through New England, conjuring up large and passionate crowds. He was becoming as famous in the New World as he was in England. In Boston, tens of thousands came out to hear him preach on the Boston Common. He preached on the campuses of both Yale and Harvard, where again large crowds collected, most of them students. Whitefield condemned the students for studying dangerous and harmful books and declared that a minister needed more than just education to lead his flock: he needed the grace of the Lord. He needed to be a man who had converted to the true faith. A saved man. A man who had heard the word of the revival and succumbed.

This would be a recurring theme of Whitefield: the worthiness—or worthlessness—of the established clergy to lead their increasingly lost flocks. He condemned many of the local ministers for hypocrisy and faithlessness in his sermons across New England, and claimed, "Many, nay *most* that preach, I fear do not experimentally know Christ."[6]

The obligations of a minister were of concern to the Reverend Lowell, as well. He saw the relationship between congregation and minister as a sacred joining, with defined duties ascribed to each side of the union. The minister must always "express every godlike virtue in our lives and Conversations, a disinterested benevolence to mankind, by Charity Condescension, and Compassion, by Meekness and Patience, and overlooking the haughtiness of Men." Lowell himself acted with propriety, steadiness, and care: "A careless affected Air, void of apparent seriousness and Devotion would justly offend." As for the parishioners, Lowell preached to them to "overlook his [the minister's] infirmities, be tender of his Name and Reputation, esteem him very highly in love, and account him worthy of double honor . . . Be thankful for all God shall make him to you and endeavor by your profiting under his Ministry, make him gladly spend and be spent for you. . . ."[7]

Whitefield's methods of preaching did not fall within the parameters defined by Lowell; the rowdy crowds and emotional exhortations of open-field meetings were far from the relationship between pastor and penitent that Lowell aspired to and seemed more like a carnival. When Whitefield condemned New England clergy and admonished students for too much book learning, Lowell's unease over Whitefield's methods grew. And yet Lowell's curiosity about the man outweighed his trepidation, and he waited with excited anticipation for the arrival of Whitefield in Newbury.

An overflow crowd attended Whitefield's sermon at Lowell's Third Parish Church. Not only the usual congregation was present but also people from other churches in and around Newbury, who streamed into the packed pews and standing-room-only aisles of the church. No record was taken of his sermon, but note was made of the collection taken up following its conclusion: eighty pounds and change. This amount was more than half of Lowell's own yearly salary. Whether John Lowell begrudged the English pastor his takings or supported the generosity of his congregation also remains unrecorded. He did welcome Whitefield into his home for dinner and to spend the night.

Whitefield passed the evening with Sarah and John, then left the next morning to further spread his gospel through the northern colonies.

The pulpit of the Third Parish Church was kept open to visiting preachers over the following months. Lowell was anxious to see a response in his congregation and hopeful of a renewed faith and sense of community. The one night of preaching by Whitefield had added over one hundred new parishioners to his congregation, and Lowell was happy about that. And yet aspects of the revival—called "the Great Awakening"—began to trouble him. The nature of the preaching, the character of the preachers themselves, and the impact of both on the gathered crowds was giving the Reverend Lowell, a tolerant man, pause. He loved to indulge in the emotions of music in his preaching, but the new reliance on exaggerated and melodramatic oratory and the passions it aroused in listeners were disturbing. Theatricality was not godliness; hysteria was not faith.

Lowell had always strived to be an example to his people: "it is not sufficient that Ministers have the Testimony of their own Consciences, that they are pious and virtuous, but that they are the Lights of the World, and should therefore shine before men." But shining was not burning; shining implied steady light, not a blazing that would soon enough burn out and smolder, leaving only ashes behind. He preached, "those that are wise shine as Brightness of the Firmament, and those that turn many to righteousness, [are] as the Stars forever and ever."[8] Whereas those who turned to melodrama, no matter the purpose, were leaders only to chaos. And the way of the Lord, the Reverend Lowell believed with all his heart, was the way of peace, not chaos.

A preacher named James Davenport had taken to extreme behavior in his sermons, stripping from the waist up and railing against education as a barrier to godliness. During one meeting, he presided over the burning of hundreds of books, calling it a "bonfire of the vanities." He set fire to another pile made up of material goods that to him seemed to be a symbol of the decadent age: "Scarlet Cloaks, Velvet Hoods, fine Laces, and every Thing that had two colours,"[9] along with shoes, wigs, jewelry, cloaks, and nightgowns. As the pile burned, he took off his own pants and threw them into the flames.

News of the bonfires spread. Descriptions of the crowds attending Davenport's gatherings and the revivals were published: "some would be praying, some exhorting, some singing and clapping their hands, some laughing some crying, some shrieking and roaring out."[10] Jonathan Edwards cautioned Davenport and his followers not to take Scripture and judgment into their own hands, and yet Edwards admitted that the so-called New Lights revivalists were inspiring a new adherence to piety—and was that such a bad thing?

The Reverend Lowell was horrified. He began to see revivalism, with its wild sermons and dependence upon even wilder emotions, as a very real threat to the stability of his community as well as to their faith. The movement simply went too far. For Lowell, revivalism had become less about religion and more about spectacle. But even worse than the itinerants like Davenport, who were at least educated in theology (Davenport received his divinity degree from Yale), were those ever-multiplying so-called preachers who proselytized widely and yet had received no education in religion or much of anything else. John Lowell had spent seven years training to be a minister. He had studied divinity at Harvard and knew not only the Bible but also the teachings of centuries of scholarship on faith, piety, and salvation. How could any person unschooled in theology and unbound by the rules of an established congregation lead lost souls to salvation?

These lay preachers included farmers, tradesmen, Indians, and women, all claiming to have been divinely inspired and to be in direct contact with God. They eschewed any need for theological study or debate; they claimed that what they knew of religion came directly from God in the daily and intimate communications they received from Him. These itinerant preachers made a regular practice of going into trances and claiming divine visions, and then crying out for repentance by all before it was too late. Traveling from town to town, and from house to house, they performed their scripts of vision, rapture, and exhortation, and then gathered donations. Supporters often joined them, leaving their homes and farms behind to follow the preaching itinerants across New England.

Bathsheba Kingsley was from the small village of Westfield in the Connecticut River Valley, a mousy woman, thin and pale, with washed-out lips and gray eyes. But when she began to talk about the dreams and visions she'd experienced, all of them directives from heaven, people stopped and listened. Bathsheba came alive when talking about the conversations she had with God. Her eyes fired with passion and her cheeks grew pink with exertion. Golden red hair fell out from beneath her white cap, falling in waves around her face, framing her in a kind of ecstasy. She went manically from house to house in her village, ministering to her neighbors with teachings she claimed came directly from God. Her husband tried to keep her at home, but she ignored him and carried on. She even stole his horse so that she could travel farther afield, carrying her message from town to town, a mouse turned lion, raging across the fields of Massachusetts.

Jonathan Edwards was one of the ministers who sought to sanction and silence Kingsley. Edwards was now following the lead of Lowell; he also had become increasingly concerned with the excesses of the revivalist itinerants. To him, there was no itinerant so dangerous and hateful as Kingsley, a woman who "is rugged, daring and presumptuous, and trusts to herself." He reported that "she has exceedingly departed from the way [of] her duty . . . her behavior has in general been exceedingly contrary to that Christian gentleness and meekness that becomes a follower of the Lamb of God, especially in treatment of her husband . . . [for she is guilty of] praying that her husband might go quick to hell."[11]

In a sermon preached by the Reverend Lowell for the funeral of a Newbury woman, he had listed the traits of "a laudable woman" to include "one who is meek, not soon angry, or hurried away by boisterous Passions . . . she is clothed in humility . . . she is one who is greatly Temperate . . ." Kingsley was most certainly none of these things, and so not a laudable woman—and yet she was so sure of her divine inspiration that she inspired others to believe her and follow her. She went from house to house, preaching the Gospel as she wanted. Again, how contrary to the Reverend Lowell's descriptions of a laudable woman: "She is no Tatler from House to House, no Common Censurer of others failings . . . she sees enough in herself to impose Silence upon her Tongue . . ."[12]

Silence upon her tongue. The punishments of the last century—banishment, fines, stock, and whip—could no longer be used to silence those who spoke out against their pastors. The only thing that could be done was to close the doors of churches, shut down the pulpits to Kingsley and others like her.

In 1744, John Lowell silenced the words of revival in his church: "He suddenly halted in his course as one out of breath, and turned aside to walk more quietly in a different path." He forbade the use of his pulpit in the Third Parish Church by any preacher not invited by him; he suspended all evening meetings of his congregation as "tending to disorder."[13] He withdrew himself and his church from the evangelizing craze. He returned to—although he had never really strayed away from—his weekly sermons based on the importance of good works, exhorting his flock to follow lessons found in the Bible, and promising them ultimate salvation: "Be steadfast, unmovable, and always Abounding in the Work of the Lord, as knowing that our labour shall not be in vain . . ."[14] He cautioned against unseemly or showy emotions and advised instead that faith be quiet and sure. He replaced the tuba of Whitefield with the bass of reassurance: Let comfort be felt, far and wide; hold back judgment, and keep the heart open. *For this is the word of the Lord.*

The Reverend Lowell founded his faith on such tenets, and his allegiance to the word of the Lord was rewarded. Another son was born, another John. This son thrived and grew.

Not everyone in his Third Parish Church was pleased with Lowell and his leadership. There were many in his congregation who had enjoyed the sermons

of traveling revivalists, especially the marvelous Whitefield. Discontented parishioners, over one hundred of them, withdrew from Third Parish and began
a campaign to form their own church. The General Court of Massachusetts
had to intervene, as things became heated between the parties. Harvard sided
with the Reverend Lowell and submitted papers on his behalf. The overseers
of the college were no supporters of the revivalists after Whitefield had called
their institution "Godless Harvard."[15]

In the end, the complaining parishioners were allowed to leave the Third
Parish and to convene as the First Presbyterian Church of Newburyport. They
were granted exemption from paying parish dues to the Third Parish Church
and Lowell was compensated for the lost income by being granted the right to
charge rent for pews in his church. Lowell's work could carry on, funded in a
new manner; down the road, the new Presbyterians set up and funded themselves. A few decades later, after George Whitefield died while in Newbury on
yet another evangelizing mission, his funeral service was held in the First
Presbyterian Church. Tears flowed and yet those in attendance rejoiced that
their inspiration, George Whitefield, was now "present with the Lord."[16]

After the schism with the Presbyterian adherents of his congregation, a painting was commissioned by the Reverend Lowell from Goodman Shattuck, the
local blacksmith and an aspiring artist. The painting features seven ministers
of Newbury, all of different denominations—Presbyterian, Anglican, Congregationalist, Baptist—sitting together, amicably and easily, at a long table. The
table is covered in an opulent tasseled cloth; the chairs are high-backed and
elegant. The men are dressed up in black gowns; most of them are wearing
wigs and all have white bands around their neck, with ruffles falling down
over their chests. The faces of the clergymen range in expression from stern to
quite merry. The Reverend Lowell sits at the head of the table, his head tilted to
the side and his mouth turned up in a smile. His wig is well powdered and tightly
curled; one long, elegant finger extends from his left hand, pointing to the Bible
on the table. Alongside the Bible, close to hand for the gathered clerics, are pipes,
tobacco dishes, and ale pots.

An inscription across the top of the painting reads, in Latin, *In necessariis
unitas; in non necessariis libertas; in utrisque charitas*. In essentials, unity; in
nonessentials, liberty; in both, charity. Reverend Lowell felt it was his duty to
make it so. Hope, not fear. Faith, not despair. Peace, not chaos.

6

1755–1759

Go on and prosper,
a Blessing to this Place . . .
a burning and shining light
in this Golden Candlestick . . .
—THE REVEREND JOHN LOWELL

The Reverend John Lowell steeled himself. He had a sermon to write and much was at stake. A year earlier, in 1754, English soldiers led by a young George Washington had attacked French holdings along the Ohio River; the French retaliated by attacking Washington at Fort Necessity and forcing him to surrender. By the summer of 1755, the Seven Years' War was fully under way in America. The French threatened to usurp English rule over the colonies of New England and replace the Protestant King George II with their French King, the Roman Catholic Louis XV.

For the first and last time in his career, the Reverend Lowell would preach not for peace but for war. Not for the chaos of war but for the unity he hoped it would bring. Unity to his New England, and to his corner of America. In England, the Crown and Parliament called upon the colonists of New England to fight. The colonists took the command willingly. From New Hampshire, Connecticut, and Massachusetts, thousands of soldiers amassed. The town of Newbury offered up more than her share of men—over two hundred—to fight against the French. Now it was up to the Reverend Lowell to exhort them to battle while also reminding them of faith and its attendant value of mercy.

He worked for days on the sermon. He searched his soul for how war could be justified, fighting could be condoned, killing allowed. He turned to his volumes of John Locke, and considered the liberty of man and the nature of tyranny. He turned to his Bible and paced through passages, seeking an absolution for war. *But if the watchman see the sword come, and blow not the trumpet, and the people be not warned; if the sword come, and take any person from among them, he is taken away in his iniquity; but his blood will I require at the watchman's hand.*[1]

On the morning of May 22, 1755, the soldiers of Newbury and their families gathered at the Third Parish Church. The Reverend Lowell walked along the rows, turning to greet them one by one. He stopped beside Moses Titcomb, long a member of his congregation. Moses was easily the largest man in town but also one of the kindest; now the Reverend Lowell took Moses' hands in his, and the two men contemplated each other for a moment. Then the minister passed on, taking his place in the pulpit. His son John, twelve years old, would leave Newbury the next year to study at Harvard, like his father had before him. But for now, he was still at home and he sat in the family pew, looking up at his father.

"For the Lord your God is he that goeth with you, to fight for you against your enemies, to save you," the Reverend Lowell began. His eyes closed and he recited silently, *When thou goest out to battle against thine enemies, and seest horses, and chariots, and a people more than thou, be not afraid of them: for the LORD thy God is with thee, which brought thee up out of the land of Egypt.*[2]

Opening his eyes, the Reverend Lowell looked out over the crowd that had gathered. Men from his congregation, yes, like Moses Titcomb. Moses, with his family gathered around him, wife and four children, all boys growing up like their father: thick as elms and just as tall. But there were also folk from other churches of Newbury, come to hear the Reverend Lowell sing one last time before their men headed out to war. Lowell would sing—he had his hymn prepared—but first he would preach. There had been a period of peace for Newbury, between the terrible King Philip's War and now this one, brought upon them by outside forces. England against France, and they were Englishmen. They would fight for England.

"God is never neutral," the Reverend Lowell declared, his voice reaching all the way to the back of the church. "He always helps one side or the other in every war." And in this war, Lowell was certain, God was on the side of England. On the side of liberty, and of freedom. The colonists were willing to fight for liberty and freedom. (England should have been paying better attention.)

Lowell went on: "If you should be Successful, let me entreat you to shew those [French] Roman Catholics what an happy Influence it has had upon your Tempers and Behavior that you have had Liberty from your Childhood . . . Would you be under a despotick Prince? Would you be dragooned and perpetually pillaged? Would you see an End to Law and everything depend upon the Will of him that had the power over you?"[3]

Then came the hymn. All the voices in the church joined in, trebles and altos and sopranos of varying potency adding to the bass of the Reverend Lowell.

Thou hast redeem'd our souls with blood;
Hast set the pris'ners free;
Hast made us kings and priests to God,
And we shall reign with thee.[4]

Moses Titcomb died four months later in the wilderness beside Lake George
in New York (the lake had just been renamed, changed from the French Lac
Saint Sacrement, in honor of the English king). Titcomb and his troop of
Newbury men had been set upon by a group of French soldiers and their Native American allies: "hailstones from heaven were never much thicker than
their bullets came."[5] In the bloody battle that ensued, dozens of men fell from
both sides, including Moses. But the English carried the day, driving the
French to flee and leave their dead behind. The bodies of the dead enemies
were thrown in a marshy pond fed by the waters of the lake. The pond would
be forever known as "Bloody Pond."[6] The body of Moses Titcomb was carefully laid to rest under a gathering of pines at the shoreline of Lake George. No
marker was laid, save for a nest of small stones.

It took two weeks for a relay of messengers to deliver the news back to
Newbury. No one wanted to be the one to tell the people of the town that their
mountain of a man, Moses Titcomb, had fallen and would never be returning.

"Moses, my servant is dead," Lowell preached at the memorial held for
Moses Titcomb in Newbury. "Seldom was any man more generally beloved,
and the whole country shows that his death is a great public loss . . . such a
hero will be very much missed." And while Titcomb's body would never be
returned to Newbury, God would take good care of his soul and welcome the
resurrection of his body: "The dust shall not be lost, not a particle of it that at
last He may rebuild the fabric, more glorious at the resurrection of the just."[7]

The minister stooped in his pulpit then, feeling himself grow older, years
lost in the passing of only minutes. The tearstained faces of his congregation
were turned up to him, looking for counsel and for comfort. He could only
offer words, words and his own fervent prayer for their relief. *Yea, though I
walk through the valley of the shadow of death, I will fear no evil: for thou art
with me; thy rod and thy staff they comfort me.*[8] Words passed on and repeated
through centuries, prayers made in the moment. But never quite enough to
quell the pain.

The English dealt a decisive blow to the French in 1759 at the battle fought on
the Plains of Abraham, outside the city of Quebec. The commander of the
forces that defeated the French at Quebec was Gen. James Wolfe, who died
from wounds received there. William Davenport of Newbury had been one of

the soldiers serving under Wolfe's command. He returned home after the victory and opened his house as a tavern for travelers on the Boston to Portsmouth road. In honor of his fallen hero, he named his tavern Wolfe Tavern. Over its front door, he hung a large wooden sign featuring a portrait of General Wolfe. Wolfe Tavern became a well-known watering spot throughout coastal New England, and would be a favorite meeting place for the Massachusetts revolutionaries in the decades to come.

One night, two men coming out of Wolfe Tavern made a bet: If they were to wake the Reverend Lowell at that moment, at three o'clock in the morning, would he or would he *not* be found with pipe in hand? Together under the light of the moon, they went to the house on Greenleaf Street. They banged upon the door. After a few moments, the door was opened by the Reverend Lowell. His lips were formed into a gentle, inquiring smile, his high forehead was wrinkled with concern. And in his hand, he held a pipe. One man was surprised by the pipe, already lit: He had lost the bet. But neither man was surprised that Lowell had opened the door. They knew that he would, no matter the hour.

A victory party celebrating the defeat of the French was held on the triangular green outside the Third Parish Church. A "huge gridiron [was] erected and an ox was roasted."[9] Songs were sung, ale drunk, and prayers offered for those who had safely returned and those who would never come back to Newbury but would be forever remembered. The men of Newbury, along with hundreds of other New Englanders, had fought against the "despotick Prince" of France, willingly and with bravery. And when England started to bind and burden the colonists with laws and taxes and strictures they had no part in, and no voice in, the people of New England would recognize a new "despotick Prince." And would vow to fight against him, just as willingly and bravely.

Part Three

REVOLUTION

I first drew in New England's air, and from her hardy breast

Sucked in the tyrant-hating milk that will not let me rest;

And if my words seem treason to the dullard and the tame,

'tis but my Bay-State dialect—our fathers spake the same!

—JAMES RUSSELL LOWELL,
"ON THE CAPTURE OF FUGITIVE SLAVES NEAR WASHINGTON"

7
1765–1774

No grief or Pain shall wreck your Breast,
With Angel's Conversation Blessed;
Survey this spacious Garden round,
Whatever pleasure can be found, Enjoy . . .
—JOHN LOWELL, ESQ., "CREATION AND THE FALL OF MAN"

John Lowell, son of the Reverend Lowell, walked down High Street in Newburyport on a blustery day in late September 1765. He was five years out of Harvard College. Beside him strolled Jonathan Jackson. Both men were oblivious to the chill wind that swept up from the Merrimack River, caught up as they were in their conversation. Lowell was tall and sturdy, elegant in a high-collared dark green jacket and snow white neck piece that came out in waves below his broad chin. Jackson, shorter than Lowell, was a gangly branch of a man in brown jacket and breeches. Slighter he might have been, but he was Lowell's match in energy and ambition.

The two men were the closest of friends, a strong affection having formed between them as college students in Cambridge. Now they were housemates in Newburyport, having moved in together when Lowell returned to his hometown to start up a law office. Lowell had no interest in following his father into the church. He had spent the past five years in Boston, working under a seasoned lawyer and learning the trade. There were no law schools or books on law to be studied in the mid-1700s; the only way to learn how to be a lawyer was to practice.

Lowell and Jackson vowed to each other a life of eternal celibacy and devoted companionship. Lowell would pursue the law, and Jackson would tend to business. Together, they would prosper. They'd chosen a neat white house to live in, simple and spare but for the elegant parlor, which boasted a wide carved mantelpiece and a baroque china cupboard. On display were cups and saucers of finest white china etched in various decorations of gold. The china pieces had come from Staffordshire, England, imported on a ship built in one of Newburyport's own yards; one portion of the fine china had been given to the shipbuilder in partial payment for the ship itself and another portion went to the merchants who had arranged the trade, including Jonathan Jackson and his firm.

The close friendship between Lowell and Jackson did not mean they were in agreement on all issues all the time. On this evening in 1765, Lowell was adamantly arguing that the Stamp Act recently enacted by Parliament fell hardest on him and his fellow lawyers, for the highest levy was upon attorney licenses; all court papers were to be taxed, as well. But Jackson countered that the entire colony suffered under the act, as every parchment or paper upon which anything was printed or written would be taxed. His business as a merchant would be hurt, for in trade, every transaction went on paper, every promise or agreement or contract. Jackson couldn't move a barrel of molasses without at least five documents to accompany it down its happy road to becoming rum—and every one of those documents now would be taxed.

The lawyer under whom Lowell had trained after college was the renowned pamphleteer Oxenbridge Thacher. While working for Thacher, Lowell imbibed deeply of his many anti-Parliament diatribes. Thacher was particularly known for his antitaxation pamphlets, including *The Sentiments of a British American*, and for his *Address to the King and Parliament*, which he had written in 1764:

> We have learned . . . to consider ye rights of Britons as sacred & inviolable. And we cannot conceive that the colonists have forfeited [such rights] by their emigrating a thousand leagues, subduing immense forests, filled with savage beasts & men . . . [and] protecting at their own expensc the British subjects at ye great distance from the capital . . . Now we have ever supposed this to be one essential right of British subjects, that they shall not be subjected to taxes which, in person or by representative, they have no voice in laying.[1]

England had begun imposing more and more taxes on its colonies to cover the many costs associated with the Seven Years' War. Great Britain won new territory in the war, including New France and Spanish Florida, additional islands in the Caribbean, and the coastline of Senegal in Africa. But the waging of war had incurred large debts for the growing empire, and the costs of maintaining that empire were rising all the time. Loyal subjects in England couldn't be taxed nearly enough to cover all the costs of paying off those debts. Taxing the colonies was the answer.

Parliament had attempted in the past to levy a tax on the colonies, in the form of a molasses tax imposed in 1733. But that tax was never enforced, largely because colonists evaded it through rampant smuggling conducted right under the noses of English officials. Molasses kept arriving in larger and larger amounts to feed the rising number of rum distilleries, and there was little the royal authorities could do about it. Parliament made clear that the sugar tax imposed in 1764 and now the Stamp Act of 1765 would not be so laxly enforced. Collectors would be appointed, offices built and outfitted, and taxes and duties collected.

John Lowell and Jonathan Jackson met often with other men from Newburyport at Wolfe's Tavern, sitting down over pots of rum and mugs of ale to discuss the unfairness of British policies in the colony, and to lament the growing conflict between England and New England. Issues were debated, ideas thrown out and discussed, options for securing the rights of the colonists evaluated. The men couldn't forget the legacy of the man for whom the tavern had been named. While in college, Lowell had written a poem in Wolfe's honor:

> No pangs he felt but what his country gave
> For fate awhile detained him from his grave;
> Soon as the happy Conquest reached his ear,
> And wry gale through glorious tidings bear,
> "Tis all I ask of the scriptures," he replies,
> And a gentle slumber closed his eyes . . .[2]

On that blustery night in September, as John and Jon made their way into the tavern, Lowell pointed to the portrait of Wolfe on the tavern sign and commented that the beak-nosed general looked properly pained and in need of a good drink: He had fought for Britain, and now the mother country treated her colonists like *this*? By installing a new tax collector in the town and giving him vast powers to collect revenues for the Crown? The two friends moved to the back of the tavern to meet up with the other men of Newburyport, everyone concerned that under the Stamp Act, "Our Commerce would Stagnate and our Laborers Starve."[3] Proprietor William Davenport gave the men their own meeting room, promising supplies would be sent in. Soon enough, he came in himself to set down bowls of hot rum punch, cups of egg toddy, mugs of ale. Supper was served: roasted chicken legs, bread warm from the oven, pudding thick with drippings. More bowls of punch, a double bowl of "toddy" and "egg toddy," and then "a thrible bowl," then another double bowl.[4]

Guy Fawkes Day was still over a month away, the date on which Englishmen celebrated the failure of Fawkes and his Catholic coconspirators to blow up Parliament and kill King James I. No longer were witch marks carved into

floors to keep evil Catholics at bay, as had been done in the time of Percival
Lowle back in Bristol. But the century-old tradition of setting bonfires and
burning effigies of Guy Fawkes had persisted. As the men in Wolfe's Tavern
became more and more incensed over the taxes imposed by England, the idea
of burning a different kind of effigy was proposed, and applauded.

What was needed was quickly searched out: a stocking here, a torn che-
mise there, a stained glove, a forlorn pair of discarded breeches, a hat that had
been trampled by a horse and still bore the mark of the iron shoe, lumps of
straw and a bit of string. Then an effigy was made. Guy Fawkes had been replaced with a new straw man for evil: John Boardman, the town's new tax collector. The figure, all dressed up and ready to go, was hoisted up above the
crowd and carried ceremoniously outside, men from the tavern streaming
alongside and cheering.

Tar barrels stored behind the tavern were rolled out and placed below a
high branch of the old elm tree that stood at the foot of King Street. A scrap of
a man, carrying the effigy on his back, shimmied up the tree and hung it with
a rope from the high branch. The effigy swung in the wind; the motion of its
waving arms and the swaying of its feet made it seem almost alive, as if it were
struggling to get away, aware of the fate that awaited. The barrels were set afire
and then the straw man was cut from his noose. The effigy fell into the flames
and began to dance about in the heat. Soon the entire bundle was engulfed, a
rolling torso of bright flames underneath a dark sky.

"I am sorry to see that substitute," Jackson said to Lowell as they watched
the straw smolder and smoke, flames shooting from the lopsided head in licks
of orange and yellow. "I wish it had been the original."[5]

Effigies burned throughout Massachusetts during that fall of 1765. In Boston, colonists took an old boot, in reference to Lord Bute, former prime minister of England, and filled it with a putty figure of the devil. The stuffed boot
was hung from the Liberty Tree close to the Boston Common and set aflame.
Another effigy was made, this one resembling the royal stamp distributor, Andrew Oliver. It was burned in front of Oliver's house, after being heaped upon
a bonfire built from scaffolding that had been torn down from the building
site of the new stamp collector's office in Boston.

Lowell and Jackson watched their local effigy burn and then headed for home.
Many of their companions, however, began to parade through the streets,
stopping every person they met in the dark and demanding, "Stamp or no
stamp?" Beatings were dealt out to anyone replying "Stamp" and even for any
poor fool who waited too long before uttering the correct reply.

"I am as you are!' cried one seized-upon passerby. The reveling marauders took a moment to understand his meaning. Then with a cry, they clapped the fellow on the back and sent him on his way, cheering loudly as he hurried away.[6]

John and Jonathan arrived home to their snug house, full of food and drink and tired from the events of the evening. But they could not yet settle down to sleep, and stayed up talking beside the fire, splitting an apple between them to settle their stomachs. Calm the mind, calm the belly, and then sleep will come. They turned in finally, for the next day was a day of business, and the only way to prosperity was through hard work. Hard work needed a good night's sleep. Taxation would be fought, but in the meantime, there was money to be made.

The town of Newbury had split into two in 1764, with the more prosperous portside part of town, populated by ship owners, traders, merchants, and lawyers, becoming the town of Newburyport. The Reverend Lowell's Third Parish Church, situated close to the river, had become the First Church of Newburyport. Churches of other denominations arrived in town, filling their own pews with the faithful and full of their own ideas of what it meant to be spiritual. And yet the Puritan practices of sobriety, religiosity, and self-denial were imprinted upon the character of New England, no matter the church. There was no question that what saved a man was hard work. Not only in the hereafter but in the here and now. Nose to the grindstone: Get the work done, and flourish.

John Lowell did work hard and he did flourish. He became well known for the commercial cases he handled for Jonathan Jackson and his business partner, Nathaniel Tracy, as well as for cases he took on for other merchants and traders around the colony. Lowell also became skilled in criminal defense work. Perhaps his work defending the criminally accused didn't garner the fees that his commercial work did—he was often appointed by the court to represent a client of little means—but the cases more than made up for lack of fees by granting him largesse of fame. When John Lowell took to a courtroom, he seized judge, jury, and the watching public in his very capable hands and landed them wherever he wanted, most often with a finding of not guilty.

The Stamp Tax was repealed in 1766, but it brought little relief to the colonies, for almost immediately the Declaratory Acts were imposed, stating plainly that only Parliament had the power and authority to "make laws and statutes of sufficient force and validity to bind the colonies and people of America, subjects of the crown of Great Britain, in all cases whatsoever."[7] Then, in 1767, the Townshend Acts were passed. Heavy duties were levied on all imports of paper, glass, paint, lead, tea, and other daily necessities. Everyone in the colony felt the brunt of these new duties, from the fat merchants of Boston sitting in their brick warehouses to the skinny fishmongers on the pier, from the wigged lawyers in town to the apron-bibbed tavern owners on the road.

The merchants of Boston demanded an immediate boycott of all goods imported by British traders. The people of Boston strove to comply. Pamphlets, newspapers, and street orators urged the colonists on: Buy local, trade local, sell local. No more fancy imports of lace and fine furniture, no more perfume or embroidered gowns, no more Indian tea, Oriental spices, or French milled soap. Those goods were for loyalists; patriots knew how to make do with what they could make (or smuggle) themselves.

Organized groups, calling themselves the Sons and Daughters of Liberty, sprang up in and around Boston, and in towns like Newburyport. The groups urged their fellow colonists to resist the tyranny of England by joining in the boycotts, writing pamphlets, holding meetings. Poems and songs burst from busy pens, exalting the fight for freedom, stirring others to join in: "In freedom we're born and like sons of the brave,/ We'll never surrender, But swear to defend her,/ And scorn to survive, if unable to save."[8]

On May 17, 1767, the Reverend John Lowell died at the age of sixty-three. His son and his second wife, Elizabeth Cutts Whipple, sat in the front box pew to hear the funeral sermon.* Behind them, the pews were crowded with parishioners and townspeople. After the service, the large group of mourners walked side by side with the family, all following as the casket was carried from church to graveyard. The Reverend Lowell was buried on the hill overlooking his Third Parish Church and the Merrimack River beyond. A simple stone was placed to mark his grave. No more wolf stones—wolves were rare in town now, having been killed off by the colonists one by one. The Reverend Lowell could lie undisturbed on this high hill overlooking the town he had loved, and had been loved by in return. He bequeathed to his son, John, a ring bearing the family coat of arms registered by Richard Lowle of Somerset back in 1591. He also left to his son a family motto, coined by the reverend himself. *Occasionem Cognosce*. Seize the Opportunity.

---

* The Reverend Lowell had married Elizabeth Cutts Whipple in 1758. She brought to the marriage both goods (fine works of silver, wrought by the father of Paul Revere) and experience—her dead husband had been pastor in Hampton Falls and thus she was well versed in the duties of a preacher's wife. She would live through the days of the American Revolution and the new republic, although she could never reconcile herself to the break with England. On days celebrating the colonists' victory, she wore black.

Opportunity arrived in the form of a woman—or rather, two women, both from Salem. It was Jonathan Jackson who first decided to marry, after meeting a young woman named Sarah Barnard from the town of Salem. Jon had pledged eternal celibacy to his friend, but needs must. Lowell followed suit. What his good friend Jonathan did, he would do, too. He met Sarah Higginson, also from Salem. John wooed his Sarah and pledged himself to her. The joint vow of celibacy made by the two young men never really had much of a chance. Puritan strictures against bachelorhood were long gone, but the mandate in the community still existed: Marry and have children. Lowell and Jackson, best friends for life, complied.

Jon and John were married to their Sarahs in 1767 in a double wedding. The morning of the event, they paraded through the town of Salem, their brides on their arms, in compliance with the old ritual of "walking out": betrothed couples cheered on by neighbors as they made their way to the meetinghouse to be married.[9] Flowers were brought forth by little girls and given to the brides, posies of sweet william and phlox wrapped in ribbons and string.

John Lowell was a man of the law. He practiced the law with a reverence even greater than that he held for his king. For no man rises above the law, as every Englishmen versed in the Magna Carta knew: *Nemo est supra legis*. Through law came order, and with order, opportunity. Having been elected a selectman for Newburyport in the fall after he was married, he saw his duty as protecting his community and promoting her prosperity, all under the law. He was part of the elected elite now and he would do his utmost to care for those who counted on him.

Late in the year of 1767, the merchants of Boston sent a letter to the town of Newburyport, asking that they support Boston's boycott of English goods. John Lowell met with his fellow selectmen to consider the response. Newburyport depended upon shipbuilding more than any of its other industries. Fishing, whaling, trading, distilling: All were secondary to the business of building grand sailing ships. These ships were mostly bought by English traders and paid for entirely with English goods. A boycott of goods from Britain would hit Newburyport coming and going: traders without trade didn't need new ships built, and any ships that were purchased would be paid for with British goods, which couldn't be passed on due to the boycott. The selectmen of Newburyport did not want to join the boycott, but how to reject the request from Boston without angering their fellow colonists?

Lowell took charge. Using his legal skills, he crafted a response to the men of Boston that was both diplomatic and unambiguous:

We have regarded Great Britain with all the respectful affection of a Child to its parent, but due to some recent measures undertaken by Parliament—which seem to be highly misjudged—there has arisen a cloud which obscures the true interests of those over here, from those over there. . . . we expect—we impatiently desire!—that the measures and the cloud soon be removed, and a mutual confidence restored between Great Britain and her colonies. . . . The question, of course, is what a boycott will achieve for removing the cloud, and at the same time, what will it do for the town of Newburyport?[10]

Lowell promised the merchants of Boston to "be watchful against any Encroachments on our Rights as Englishmen or Freemen and to be uniformly and resolutely determined that these shall not be infringed while our Fortunes or even our Lives continue."[11] John Lowell still believed in the rule of law, and in his duty to his king and country.

But within the year, most of his fellow selectmen and townspeople joined the boycott. Distrust of the English was growing, and even more important, money could still be made in trading goods—maybe not through the English-mandated trade routes, but through the increasingly profitable illegal running of goods in and out of Newburyport. As the tide in the town swung toward supporting the rebels, anyone harboring what were deemed royalist loyalties was viewed with suspicion—or worse.

On a September morning in 1768, Lowell witnessed firsthand the kind of justice the patriots of Newburyport meted out to those who had not joined their cause. Joshua Vickery, a ship carpenter, was accused of passing information to British customs officials about ships carrying illegal goods into the harbor. A mob descended upon his shop and carried him by his arms and legs to the public stocks. There he was forced to sit "from three to five o'Clock in the Afternoon, most of the Time on the sharpest stone that could be found, which put him to extreme Pain, so that he once fainted."[12] He was then carted through the streets of Newburyport and pelted with eggs, gravel, and stones. There would be no tolerance of those who parlayed with the British.

Elizabeth Cutts Whipple, the widow of the Reverend John Lowell, moved back to her hometown in New Hampshire and John and Sarah Lowell moved into the family house on Greenleaf Street. Sarah set to work on the neglected kitchen garden, putting in rows of beans, peas, tomatoes, and squash. John took over the flower beds, tending to the lemon yellow lilies along the front of the house and planting stands of purple strawflower and orange yarrow against the fences.

A daughter was born in 1768. John and Sarah named her Anna Cabot Lowell and called her "Nancy." A year later, a son was born. He was named John Lowell, Jr., and John senior was over the moon with pride.

John Lowell, Sr., and Jonathan Jackson purchased together a double lot of land on High Street in Newburyport. They built side-by-side matching mansions, three-storied and square, with elegant rooflines and firm foundations. Into Lowell's mansion came the Staffordshire cups and saucers (a gift from Jackson), along with silver pieces made by Paul Revere and passed down from the Reverend Lowell; fine chairs crafted in Connecticut from cherry and pine and carved in rococo sinuosity; and a bow-legged table, made of maple and eastern pine, from a workshop in Rhode Island. John Adams stopped by Lowell's new home on a visit to Newburyport and wrote back to his wife, a green tinge of jealousy spreading across the page: "He has built himself a palace like a nobleman's, and lives in great splendor."[13]

A third child was born to John and Sarah in 1771, and they named her Sarah for her mother. The joy at Sarah's birth was to be tempered by sorrow, for her mother died the following year. Sarah Higginson Lowell was buried on the hill beside the old Third Parish Church, not far from the stone marking the grave of the Reverend Lowell. From the hill, mourners could look out over Frog Pond, where Sarah had gone often with her two older children to hunt for tadpoles on warm summer mornings. The children now stood with their heads bowed, all thoughts of tadpoles gone, for they had grown suddenly older without their mother. John Lowell mourned for his Sarah but thought of his three children and knew he had to marry again.

In early 1773, a pamphlet began to circulate through the colony, laying out the story of a "Negro who had accompanied his Master from the West Indies to England and there sued and obtained his freedom."[14] James Somerset had been a slave of Charles Stewart, an English customs officer stationed in Boston. When Stewart returned to England, he took Somerset with him. Somerset attempted to run away and Stewart arranged to have him sent to Jamaica and sold. Somerset turned to the English courts to protect him. Lord Mansfield, chief justice of the King's Bench, heard the case and then ordered that Somerset be released as a freeman. He stated that slavery was "so odious" that it could be allowed only if a statute or law provided for it, and since no such statute or law existed in England, "the black must be discharged."[15]

John Lowell was approached by local slaves, emboldened by the story of James Somerset's delivery from servitude. They asked him what were there chances of winning their freedom in a colonial court of law. Lowell carefully considered the answer to such a question.

He himself despised slavery. Amid all the clamoring for liberty and freedom by his fellow colonists, he was struck by "the inconsistency of pleading for our own rights and liberties whilst we encouraged the subjugation of others. . . ."[16] How ironic it was that in Great Britain, a black man held as a slave could be made free, and yet in the colonies, a slave had no rights to freedom at all. In Massachusetts, the laws were explicit when it came to slavery. Slavery was allowed and regulated as any other kind of business. Duties were imposed on the importation of slaves; bonds were required to manumit a slave; the ability of a slave to marry or own livestock or travel was all strictly controlled.

Lowell read of a black slave living in Boston who submitted a petition for freedom to the General Court of Massachusetts. In his petition, which was ignored, Felix Holbrook laid out the plight of all enslaved people: "neither they, nor their Children to all Generations, shall ever be able to do, or to possess and enjoy any Thing, no, not even Life itself, but in a Manner as the Beasts that perish. . . . We have no Property! We have no Wives! No children! We have no City! No Country!"[17]

Lowell knew there were about five thousand blacks in Massachusetts. As a diligent selectman, he reviewed all government documents that came across his desk, including the latest census figures of 1763. What he did not know was how many of these black inhabitants were slaves. He saw slaves every day in Newburyport. They worked in homes or in warehouses or on the docks. They lived with their white owners and, as far as Lowell could tell, were treated as members of the household. Slaves and family ate together at the same table, slept in the same house, read from the same Bible. Black slaves were taught to read, write, do sums. Jonathan Jackson's slave Pomp was Jackson's right-hand man, trusted and respected. But Lowell knew that these enslaved men and women could not be truly happy, not when their very person was defined as property.

He despaired of the government of Massachusetts passing legislation that would end slavery in the colony. It would never happen so long as slave owners like John Hancock and compromisers like John Adams ran the General Court. Lowell would not give up fighting for legislation (in 1777, he would push for passage of an act "preventing the Practice of holding persons in slavery"[18]) but for now, he recognized that the venue for freeing slaves was not the legislative hall, but the law court. And he felt very comfortable in a law court. John Lowell., Esq., set to work.

The case of *Caesar Hendricks v. Richard Greenleaf* was heard in Essex Inferior Court in October 1773, before a civil jury, the Honorable Judge Peter Frye presiding. Caesar Hendrick, a black man, brought suit against Richard Green-leaf, a white man, for trespass: "With force and arms assaulted the plaintiff then and there being in our peace, and then and there with force aforesaid falsely imprisoned him and so with force as aforesaid and against the plaintiff's will, hath then help kept and restrained him in servitude as said Richard's slave . . ."

Daniel Farnham, attorney for Richard Greenleaf, alleged owner of Hendricks, argued his defense. "The Egyptians, Grecians, Jews, Romans, held many in slavery . . . law shows there were many slaves in the province . . . to be held in slavery, and not to be manumitted . . ."

John Lowell, attorney for the plaintiff, stepped forward to respond. "Villeins [feudal tenants] were known in English law. We have nothing to do with any other laws. Those of Egypt, Greece, or Rome are nothing to Englishmen."

Lowell then continued: "No human tribunal can take away natural rights so fundamental. The precepts of revealed law, golden rule of the gospel, are that we are not to sell our brethren, that we are to do as we would be done unto."

Finally, he argued, "Even villeinage is abolished by English law. The Common law abhors slavery. The Somerset case shews every one setting his foot on English ground, to be free, wherever he came from."

Judge Frye asked of the jury: "Shall this humanity be taken?"

The jury replied, "No."

Caesar Hendricks was ruled a free man, and Greenleaf was ordered to pay eighteen pounds in damages and costs.[19]

John Lowell brought more and more cases, pleading for the freedom of slaves. Slave owners argued that they had purchased "their Negroes in Open Market and bills of sale could be produced in evidence," and that "the Laws of the Province recognized Slavery as existing," but Lowell was swift and sure in his response: "The Charter explicitly declares all persons born or residing in the Province are as free as the King's subjects in Great Britain. . . . the laws of England are that no man can be deprived of his liberty but by verdict of a jury . . . the laws of this province respecting that evil of slavery and attempts to mitigate or regulate it, do no authenticate it . . . slavery is not legal and cannot be allowed to stand."[20]

The juries fell to Lowell's side, one by one. As John Adams noted later in writing about the freedom suits, "I never knew a Jury by a Verdict, to determine a Negro to be a slave. They always found them free."[21]

"The differences among men are not great," Lowell wrote in a letter to his best friend, Jonathan Jackson. "Men are influenced and molded by external, or accidental, circumstances. Inside, we are more similar and we want the same things. We are all motivated by the same desires."

"No," Jackson wrote back. "The peculiarity of each man is the result of an original bent of tendency, an inherent, and not always good, quality of character. Our desires are not the same, our qualities either."[22]

The age-old argument between friends: Is man born good or evil? As his father, the Reverend Lowell, had found before him, John Lowell always found some proof of goodness in his fellow man, black or white.

Such belief in goodness may have been why Lowell found it so hard to join other colonists in the rebellion against England. He trusted Great Britain to behave in the interests of its citizens, whether on English soil or far away in the colonies. He relied on the beneficial stewardship of Parliament and believed in his king; he embraced his duty as a royal subject. In 1760, when King George II died and King George III ascended to the throne, Lowell had written a long poem in commemoration of the event:

> GEORGE shines unrivall'd in the list's of fame;
> For while he reign'd, each virtue, ev'ry grace,
> Beamed from his throne, and sparkled in his face—
> While justice, goodness, liberty inspired;
> And Britain's freedom all his conduct fir'd.[23]

When the Court of England moved to free the black man James Somerset from slavery, Lowell had become even more fervent in his allegiance. He was quick to point out to his friends agitating for freedom from England that, in fact, it was England that guaranteed freedom—and colonists who owned slaves. Lowell applauded when Caesar Sarter, a free black man from Newburyport, published an essay in the local papers criticizing colonists for what he called the "absurdity of your exertions for liberty, while you have slaves in your houses."[24]

Lowell urged his friends, including Jonathan Jackson and old Patrick Tracy, father of Jackson's business partner, to free their slaves. Jackson, having "long felt [the impropriety] in holding any person in constant bondage—more especially at this time when my country is so warmly contending for the liberty which every man ought to enjoy," finally agreed. He went to Lowell's office and drew up the papers officially manumitting those he had held in slavery.[25]

John Lowell met another Salem-born woman named Susanna Cabot, and on May 31, 1774, they were married. Susanna came to live in the house on High

Street, taking over care of John's children. By April of the next year, John and Susanna's first child would be born. They would name him Francis Cabot Lowell and call him "Frank." Older sister Nancy would adore baby Frank. She would sing to him out under the apple trees growing behind the house on High Street, where pink blossoms rained down on them in May and in summertime, the trees' dense leaves brought shade. By the fall of 1775, little Frank would be able reach up to the darkening apples, and Nancy would make him sweet sauce to eat.

Long before the Boston Tea Party, a boycott of English tea had spread throughout the towns and villages of New England. Refusing to allow any profit at all to the English, industrious colonials got to work making tealike concoctions with ingredients found in their own gardens, everything from the four-leaf loosestrife to ribwort, from strawberry leaves to currant leaves and sage. Nothing tasted as good as the real thing, but patriots gritted their teeth, then opened wide and drank down what they called their "liberty teas."[26]

Then temptation arrived in the shape of three British-owned ships, each bearing cargo of good Chinese tea. The tea was owned by the East India Company, which had just been granted a monopoly over tea in the colonies. Samuel Adams worried that the colonists, wearying of their homemade concoctions, wouldn't be able to resist the influx of good-tasting tea, especially if the prices were set attractively low. John Hancock worried for another reason: He stood to lose a bundle on his own tea trade if duty-free East India tea flooded the market. And so together with their local band of the Sons of Liberty, Hancock and Adams planned a raid on the tea-bearing ships. Late on the night of December 16, 1773, Adams led a band of colonists dressed as Mohawk Indians aboard the English ships. Working feverishly through the night, they dumped over ninety thousand pounds of East India Company tea into Boston Harbor by morning.

Great Britain reacted to the Tea Party by shutting down the port of Boston. Nothing could come in or out until all the lost tea was paid for. Parliament also passed the Coercive Acts, which prohibited all town meetings in Massachusetts, declared British officials immune from criminal proceedings in the colonies, and required the people of Boston to house and quarter British troops. That could mean only one thing: *Troops are on their way.* And so they were—under the command of General Gage.

General Gage, who had fought beside George Washington against the French, was used to undertaking hard measures to get things done. With Thomas Hutchinson dismissed as royal governor and Gage installed in his place, Gage prepared to bring the rebel colony of Massachusetts to heel. But the colonists were not so easy to corral. The tea had been dumped and there was no going back. As John Adams described the situation in a letter to James Warren, "The dye is cast; the people have passed the River and cutt away the bridge. . . ."[27] Angry New Englanders called the new acts of Parliament "the Intolerable Acts" and vowed noncompliance. By the summer of 1774, they were laying plans for the First Continental Congress. The purpose of the congress was to seek "restoration of union and harmony between Great Britain and the Colonies, most ardently desired by all good men." But the underlying threat was clear: The colonists would not stand for the current British plan "to alter the free Constitution of civil government in British America . . . and reduce the inhabitants to slavery."[28]

John Lowell added his signature to a letter greeting and welcoming General Gage when he first arrived in Boston in May 1774. Governor Hutchinson left in June with a similarly ingratiating letter in his pocket, this one signed by a group of twenty-four lawyers, including John Lowell, Esq. Similar in praise, similar in nature, the letters complemented incoming Gage and outgoing Hutchinson as being exemplary representatives "of the paternal goodness of our most gracious Sovereign."[29] The lawyers asked Hutchinson, when back in England, to exercise what influence he had at court "for the relief of the town of Boston from its present distress."[30]

Motivated by what he saw as the interests of his constituents, both the townspeople who had elected him and the commercial clients who hired him, Lowell had signed both letters without hesitation. The letters, after all, were not so different from the appeasing gifts sent by the merchants of Bristol to James I back in 1603. But when the Newburyport public discovered what Lowell had done, the only motivation ascribed to him was that of treason to the cause of liberty. Lowell was accused of being a royalist, a Tory, a betrayer of his town and his American brethren. There was no longer any place for a "paternal sovereign," not in the great colony of Massachusetts in America. Perhaps there was no longer any place for a Lowell in Newburyport.

John Lowell continued to walk every morning to the office and home again to his house on High Street in the evening. But now the backs of townspeople were turned to him as he passed by, tavern doors closed, and even friends scurried away when they saw him coming. Only Jon Jackson still welcomed his old friend. But even Jackson was losing any hope for reconciling with England. He'd been chosen to represent Newburyport at the First Continental Congress and would be leaving soon for Carpenters' Hall in Philadelphia. Delegates from twelve of the thirteen colonies gathered together to plot their future and the future of all colonists. Independence or reconciliation? Jackson believed the time had come for the colonists to stand against England.

Lowell still hovered between conflicting duties, those owed to his king and those owed to his community.

On October 14, 1774, the Continental Congress released its "Declaration of Colonial Rights." The declaration proclaimed that "the inhabitants of the English colonies in North America, by the immutable laws of nature, the principles of the English constitution, and the several Charters or Compacts . . . are entitled to life, liberty, and property" and would do whatever "peaceable measure" was necessary to protect those rights "in hopes their fellow subjects in Great Britain will . . . restore to us that state in which both countries found happiness and prosperity. . . ."[31]

Alongside the cheers heard up and down the streets and alleys of Newburyport, along the wharves and in the warehouses, there were murmurs.

What of Lowell? Is he with us? Or against us?

By year's end, they would have their answer.

8
1774–1777

New occasions teach new duties;
Time makes ancient good uncouth;
They must upward still, and onward,
who would keep abreast of Truth . . .
—JAMES RUSSELL LOWELL, "THE PRESENT CRISIS"

On December 26, 1774, John Lowell made his apology to the people of New-buryport via a letter sent to two newspapers, the *Merrimack Packet* and the *Essex Journal*. It was the day after Christmas, season of hope. A child is born; a patriot is declared. Lowell was no Tory, no royalist. He was a colonist, and an American, and committed to the future of change. Committed to a new world.

"[I am] heartily sorry," he declared. "I never wished any of your liberties abridged, or any unconstitutional power submitted to, but on the contrary, am ever ready to join in preventing such mischief . . ."[1]

The arms of Newburyport, which had been crossed against him, now opened wide. He was reelected to the office of selectman and welcomed back into the meeting rooms and taverns where patriotic fever stirred and rebel ale was brewed. The protest against British-brought tea had extended to other drinks. Now spirits of all sorts, though distilled in America, were seen more and more as vestiges of the colonial yoke. "Beer and cider are the companions of those virtues which can alone render our country free and reputable," read one of the pamphlets produced by the local liberty committee. "Spirit liquors are the broth of oppression, and we must consider them the companions of all those vices which are calculated to dishonor and enslave our country."[2]

Lowell shook his head when he read the pamphlet, remembering the bowls of rum that had fueled action against the Stamp Act. How times had changed. He'd just heard gossip that John Adams took a full tankard of hard cider before breakfast every day.[3] Lowell had too much business at hand to imbibe in spirits or cider or ale, and a family that was growing ever larger and more needful of his attention. By the spring of 1775, he had four children, and new work had to be found to support the family. He was a rebel, but a rebel still had to make money. That he would find work that could support a new nation and his growing family, Lowell could not have foreseen.

One of General Gage's first priorities upon arrival in the colonies in 1774 had been to locate and secure guns and ammunition. Ever since the first patriot assemblies were called for by Samuel Adams in 1772—"Let Associations and Combinations everywhere set up to consult and recover our just Rights"[4]— the colonist rebels of Massachusetts had been gathering and then hiding caches of arms and ammunition, preparing for whatever confrontation was to come. Gage was determined to root out and confiscate the hidden stores of guns and powder. But there were eighty wharves and dozens of brick warehouses in Boston alone, with dozens more up and down the coastline and inland. Searching through each and every one was impossible. Gage turned to local men who knew their way around—colonists who remained loyal to their king and would turn over much-needed town secrets to prove it.

Daniel Bliss was a Harvard classmate of John Lowell, and there were many similarities between the two. Like John, Daniel apprenticed at law and then returned to Concord, his hometown, to practice. Like John's father, Daniel's was a minister, and the Bliss family was well thought of in Concord. In 1774, Bliss had been hired as Governor Hutchinson's legal adviser, and when General Gage replaced Hutchinson, Bliss welcomed him as well, much as Lowell had. Bliss's enthusiasm for the rule of Great Britain, unlike Lowell's, never wavered. Bliss called his patriotic neighbors "fools" whose revolutionary activities were "madness, folly, deserving of nothing but scorn . . . the colonies are England's dependent children . . . cut off from Britain, they will perish."[5]

When Gage went looking for information on hidden caches of guns and ammunition, Daniel Bliss obliged. He knew where the patriots of Concord had hidden away twelve cannons and plenty of powder, and he told one of Gage's officers where the contraband arms could be found. Late on the night of April 18, 1775, a legion of seven hundred redcoats set out to hunt down the hidden caches revealed by Bliss, and to arrest the treasonous troublemakers John Hancock and Samuel Adams. The British plan was to first march on Lexington and then continue on to Concord. But rebels colonists spying on the redcoats discovered the movements of Gage's troops and dispatched warnings. Lanterns were hung from the tower of Boston's North Church to signal an impending attack. Paul Revere set out on his historic ride and women and children fled from their homes, while men gathered in motley, disorganized crews. Ammunition and guns, cannons and powder, were spirited away from Concord to be stored out of sight in other towns; John Hancock and Samuel Adams fled Lexington to go into hiding.

Another John Lowell took the stage to aid Hancock in his flight. John Lowell of Charlestown was the son of Michael Lowell, the Reverend Lowell's younger brother. This John's sister Elizabeth was married to Ebenezer Hancock, little brother to John Hancock. John Hancock had a trunk with him in Lexington that was filled with materials that would have proved him once and for all to be a traitor to the king. John Lowell of Charlestown took charge of the trunk, hauling it from Lexington to Woburn and keeping it safely hidden for years.

When British soldiers arrived in Lexington at dawn on April 19, they were met on the green by a force of fifty-some revolutionaries, dressed in "rustic, homespun clothes," carrying "clumsy muskets," and operating under a "ragged discipline."[6] And yet it was the raggedy, outnumbered ones who carried the day: The British were turned back from Lexington and stymied in their march to Concord. Neither Adams nor Hancock was captured that day, only two cannons were confiscated, and although forty-nine Americans were killed and thirty-nine grievously wounded, the British losses were far greater: 73 of the king's soldiers killed, 174 wounded, and 26 missing. Lord Percy, who led the British troops back to Boston, understood the rebels: "whoever looks upon them as an irregular mob will be much mistaken."[7]

The colonists, buoyed by their victory at Lexington, raised the call to rebel militias from up and down New England. The colonial forces converged on the hills above Boston, determined to take control over the British in Boston and to hold them there. The War of Independence had begun.

In June, King George issued his proclamation that the colonists must lay down their arms and swear allegiance to king and country, or forever be branded as traitors. Three more generals were sent from England to marshal British forces against the colonists—William Howe, John Burgoyne, and Henry Clinton—and to manage the defeat and surrender of the rebels. But there would be no laying down of arms, no allegiance sworn to any king of England. Rallying together under the leadership of their Commander, Gen. George Washington, the American militias dug into their positions above Boston Harbor. They were determined to hold Boston under siege, the British soldiers and loyalists confined there without supplies or support.

Within days of the attempted raid on Lexington and Concord, the townspeople of Newburyport had their own redcoat scare. A frantic man came riding into town, his horse lathered in sweat and his face red and streaming under the heat of the spring sun. He'd ridden hard from the outskirts of Boston, having overheard rumors in one of the army camps. He took his horse to the triangular green and began to yell, bellowing with all his might. A crowd gathered to listen.

"Turn out, for God's sake, turn out! Lobsterbacks are on the way!"

Men ran back to their homes, searching for their muskets or any other kind of weapon that might be used to halt the rampaging British. Women and children took to their heels, grabbing whatever household goods they could carry and heading out of town into the meadows to hide amid the copses of trees or in farmhouses set far back from the road. One woman ran for over a mile before stopping to catch her breath, and to check that her baby, clutched in a satchel to her breast, was all right.

She opened the bag, then shut it again and began to wail. Her words amid the cries were unintelligible at first, but then gradually her moans grew to whimpers, and her voice became more clear.

"My baby's not here. . . ."

She opened her bag to show the house cat, a small tabby, ensconced within the folds of a torn blanket. She'd grabbed the cat and left the baby.[8]

The alarm raised in town turned out to be a false one. No British forces were on the march to Newburyport, and the refugees returned home. The baby was fine, as was the cat. But the people of Newburyport vowed never again to be caught unawares. Two companies of fighting men were formed immediately, and then four more, all under the command of Col. Jonathan Titcomb, relative of and heir to the mighty Moses Titcomb, who had led the men of Newbury twenty years earlier in the fight against the French. John Lowell was made major and adjutant of the local companies.

It was a beautiful fall day when Capt. Benedict Arnold and his troops arrived in Newburyport on their way to Canada. Arnold and his thirteen hundred men were to board the eleven Newburyport-built sloops and schooners that would carry them in their expedition to capture and hold British-held Quebec. Well-dressed crowds turned out as if for a party, lining up along the streets of Newburyport to listen to the fife and drums play. They cheered and clapped and whistled as the militiamen passed by. John Lowell stood by with his company, all of them standing tall and still in honor of Arnold and his men. Banners flew from windows and rooftops, dyed linen and muslin fluttering in the breeze, their slogans rippling the word LIBERTY against brick and stone.

Down by the water, people piled up against the piers, from gentry to ragamuffin, eager to see Arnold and his men off. The waiting boats tossed and pitched on the tide, skittering about as if joining in on the excitement. Yet underneath it all, a somber truth: These men were going to war and might not come back. As Joseph Ware, militiaman from Needham, noted in his diary, "Early this morning weighed anchor with a pleasant gale, our colours flying, drums and fifes playing, and the hills all around covered with pretty girls weeping for their departed swains."[9]

The capture of Quebec proved to be elusive. Arnold lost many of his men in the months-long effort to take the town, struck down not only by musket fire but also by smallpox and other diseases that set in during the winter months. What had begun on festive day of sunshine, fife and drum, ended in a cold misery of snow, disease, and defeat.

In June of 1775, the rebel troops holding siege over Boston were low on everything, from uniforms to blankets, from food to fuel. What they needed most, and lacked most dearly, were arms and ammunition. The only way to secure what was needed was to attack the ships supplying the British troops and plunder and steal their cargoes. But outfitting a navy would take time, and supplies were needed now. And so General Washington and his officers turned to the age-old practice of privateering to get what they needed. Unlike on land, where looting of private property by enemy soldiers was seen as violating rules of war, on the high seas, international law encouraged the use of privateers to attack and loot enemy ships. There were complex rules governing how this was to be done; for example, before a ship could set to sea and begin plundering, the sovereign nation it served had to grant it a privateering commission in the form of a letter of marque and reprisal. With that commission in hand, a privateer could go after cargoes of the enemy, and if crew members from the privateer were captured, they were to be treated as soldiers. Unlike pirates, who could be hanged immediately, privateers caught by enemy forces were treated as prisoners of war.[10]

Washington's use of privateers was risky. In order for the crews and vessels to be recognized as privateers and not pirates, there had to be recognition by other nations that the American colonies were a sovereign nation and therefore had the right to issue letters of marque and seize goods from their wartime enemies. The test would come, but for now, Washington did not hesitate. He authorized the commission of hundreds of schooners, sloops, shallops, and brigs, most hailing from New England, to take the battle for independence to the seas. New England captains and crew got to work harassing British war vessels, burning down lighthouses and other navigation markers, and plundering the islands of Boston harbor of forage and cattle. But the biggest goal by far was the capture of British ships and the taking of their cargoes for the benefit of the colonists' troops.

In November 1775, the British brig *Nancy*, an ordnance ship carrying tons of ammunition, thousands of muskets, and a three-thousand-pound mortar that would later be called "the noblest piece of ordnance ever landed in America" was captured by the *Lee*, a small schooner led by the "rough and ready" Boston shipmaster John Manley.[11] The *Nancy* was taken without a fight because her crew thought the *Lee* was a Royal Navy pilot craft come out to help navigate them to their mooring in Boston Harbor. The *Nancy* had had a terrible crossing over a stormy and turbulent Atlantic, and everyone on board wanted only to rest, finally, at port. When rebel sailors appeared on her deck, hopping up over the railing, the crew did not resist. They were simply too surprised and too exhausted.

News of the *Nancy*'s capture quickly spread. Initial estimates of the value of her cargo were set at ten thousand pounds, but within days the amount was revised upward. Thomas Jefferson estimated the value of the *Nancy*'s cargo at thirty thousand pounds. The *Nancy* carried arms for the army and goods to be sold, gathering profits for all concerned, including the *Lee*'s owner and crew. But first the expenses of running the ship had to be taken out of the profits. Bills would also be submitted by all sorts of subcontractors, including for the costs of storing the cargo pending its disbursal, for housing the crew of the *Nancy* pending their return to British territory, and for all attendant costs of their care, including laundry and needed medical services. If anyone died while being held, the digging of the grave counted as an additional expense. The allocation of prize money and paying out of claims was a complicated transaction, covered by a myriad of intertwining international laws and regulations. Such a complex legal enterprise was well suited to a savvy, ambitious lawyer. A lawyer like John Lowell.

By March 1776, Congress proclaimed that all vessels belonging to Britain were "fair game for civilian and Continental warships."[12] General Washington did not want long legal hassles delaying the delivery of what he needed—arms and other supplies—and he urged the provisional courts that had been set up to handle the prize cases to proceed swiftly. Not only was it important to supply the troops with items they sorely needed but, in order to encourage more and more private ships to set to sea harassing and capturing British vessels, the road to profit for those shipmasters was to be made as smooth and easy as possible. Patriotism only went so far.[13] From Jamaica to Nova Scotia, the waters churned with desire, aggression, and greed. Ships were captured, then recaptured and reclaimed. On the way to the port of choice—Halifax or Antigua for the British, Boston or Rhode Island for the rebels—ships could be captured yet again. Back and forth the prizes went.

Both the British and the colonial press printed letters and reports about the antics on the high seas that were often not quite factually accurate, but the impression they left—in lurid and compelling detail—was what mattered. A letter from a Briton in America, printed in England, stated, "These islands swarm with those vermin of American privateers. A day does not pass but they take some vessel." A press report in the *Newport Mercury* claimed that the *Glasgow,* a British vessel, was "yelping from the mouths of her canons (like a broken legged dog) in token of her being sadly wounded."[14] In fact, the *Glasgow* suffered little (only one crewman dead) when making its escape, whereas the colonists suffered ten dead and the loss of three ships.

No matter the accuracy of the reports, the news seemed to buoy the rebels and cause pain to the Britons. It was a case of Goliath—the Royal Navy—versus the pesky Davids—the "rebel pirates"—of the colonies.[15] The Davids always came out looking better. Lowell read all about it in the many periodicals that were springing up, feeding the public's need for news. The moment had come to recognize his opportunity, and to seize it.

After his first wife, Sarah, died, Jonathan Jackson married the daughter of his mentor Patrick Tracy, and sister of his good friend and business partner, Nathaniel Tracy. Nate was twenty-four years old, ambitious, and courageous. He had been one of the very first to apply for a privateering commission from the Massachusetts General Court. But before committing more and more ships to the cause, he needed legal counsel. He went to John Lowell for help.

Lowell had been studying up on the international laws governing privateering. He explained to Tracy that privateers were bound by a complex, universal, and inviolable code of rules. For example, when firing upon an enemy, an American vessel had to display its flag. For now, the fleet of the colonies flew under the tree flag. The tree flag, displaying at its center a white pine, was the banner of New England. White pines were the trees long favored by the British for the masts of their ships. So covetous was Britain of the white pine trees that laws had been imposed on the colonists, prohibiting them from harvesting any twenty-four-diameter pines for their own use; they were to be saved for the building of British ships.

New Englanders had chafed under the restrictions. In 1772, a revolt flared up in New Hampshire when royal officers tried to fine a mill owner for cutting down pine trees without authorization. In what came to be known as the Pine Tree Riot, the officers of the Crown were seized by a jeering crowd and whipped with pine tree switches. The ears, tails, and manes of their horses were cut off and the men were paraded through town, pelted with dung and stung with insults. The fines were not paid and the tree flag was born.

The pine tree flag bore the inscription "An Appeal to Heaven," a reference to John Locke and his assertion that an oppressed people, having sought through all peaceful and lawful means to secure their rights, could make an "appeal to heaven" in rebelling against the forces on earth that sought to oppress them.[16] The patriots were making their appeal to heaven—and now the privateers would sail under a flag that gave them the right to plunder from the British.

Lowell explained to Tracy that once an enemy vessel was captured, strict rules applied as to how the crew was to be treated, how the cargo and all the appurtenances of the vessel, along with the vessel itself, were to be handled, how profits from sales were split up, and where the vessel was to be taken. A prize suit, called "a libel suit," was to be brought immediately, like a sort of petition to an admiralty court, and then the petitioners had to prove that the seized cargo was British and the vessel was either British or hired by British merchants; only then could condemnation (seizure) of the enemy goods be requested. The petitioners had a right to whatever profits came from sales of the seized cargoes, with distributions to be determined by the admiralty court or as set by contract.

Impressed by his knowledge, Nathaniel Tracy asked John Lowell to be his lawyer, not only to pursue his privateering cases through the admiralty court but also to organize his privateering enterprise in the first place. Partnerships had to be formed to fund the fleet and pay for arms, crew, and supplies; and these partnerships had to be legal and binding. Contracts were needed to allocate who would get what in the event of cargo captured. John Lowell agreed to represent Tracy, and a long-standing association began.

In the years that followed, as more and more New Englanders set to sea to fight the enemy and carry away profitable cargoes, the services of John Lowell would be called upon again and again to create partnerships and syndicates, to write contracts, and to take the prize cases from start to finish through the legal system. Out of eleven hundred privateering cases brought in the Massachusetts Prize Court during the American Revolution, John Lowell handled seven hundred of them, and participated in the resolution of half of the rest.[17] He helped settle more than one thousand prize cases all together, always garnering his own piece of the settlement. He collected even more in fees for brokering partnerships and syndicates, working up contracts, and settling disputes.

The profits of the ship owners engaged in profiteering were often balanced by terrible losses. During the war, Newburyport alone lost twenty-two vessels and one thousand men. The town of Salem lost a third of its registered privateers, and Gloucester lost every single one, twenty-four boats in all. Nathaniel Tracy lost entire fleets, boats and their crews gone forever, through battle or storms. Jonathan Jackson also suffered devastating losses: Vessels he'd invested in were destroyed, shipwrecked, sunk to the bottom of the ocean. But for the lawyer involved, John Lowell, the losses did not threaten his own livelihood. Lawyers were needed to pick up the pieces wrought by bad luck and sad turns of fate as much as they were needed to parse out the fruits of those ventures that had been lucky and profitable, very profitable.

John Lowell helped his friend Jackson the best he could. In the months to come, he would counsel Jackson against lending money to the fledgling

American government, but Jackson the patriot was sure the money would be repaid once victory for the Americans had been secured. Even as his trade profits fell, stymied by the Royal Navy blockade of the harbor at Newburyport, Jackson gave what he could to the cause of freedom, "contributing money for the public needs."[18] Lowell shook his head, and Jackson hoped for the best.

In March of 1776, the town of Boston, long held by British forces, was surrendered to the colonists. General Howe of Great Britain sent a message to George Washington under a flag of truce, promising that he would not burn Boston if his troops and all evacuees were allowed to leave without being fired upon. The evacuees included dozens of colonial families that sided with the Crown, the loyalists of Boston. Many of the now-exiled families went to Halifax, in Canada, others went to the Caribbean islands of Jamaica, Antigua, and the Bahamas, and others returned to England.

Boston had been left in ruins. The patriots who returned to reclaim their city had a huge job ahead of them. Shops were shuttered, empty of goods. Streets were broken up, homes broken down, wells emptied, and fuel stores depleted. John Hancock led the rebuilding of Boston, sinking money from his own fortune into reviving the Boston Common and repairing tenant buildings; he also paid the rents of widows and orphans, and donated wood to the public almshouse. He was joined in his efforts by men made newly rich through rippling circles of profits found in privateering. These men came to Boston, moving into the grand houses left behind by fleeing loyalists, and helped to bolster the struggling Boston economy. There was room for all: merchants, traders, builders, ship owners, lawyers. Among them were the Cabots, the Lees, the Batchelders, the Tracys. When would the Lowells come?

In December of 1776, a second child was born to John and Susanna. They named her Susanna, after her mother. Too soon, her mother was gone. Susanna Cabot died on March 30, 1777. A funeral cortege proceeded through the streets of Salem, hometown of the Cabots. A March drizzle dulled already-wasted spirits. John Lowell stood beside his brother-in-law, William Cabot, as the coffin of his late wife was lowered into the damp, marshy ground.

"That lively hope with which she expected death and realized future Happiness made it selfish to wish her to stay in this scene of Perplexity, Sorrow, and Despair,"[19] Lowell wrote to William later. Now, graveside, he could only swallow back his tears. Young Francis' hand held tightly to his father's, the palm warm, like a fresh seal on paper. A covenant between a man and a boy. A promise to remember the dead and care for the living.

John Lowell packed up his five children and moved to Boston.

9

1778–1789

It takes some time for moss and vines to grow
And warmly cover gaunt and chill stone walls
Of stately buildings from the cold North Wind . . .
—AMY LOWELL, "THE BOSTON ATHENAEUM"

On Christmas Day in 1778, John Lowell married his third wife. Rebecca Russell Tyng was a thirty-one-year-old childless widow; John was now thirty-five. Happy couples come to look like brother and sister, and John and Rebecca fit the rule. Not for them the flint jaws, tight lips, and narrowed eyes of so many old New England portraits. They were characterized by curves— of the cheek, of the lips, of the hips. John balanced his torso with the width of his broad shoulders; Rebecca with the fullness of her bosom.

Alike in looks, and in spirit. Rebecca understood John, knew where his past troubles had come from (her own family had been split in fealty between king and rebels, with two brothers remaining loyalists and one siding with the revolutionaries), and what his dreams were for the future: a profitable nation, led by enlightenment, fed by faith, and committed to hard work. James Russell Lowell, a grandchild still to be born to them, would write in 1865, "Faith in God, faith in man, faith in work—this is the short formula in which we may sum up the teachings of the founders of New England, a creed ample enough for this life and the next."[1] And so it was for John and Rebecca.

Rebecca moved into the grand house on Tremont and Beacon Street that John Lowell had found for his family the year before. She settled into their life easily and happily. With no children of her own, Rebecca enveloped the five young Lowells in unchecked affection. "If ever an angel has appeared upon Earth, one has come down now!" young John wrote in his diary.[2]

The house was a place for family happiness. Large, roomy, set well back from the street, with views from every window: King's Chapel and the old burying ground to the east and a large peach orchard to the west. Lowell had taken a suite of rooms for his office. Shelves stuffed with law books, cupboards rife with papers, a large desk holding squibs and ink pots, wax and seals, boxes of onionskin paper. A window over the Common, a glance stolen from time to remind him: *Boston is my home now.* All other spaces in the house were apportioned for learning, living, sleeping, eating. The two boys were away at school, John junior and Francis Cabot at Andover, but the girls—Nancy, Sarah, and Susanna (called "Susan")—were taught at home. Reading, writing, music, mathematics. Books and letters, songs and sums.

Lowell insinuated himself easily into the political and social scene of Revolutionary Boston. He was elected as a selectman to the General Court in 1778 representing Boston, and in 1779 he was asked to join the Boston delegation to the Massachusetts Constitutional Convention. Along with John Adams, Samuel Adams, John Hancock, and his privateering partner Nathaniel Tracy, Lowell would help to write the constitution for the state of Massachusetts.

That winter was the harshest New England had seen in forty years. Boston Harbor froze, all its marshlands encased in ice: glass and marble under a cold sun. The snow fell so hard and was so deep that gardens were buried, with only the tops of trees jutting out like strangely branched bushes. Streets disappeared and paths had to be cut like tunnels through the white drifts. The work of forming a constitution—much of it falling on the shoulders of John Adams, with advice offered from the delegates—was to have been completed by the New Year. But it was late January before the group could meet again to go over what Adams had compiled.

The preamble of Adam's fifty-page document hearkened back to the ideals of the original Puritan settlements: "The body politic is formed by a voluntary association of individuals; it is a social compact by which the whole people covenants with each citizen, and each citizen with the whole people, that all shall be governed by certain laws for the common good . . ."[3] Then the articles laid out the structure of the government, and its purpose. The state would have three branches of government, each with carefully balanced powers, all clearly delineated. The purpose of government was to protect the rights of all its citizens.

John Lowell took a deep breath as he read the language that he had urged Adams to put in to the new constitution, and here it was, now before him, unequivocal and clear: "All men are born free and equal, and have certain natural, essential, and unalienable rights."[4] He had campaigned for this since his early days as a lawyer: to make all men free under the law. It was a victory to be celebrated. But not yet. Massachusetts citizens had to approve the constitution, and then the War of Independence had to be won. Because until the war was won and a new nation created, there would be no guaranteed freedom for any of the colonists.

The war was not going well. The Continental troops were low on food, arms, and men. George Washington wrote to Congress: "we are reduced again to a situation of extremity for want of meat. On several days of late, the Troops have been entirely destitute of any, and for a considerable time past they have been at best, at half, a quarter, an Eighth allowance of this essential article of provision . . . such reiterated, constant instances of want are too much for the Soldiery . . ."[5] And the quartermaster general, Nathanael Greene, in charge of provisions for the army, commented, "A Country, once overflowing with plenty, are now suffering an Army employed for the defense of every thing that is dear and valuable, to perish for want of food."[6]

Household goods throughout all the colonies were scarce, due to British blockades and disruption of trade routes. Prices for everything were rising higher and higher, and the value of the dollar sinking lower and lower as Congress printed more and more money in a vain effort to fund the war. Congress also imposed taxes to fund the war, which were less than popular with an already debt-ridden populace.

Congress and General Washington continued to push for more privateering ventures in an effort to secure needed supplies and funds. John Lowell played a role in many of these seagoing ventures. Yet the dollars he earned were worth less and less in the hyperinflation caused by continual disbursements of newly printed money. Lowell and other well-to-do men like him began spending their earned dollars as quickly as they could, buying up fine furniture from Philadelphia, commissioning portraits and miniatures from artists like John Singleton Copley, and laying in stores of Nanking porcelain from China in an effort to secure property worth more than the paper that dollars were printed on.

Such opulent living led to charges of corruption, inequity, and elitism. There was a tension and division among the rebel colonists, and Lowell felt once again the sting of public condemnation. In 1778, Mercy Otis Warren, pamphleteer from Boston, published a poem in the *Boston Gazette*, laying down charges against the wealthier citizens of Boston:

> . . . So dissolute—yet so polite the town,
> Like Hogarth's days, the world's turn'd upside down . . .
> . . . sins run rank, from levity of thought;
> Ere the big cloud that shook the north retires,
> Each generous movement of the soul expires;
> All public faith, and private justice dead,
> And patriot zeal by patriots betray'd—[7]

Lowell was enraged. To be seen as greedy, not hardworking; to be labeled corrupt and depraved, not abiding by the law and morally irresolute—these were condemnations that could not be borne. The poem had distorted the charge under which he labored. General Washington depended on what the privateers captured; Congress depended on the taxes and duties they paid; and Royal Navy and merchant ships suffered under the continual at-sea onslaughts. Thus all aspects of the war effort were increasingly supported by the work of privateering operations. Lowell prayed for the defeat of the British. Not only would a new nation be born, with freedom and equality for all, but his own name would be vindicated. For when the British surrendered, a full account of all that privateering had contributed to the war could be made; everyone would know then the role that John Lowell had played. British sea power was constrained due to the assaults by American privateers, and over six hundred British ships had been captured, with much-needed stores and stock, including arms and ammunition, as well as actual coin, seized. This path of money and supplies had been laid not only by the sailors who went to sea but also by the lawyers who smoothed the way. And it was John Lowell who led the lawyers.

In June 1780, the delegates to the Massachusetts Constitutional Convention gathered one last time. Over the past spring, delegates had gone back to their towns to present the proposed constitution and secure its ratification. Over sixteen thousand free males cast their votes. Now the returns would be counted. John Lowell was unsure of how the cumulative tabulation of the votes would fall. A previous embodiment had been rejected in 1778—and he had been happy about that, as it had lacked many provisions Lowell through absolutely necessary for a state constitution, including a bill of rights. Would this new version survive and become the binding political document for all who lived in Massachusetts?

On the night of June 15, 1780, John Lowell sat with his two boys, John and Francis, in the dining room of his home on corner of Beacon and Tremont. Dinner had long been cleared away, but their father's exuberance kept the children at the table. Light was fading beyond the opened windows, setting in relief the rooflines of the houses on the other side of the old burying ground. The bells of King's Chapel pealed, as if in celebration of a great victory. John turned to gesture at the windows, letting out his own deep whoop of joy. Then he turned back with a smile set deep in his wide, open face. The constitution had been ratified and would become the governing document for Massachusetts. He explained to his children that to him such a document was a most wonderful living thing, given its life by the people who had created it and voted for it and would now uphold it. The constitution of Massachusetts would serve as an example to the new nation when victory finally came.

Rebecca joined her men in the dining room, carrying one-year-old daughter Rebecca in her arms. Nancy, Sally, and Susan entered after her, and moved to sit at the table beside their brothers. Rebecca stood beside John and laid a hand on his shoulder. She asked him what made him most proud.

His reply: "That now there is no longer slavery in Massachusetts. It is abolished! I will use this Constitution to pursue freedom, and I will render my services as a lawyer gratis to any slave suing for his freedom."[8]

Sixteen months later, the War of Independence was won. On October 19, 1781, General Cornwallis surrendered to General Washington at Yorktown. The grand dream of a new country had come true. How that new country would be governed—under a nationally ratified constitution created to uphold equality and justice for all citizens—could be traced back to the early Massachusetts colonists, with their ideal of a community compact working for the common good. But the Constitution of the United States (largely influenced by the Massachusetts Constitution) would not be ratified until 1788. For now, the new country was to be governed by the Third Continental Congress under the Articles of Confederation, already in place in Philadelphia. John Lowell was sent to serve as Massachusetts representative to the Congress of the Confederation.

The role of representative was both an honor to Lowell and a responsibility—and he never turned away from honorable responsibility—but his attendance at the lengthy meetings took him away from home for months at a time. He wrote to his wife, "I have such ardent desire to remove the painful sensations experienced from my absence, as well as to gratify my supreme wishes of pouring my whole soul into your bosom. . . ."[9] While in Philadelphia, Lowell shared housing with James Madison, and the two became good friends. But friends could never replace family, and he missed Rebecca and the children.

Lowell was also named a judge for the new Commonwealth of Massachusetts in a florid proclamation signed by, among others, Walter Spooner, Sam Adams, and Moses Gill. The proclamation gave Lowell full responsibility "to hear and determine all and singular thefts, trespasses, Riots, Routs, unlawful assemblies, and all and singular other premises and to do therein as to Justice appertaineth . . ."[10]

A son was born to John and Rebecca in 1782: Charles Russell. The following year, a girl was born and they named her Elizabeth. The family moved to a larger home at 41 Tremont Street. They still had a view of King's Chapel, but now from a new angle. A new home and new responsibility: Lowell had been appointed by Congress to serve as an admiralty judge for the new country of the United States. He had made his fortune arguing cases involving the sea, and was more than capable of presiding over their judgment. With his stout frame, broad forehead, and cascading white curls, he looked like a kind of Poseidon seated before the lawyers, his wooden gavel a substitute for the trident wielded by the Greek god. The garb he donned—long silk robes—only deepened the likeness.[11] The court itself was a room in the Bunch of Grapes Tavern on King Street. The young nation had no funds to go around building courthouses; the local tavern would do.

In 1789, George Washington appointed Lowell to the federal bench. He left the admiralty court, as he had left the state court, with gratitude for having served and excitement for the new opportunity. *Occasionem Cognosce.* He would be reappointed to the bench under President John Adams and remain a federal judge until the presidency of Thomas Jefferson. John Lowell became known from that point on—and would forever be known—as "the Old Judge." Even his children called him that. He was hardly old, only forty when first seated as a judge in admiralty court. But his youth as a loyal English subject and then as a patriot devoted to the Revolution was behind him. What lay ahead was a new world, graced by a new nation, the United States of America.

A place for young men and women, for his young men and women. His daughters and sons. John had lost one child, Mary, in 1789. (Born in May 1786, she was two years old when she died.) Nancy, Sarah, Susan, Rebecca, Elizabeth, John, Francis, and Charles remained. The next generation of Lowells.

Part Four

ACQUISITION

A country with such energies as ours, with such
opportunities and inducements to grow rich, and such temptations
to be content with growing rich, needs saving all the time.

—JAMES RUSSELL LOWELL

10

1796–1802

No more in false seductive charms arrayed,
Some favorite vision shall enchant my mind,
For all too soon the fleeting colours fade
And leave the soul to misery resigned . . .
—ANNA CABOT LOWELL, "TO HOPE"

In the spring of 1796, Anna Cabot Lowell, eldest daughter of Old Judge Lowell, was feelings the stirrings of the season. A swelling of emotions, a rising fondness for a certain young man. Anna, known as Nancy to her friends and family, was twenty-eight years old. She lived in the country town of Roxbury, just outside of Boston, on the family estate her father had dubbed "Bromley Vale" (pronounced "Bromfield," in the English way).[1] Nancy wrote to her friend Eliza Morton about how often Josiah Quincy III came to visit her there, how comfortable he was passing the afternoon and evening with her at home, and how eager to take her out, as well. When a ball was held in Boston, Quincy had been her most faithful companion.

"Oh, Mr. Quincy. . . . he happily decided my fate for the Evening by asking me to dance, [and] I asked of Fortune no other favor . . ."[2]

But could this Quincy offer comfort to Nancy, who had recently been left brokenhearted by another man? She was making her best effort—"the pleasure of dancing with Mr. Quincy ensured my happiness for the evening"[3]—and yet still she suffered. She missed the companionship of that other man, John Singleton Copley, Jr., son of the famous artist. Young Copley had wooed her but then left her. With his leaving, he had wounded her deeply: "Love by fancy wrest, / May gild her youthful morn,/ But Ah! Within the feeling breast,/ Too oft it leaves its thorn."[4]

Writing eased the pain of that thorn. Nancy found release in letters, in her diary, and in the many poems she composed across loose scraps of paper. Her heart displayed in looping letters across the page, secured by pen and ink.

Go and deceive some tender hapless maid
When thy fair form shall her soft heart betray
She'll weep with me to see its lustre fade.
She too by sensibility misled
Shall place her visionary hopes on thee,
Then sigh to find the sweet illusion fled
And mourn her withered happiness, like me . . .[5]

Although writing was Nancy's salvation, she understood that family was her duty. Within that duty lay a most important commission: to find a single man from a good family and marry him. Over the past ten years, Nancy had had her share of young suitors, for she was not only pretty but also smart and kind and funny. She had large hazel eyes and a bowed pink mouth; her straight nose came from her late mother, Sarah Higginson, and the high, smooth forehead she got from her father, the Old Judge. When Nancy wore her hair wound up atop her head, bound with a band of velvet or silk across the brow, a curl or two always slipped out, giving the impression that she had just left off dancing at a ball or skipping around the flower gardens at Bromley Vale, or that she had just been wakened from a particularly stirring dream or interrupted in the middle of a most rousing conversation.

Bromley Vale was a home filled with women: Rebecca, wife and mother, and five daughters, Nancy, Sarah (called "Sally"), Susan, Rebecca, and Elizabeth. Charles, the youngest son, was a student at Harvard. John, the eldest son, had graduated from Harvard in 1786 and was now married and living in Boston in a home he'd made above the offices of his law practice. Francis, the middle son, a "happy genius for mathematics," graduated from Harvard in 1793, despite having been rusticated (temporarily expelled) in his senior year for having lit a bonfire in Harvard Yard.[6]

Two years later, Francis—called "Frank"—set off on a year's journey through France. The nation was in the midst of a bloody revolution, but nothing daunted young Frank; after all, it was adventure that he wanted. He set sail on a ship owned by an uncle, Thomas Russell (brother of his stepmother, Rebecca). The vessel was filled with a cargo of rice and flour to be traded for French wine and spirits. With England at war with France, and the seas largely controlled by the British Royal Navy, there was danger of having the vessel stopped. But neither captain nor crew was worried about the British-imposed embargo of goods entering France. When the ship was approached mid-seas by a British naval cruiser, it took no time at all to hide the papers indicating her intended port of call; documents listing a more acceptable destination were quickly substituted. The British captain may have been suspicious enough to conduct a thorough search, but no clue as to her French destination was discovered. And so the ship was sent on its way. It was the first of many lessons learned by Frank: Keep all necessary information close to the vest. Secrets can be hidden, if only care is taken.

Frank arrived in Bordeaux, made the required trade for Burgundy wines and French brandy, and then set about traveling through the French countryside. Despite the chaos and violence imposed by the Revolution, the French people he met carried on with their daily life. To Frank, it seemed as if they were blessed with the ability to find pleasure where they could. He marveled at the meals he enjoyed, dish after dish delicious despite the constraints of war rationing and embargo-caused shortages. He sampled wines and bought himself some French cravats, so much more elegant than anything he could find in Boston. He worked on his French until he was able to fully enjoy a night spent at the theater, in the company of interesting men and enchanting women.

He was simply having too good a time to write home to his parents and siblings back in America. The lack of news made them worry. The initial wave of public approval for the French Revolution was receding. The Reign of Terror had turned American support into fear: What terrible violence had been unleashed in France? The French Revolution had seemed like a good idea—and a flattering imitation of America's bid for independence—but now it had become something quite different. Revolution was supposed to lead to an evolution for the greater good, but in France, the Revolution was dissolving now into anarchy. The aristocracy was being massacred, churches desecrated, clergy decimated. The governmental institutions for law and order were breaking down. When the great French hero of the American Revolution, the Marquis de Lafayette, was called a traitor by Robespierre and then jailed by Danton, Americans cried out in protest. The French were no longer to be trusted.

But Frank never felt himself to be in any danger. He had numerous cousins living in France, safely and happily, and he himself was traveling with a special passport issued by the French Committee of Public Safety. Enjoying his cloak of official protection, he found French life interesting and satisfying more than demoralizing or terrifying. After witnessing mass executions of five hundred men while visiting Paris, the only mention of it he made to his father when he finally wrote a letter was about how very *quiet* the whole event had been: "One of our training days [at Harvard] made a great deal more noise . . ."[7]

Frank spent little time considering the moral or political implications of the French Revolution; instead, what fascinated him were the opportunities he saw everywhere he went, especially financial opportunities. The French were cut off from English traders and merchants, and the demand for American goods was increasing. Outfoxing the English navy could be done, and ships full of needed cargoes would be welcomed in the ports of France. Frank traveled around, gathering information and storing it away in his head, much as he would years later when traveling through Scotland and England, touring the cotton mills. The ways and means of making money: he was calculating the hows and wheres, developing plans to be put into play once he established himself in business.

The family back at home continued to worry. The Reign of Terror had ended, but now war raged in France: the royalists and Catholics, assisted by Great Britain, against the republicans. A young general named Napoléon Bonaparte had fought off the royalists and saved the republic, but what now? Was their Francis safe?

The family had a mailing address for Higginson cousins who lived in Paris, and Francis's older brother, John, wrote to him there. He scolded Frank for his failure to write more frequently—"not a line has been received since sixteen days after your arrival in France"—and told him that it was now time to come home: "The sooner you get settled in business, in my opinion, the better for your future interest and certainly better for your happiness . . ."[8] He did not add *and our happiness and peace of mind*. But Frank understood the unwritten message. Family duty over self-cultivation. He returned to Boston in June 1796.

To the relief of his family, Frank returned unscathed from the troubles in France. Even better, he was now quite knowledgeable about the ports of Europe. He had taken note of the goods desired by Europeans, and, in turn, the European cargoes that appeared to sell well in the United States. He planned to get started in business, working from the ground up to become a merchant trader. Perhaps he thought back to his ancestor Percival, so busy on the wharves of Bristol, as he himself walked the docks in Boston looking for a spot to set up shop. By the fall of 1796, his offices at number 60, Long Wharf were up and running. Frank settled in to build his fortune. It was his duty and his opportunity.

John Lowell was now in his fifties. He was still a practicing judge and a sometime lawyer, meeting with old compatriots pursuing claims and advising his son John on his own growing law practice. The Old Judge dressed for court, as he always had, according to current standards of style and elegance. But he added a flourish of something beyond style—his own personal panache: hair smoothed back and curled under, wearing a silk robe of a vibrant color, his gouty legs hidden within silk breeches and blinding white stockings, and his leather shoes always polished to gleaming. In old age, the judge had softened from looking like a looming Poseidon to looking like a more benevolent version of George Washington. His hair was as white as the general's but more full and luminous; his eyes were bigger, his nose gentler, his chin rounder.

Judge Lowell gave Frank money to invest, confident of his son's merchant endeavors. He was sure Frank would spend the money well and bring in profits for all the family. Until then, the Old Judge's other investments were paying him back in huge dividends: the building of bridges, canals, roads, and turnpikes throughout New England. The growing wealth of the family was reflected in the elegance and abundance of Bromley Vale, their Roxbury home.

The old farmhouse on the ridge that Lowell had purchased in 1785 had been transformed into a mansion. Inside, the rooms had been extended and made large and airy, with tall windows; outside, a sharply pitched roof had been added, along with a porch. From there, Judge Lowell could look out over green country hollows to the west and the growing town of Boston to the east, its busy "bays studded with the white sails of ships and brigs."[9] Town and country, business and leisure, sociability and meditation. The situation suited the Old Judge perfectly.

Long meadows surrounded the house, alongside elaborate flower gardens and row after row of fruit trees. Inside, the house was furnished in velvet and silk, holly and cherry and mahogany; walls were lined with portraits, landscapes, and tapestries. Shelves displayed the Staffordshire china given by Jonathan Jackson, along with the Revere silver left by the Reverend Lowell. The cellar was well stocked with French wines, Madeira, and rum. The rooms included two parlors, six bedchambers, and a library housing over nine hundred books. All the rooms had astral lamps; fed by expensive sperm oil, they provided the latest advance in lighting. The dining room was the largest room, oversized to contain all the Lowell offspring. The room was lined with mahogany cupboards holding supplies: "three punch bowls, twenty-one decanters, four dozen wineglasses, and forty-one for that rather unattractive ladies' drink, syllabub—the Federalist anticipation of a milkshake with a stick in it."[10]

Among the servants at Bromley Vale were two black women, possibly former slaves whom John Lowell had helped free. The younger of the two, named Phillida, doted on the youngest Lowell son, Charles, and sent weekly packages of fresh-baked cakes to him at Harvard. Accompanying the cakes were verses she had written, rhymed accounts of the daily happenings at the estate on the hill.

Most days began with old John taking a walk around the grounds of the estate, checking on his fruit trees and flower gardens. But gout had become a recurring source of discomfort and even pain. John eased himself into the most comfortable chair in the library after his daily stroll and remained there,

receiving visitors with as much energy as ever but perhaps a bit less enthusiasm for the drinks and food that had always accompanied visits to any Lowell
home. Guests included Aaron Burr and Alexander Hamilton (in happier
times, before their ill-fated duel, which would leave Hamilton dead); James
Winthrop, librarian at Harvard, and James Bowdoin, former governor of Massachusetts; George Cabot, senator, and his wife, Elizabeth; and the Josiah
Quincys, father and son.

The Lowell family had never approved of Nancy's romance with John Copley. Rebecca, her stepmother, was sympathetic to her involvement with the
man; he was handsome and interesting and ambitious, after all. But her father
wanted his daughter to form an alliance within the family connections—a
Gardner, a Putnam, a Higginson, a Cabot—and not with the son of an artist,
no matter how esteemed. John Singleton Copley, Sr., had painted a miniature
of the judge. All the family thought it a perfect likeness. Lowell was portrayed
wearing his full wig, dusted white, and a blue silk robe. In the background,
trees and a temple, and two angels. The miniature would pass down through
generations of Lowells—a revered heirloom—but a marriage compact with the
Copley family was not to be.

Four years younger than Nancy, John Singleton Copley, Jr., had been
born in Boston but schooled in England. He studied law at Cambridge and
became an English barrister. His father, working then in England and Europe
on painting commissions, sent his son back to America to attend to family
legal affairs. It was during that visit that John Copley met Anna Cabot Lowell.
Met her, courted her, and then left her. He returned to England and an increasingly brilliant career. Three times he was appointed lord chancellor of England,
by George IV, William IV, and Queen Victoria, and he was knighted and later
raised to the peerage as the Right Honorable Lord Lyndhurst. He became an
English gentleman, through and through, and left Nancy, his American love,
behind.

Josiah Quincy III was more in keeping with Lowell family expectations:
He descended from two old New England families, the Quincys and the Phillips; had been educated at Phillips Andover and Harvard; and was thoroughly
committed to New England and Boston (his father had been a leader in the
Sons of Liberty). He was an up-and-coming lawyer, and a very social fellow.

Nancy found Quincy charming and interesting, yet she could not help
noticing that he was a bit homely, with close-set eyes, a pointy nose and chin,
and a protuberant lower lip. The unruly curls on his head were thinning, be-
traying a freckled scalp. He could not compare to her beloved Copley. Copley
was a successful barrister, a man of passion and determination, and very good-
looking, with his dark, piercing eyes, perfect Roman nose, sensuous mouth,

and ample wavy hair. He'd attracted Nancy not only with his achievements, mental and physical, but also with his presence. Being around him made her mind jump and her thoughts hop; she felt alive with him, every nerve brightly lit and heart drumming. Now his absence caused her pain; even worse, she felt dull and dispirited. Yes, Quincy was kind and easy in personality but he was perhaps far too pleasant to *everyone* he met. Nancy wanted to be special, singled out.

As summer turned to fall, Nancy found herself falling into a state of melancholy. She tried to blot out the "gloomy November sky, uncheered by sunshine, a chill bleak wind, which is robbing the trees of their last withering leaves. . . . Let me blame the weather for this disorder of my nerves and hope that tomorrow I shall smile and be happy . . ."[11] Dedicating herself to her duties as the eldest daughter, she focused on her role as a second mother to the younger ones. She wrote to her brothers away at school, scolding them and advising them and teasing them, much as she would treat her nieces and nephews in the years to come. Her younger sisters she endeavored to keep entertained and busy, planning outings and inviting friends over often. What free time she had, she sought to fill with the company of Josiah Quincy, hoping to forget Copley. But the heartache persisted.

> Where now is fled that sentiment and truth
> On which my listening ear enraptured hung?
> Where all the graceful modesty of youth
> Which flushed thy cheek and flattered on thy tongue?
> Where that engaging purity of mind,
> Which gave thy manners a peculiar charm
> That dignity of soul, that thought refined
> That heart with tenderness and feeling warm?
> And is the excellence my soul admired
> Alas so greatly changed? Or must I deem
> Those radiant virtues which my love inspired
> The gay creation of a youthful dream?[12]

Nancy traveled to Portsmouth, New Hampshire, to visit an old governess, hoping that a change of scenery would lift her spirits. But try as she might, she could not erase the memories that still held her hostage: "highly as I think of the pleasures of memory, I sometimes would be willing to forego them, could all the past be buried in oblivion . . ."[13] she wrote to her brother Frank, describing her mistake in relying upon the love she had been so sure of in Copley. She envied Francis for the security of heart and mind granted by

masculine gender: "your sex are in less danger of suffering from these indul-
gences than ours since it is infinitely more in your power to decide your own
fate."[14]

Frank had started out in business by supplying local grocers with the goods
they needed: raisins, chocolate, molasses, sugar, rum. Urban markets were
growing as the town's population grew. These new urban households were no
longer self-sufficient (in the country, they'd had room to grow and make much
of what they needed) and people were eager to try new goods, as well as find
old necessities available in the local grocer's shop. Frank worked to supply what
they needed. It was part of his plan to begin modestly, create contacts, build a
reputation for delivering what he promised. Now his business was growing
and his interests, as well. Investments could be sought, on his behalf and on
behalf of others, in ventures that involved traveling to new ports, seeking new
goods to trade. The Eastern trades were wide open—China and India—and
there was money to be made.

Frank modified his business model only slightly when it came to love. The
woman he pursued was Hannah Jackson, daughter of his father's oldest friend,
Jonathan Jackson, and sister of his own best friend from Harvard, Charles.
Frank started modestly, using his contacts, including Charles, of course, to see
Hannah and encouraging his parents to extend more invitations to the Jackson family. Whenever a meeting could be arranged, he attended to Hannah
with kindness, humor, and persistence. He offered his services—eagerly taken
up—to the Jacksons in guiding them on investments. Hannah grew to like
him quite a lot, and her family trusted him with what remained of their life
savings.

It was not much that remained to them. Loans Jonathan Jackson had
made to the Revolutionary government had never been repaid. Those debts,
along with the money Jackson lost in privateering ventures at sea and his failed
trading business, brought the family to the edge of financial ruin. Jonathan
and Hannah moved into rented lodgings in Charlestown, and their nine
children were scattered all about. The eldest son went to sea, Charles was in
Newburyport working as a lawyer, another brother was struggling to become
a doctor, and the youngest, Patrick Tracy Jackson, had been apprenticed to a
merchant. The youngest daughters were put in school in Hingham as boarders. Their sister Hannah also moved out to Hingham, renting simple lodgings
there.

No matter where Hannah was, Frank managed to spend a fair amount of
time with her. The affection she felt for him was growing into something more,
fed by Frank's sincere and steady attention. Their courting became official and

Charles Jackson, along with the rest of his family, happily approved. The faith the Jacksons had in Frank carried over to finances. Jonathan Jackson needed help, and Frank gladly offered to manage what money the family had left. He promised Hannah's father, as he promised all his clients, that he would deliver profits in return for the confidence Jonathan had in his abilities.

The population of Boston had changed in the years since the fight for independence had been won. So many families had left New England, loyalists migrating to Canada, the Caribbean, and England. Even with the influx of country folk, seeking new ways of earning a living, and of merchants, lawyers, and ship owners from the northern port towns, Boston was now smaller in population than Philadelphia or New York. All of New England accounted for less than a quarter of the population of the new nation of the United States. But while rankings went down, prosperity and jollity went up. Boston had recovered from the worst of the war, with newcomers like the Lowells, the Cabots, and the Tracys helping to rebuild her economy, old-timers like Paul Revere and John Hancock opening their purses to gussy up her streets and parks, and the revived upper class determined to enjoy themselves.

The social life of the upper classes after the war became a round of balls and dances, orchestrated outings to the countryside, and intimate soirees at home. Nancy wrote of a party she had organized with her sister Sally, a night of dancing at their home in Roxbury. Even the gouty Old Judge joined in to dance "several dances." The sisters had arranged for food and wine that could tempt any sweet tooth or savory connoisseur: "frosted Plumbcake ornamented with large bunches of artificial flowers and surrounded by small baskets of fruit . . . cold meats, puddings, pies, jellies." And after all the food was consumed and the wine drunk? "More dancing."[15]

Theater came to Boston, after years of playhouses being banned by the Puritan-minded authorities. Actors walked the boards, bringing the works of Shakespeare and other plays to grateful audiences, and the seats were filled to capacity. One evening, Frank escorted Hannah Jackson to a performance of *Know Your Own Mind,* a comedy written by Arthur Murphy, English barrister turned playwright. If Hannah laughed at the play, Frank would have laughed beside her, perhaps taken her hand. There was no doubt he knew his own mind: He wanted to woo and win Hannah. He was well on his way.

Fun, a concept long regulated (and frowned upon) was now up for grabs in Boston, and there were many takers. As Nancy described in a letter to Eliza after her return from Portsmouth, "Boston is beginning to be very gay," and indeed it was. Nancy took advantage of the opportunities on offer: She enjoyed the many "plays, assembleys, and sometimes private balls" put on for the delight of the rising upper class.[16] In this new, post-Revolution world, women—those with the financial resources to be excused from housework—were freer to move about socially and have fun, and Nancy took advantage of the opportunity.

At the same time, she was well aware that the fate of women in this new country had not changed much. Schooling was limited, careers unheard of (work a necessity for many but not for a daughter of Judge Lowell), and talents more often shared only with family, rather than with the world at large. Her contemporary Mercy Otis Warren used her talents to write propaganda plays during the War of Independence (and the poem that had horrified Nancy's father); Warren also wrote a history of the war in the years that followed, and she became known and respected as the Revolution's resident historian. While Nancy was also a writer of acute observations—demonstrated in her prolific letter writing to others and the poems she kept for herself—she was not ambitious for herself. Only for her family. And her family would have been scandalized if she had attempted to make a living at her writing. Her living was to be found at home.

A woman's preferred status was still that of a married woman with children: "to what purpose are girls now educated, their minds accomplished & their manners refined, unless it is to love and to be loved . . ."[17] But Nancy's relationship with Josiah Quincy was causing some queasiness on her part, a vertigo of misgivings. She had begun to doubt Quincy's affections, as well as the truth of her own feelings. She wrote to Eliza of her efforts at "correction of my own heart—I have been trying to banish from it all flattering hopes, all idle wishes. I have been endeavoring to withdraw its affections from some of the objects of this world and to fix them on something better—something which cannot change. . . ."[18]

Quincy could please her, and she admitted wonder at the nature of her feelings for the man: "I felt a happiness for which I could hardly account [in his company], and should find it difficult to define."[19] Having set herself to heal from a broken heart, she was now just as determined to form a new emotional tie. With just a bit of trepidation, she hoped to be firmly moving ahead on a path that would lead to marriage. A path without passion perhaps—"Go idlest passion of the human heart/ No more they meteor-form shall guide my way"[20]—but with a defined end goal and a steady plan of action.

Frank continued to steadily build his business. He'd expanded far beyond supplying the grocers of Boston (although he still did that, as well) by investing in imports and exports. He brought in wine, brandy, tea, coffee, molasses, sugar, rum, pepper, coffee, salt, figs, cinnamon, textiles from England, China, and India, and books from all ports. Over just a few years, he had customers not only in Boston but also in Philadelphia, New York, and Baltimore. He commissioned a shipment of books to Aaron Burr in 1797; the total bill included the costs of the books themselves, import duties exacted, shipping and freight, and the postage of a letter confirming the sale.[21] Every cost was accounted for and entered into the appropriate ledger.

Frank exported cotton, lumber, tobacco, flour, rice, coffee, cocoa, and pepper. He had agents working for him in ports from Calcutta to Bordeaux and from Rotterdam to Barcelona. He began to buy into the trading vessels themselves, becoming owner or partner in Yankee ships that went up and down the coast of the United States, to the West Indies and South America, and on to the farthest corners of the world. Everything he did went into his ledgers, money paid in and taken out, cargoes spoken for and cargoes delivered, ships partnered on, commissions and profits and losses. But the losses were few, and the profits ever growing. The fortunes of those who had invested with him, like his father and the father of his beloved Hannah, Jonathan Jackson, rose also. Frank had offered promises, and delivered.

Josiah Quincy visited Bromley Vale one evening early in the year 1797. He told Nancy that he would be going to New York for a visit. He expressed regret at leaving her but hoped that she would write to him there. Nancy assured him that she would, and told him about a friend of hers in New York, Eliza Morton. She asked him to carry a letter to Eliza, for the best way to ensure prompt delivery of a letter was not through the post but through the kindness of friends and family traveling in the desired direction. Quincy took the letter from Nancy and then made his good-byes.

He was away for weeks. Nancy stayed busy with her sisters, went out to see her friends George and Elizabeth Cabot from time to time, or invited them to Roxbury for a visit. The winter passed quietly, the weather cold and steady. Boston was encased in snow and ice, and fires needed constant tending at home.

When Quincy returned, Nancy quickly perceived a change in him. They talked of what he had done while he was in New York. He'd gone to parties, seen a good deal of that young woman to whom Nancy had asked him to deliver a letter. *Eliza Morton?* Quincy nodded. Nancy questioned Quincy further. He was coy, smiling and demurring, and offering no simple answers to her queries. Nevertheless, Nancy understood what had happened in New York. Nancy's Eliza was now loved by another. By someone who had once loved her.

She dashed off a letter to Eliza: "of what nature the impression you have made on him I have not been able to discover but it is surely indelible . . . I shall pronounce this to be love yet I can bring him to no confession . . ."

Nancy then straight out asked her friend simple questions, pleading that Eliza "answer my enquiries with sincerity . . ."[22]

Do you love him then? And does he love you?

The answer came by mail.

Yes, and yes.

Nancy hid her own feelings and generously opened her heart to share Eliza's happiness. "How many charming things he said of you—he desired me to tell you that when he had once proposed an attachment, he knew no change . . . [he] beg'd me to ajure you of its constancy—no selfish sorrows can so far chill my heart but it will be open with warmth and gladness to receive the communication of your felicity . . ."[23]

She tore a page from her journal and wrote quickly across the page, a note she meant for just herself, for once she'd written it, she folded it over and over and over, until it was like a tiny wound in her hand. She placed the folded note deep in the pocket of her skirt. During the days that followed, she would reach in and, with the soft pads of her fingers, touch its sharp-cornered folds and remember. "Since Sad remembrances wakes the heart to woe/ Calm resignation vainly lends its aid/ To wipe the tear which misery taught to flow . . ."[24]

Josiah Quincy and Eliza Morton were wed that June in New York. Nancy took part in their celebration and then returned north to Boston. A rough journey by stagecoach over bumpy miles, the constricted space within shared with strangers. Nights at crowded inns, then up early for the continued journey. Nancy would have traveled accompanied, but still she was alone and lonely in her thoughts. Perhaps the long trip gave her the time she needed to think. Time to shape and pare her feelings, to create the impression that she would give to others. Time to bury deep within herself whatever sadness—or relief—the event of her friends' marriage had caused.

"The present moment is all of life I permit myself to dwell on," she scribbled in her journal when she returned home. "I enjoy its blessings, and endeavor to support its sorrows with resignation . . ."[25]

She looked up from her writing desk. Walked to the window and looked out over the green meadows of Bromley Vale, lined now with flowering rosebushes. Velvet petals of pink and orange and red grew from thorned branches. She returned to her seat and began a new letter to her Eliza, now Eliza Susan Morton Quincy.

"I feel as much affection as jealousy permits me to feel . . ." she wrote. "I shall go on feeling only affection for my dear friends, no matter what I might have hoped for myself. I can only hope that they keep my place in their hearts, as warm and constant, as I do theirs in mine."[26]

In the back of her mind, lines to a poem buzzed, like the bees outdoors, dipping in and out of the rosebushes. She pulled another leaf of paper from the box beside her, one that was fresh and clean, unmarked ivory ready for her words. She began again to write.

> On this green slope, reclin'd I may gaily dream.
> Ah! And like her I passed the blissful hours
> And strewed the path of life with fancied flowers,
> Till sad experience on this wounded breast
> This painful truth indelibly impressed
> Vain the sweet hope the feeling heart would form
> Of friendship perfect and Love ever warm.
> We ne'er shall find beneath Heaven's azure vault
> Love ever young or friends without a fault.[27]

In the months that followed, more weddings were celebrated: Rebecca, Nancy's younger sister, was married to a Gardner, a match that met with all the family's approval. Samuel Pickering Gardner and Rebecca would have three children, including a John, who would become father of another John, John Lowell Gardner II, who married Isabella Stewart; Isabella Stewart Gardner would become known for her scandalous neckline and her magnificent mansion filled with treasures of art.

It was no surprise when Frank asked Hannah Jackson to marry him. They were married on October 31, 1798. The greater surprise was the birth, only six months later, of their first son. They named the boy John Lowell, Jr. Another John for a family chock-full of Johns.

The wedding of Frank and Hannah was a happy event. The two old friends John and Jonathan were well content to see their families united, and the younger generation was happy to have an occasion to dance, drink, and eat. Nancy considered Hannah a close friend, along with her brother Charles; she'd known them both all their lives. She was content to now call Hannah her dearest sister, and to welcome her into the Lowell family.

"The morning rose bright and unclouded as I trust their fate will be whose union it celebrated. Everything looked cheerful as the smiling countenance of our Hannah, and everything proved propitious. . . . there is nothing like having one's feelings attuned to happiness. Some of the ladies appeared in the character of shepherdesses with straw hats tied under the chin, with wreaths of flowers and wreaths around the crown . . ."[28]

Another wedding, at the beginning of a new century. Cousin George Higginson was married to Martha Babcock. Nancy attended the party celebrating the match, dancing six dances with President Kirkland of Harvard before retiring from the dance floor. She then sat by as the younger generation, "thirty young girls from fourteen to eighteen, in the very season of their bloom, innocence, and gaiety, and young men from seventeen to twenty-one, formed a lovely set of dancers . . ."[29]

At the age of thirty-two, it was unlikely Nancy would be married. It wasn't unusual to be unmarried—her sister Sally, three years younger than Nancy, was still living at home, with no prospects for marrying. But it was undesirable. Without a home of their own or children, the sisters would be relied upon to care for the family home, their father, their younger siblings, the children of their brothers. Their sister Elizabeth was still only a girl, and their brother John's children, Amory and John, still toddlers. All needed watching over. Their father was growing older and more needy, although his third wife, Rebecca, happily handled most of his care.

The fortunes of the unwed sisters had no chance of accelerating unless their father—and then their brothers—managed things so that the women could live free of want, with no debt or favors to be paid. But even more than the financial insecurity and dependence of an unmarried woman, there was the emotional vacuum. More lines forming in her head, Nancy committed words to paper:

> Ah! Since, full many a gloomy hour has flown
> And passing bade some flattering prospects die,
> then full many a pang my heart has known
> And many a tear has glistened in my eye . . .[30]

In May 1802, the Old Judge died at home. Although he had been suffering from gout for a long time, his death was sudden and unexpected. Rebecca, his wife, was overcome with sorrow. The daughters living at home felt his absence keenly. They had lived their entire lives under his benefice, his protection. Now the house centered around a coffin, laid out on a table strewn with sprigs of rosemary and tansy. A dead man. A departed father and husband. Cloths were draped over mirrors and paintings. Curtains were drawn. No light to be let in or reflected out. Only gloom.

It was a somber gathering that followed the coffin of John Lowell across the Boston Neck and onward to the Burying Ground on Boston Common. Rain came down on the procession, steady and cold. The sisters huddled together; the brothers walked with their wives. Judge Lowell would be buried

among Revolutionary patriots; companion to bones and ghosts. Rebecca bent her head to pray for the final reunion with her beloved husband in heaven: *Delight thyself also in the Lo rd; and he shall give thee the desires of thine heart.*[31] John Lowell, lawyer and judge, died without a will. The properties and investments he left behind, including eight trading ships under the management of his son Frank, were divided up among all the sons, with money set aside for his wife and daughters. The properties were mostly sold off, except for Bromley Vale, which John, the eldest son, took for himself. His unmarried sisters, Nancy, Sally, Susan, and Elizabeth, along with his widowed stepmother, Rebecca, continued to live at Bromley Vale until 1810, when those left unwed— Elizabeth and Susan would marry—moved to Charlestown, to a home of their own on Common Street.

The Old Judge left behind less money than might have been expected but certainly more than any Lowell had ever accrued before, in the Old World or the New. Mother and sisters would be largely dependent upon how their funds were managed by the brothers. For the time being, Frank would look over their interests. He would do what he could for them, while he could.

John Lowell, Jr., lost not only a father when the Old Judge died but also his mentor and his adviser. His inspiration, his ally, and his companion: They'd addressed each other as "Dearest Friend" in their letters back and forth. He was devastated by the death, and wrote to his brother Francis of the great "agitation" of his mind, caused by the "unexpected death of my excellent father."[32]

John had a mourning ring made, a golden band with a coil of his father's hair encased in a glazed bezel and surrounded by fifteen faceted amethysts. Inside the band was engraved his father's name and the date of his death and his age at the time: fifty-eight. So much had been achieved in so little time on earth, so much witnessed. John junior had aspired to be what his father had been: a man who promoted and protected his family and his community through the practice of law, through submission to the rule of law. John junior believed, as his father had, in the power and duty of a strong central government, led by an educated and faithful elite, to protect and unite the community, ensuring stability and thereby promoting a flourishing economy.

These were ideals that could be traced back to the early strictures of Puritan life, and John junior believed in them, heart and soul. Together with his father, he was part of the Essex Junto, a band of Massachusetts men committed to maintaining New England's political and economic primacy through exercise of the old Puritan political philosophies: a government conducted by the chosen elite, buttressed by faith, and led for the common good.

But the definition of the "common good" was changing. Those of New

England Puritan stock were no longer in charge. After leading the colonies for over one hundred years, now New England was just one region—one part—of a dynamic new country, the United States. Three more states had been added to the original thirteen: Kentucky, Tennessee, and Vermont. The older order was being challenged by a rising Republican Party. The Federalists, long the governing elite of New England—led by the Pickerings and the Cabots, the Lowells and the Adamses—were being challenged by the Republicans, led by Thomas Jefferson.

With whom could John junior discuss New England's political prospects? He'd always looked to his father for engagement. His brother Frank cared little for the politics or political philosophies; business was all that mattered to him. His brother Charles, having graduated from Harvard, was now off in Scotland studying theology. Nancy followed political currents and could discuss matters as well as any man, but she was busier than ever with her home duties, entrusted with the care of her sisters, her stepmother, and a growing number of nieces, nephews, and young cousins.

John junior would have to navigate the political currents of New England alone—but not all alone. He had a trusted and beloved ally in his wife, Rebecca Amory Lowell. He would need her more than ever as the nineteenth century settled in.

11

1802–1812

... possessed of competence, and health,
He leaves Ambition to the vain and proud,
Friendship, and Love, shall constitute his wealth,
And Life's calm Evening set without a cloud ...
—ANNA CABOT LOWELL, UNTITLED POEM

John Lowell, Jr., met Rebecca Amory through her brother Rufus Amory, a clerk in the Old Judge's law office. The Amorys were an established New England family who had suffered in the Revolution when their father's loyalty to the rebels was called into question. John Amory had had the bad fortune of being in England when war in the colonies broke out. He'd gone on the trip with his wife, Katherine, leaving his children behind in the care of his brother and business partner. The family name was put on the Banishment Act list and John Amory was forbidden from returning to America to claim his house, his property, his family. John Lowell, Sr., had rented the deserted Amory house on Tremont Street in 1776, bringing with him his five orphaned children. But a few years later, he would lend his lawyerly skills to the task of getting John Amory back to Boston. Finally, after much legal maneuvering, John Amory was able to reestablish his allegiance to the colonies and return to Boston.

The courtship of Rebecca Amory began in the spring of 1789. John junior escorted her to dances and get-togethers around Boston and visited her often at home. He also sent to her a steady stream of letters, especially once it became clear that she returned his affection. John, like his sister Nancy, was a devoted letter writer. He exhibited all sorts of rhetorical flourishes in his writing, including the use of repetition and third-person pleading. He was, after all, a skilled lawyer and well versed in presenting his case, ad nauseam if so required. "He can add with sincerity that it shall ever be the happiness of his life to afford her [Miss Amory] the smallest gratification," he wrote to Rebecca in 1789, using the somewhat annoying affectation of referring to himself in the third person. He promised Rebecca that her company alone would "gratify one whose highest gratification is to render you happy."[1]

Rebecca found herself happily won over by his long letters. Within months, he was writing to her in terms familiar and warm, and confessing his love without restraint: "Becca! I love you too well. . . ."[2] They were engaged in 1791, and he wrote to her promising undying love: "Yours forever and in all situations . . ."[3] To his father, John explained, "I have the consent of Mr. J. Amory to form a connection with his second daughter, whenever my circumstances will warrant me in making such a connection."[4] He worked harder than ever at building up his legal practice, and the two were married two years later.

They first lived in rooms above John's office in Williams Court in Boston, just off Court Street. With the family expanding and John's law practice growing, they moved to a larger house on School Street. A girl was born in 1794—another Rebecca—and a boy was born in 1798—another John. Another girl was born in 1801, named for John's sister Nancy: another Anna Cabot Lowell. All was well and as it should be. John's duty was to his children, to his law practice, and to his wife, whom he loved above all else and from whom he hated to be separated: "Every mote that floats between us is a beam—every mole hill a mountain—every innocuous insect the most formidable monster of the forest. . . ."[5]

In the summer of 1801, John joined Harrison Otis Gray, one of his father's former law clerks, in representing a young man accused of murder. Jason Fairbanks was twenty years old and his lover, Betsy Fales, whom he had allegedly murdered, was eighteen. They had been sweethearts for years, but Betsy's father disapproved of Jason. The couple often met in secret, and on May 18, 1801, they had planned a furtive assignation in the fields behind their village of Dedham, in a place called Mason's pasture. Betsy left her house after lunch, intent on her rendezvous with Jason. Two hours later, Betsy's mother was startled by the sight of Jason staggering up to the Fales home. He had gaping wounds on his chest, and he was covered with blood.

"Betsy has killed herself and I have killed myself too," he managed to say before falling to his knees at Mrs. Fales's feet.

Betsy's father ran to look for his daughter and found her lying with her head against a hard stone, her throat slashed, and wounds in her chest and arms. He cradled her in his arms. She gazed up at him, her eyes still open but losing all focus.

"Water?" he asked.

She nodded, but within moments she was dead.[6]

Fairbanks was indicted for murder and the trial was set for August, to be heard by the Supreme Judicial Court of Massachusetts when it sat in Dedham. John junior and Harrison Gray Otis quickly got to work preparing their defense. They interviewed witnesses, including family, friends, and enemies of the young Fairbanks. They spoke with the doctor who had examined Betsy; they spoke with another doctor about the severity of Jason's wounds. One of the stab wounds in his abdomen had turned septic, and Jason had suffered through a terrible bout of tetanus, or lockjaw.[7]

Jason was a sickly young man and had been for years. He was permanently damaged by the mercury treatments he was given as a boy after coming down with smallpox, and was left partially paralyzed in his right arm and shoulder. Any kind of physical exertion led to headaches, fever, and coughing up of blood (indications of tuberculosis). Unable to work on the family farm, Jason had gone to school but the class work caused terrible headaches. He returned home and found refuge from his pain and isolation in reading. He settled into "a life as a sickly, small-town dilettante of literature and music."[8] There were many in town who found him suspect for his tastes in books, his infirmity, and his failure to work the fields as most men did. In their eyes, he was not a man, but a weasel.

According to Jason, he and Betsy had loved each other but were frustrated by her family's refusal to allow Jason to court Betsy and marry her. Betsy had killed herself because she feared the two would never be allowed to be together. Helpless to stop her because of his own infirmities, Jason had taken the knife to himself after Betsy fell to the ground from her self-inflicted wounds.

Both Harrison Otis Gray and Lowell believed their client. Everything he said could be collaborated by the witnesses they'd spoken with, by the doctor's account of Betsy's wounds and Jason's wounds, and by Jason's existing physical condition of disability and weakness. The lawyers were confident of their case in Jason's defense. They believed what they had seen so clearly—his innocence—would be seen by the jurors and that Jason would be set free.

The crowd gathered in the Dedham courthouse on a hot, humid day in August was so large that the case was moved to the meetinghouse down the street. Following jury selection, the two sides, prosecution and defense, began to make their cases. James Sullivan, attorney general for the state of Massachusetts, argued that Jason had hoped to "violate her chastity or run away" with Betsy that day in May, and when she resisted, he had become enraged and killed her.[9] The stab wound in her back proved that Jason had attacked her. How could a girl reach behind to deliver such an injury?

Lowell and Otis presented the defense that the couple had truly been in love. Friends of Betsy testified that she had cared for Jason, that the two were often together, and that they had been "very fond of each other . . . and would go through fire and water to be together."[10] One witness said that both Jason and Betsy were romantic, dreamy types, and that the very day Betsy died, she had spent time reading the novel *Julia Mandeville*, in which star-crossed lovers die, one killed in a duel to defend the other's honor and the other killing herself in despair. When Jason and Betsy met in Mason's pasture to discuss their future that day, Betsy had grown hysterical over the difficulty of their situation and began to stab at her own torso. She was so desperate to reach her heart that she had even tried to stab herself in the back. (Otis demonstrated the possibility of such a maneuver so effectively—and with a real knife—that he almost stabbed himself in the back.) Given the weakness of Jason's right arm and shoulder, he could not have inflicted the terrible injuries on Betsy, the defense stated. He watched helplessly while she hurt herself, and when she fell to the ground, he had taken the knife and turned it upon himself, hoping to die beside her.

Lowell and Otis took six hours to make their closing argument, "a torrent of eloquence with all that ingenuity, sagacity, and learning which the genius and wisdom of man could invent."[11] After they finished their summation, Lowell felt confident. The arguments had been well made; the flaws in the prosecution's argument were exposed. The jury would not be led astray now that they had been shown the correct path to follow. John Lowell had no doubt that Jason would be absolved of guilt.

On Saturday morning, the jury returned from their deliberations. Jason Fairbanks was found guilty of murder. Chief Justice Dana delivered the sentence: "that you Jason Fairbanks, be carried from here to the gaol from whence you came, and from there to the place of execution, and there be hanged by the neck until you are dead, and may God Almighty have mercy on your soul."[12]

John Lowell was dumbfounded. The verdict was inconceivable to him, because he believed there was no question of Jason's innocence. The case he and Otis had presented had been solid, with no weaknesses. If Jason were to be hanged, it was because justice had failed. Because the law had failed. Certainly John had seen miscarriages of justice before. He had lost cases he should have won, and had seen others pay for losses they were not responsible for, punished for acts they had not committed. But to die for a murder not committed? To die because the woman he loved had taken her own life out of love for him? Jason had witnessed a terrible act and now he would live with that vision forever before him. *But dear God, let him live,* John prayed to himself. *Let him live.*

On the night of August 17, Jason Fairbanks broke out of Dedham jail with the help of two accomplices. The trio took off on horseback for Canada. A posse set off, hot on Jason's trail. Jason was captured the next day by Lake Champlain, just miles from the Canadian border. He was brought to Boston to be held there in a secure jail until the date of his execution. On September 10, he was taken back to Dedham and, in front of a crowd of ten thousand onlookers (more than five times the population of Dedham at the time), led to the gallows. A malfunction in the mechanism delayed the hanging. It was fixed and Jason Fairbanks was executed.

There were those who mourned for Jason Fairbanks, including the attending vicar, the Reverend Thomas Thacher of the Third Parish Church in Dedham. But most in the crowd carried on as if the event were a public holiday. Men, women, and children eating and drinking, laughing and playing beside the gallows; as reported later, it was more like "a celebratory national festival" than a solemn execution.[13]

John Lowell returned to his law practice in Boston but his heart was no longer in his work. Or rather, his heart had been cracked almost in two by his work. The Lowell heart—sure and resolute—was now in fragments, held together by the slenderest of connections. He could no longer claim belief and trust in the law. Rebecca urged him to take time off, to restore his energy and spirit by traveling with her to one of the popular spas, either at Ballston or Niagara. She could leave the children with their aunt Nancy at Bromley Vale. But John shrugged off her suggestions. If he felt no desire to work, he could pretend that he did; he could pretend that it mattered, because work *had* to matter. Work was the backbone of his existence; his duty to family and community was demonstrated through the law he practiced. That he no longer believed in the law could not be an excuse. Perhaps if he faked it hard enough, the faith would come back: faith in justice.

On October 25, John and Rebecca's little daughter Anna died. When his father died in May of 1802, John mourned and suffered. His best friend was gone. But to lose a child: What comfort could be found? "Have we not enjoyed much pleasure in the time this child was shared with us, and ought we to repine because it has pleased God to let us have it no longer?"[14] Later, he would write that it was a solace to know that the dead child would be spared the sorrows that come with living, "above all, what I feel to be the greatest pain on earth, the loss of children of her own . . ."[15]

Anna was just one year old, too young to leave him. He had named her for his sister Nancy, with all the hopes such a name harbored, but now the child lay buried in a grave—like his father, like Jason. John spiraled deeper and deeper into despondency. His confidence in law, in family, in faith—all suffered. But it was his confidence in himself that suffered most. He was by nature intense, self-exacting, and judgmental. By his judgment, he had failed to protect those confided to his care. He had failed in law, in fealty, in fatherhood. And he had been failed as well by the things he had believed in like his father before him. Justice and order. Hard work and great rewards. Individual sacrifice for communal good. The tenets by which he had lived.

Rebecca worried about her husband's health. As she understood it, his internal humors were all out of order. Those humors, the vital fluids that circulated in the body, were in chaos. His body and mind were out of balance. She saw that he was both restless and tired at the same time, overwrought and depressed. Was he suffering from the malady of "a morbidly overstimulated state of bodily excitement"? Rebecca spared him the usual treatment of bloodletting and purging.[16] Instead, she enlisted the help of John's doctor to convince John to take that much-delayed rest cure, to travel away from Boston with her and find some peace.

John finally acquiesced. He handed over his ninety-three active cases to Warren Dutton, a law clerk in his office, and withdrew from the practice of law. He would never return.

John and Rebecca left for London, accompanied by their eldest daughter, Rebecca. Their son, named John Amory, after Rebecca's father, remained behind in the care of his aunts. On the way over to England, the vessel the Lowells traveled on was stopped and searched by a British frigate. War was back on between France and England, and the English naval officers were looking for seamen who had deserted the cause. None were found; the Lowells continued on their way.

They arrived in London, and there they remained throughout the winter. In the spring, they traveled north to Edinburgh to visit John's brother Charles, who was still studying theology at the university. Charles was happy in Edinburgh, and pleased to have his brother as a tourist to be shown around. Joined by Charles and by their young son John Amory, John, Rebecca, and their daughter left for Paris, then Bordeaux, Genoa, Milan, Florence, Rome, Naples, and Sicily. They returned to Rome in November 1804 to pass the winter months in the relative warmth of the south.

John had asked his brother Frank to manage his funds while he and his family traveled. He wrote to Frank often, always with directives on which properties to sell and how to handle his investments. He needed money, he wrote; he complained to his brother of how expensive London and the Continent were proving to be. At the same time, John spent freely. He sent back to Boston almost monthly shipments of wine, seeds, trees, books, art, home furnishings, a piano, and even merino sheep—not for trade, but for his own stock. John was having his town house in Boston renovated, and the estate in Roxbury he had inherited was also being prepared for his eventual arrival. Bromley Vale was his now and there were improvements that he wanted made before he returned home.

The hardworking, money-earning lawyer appeared to have turned into a pleasure-loving aesthete. But it was not pleasure or beauty that he sought in his travels and purchases; it was balance. He was trying to restore equilibrium after years of working too hard and enjoying too little, of working out of duty alone and for money alone. John warned Frank now of the dangers of work, even as he demanded that his brother attend more and more to his financial affairs.

"Believe me, for I speak the words of sober experience, no pecuniary reward can compensate for the loss of health. Be indulgent to yourself. . . . I have suffered by the errors of which I now warn you to beware, and I am now profiting by the example I recommend you to follow. Many an active, vigorous young man has sacrificed his health to the attainment of property and because he had not the resolution to quit his golden pursuits has fallen a victim to his thirst for acquisition."[17]

Traveling through Europe in the early 1800s meant coming face-to-face with the reality of Napoléon Bonaparte. Napoléon was crowned emperor of the French on December 2, 1804, and maintained a strong hold on territories in Italy, the Netherlands, Switzerland, and the Rhineland. After winning a stunning victory at Austerlitz in 1805, he secured his domination over much of Europe. Was Great Britain next? John shuddered to think of it.

As John traveled through Italy, he was struck by what he called the "impoverished, powerless hordes" ruled over by what he saw as an overbearing elite, including cosseted Catholic priests and an arrogant emperor. In France, he found the French citizens to be "a very gay, lively people, possessing a sensibility which renders them alive to every thing . . ."[18] He thought little of their clothing—"the most ill-dressed people I have ever seen"—and less of their manners: "they appear to think any stranger a savage who does not speak it [French] well, and to increase his embarrassment by laughing at and ridiculing him . . ."[19] But he also found them hardworking and good-tempered: "In the country or the city, you will find few nations more ardent in their Industry than the French . . . [while also] enjoying that eternal gaiety of heart. . . ."[20]

When it came to Napoléon, Lowell saw nothing that he liked. Napoléon was an ambitious tyrant. He was the Antichrist, a destroyer of decent religion and ancient rules of propriety, and a purveyor of empire. Napoléon's goal was clear: to create a new world order that would threaten both the United States and England. It troubled John that President Jefferson back at home did not understand the threat Napoléon posed.

Already in the late 1700s, the division between the Federalists, of which party both John Lowell, Sr., and John Lowell, Jr., were prominent members, and the Republicans, as represented by Thomas Jefferson, had split over the question of France. For the Lowells, it was a fight that went back to the concept of revolution: Was revolution a change that maintained law and order, or a change that disrupted it? They had been relieved with the outcome of the American Revolution. Independence had led to the establishment of a government that would uphold freedoms, support justice, encourage commerce. A government that would work the way the English government was supposed to but had failed to, especially in the colonies.

At first, it appeared as if the French Revolution would follow the American trajectory: freedom from tyranny; establishment of a representative government; liberty and order coexisting. But then the Tribunals began and the Reign of Terror, and the killing of thousands. The Jacobins had condemned even America's Revolutionary War hero, the Marquis de Lafayette. Now Napoléon was rising, intent on implementing his megalomaniacal plans for empire. How could the United States government fail to support the British in their fight against the French? The answer was simple in John junior's eyes. Thomas Jefferson, president of the United States, was a Francophile. He had even named his party after the République française: the Republicans.

John junior suspected Jefferson had a plan to alter the balance of order in the United States, giving more power to the southern states—the slave-owning states—and taking away the leadership long exercised by New England. The Louisiana Purchase, in 1803, was part of Jefferson's nefarious plot to build up the South at the expense of the North. Jefferson's continuing neutrality in the war between France and England was further proof of his intent. Not only was England a necessary trading partner for New England but, as Napoléon's power grew, Lowell and the Federalists believed, it was England that protected the United States from the tyranny of France: All that stood between the United States and the insatiable forces of Napoléon was King George's Royal Navy.

And yet Jefferson would not take a stand against France, would not alter the American position of neutrality. Clearly, in Lowell's view, Jefferson was a demagogue who valued Voltaire over the Bible, the South over the North, and radical ideas over practical applications of law and order.

Lowell's dislike of Jefferson was matched by Jefferson's distrust of Lowell, and all the associated men known as the Essex Junto. These were the powerful men from Essex County, Massachusetts, including George Cabot, Timothy Pickering, Stephen Higginson, Jonathan Jackson, Nathaniel Tracy, and John Lowell—all from old colonial families, established and influential. They had originally banded together in 1778 to defeat the first proposed Massachusetts Constitution and to develop and successfully ratify the second one. They'd stayed together in support of Federalist politics and New England.

In Jefferson's view, the Essex Junto was "an Anglo-Monarchio-Aristocratic party" that needed to be defeated; a threat to "the liberty which we have obtained by so much labor and peril. . . ."[21] He grouped together under this party all the old Tory sympathizers; "American merchants trading on British capital"; "Speculators and Holders in the banks and public funds"; and "Officers of the federal government with some exceptions."[22]

Jefferson may have regarded the Federalists as mad men—"Their leaders are a hospital of incurables, and as such are entitled to be protected and taken care of as other insane persons are"[23]—but there was no denying their authority and influence, especially in New England. It was one of Jefferson's primary goals when he was first elected president in 1800 to remove as much of their influence as possible from the federal government. He moved quickly to abolish judicial appointments and other governmental offices filled by Federalists under the previous president, John Adams, including John Lowell, Sr.'s role as chief justice on the First Circuit. The Old Judge had been ousted from office with barely enough time to raise his gavel.

Jefferson enjoyed a sweeping win over the Federalists in the elections of 1804. He even carried the state of Massachusetts in his reelection bid, demonstrating just how effective his anti-Federalist program had been. In his Second Inaugural Address, on March 4, 1805, Jefferson pursued his vision of a truly Republican government and a new order of business: "that the public efforts may be directed honestly to the public good, that peace be cultivated, civil and religious liberty unassailed, law and order preserved; equality of rights maintained, and that state of property, equal or unequal, which results to every man from his own industry, or that of his fathers."[24]

Instead of directly taking on the New England faction he so despised, Jefferson spoke about his policies with regard to "aboriginal Inhabitants" and explained how within the Native American clans there existed "interested and crafty individuals . . . who feel themselves something in the present order of things, and fear to become nothing in any other." He condemned such conservative types who desired only to keep "things in their present state, who dread reformation, and exert all their faculties to maintain the ascendency of habit over the duty of improving our reason, and obeying its mandates."[25]

John Lowell, Jr., still abroad, felt the sharp sting of Jefferson's oblique but pointed accusation. Jefferson was not only referring to the Native American tribes when he described their sense of duty as "sanctimonious reverence for the customs of their ancestors; that whatsoever they did, must be done through all time; that reason is a false guide, and to advance under its counsel, in their physical, moral, or political condition, is perilous innovation; that their duty is to remain as their Creator made them."[26] Jefferson's words were an attack on the Lowell family and all other New Englanders who were proudly bound by tradition, religion, and duty.

It was both reproof and challenge. The time had come for John Lowell to return home. To leave off accumulating European experiences and goods, incurring European expenses and paying European bills, and get back to the country that needed him. Lowell was feeling strong again, mentally and physically. He would take those strengths and direct himself to a certain goal: defeating Jefferson and the Republicans by supporting New England and her long-held values of law and order.

John returned to Boston, to Bromley Vale in the country and Colonnade Row in the city, and took on the challenge laid out by Jefferson: Did New Englanders care about the union of the United States? Or were they, as Jefferson accused, just out for themselves and their own interests? Lowell sat down to his desk and took pen in hand. He would use words to fight Jefferson, not the law. He was no longer a lawyer; he was a writer. It was a liberating role for him and one he took to like a cat to cream, and with as much appetite. Not restricted by rules of court or law, he could let his words flow freely and at great length—and he did both. His missives stretched to thirty pages or more. His arguments were cohesive and well ordered, his style ornate. He wrote with many rhetorical flourishes; long sentences prevailed over shorter ones; and even the titles were of a length that taxed an ordinary reader:

Analysis of the late correspondence between our administration and Great Britain and France: with an attempt to shew what are the real causes of the failure of the negociation

The New-England patriot: being a candid comparison, of the principles and conduct of the Washington and Jefferson administrations: the whole founded upon indisputable facts and public documents, to which reference is made in the text and notes

The antigallican; or, The lover of his own country: in a series of pieces partly heretofore published and partly new, wherein French influence, and false patriotism, are fully and fairly displayed[27]

When Lowell was asked to speak at a local agricultural fair to get the event started, his twenty-two-page speech took over an hour to deliver.

Writing about his community and his country—his United States—was John Lowell's new mission. A new duty discovered, an opportunity seized. And along with his newfound role in life, he was christened with a new name, one by which he would forever more be known. John signed his works by various pen names: a Yankee Farmer; The Roxbury Farmer; a Citizen of New England; a Friend to Peace. But the name that would become revered by all the future Lowells, and the one they used when referring to him, was the Boston Rebel. He was no longer just John. He was John the Rebel. He was not fighting against law and order. He was a rebel fighting for it.

Bromley Vale was a fine place for a self-proclaimed rebel. Lowell had a stone castle constructed on the grounds to remind him of old England and his travels there. He had more greenhouses built, into which he installed long rows of plants and flowers, seeded by the many packets he'd sent home during his three years abroad. A windmill was constructed to aid with the irrigation of his new plantings. The trees he'd imported were placed in rows along the ridges of Bromley Vale, and the imported merino sheep roamed free behind the barn.

John would be left alone at Bromley Vale with his wife and children, Rebecca and John. His stepmother, Rebecca, and two sisters, Nancy and Sally, were planning a move to Charlestown to live closer to Judge Russell, Rebecca's father. John's youngest sister, Elizabeth, had left home in 1806, after marrying John the Rebel's former law clerk, Warren Dutton. Their wedding ceremony had been performed by John's brother Charles, recently returned from Scotland and the newly appointed minister at West Church on Cambridge Street in Boston.

John would miss his sister Nancy when she left. She was a doting and yet disciplining aunt to his daughter, Rebecca, and also to the terror that was young John Amory Lowell, whom Nancy called "the little rogue."[28] And John loved discussing issues with his sister, whom he considered smart and knowledgeable about current events. Nancy was less vexed with Napoléon than John was, and less impressed with the French. She'd traveled to Paris herself in 1803 and found little to admire. Even a tour of art treasures owned and displayed by the French had left her disdainful. Although the paintings by "the sublime Raphael" provided her with great pleasure, the statuary was an "outrage upon Modesty by the exhibition of Naked Figures as large as Life."[29]

As far as Napoléon's ambitions, Nancy wasn't as worried for the safety of her country as her brother was. "If Frenchmen had not a sort of hydrophobia, I think we should soon be dragging at the wheels of the Conqueror [Napoléon]," she wrote in jest to her good friend Eliza, living now in Boston with her husband, Josiah (as devoted a Federalist as John the Rebel). "As it is, he will probably content himself with bribing our great men with some feathers that now adorn his horses, depend upon it you will see them in a French

Costume, they will wear his livery and he will govern our nation and manage our revenues . . ." As long as Napoléon "let a few of us Yankees sit under our own elms & bake and eat our own hasty pudding quietly, I think it will be as well to be governed by Napoleon as Jefferson."[30]

On June 22, 1807, the American ship *Chesapeake* headed out to sea, setting sail from the Washington Navy Yard, bound for the Mediterranean. Just as it passed the three-mile limit marking the territorial waters of the United States, a British naval ship, the *Leopard*, approached. The British officer, Lt. John Meade, asked to board the *Chesapeake*, and its captain, Commodore James Barron, acquiesced. Meade explained that he was looking for deserters from the Royal Navy. The ongoing war with France was taking its toll on the British. Deserters were frequent, with sailors running off to America to escape harsh treatment on board, as well as the perils of war. Barron refused to allow Meade to search the vessel. Meade left without a word, and within minutes of his reboarding his own vessel, the *Leopard* attacked the *Chesapeake*, firing twenty-one cannons. One man was killed on board the *Chesapeake* and eighteen were wounded, including Commodore Barron. Barron surrendered, and his vessel was boarded once again by the British. The ship was searched and four sailors were taken away as deserters. The *Chesapeake* was then allowed to return to port, badly damaged and with some officers wounded, one dead, and all its crew humiliated.

Outrage on the American side of the Atlantic was immediate and vociferous. How dare the British board a neutral American vessel! The United States government quickly issued a formal protest, demanding explanation and reparations. The Virginia port towns of Norfolk and Portsmouth passed resolutions denouncing the Royal Navy and declaring that no British ship would ever again be allowed into their ports for supplies or repairs. On the streets, Americans cried for revenge against the British. Not only was the boarding of American ships to look for deserters not to be tolerated but the increasing practice of the British to board ships looking for sailors to impress into Royal Navy duty was an affront to the sovereignty and liberty of the American people. Journalist William Duane called for the United States to attack Britain by marching into Canada and capturing Halifax, and by invading Jamaica and Newfoundland by sea.

President Jefferson ordered all British ships out of American waters and called for the mobilization of the American militia to enforce his order. He sent out a band of soldiers to capture the *Leopard* and bring her to America. When the British vessel was seized and brought to port, Jefferson allowed the British crew to return home. The vessel, however, he kept as ransom for his demands on Britain. Britain eventually returned three of the four sailors who had been taken from the *Chesapeake* (the fourth was hanged for desertion in Halifax) and offered to pay for boat repairs and other costs.

John Lowell was fearful that the *Chesapeake* incident would lead the hawks in Congress, led by Henry Clay of Kentucky, to push Jefferson into a war against Great Britain. He set to work writing. His pamphlet *Peace without dishonour, war without hope: being a calm and dispassionate enquiry into the question of the Chesapeake, and the necessity and expediency of war* (authored by "a Yankee Farmer") offered justification for the British attack. Lowell explained that it had been a "necessary act" for a country at war. England had to seek out deserters and punish them. The United States was right to be offended, but on the other hand, the Royal Navy was protecting U.S. citizens from the French: "Do we really want to punish our protectors for a mistaken transgression, or even worse, go to war with them?"[31]

"If we succeed in the war," Lowell argued, "we gain the right to cover a few British deserters, whom we do not want, and which . . . will bring little profit; but we hazard our lives, our liberties, our government."[32]

The United States would not go to war with Great Britain—not yet. But Jefferson convened Congress to enact other measures that he felt were necessary. Dangers on the seas were increasing, with threats from the French as well as the British. Jefferson considered that the best way to protect American interests was for American vessels to simply stay home and out of harm's way. In December 1807, he persuaded Congress to pass the Embargo Act. The act prohibited any American vessels from leaving U.S. waters to go anywhere at all. All exports by ship (and later, this was amended to include by land, as well) were prohibited. The merchant fleet of New England, the whale of an engine driving the economy of the entire region for over one hundred years, was beached; stranded, docked, laid to rot.

Now the pen of John the Rebel truly set to work, his words firing across paper like the English shots across the bow of the *Chesapeake* and accusing Jefferson of leading a conspiracy to bring down New England; Jefferson, he claimed, was in cahoots with the South and France to make the northern states suffer. It was true, after all, that the economy of New England was faltering terribly under the embargo. Almost overnight, its shipbuilders went out of business. Merchants' houses went bankrupt. Ships floated at deserted docks, rotting away on their lines. Sailors were unemployed by the thousands. Trade fell to a dead standstill and nothing of value moved (except by smuggling, the practice of which required more and more skilful and daring maneuvers). One hundred sailors, suddenly out of work, marched on the home of Massachusetts governor James Sullivan, demanding "bread or work." Soup kitchens were organized in Boston to feed the hungry.[33]

One distraught Bostonian wrote to Jefferson in the White House: "How much longer are you going to keep this damned Embargo on to starve us poor people. One of my children has already starved to death of which I am ashamed . . . I have three more children which I expect will starve soon if I don't get something for them to eat which cannot be had."[34] Misery prevailed where before commerce had reigned. In Lowell's eyes, it was all the fault— indeed, the plan—of Jefferson and the Republicans.

Francis Cabot Lowell, meanwhile, appeared to deal with the circumstance of the embargo as calmly and cleanly as possible. He closed his import business and turned his investments from goods to property. The family belt was tightened a bit, and Hannah schooled the children—Susan, John junior, Francis junior, and Edward—on frugality. Frank was determined to find a way out of the embargo beyond the shoring up of property holdings and turnpike investments. The values in both were falling anyway, due to the failing economy.

Without the imports of British goods, including all sorts of cloths from India and China, was there a vacuum that could be filled? Frank began to think that it was in *creating* goods, rather than in trading them, that fortunes could be made. It was time to turn the small-scale manufacturing enterprises of New England into something more impressive. The mills operating now, like the one operated by the Cabot family in Beverly, Massachusetts, were too limited in scope to make money. Based on horsepower—wheels turned endlessly by mules—the Beverly Cotton Manufactory was simply never able to turn out the large amount of cloth in the short time that was necessary to cover the costs of building and operating the mills. The company went bankrupt, despite numerous bailouts from the state. Investments made by members of the Cabot and the Lowell families were lost.

Frank thought there had to be a better way to power the factories, and to run them. He knew that England was the leader of the textile industry worldwide. What were they doing over there that the Americans were failing to do over here? Using the excuse that he was in need of a rest cure—a vacation to shore up his health—Frank planned a trip to Europe much like the one his brother John the Rebel had taken after the Jason Fairbanks trial. A long trip through the British Isles would do him much good, he told friends and family. That such a trip would also afford him the opportunity to look into the manufacturing techniques and management styles of the booming British textile industry was just an added bonus that he kept to himself.

The embargo was not popular anywhere in the United States. Trade and commerce were impeded everywhere, including in the South. Southern harvests of tobacco, rice, cotton, and wheat could no longer be transported to necessary foreign markets. People around the country suffered from lack of goods, loss of jobs, and rising debt. Republican politicians took hard hits as the party behind the embargo, losing seats in local elections. The Federalist Party surged. The Republican Party, still in control of Congress, grew nervous about their national popularity. In March 1809, Congress repealed the Embargo Act.

John the Rebel rejoiced. It was a victory for pen and party. But neither Lowell nor the Federalists could rest. The battle against the Republicans was far from over. War against Britain still loomed as a possibility. James Madison, Jefferson's chosen successor to run for president in 1808, would not hesitate to move against England if the British navy, still at war with France, continued to harass American ships.

Madison won the election handily, with the Federalists' candidate, Charles Cotesworth Pinckney, barely putting up a fight. Lowell knew that Madison was even more intent on war with Great Britain than Jefferson had been. What could be done to avert war and keep peace? Republicans, with their "dream of a war-free world" had become warmongers, while the Federalists sought peace—but only with England.[35]

Nancy died at the end of the year 1810. She had been busily packing up her belongings, along with those of her stepmother and her sister Sally, to finally implement the long-talked-of move to Charlestown, when she fell ill. She was buried beside her father and the little niece who had been named for her, in the family tomb at the Burying Grounds on Boston Common. Two more namesakes would live on, for John the Rebel had named another daughter for his sister, and Eliza Morton and her husband, Josiah Quincy,* Anna's old beau, also named a daughter for their friend. Anna Cabot Lowell, born in 1808, lived a long and fruitful life, becoming known for her wit and intelligence, and for her voluminous writings on all sorts of topics. Anna Cabot Lowell Quincy, born in 1812, would grow up to be a famous memoirist, a keeper of the pen and another living tribute to the woman for whom she had been named.

John and Nancy had shared the same mother, and been raised on the same milk of discourse, disputation, duty. But he barely had time to mourn her death before another blow landed. President Madison was calling for war against Great Britain. He listed the reasons for war: British impressment of

---

* Josiah Quincy served in the House of Representatives from 1805 to 1813, and then was mayor of Boston from 1823 to 1829; in 1829, he became president of Harvard. Quincy House at Harvard is named for him.

sailors, blockades on the seas, and incitement of the Native Americans on the western frontier to wage war against American settlers. Madison asked Congress to back him in declaring war. The vote went along partisan lines, with all votes in favor of war cast by Republicans; not a single vote for war came from the thirty-nine Federalists in Congress.

On June 18, 1812, the United States declared war against Great Britain. John the Rebel stayed silent in his home on the hill. But not for long.

12

1812–1817

The Age is mad: Good taste is fled
Bold Folly Triumphs in its Stead . . .
—JOHN THE REBEL

The question of secession haunted John Lowell. The U.S. declaration of war against Britain renewed the anguish of the northern states. The fortunes of his fellow New Englanders had already been ravaged by the embargo of 1807. Now once again, the merchant shipping trade would be held hostage. By early 1813, Great Britain, with its superior naval power, effectively shut down the ports of Salem, Newburyport, and Boston, Massachusetts; Newport, Rhode Island; New London, Connecticut; and Portland, Maine, through a blanketing blockade of the American coastline. American ships rocked uselessly at their piers, more sailors were thrown out of work, and imports and exports were reduced to what could be smuggled in and out.

Francis Cabot Lowell also struggled with the economic disaster that was New England. But unlike his brother, who was contemplating a radical political solution, Frank was planning another kind of revolution. John wanted to fix the government in order to get New England working again; Frank wanted to fix the way New England worked. Two brothers, two different solutions to the problem of war.

John the Rebel took after his father politically, but physically, he looked nothing like the Old Judge. Whereas the Old Judge had been round and generous, John was sharp and spare. His constantly whirring mental energy was reflected in the energy of his body; always with a foot tapping, leg shaking up and down, or fingers drumming, John never stood still. Frank combined the energy of his brother with the affability of his father. Physically and mentally, he could be both generous and sharp. He was a charmer with a purpose—and what he set his mind to, he accomplished.

When the United States declared war, Frank was in Great Britain. He and his family had been living for months in a grand old house in Edinburgh, in the fashionable area around St. Andrew Square. Edinburgh was a large town, four times the size of Boston, and yet the Lowells felt comfortable and at home in the old city. With weekly balls hosted by established families and evenings spent at the theater or taking part in small gatherings, the Lowells immersed themselves in the local high society and made new friends.

It was through these contacts that Frank was able to satisfy a singular desire: to get inside an English textile mill and take a good look around. He confessed his secret plans to Nathan Appleton, an old Boston friend, when Nathan was in Edinburgh for a visit. He explained that he planned to use his visits to English mills to school himself on the ins and outs of English cotton manufacturing. Frank wanted to understand, from start to finish, how the British mills, with their new machinery and innovative methods, worked.

Once he understood, he planned on taking everything he'd learned back to Massachusetts, where he would set about improving upon English methods and machines. The final goal? To introduce large-scale manufacturing to New England. Frank promised Appleton that New England manufacturing would be bigger and better than anything seen in England.

Appleton did not hesitate. He pledged his support to Frank's plan. He was well aware of Frank's successes in trade and property, and was only too happy to pledge his cooperation to the fulfillment of Frank's manufacturing dream.

Back in the United States, John the Rebel was considering whether the time had come to cut off relations with the Republican-loving Jeffersonians of Virginia, the Carolinas, Georgia, and Louisiana, and sever ties with the southern states. The United States was yet a new country. The bindings between states were not so tightly woven, Lowell reasoned, the allegiances between citizens not so widely held. In order for New England to revive its "ancient prosperity," the northern states would have to start looking out for themselves. Massachusetts could lead the way.[1]

By July 1812, one month into the war against Great Britain, fifty-three towns in Massachusetts had signed a petition to President Madison, declaring the war to be "neither just, necessary, nor expedient." They demanded that a quick peace settlement be achieved. Throughout Massachusetts, and followed by regiments in Connecticut, New York, and Rhode Island, militia refused to show up for their assignments for planned forays into Canada, and some companies had no men at all. An antiwar rally was held in August in New York City. Its mayor, DeWitt Clinton, a Federalist, denounced the war, and hundreds cheered him on.

New England ship owners refused to engage in privateering—so lucrative for them during the Revolutionary War—and the state of Massachusetts went so far as to impose a forty-day quarantine on any captured British vessel (and its crew) to discourage privateering by others. There were sightings of mysterious blue lights along the Connecticut coastline, leading many to suspect that locals were alerting the patrolling Royal Navy about American ships seeking to evade the British blockade. New England was not behind Madison's war.

John the Rebel was the first to describe the war against Great Britain as "Mr. Madison's war." Within days of his published pamphlet, that was the way all Federalists referred to it.[2] It was not a war of the people; it was a personal war of the president, fought not for the interests of the United States, but for the interests of Francophile James Madison and his supporters in the South. John the Rebel poured words onto paper—thousands of words, hundreds of pages—to make his case.

"From the moment war was declared those who had conscientiously opposed its declaration have the right, and . . . are bound to endeavor to bring about a peace by showing the folly, the wickedness, and the evils of war," John the Rebel argued. "It is a sacrifice of our commerce, our agriculture, our money and our lives, for no other good than to make a diversion of the British forces favorable to France"; it is "one of the most alarming attempts ever yet made against whatever little there is left of liberty, virtue, and religion in the world." From such folly and wickedness, only great evil can result: "an oppressed, and impoverished, and desperate people."[3]

And make no mistake, Lowell added in a final argument, a high price will be paid for Mr. Madison's war:

"Tax bills . . . will be passed, or if not, an immense debt (if they can procure loans) will accumulate and then the only boon we shall have will be that our children are taxed instead of ourselves . . . The People, particularly of the Northern States, are now in fact taxed for the war, and will soon feel its pressure by the diminished value of their real estates, by the reduced price of labor, and the difficulty of finding employment, and by the dreadful increase of the price of all foreign commodities, which have become almost necessaries of life."[4]

The only solution was to oppose the war in whatever way possible: "My fellow farmers, who with me think that the war is neither just nor expedient and who know it will be ruinous, will leave no constitutional measure untried to put an end to so fatal a measure" as war against Great Britain.[5] The only question to be asked: Was secession a constitutional measure?

The very successful cotton and wool industries of Great Britain were fiercely protected by the Crown and Parliament. Since the 1700s, there had been explicit laws in place to protect and hide the processes and innovations of British manufacturing from foreigners. Cotton workers, along with woolen, mohair, and linen workers, were prohibited from emigrating out of England, and those who tried to entice English workers to leave for foreign mills were subject to fines and imprisonment. Laws prohibited the exportation of any machinery involved in textile manufacturing, and any mechanic or engineer with knowledge of operations was not allowed to leave the country, upon risk of arrest. Mill employees were forced to take loyalty oaths, factories were designed "with the defensive features of a medieval castle," and machinery was built to look more complicated to operate than it actually was.[6]

And yet somehow Francis Cabot Lowell managed to worm his way into factories all over Scotland and England. Glasgow. Lancashire. Shropshire. Worcestershire. He went to Manchester, nicknamed "Cottonopolis" for its world dominance in textile manufacturing. Wherever Frank was allowed in, he spent hours walking around and then stopping to observe the machines at work. He studied the power looms, the spinners and bobbers, the dressing machines and roving machines. Studied and stored away all the minute details caught by his laser eyes. He wrote nothing down and when he asked questions, he did it in such a way so as to appear merely polite but not especially interested. He smiled charmingly and let the British think him a tourist only; a sweet American bowled over by British brilliance.

It wasn't only the machines and the manufacturing operations of which Frank took mental note. He also examined the workers employed to keep the mills going, the legions of men, women, and even children brought in to work. From what Frank could see, they were paid little and trained even less, treated as replaceable labor of little worth. They worked long hours in miserable conditions and went home to hovels that were even worse. The laborers appeared to be undernourished and dirty, and were ill-mannered and hostile. Frank believed it was not the work itself that made the workers "of the lowest character, for intelligence and morals,"[7] but the conditions in which they worked. He would make certain that the environment in any mill he designed would be of a different order entirely.

Riots broke out in Nottinghamshire while Frank was in England. Started by the highly skilled artisans who created cloth by hand, the croppers were quickly joined by other textile artisans in what came to be called "the Luddite rebellion." The rioters protested not only the annihilation of their artisan trades and the low quality of cloth produced by machinery but also the terrible wages and miserable conditions associated with machine-equipped mills. The rebellion quickly spread to Yorkshire and Lancashire, where it turned violent. Mills were attacked and burned to the ground, machines smashed, bolts of finished cloth set on fire or cut to shreds. The British military intervened and leaders of the rebellion were eventually rounded up. Fourteen men were hanged for the insurrection; countless more were exiled to Australia. All of it was reported in the papers throughout Great Britain. Frank was well aware of the bloody events, and their causes.

Thirty-five miles from Lowell's house in Edinburgh, a visionary named Robert Owen operated a very different kind of mill. Owen was a social reformer who believed in the possibility of improving mankind's lot through cooperative work and effort. His workers at the New Lanark Mill lived in company-owned housing that was clean and well maintained; tenants had running water, windows, light. The children of working families were sent to a mill-owned school. Food and goods were purchased at low prices at the mill-owned store. Alcohol consumption was strictly regulated and moral behavior rewarded. The workday was restricted to ten hours (and later, eight). The mill's success brought it many visitors and also accolades; Owen's "experiment" was held up as a success of paternalistic manufacturing.[8]

Frank took everything in, turned the information over in his mind, applied his analytical skills. How to make the machines work faster and more efficiently, how to keep mill operations running smoothly, how to treat employees, how to keep the surrounding communities supportive. Everything would be different in New England, he vowed to himself. Everything would be better. He had a plan.

Now that war had broken out between England and the United States, it was time to go home. Time to make his plan a reality. He and Hannah and their four children booked passage on the American ship the *Minerva* and headed west to Boston. Halfway across the Atlantic, their ship was stopped by a British frigate patrolling the high seas. The vessel and all her crew and passengers were taken to the British port of Halifax. The Lowell family was held for days, their baggage repeatedly searched and the Lowells themselves questioned.

All the searching and questioning in the world would do no good. Francis Cabot Lowell carried with him precious information, a treasure of blueprints and ideas for the manufacturing of textiles. Blueprints and ideas he'd stolen away from the British. But the British agents would never find them. The purloined information was stored away in Frank's brain. No investigator would be able to open the vault. Frustrated but finding nothing to make their wavering suspicions concrete, the British officers finally had to let the Lowells go. The family was free to leave Halifax and return to the United States. When the family arrived safely into Boston Harbor, a relieved Hannah wrote to Anna MacVicar Grant, a friend back in Edinburgh, "I decided on entering Boston that it was more beautiful than anything I had seen in my absence."[9]

Frank got to work immediately. Pulling every detail of the power loom out of his head, he reconfigured all that he had seen and created blueprints that were startling not only for their clarity but for their specificity. Far beyond just re-creating the power loom he'd seen in Great Britain, Frank had made the machine better—much better. He turned his thoughts now to how his new and improved machine could be powered. Water was the answer, constant and strong and cheap. Any factory he planned would have to be sited near a powerful source of water, like the mills of Robert Owens he'd seen at New Lanark.

But Frank knew that the key to success in manufacturing wasn't only how the machine was designed and how power was supplied. The way in which the factories themselves were planned and built had to be radically changed. And the manner in which workers were employed and compensated also had to be brought up to standards of what Frank considered simple decency. He would never treat a fellow American the way in which the mill workers of Nottinghamshire, Yorkshire, and Lancashire were treated.

The idea of building a strong manufacturing sector in the United States was not new. Alexander Hamilton had proposed its establishment decades earlier—"everything tending to establish *substantial* and *permanent order*, in the affairs of a country, to increase the total mass of industry and opulence, is ultimately beneficial to every part of it"[10]—but with the advent of the Jeffersonians around the turn of the century, favor had turned to the farmer and the agricultural/agrarian model for the United States. Thomas Jefferson stated in 1785, "Cultivators of the earth are the most valuable citizens . . . I would not convert them into mariners, artisans, or anything else . . . I consider the class of artificers [manufacturers] as the panders of vice and the instruments by which the liberties of a country are generally overturned."[11] When Jefferson became president, he put his agrarian favoritism in practice with regard to the policies of the United States: "for the general operations of manufacture, let our workshops remain in Europe. It is better to carry provisions and materials to workmen there, than bring them to the provisions and materials, and with them their manners and principles."[12]

Now Hamilton's industrial vision showed itself as both prescient and presently necessary. With war declared between Great Britain and the United States, Americans needed local sources of cotton cloth; home weaving was not enough to satisfy the demand. Southern planters also needed new markets for their cotton now that overseas markets were shut down due to embargoes and dangers on the high seas. Even Jefferson admitted that "to be independent for the comforts of life we must fabricate them [textiles] ourselves. . . . Experience has taught me that manufactures are now as necessary to our independence as our comfort."[13] At his estate in Monticello, he set up a minifactory of one hundred spindles spinning yarn to make cloth.

National industries could address clothing shortages while also providing a market for southern cotton. Frank recognized another problem that
could be solved by creating a strong manufacturing sector. The merchant class
of New England needed a new direction. The adventurous and lucrative sea
trade was becoming riskier in all ways. Ships were plundered, sunk, taken
away. Crews were lost, cargoes seized. Insurance rates were going up; profits
were going down. Frank had weaned himself from the merchant trade by investing more in property, and in the building of canals and turnpikes. Now
he and his Boston brethren needed a new, longer game. And what about the
job needs of the growing population of ordinary people? Not everyone could
be a farmer.

Frank's grand manufacturing plan would satisfy everyone's needs by supplying needed cotton textiles to Americans, ensuring a market for the southern growers, providing a new source of wealth for New England merchants
and traders, and creating new jobs for ambitious workers. Frank wanted to
build an industrial factory that included within its operations every step necessary to creating the final product, from importing the raw cotton to carding,
to spinning, and then to weaving. Cotton would come in tied up in bales and
leave as finished bolts of cloth. American-made, from start to finish. All in
one physical plant, one single location. Never before had such an operation
been attempted.

The innovations did not stop with the plan of integrated production. For
the first time, all carding, spinning, and weaving would be done by machines,
not by individuals at their loom or carder or spinner. The machines would be
powered by giant waterwheels. The work of the machines would be overseen
by workers who lived on-site, housed in convenient, clean, and safe buildings,
with room and board provided at low cost. Workers would be paid in cash.

The manner in which Frank would fund his grand plan was also innovative. Instead of a partnership, where each player had a role in operations, Frank
sought to set up the factory as a joint stock company. Partners would buy
shares and leave day-to-day operations to be run by a management team.

In February 1813, the General Court of Massachusetts approved Francis
Cabot Lowell's application for incorporation of the Boston Manufacturing
Company. He was authorized to raise funds up to $400,000 to buy property,
build the factory and housing, and construct the machines necessary for the
carrying out of the stated purpose "of manufacturing Cotton, Woolen, and
Linen goods."[14]

Frank was off and running.

But when he approached members of his own clan, the Lowell family, to
buy shares in the Boston Manufacturing Company, they balked. It was too

innovative, too risky. Despite all of Frank's previous successes, his own brothers thought it to be a "visionary and dangerous scheme."[15] Perhaps their trepidation was due to the failed mills started by the Cabot family in Beverly; the Lowells had lost money on that venture. As John the Rebel explained to his brother, "despite our faith in your full strength of mind, the accuracy of your calculations, your industry, patience, and perseverance . . . we just still all think you are mad."[16]

Frank had to find some other investors to take stock in his company. But where?

John the Rebel had once again become obsessed. He'd been obsessed when representing Jason Fairbanks, and again when writing up his pamphlets against the Embargo Act. Now the political future of the country became his obsession. Would it be a united country or one divided into two nations, North and South? Would the North secede from the South? A convention was called by the Federalists to be held in Hartford, Connecticut, in December 1814. The purpose of the convention was to consider how best to mobilize New England's opposition to President Madison and his administration. Twenty-six delegates from Massachusetts, Connecticut, Rhode Island, Vermont, and New Hampshire would meet in sessions that would be conducted in utmost secrecy. No notes would be taken and no records kept.

One of the issues rumored to be on the agenda of the convention was the question of secession. There was talk of a new northern states alliance, which would be supported by Great Britain. This new country of New England would once again take to the seas and assert its shipping and trade prowess, protected by its new ally Great Britain, and the British Royal Navy. John Lowell had to answer the question, now and for good: Was he behind the unified United States or for a new country of New England?

When the Jackson family had been in dire financial straits, Frank was there to help them. He invested Jackson funds profitably; sent legal business to his friend Charles; helped to pay for brother Jonathan's medical schooling; and brought Patrick, Hannah's youngest brother, in as a frequent partner on deals and ventures. All three of Jonathan Jackson's sons had worked hard, and now they were financially secure: lawyer, doctor, merchant. They were grateful to Frank for having helped them when they were down. When Frank asked them for money to fund his grand plan for New England manufacturing, the brothers did not hesitate. Patrick was so excited about the plan that he asked to come in as Frank's assistant, and Frank agreed.

Frank also asked his brothers-in-law, Warren Dutton (married to sister

Elizabeth) and Benjamin Gorham (married to sister Susanna) to buy shares in his company. They did so without question, their faith in Frank strong.

Frank and Patrick Tracy Jackson went looking for the machinist they would need to build the looms and spinners for the factory, and also to design the massive waterwheel they would require for power. Frank knew whom he wanted: Jacob Perkins, a renowned inventor and machinist. Everything mechanical interested Perkins and he excelled at coming up with better ways to make everything work, from the manufacturing of nails to the launching of cannonballs, from the printing of books to the printing of money, and how to manipulate steam energy efficiently and with maximum power.

Unfortunately, Perkins was just about to leave the country. He was going to England in pursuit of new investors interested in his currency-engraving methods. Frank did not despair upon hearing of Perkins's imminent departure. While his brother John, a man of fiery passions, might have lodged complaints and employed all sorts of arguments to keep Perkins in Boston, or his brother Charles, a man of faith, might have tried gentle persuasion and the application of prayer, Frank did what he always had done when faced with an obstacle. He analyzed it, sought out solutions, and when no solution could be found, he found the silver lining. He turned every obstacle into an opportunity.

In the case of Perkins, the benefit of an expert machinist going off to England was obvious to Frank. Perkins could become his transatlantic spy. Perkins could easily secure invitations to tour English factories, and with his sharp eye and trained mind, he might see more than Frank had seen during his tours. As long as Perkins promised to keep all observations to himself until he returned home, the boon to Frank could be huge. The more information Frank had, the better he could build his own machines, his own factories, his own empire. And before Perkins left, he agreed he would design a waterwheel that would match in magnificence Frank's plans for his mill.

It might have been Perkins who recommended Paul Moody to Frank and Patrick as a replacement machinist for building the looms and other machines Frank would need. Moody had worked for Perkins in his nail-manufacturing plant. He was smart, hardworking, and, like Perkins, he was from Newburyport, always a lucky place for the Lowells. Moody signed on eagerly with Frank and got to work designing machines built to Frank's specifications.

More investors came on board. Nathan Appleton, the early enthusiast, bought only ten shares of the enterprise, but he was so well respected that he attracted other investors, including the Israel Thorndikes, father and son. The Thorndikes had lost money in the Beverly mills operated by the Cabots, but they were all in with Frank. Well-seasoned traders in cloths from India and China, they'd struggled for years with embargoes, wars, and other risks of sea trade. They knew that Frank had pounced on a good opportunity: to make American textiles that were less expensive, of better quality, and more easily available. With Frank at the helm, the Thorndikes would move away from shipping—the merchant trade—and help establish a new source for themselves and for New England: manufacturing.

Frank found the site he needed for his dream factory in the sleepy village of Waltham. A paper mill, built beside the Charles River at the juncture of a series of powerful waterfalls, had foundered and was sitting empty. The site was ten miles away from Boston, but Frank wasn't concerned about locating his factory close to a labor force. Under his plan, the workers would come to him, living within the factory compound and getting everything they needed from the community there.

Frank picked up the fifty-seven-acre property "for a song" and construction began almost immediately.[17] A huge waterwheel, designed by Perkins, was constructed to harness the power of the falls. Factory buildings were built, and housing for workers. The machines themselves were built on-site in a special machinery barn, with parts purchased from around the region and other parts constructed from scratch. The power loom designed by Frank was carefully constructed by Moody, then tested again and again. Tweaks were made, and it was tested yet again. Finally, the design had been perfected, and the looms were installed. By the end of 1814, the factory site was ready.

Nathan Appleton was one of the first to be taken on a tour of the site, accompanied by Frank and Patrick. The tour began in the well-kept machine shop, low-roofed and red-bricked on the outside and well lit and clean on the inside. The three men walked by the worker housing, three-story dorms of red brick with large windows that sparkled in the morning sun. They followed the manicured path that led along the river, Appleton pausing to admire the trees that had been planted, the beds of flowers that had been dug—bulbs already planted for the spring—and the pleasant village-like aspect of the layout. The center of it all was the redbrick factory, five stories high and with a white cupola on top holding a bell made by Paul Revere. The building was the epitome of New England: bold, strong, and yet traditional. Appleton felt himself to be on the campus of a university, not a factory.

Before entering the factory itself, Frank wanted to take Appleton down to the river to see the giant waterwheel. Standing alongside a fence, the men pressed themselves forward to look out over the water of the river as it churned its way through the flumes and raceway. The noise was thunderous. So much power, garnered in the flow of water. How would this power be used? Frank led the group back toward the factory. Paul Moody joined the men as they came onto the manufacturing floor. The loom was his baby and he would be the one to demonstrate it to Appleton.

The power loom was massive, tall and wide, gorgeous and gleaming. Polished iron wheels protruded from its sides and within were held the long, smooth cylinders upon which the fabric would be woven. The structure rested upon a series of slender iron legs, like rows of soldiers proudly proclaiming a revolution. And it was a revolution. The manufacturing of cloth would never be the same again. The loom moved smoothly into action—a rotation of wheels and an orchestrated dance of cylinders, a clicking and humming of moving parts. The machinery purred, then roared. The men turned to one another and broke into cheers. Hands were shaken all around. They turned again to watch the beautiful movement of this new and wonderful machine. The world was changing right in front of them and they couldn't move from the spot, transfixed by all the possibilities.

Skilled machinists and technicians had already been hired for the mill. It was time now to bring in the unskilled labor, the masses of people needed to run the machines. No great strength or in-depth training was necessary. Sharp minds and a willingness to work—those were the only requirements. It was Frank himself who decided where such workers could be found: on the farms of New England. Not the farmers themselves, but their daughters. In Frank's opinion, the farm women of New England were hardworking as well as "well-educated and virtuous."[18]

Frank set out on a tour of country villages, talking to farming families and telling them of his plan. Not only could he ensure that the young women would be fully supervised by matrons of good moral standing, that they would be kept to high standards of dress and cleanliness, and that they would be required to attend church on Sunday; he also promised the women and their families that they would be working and living in clean conditions, that there would time off in the evenings for self-improvement, and that the wages would be high and paid in cash.

The pay offered was more than what a typical schoolteacher made, the hours were similar to those required for farmwork, and the independence—even with supervising matrons—offered by living away from home was all too good to pass up for the young women of New England. They were used to living hemmed in by family and farm duties, with no money or time to call their own. Frank offered them a way out. And so countrywomen flocked to Waltham, eager to apply for the chance to work in the mills. Some who came were in their teens; others were into middle age. All were welcome, so long as they were of "good moral character and industrious—those in the habit of profanity and Sabbath breaking are not invited to apply."[19] A handbook of rules, written by Lowell himself, was distributed, with the admonition that its adherence would be strictly monitored and enforced without exception.

By the end of the year 1814, the Boston Manufacturing Company was ready for business.

The union must stand. John the Rebel made his decision: He would not revolt against the nation his father had helped to form. A separation of the United States into two entities would be "one of the greatest evils," not to be countenanced now or ever.[20] He placed his faith in union and hoped for the best from Madison.

And yet when the war with Great Britain finally ended with the signing of the Treaty of Ghent on December 24, 1814, John Lowell, Jr., found himself herded with all the other Federalists into a group generally despised. Across the country, the Federalists of New England were called traitors for opposing the war against Great Britain, but even worse names were offered up: "British bootlickers," "monarchial aristocrats," and "Lobster princes."[21] Under the assault of public condemnation, the strength and will of the Federalist Party faded away. Only a few seats were still held by Federalist politicians in the local and state governments of northern states. New political parties would rise in New England, but the Federalists were done.

John the Rebel retired his pen and returned to farming. Inflamed and enraged by the government of Republicans for so long—for too long—he had burned out. As he once turned away from the law, he now turned away from politics. He stayed at home at Bromley Vale and looked to nature and family for his satisfactions. Above all, he turned to his wife: "It is perfect nonsense for two people who have so much and so good reason to be attached to each other ever to be apart; who is there on earth who cares for them half as much as they do for each other? Who can ever learn to care for them after they have arrived at our years?"[22]

John was content in the house on the hill, and in the gardens and groves he tended so carefully. In a strange parallel to his nemesis at Monticello, John at Bromley Vale became the agricultural advocate and model for all of New England, much like Jefferson was for the South. He was nicknamed "the Columella of the Northern States," a reference to Lucius Junius Moderatus Columella, a first-century A.D. writer famous for his twelve-volume treatise on Roman agriculture.[23] That John the Roxbury farmer would be drawn from his gardens and once more take his place in the public arena—impassioned one more time—he could not foresee. It would not be for law or for politics, but for something else entirely.

Peace with Great Britain threw a shadow across Francis Cabot Lowell's dream for American manufacturing. English merchants made no secret of their plans to flood the newly reopened American markets with cheap textiles from England, India, and China. But Frank did not panic. He was suffering from ill health, and in mourning still for his wife, Hannah, who died in May 1815. Her death was followed by the death of his sister Susan Gorham in February 1816. Nevertheless, in April 1816, Frank gathered his strength and traveled to Washington, D.C., to pursue protection for national industries. With the support of southern representatives, who were looking out for their own cotton interests, Frank successfully worked to convince Congress to pass a protective tariff that would ensure the northern manufacturing plants a competitive advantage over cheap imports.

The Boston Manufacturing Company was already turning a profit. The cloth made at the Waltham mill, a durable and rough white sheeting, had become a favorite with rural families. Demand was growing. Sales were going up. Returns on investment were high. In addition to making textiles, the machine shop was gaining renown for its products, including a new kind of dressing machine (preparing material for weaving), a double speeder for making roving (carded material), and a machine for spinning directly onto bobbins.

The rest of the Lowell family was finally ready to commit to Frank's grand manufacturing scheme. They understood now the huge potential for profit in what would come to be known as the Waltham-Lowell factory model. Locate a factory close to a power source; house workers on-site and treat them well; complete all operations of the manufacturing from start to finish in one location. Francis Cabot Lowell had envisioned it and made it a reality. Now the rest of the family would climb on board, investing hugely. Importing cotton from the South, turning it into fabric, selling it to the world. Everything was going just as Francis Cabot had planned.

In August 1816, John the Rebel's five-year-old daughter, Sarah, died. Her body was interred in the Burying Ground on Boston Common, close by those of her grandfather; her aunt Nancy; her sister, the first Anna; and her aunt Hannah, wife of Francis Cabot Lowell. John berated himself for his overwhelming sorrow for this child—"the wickedness of cherishing grief"—and wrote to his wife, Rebecca, that his only consolation was that he had done his best to "render her abode in this world . . . sweet." He reasoned that God had "afflicted us to remind us of our own mortality, and of the frail nature of all our earthly possessions, and to induce us to quicken our exertion in performing well our duties on this earth . . . the highest of which is toward each other and the next highest toward our remaining offspring. . . ."[24]

Rebecca Russell Lowell, widow of the Old Judge, died in September 1816. Another death to grieve: cloths over windows, black armbands, a mourning ring of gold and amethyst and twisted locks of hair. Rebecca was buried, like little Sarah, on Boston Common beside those she had loved, now joined in the earth and, as she had so fervently hoped, in heaven.

Frank's health grew worse. He began to suffer from bouts of weakness and dizziness. He tried the waters at Ballston Spa and Niagara Falls, but to no avail. His health continued to deteriorate. He returned to his home in Boston and gathered his children around him: Susan, John junior, Francis junior, and Edward. On August 10, 1817, Francis Cabot Lowell died. John the Rebel was away in London when his brother died, taking care of business for a friend. When he returned, Frank had already been buried, laid to rest beside the others in the Burying Ground on Boston Common. John walked on his own to the collection of graves and stood silently before the spot, marked by the recently disturbed soil. A hymn came to him then, one he'd heard often at King's Chapel close by: *Remember, Lord, our mortal state,/ How frail our life, how short the date!*[25]

He couldn't remember the rest of the words. He dropped to one knee and bowed his head. A blessing on them all. Then he rose and turned to walk home, just a few blocks down along the Common to number 19 Colonnade Row. Rebecca was waiting for him, along with his daughters Anna and Amory (named Rebecca Amory for her mother, she went by her middle name). Tomorrow they would leave for Bromley Vale. He was so weary. He hoped that there, amid his flower gardens and his fruit trees, working the earth under a warm sun, he would find the rest he needed.

13
1817–1829

We shall recur to the history of New England, and trace,
in the stern virtues of its founders, the cause,
at once, of our institutions and our success.
—JOHN AMORY LOWELL

When Frank died, John the Rebel and Charles were the two sons remaining, the eldest and the youngest boys of the Old Judge. With thirteen years between them, they had never been particularly close, but they did like each other. They were joined by the love they had for their father and for Charles's mother, Rebecca. John would never forget how kind Rebecca had been to him when he was a child, and he saw in Charles much of his stepmother's gentle kindness. He also saw a bit of himself there, for the two brothers shared a physical resemblance.

They both had broad, square shoulders, but Charles's were not held so tightly as John's; Charles's chin was strong, as John's was, but he never thrust it forward so aggressively; and his arms swung freely as he walked, not held rigidly to the side as John's were. Charles's large brown eyes were just as focused as John's but seemed warmer and wider; his eyebrows were rounded, not arched; his nose was less sharp and his mouth was more often turned up at the edges than tight with reproof.

It was temperament that accounted for the differences between them, for in temperament, the two men were opposites. The Reverend Charles Lowell was calm, content, rarely ruffled. His sermons, delivered weekly and at all sorts of special events, from funerals to ordinations to weddings to community meetings, were short and to the point, quite unlike John's loquacious, demanding, and argumentative briefs and pamphlets.

Charles never tried to harangue a man into submission. He convinced his parishioners with plain speaking, promises of peace to come, and his own always-open arms. Students under his tutelage were encouraged to study for the lasting gift of faith but were also promised a temporal gift—a copy of Thomas Bewick's *History of British Birds*—for Lowell believed there was as much to learn in the beauty of birdsong as in the words of man. Lessons of patience, simplicity, endurance, and loyalty: *Even the stork in the sky knows her appointed seasons, and the dove, the swift, and the thrust observe the time of their migration . . .*[1]

One man, clear and soothing like water bubbling through a forest brook; the other man as rough and abrasive as the sharp pebbles found deep below. Charles the youngest brother, and John, the eldest.

Frank had left a small fortune to be divided among his four children, and an even greater legacy, the concept of the mill town. John Amory Lowell, son of John the Rebel, took hold of that concept in 1822 when he married his first cousin Susan, daughter of Frank. He took on all her interests in the Boston Manufacturing Company and set out to create a manufacturing empire. *Occasionem Cognosce.*

As a senior at Harvard, John Amory Lowell had considered the question, "Whether prosperity and the increase of wealth have a favorable effect on the manners and morals of the people."[2] John had no doubts as to the affect of wealth on the Lowell family: it was all to the good. When he graduated from Harvard in 1815, he immersed himself in the world of cotton manufacturing, working at Kirk Boott & Sons in Boston. He walked the four miles to work every morning, from Bromley Vale to 30 State Street, and then walked back home again in the evening.

In 1822, in addition to taking on the Boston Manufacturing Company, he formed the Merrimack Manufacturing Company, also with the aim of building cotton mills and other manufacturing industries. The waterpower generated by the Charles River at Waltham was no longer adequate to supply the number of mills that John and his partners wanted to build. There was huge demand for cloth throughout New England and beyond, and the men wanted to meet that demand. A new site for manufacturing would have to be found, close to a new and stronger source of waterpower.

East Chelmsford, Massachusetts, was a sleepy village on the banks of the Merrimack River when John Amory Lowell, Nathan Appleton, and Patrick Tracy Jackson showed up to take a look at Pawtucket Falls, the huge waterfalls that fell close by. Within months, they had bought up all the riverfront properties in the village and begun construction on a series of mills both for the Merrimack Manufacturing Company and the Boston Manufacturing Company. By the year 1824, the village was transformed into a thriving mill town of redbrick factories and dormitories, machine shops, rope factories, company stores, a bank, a theater, and a church. The village of East Chelmsford was renamed Lowell in honor of Francis Cabot Lowell. This new town of Lowell would become the heart of the cotton industry in New England, and it was John Amory Lowell, spare and tall, who would keep that heart pumping.

John had the strong Lowell chin but in him, it was pointed, just like his ambitions. He was certain of the direction in which he moved, led by heart and mind and chin: always straight ahead, never wavering. He didn't question his role or his duty or his ambition: to take care of his family by making them financially secure. And then some. He became a director of the Suffolk Bank in 1822 (a position he would hold for the next fifty-nine years), thereby organizing not only the manufacturing of cotton but the financing required for every step in the process: plantations in the South, transportation systems that ran north and south, mills throughout New England, and trading ventures that went even farther, carrying cotton products around the world, as far as Russia, China, and India. He was the face of the New England cotton industry, and his chin was the pointer, always going full steam ahead.

"I am looking for the man who gives short sermons," said the traveler. He was a visitor from the country, wandering through the streets of Boston, and when a local man asked him for what or whom he searched, he repeated his simple entreaty: "Where can I find the man who preaches short sermons?"

The Bostonian was happy to comply, for he knew the answer. The man the traveler was searching for was the Reverend Charles Lowell, and the path to his church, West Church on Cambridge Street, was easy to point out. The Bostonian asked if the visitor might not want to hear another preacher, one who gave longer and perhaps more comprehensive sermons.

The visitor shook his head vehemently. It was Reverend Lowell he was looking for. "I never heard him preach but once . . . but I remembered every word of his sermon as if I had preached it to myself, and my wife and I had something to talk of for a week after. I tell you, stranger, that after he has preached his short sermon, there is not much more to be said on the subject."

And with that, he made his way to West Church.[3]

Charles Lowell had been pastor of the church since 1806, when he returned from his theological studies abroad. The sermons he gave *were* short: four or five pages at most, delivered in less than thirty minutes or so. His favorite themes recurred often but never for long duration: The eye of God is always upon us. God is all sufficient. Good works shall grant you peace forever. And his favorite theme, God's shared gift: "May we be partakers of the same faith, that we may be partakers of the same joy!"[4]

Charles nudged his parishioners along toward goodness by emphasizing the promise of heaven and the power of self-determination. He asked them, "Are you sowing such seed as that when your spring increases into summer, you will bear the fruits of knowledge and piety; and when autumn comes, reap a harvest of satisfaction and comfort?"[5]

He was the kindest of preachers, all his congregation agreed. He was patient with the old ones, who had grown hard of hearing and a bit tumbled in the brain. He took on the teaching of the young ones when he started one of the first Sunday schools in Boston and taught there himself (Louisa May Alcott was one of his students). Even the smallest of parishioners felt his gentle touch. Early in his ministry, he'd changed the centuries-old practice of baptizing babies at the end of services to allowing them to be baptized first, so "that they might not be so long separated from their parents."[6] Had no other preacher ever given a thought to the comfort of the child or the parents?

Nor were his kindnesses reserved only to members of the parish. He was known for going into the darkest pockets of poverty, the miserable, crowded neighborhoods of so-called Nigger Hill in the West End and the strangled alleys and streets of the North End. During the depression brought on by the Embargo Act and the War of 1812, the Reverend Lowell made it his duty to care for the poor of Boston. As the years passed, his compassion grew to provide for the waves of new immigrants, living in poverty as they struggled to make a foothold in the New World. The Black Sea, a red-light district, sprang up along North Street after Mayor Josiah Quincy (Nancy's former beau) drove the prostitutes out of Beacon Hill. Drinking clubs, dance halls, and brothels were so numerous and crimes so frequent that most Bostonians feared the North End, especially at night.[7] And yet the Reverend Lowell made it his duty to go there and bring what help he could, offering counsel, food, and clothing.

When Charles asked that his church be listed as "Independent Congregational," his parishioners assented in his wishes. They would no longer be bound by the orthodoxy of the long-established Congregational Church. Membership in the club—those elected to go to heaven—was no longer to be determined by fate. How a man chose to live his life was most important. All who attended West Church knew that what they did mattered more than who they were. And yet who they were was of no little matter. They comprised the wealthiest families of Boston, merchants and ship owners and manufacturers. Men of property, women of privilege, families upright and closely knit, enclosed within a circle of like-minded, well-heeled cousins and uncles and aunts. A circle of affluence, and influence. The Reverend Lowell preached to them to move beyond their circle and help the larger community of Boston.

"May your whole life . . . be one labor of love, the overflowings of a soul fraught with love to God and man," Charles preached, and he warned against "the absorption of the mind by worldly cares, and an unremitted devotion to worldly business." He urged his parishioners to care for others: "We are to cultivate our own powers, and improve our own light, and use our own means of religious and moral instruction, not only that we advance our own benefit, but be useful also to others. . . ."[8] To benefit the community of man, that was his message and his goal: "Happy will it be for us if we diligently improve the talents which have been given us, direct our steps by the light which has been imparted, faithfully observe the institutions which have been appointed for our benefit, and promote, as we can, the improvement and happiness of our fellow men."[9]

The Reverend Lowell didn't make much of a salary as a pastor. What he had inherited from his father in 1802 was mostly used up to fund his education in Edinburgh. When his mother, Rebecca, died in 1816, he used that inheritance to buy a house for his growing family. They moved from Boston to the village of Cambridge, into the house called Elmwood. The Reverend Charles Lowell would live there the rest of his life.

Elmwood was built in 1767 by Thomas Oliver, who in 1774 would become the last royal lieutenant governor of the Massachusetts Bay Colony. It was set at the end of Tory Row, the street where all the powerful loyalists lived before the Revolution. In 1774, when an angry mob of colonists marched to the door of Elmwood, Oliver fled out the back, never to return. During the Revolution, Elmwood was used as a hospital for American soldiers, and toward the end of the war, the Massachusetts Constitutional Convention met there to create the state's constitution (with John Lowell, Charles's father, in attendance). Who was it that scratched into the window glass of a second-floor bedroom *Libertas 1776*? A recovering solider or a hopeful patriot, carving out the words that would carry New England forward.

Set on a knoll overlooking the Charles River, Elmwood was surrounded by acres of woods, fields, and meadows. To the east, the land sloped down to the marvelous green curve of the river. To the west, the irresistible delights of Fresh Pond: skating in the winter, bathing in the summer, strolling alongside all year long. A long avenue of elms led from the door of the house to the street, giving the place its name. But not only elms grew at Elmwood. Shaggy-bark hickories, fragrant pines, and gnarled cherry trees made up the arboretum, along with a few horse chestnuts. The shelter of trees opened up close to the house, allowing sunshine to cascade over the beds of flowers planted here and there. Roses and asters, lilies and mums; stands of brides' feathers and goatsbeard in abundance, and at the back of the house, heavy hedges of lilacs in every shade, white to pink to purple. Beyond lay a kitchen garden bordered by berry bushes. Birds were drawn to Elmwood by the berries and they stayed for the hollowed trunks and long branches of her many trees: places of refuge for their mating and nesting. Orioles, bobolinks, catbirds, linnets, and robins made their home at Elmwood.

It was birdsong, heavenly notes of joy filtering through the trees, that convinced the Reverend Lowell on his very first visit to the place that Elmwood was meant for him and his family, to be their own most comfortable nest. A refuge of peace and sunlight, protected by an assembly of trees.

Charles Lowell had married outside of the Lowell clan when he chose Harriet Brackett Spence to be his bride. She was a cousin, but so far removed that it didn't count. A waif of a woman, at barely five feet tall, she was nevertheless impossible to overlook, with her red hair and luminous eyes. Harriet's family had come from the Orkney Islands, off the coast of Scotland, her grandfather having moved to New Hampshire to work as royal comptroller in 1753. During the Revolution, he'd fled to England, leaving Harriet's father and grandmother behind to fend for themselves. Harriet, born and raised in Portsmouth, New Hampshire, had always dreamed of seeing Scotland. Soon after marrying, Charles took her on a trip to the Orkney Islands. Once there, Harriet experienced a strange communion with the land—some tangible connection between the past and present, a force that rose from the ancient stones, new spring grass, and the spray of the sea. It was something not seen but most definitely felt. From that moment on, Harriet claimed an ability to commune with spirits and a gift of second sight. Not the most common of attributes for a New England vicar's wife, but Charles adored his Harriet and never found anything to condemn or regret in her behavior.

The rest of the Lowells were not quite as enamored of the red-haired Scottish beauty as Charles was. In the generations to follow, any failure to follow through on a stated plan of action was attributed to what they called "the Spence negligence."[10] They found fault with how she kept house at Elmwood, and the education that she and her husband provided for their six young children, Charles, Rebecca, Mary, William, Robert, and James. The children were schooled by their father in ornithology and dendrology: they could name a bird by its song—its true signature—and a tree by its bark or its shadow against the setting sun. They were also taught how to read the signs of weather; they could predict thunderstorms and heat spells, and calculate the exact day when Fresh Pond would be safe for skating in the winter and when the maple sap would start to flow every spring.

From their mother, the children learned the mythologies of the Scottish islands and the geography of the world. They took that knowledge into their playing fields, naming the hollows and meadows of Elmwood after real places in the world, and imagining the sprites and fairies that lived there. Harriet also taught them languages, both alive and dead. By the time they reached their teens, they would be able to read Latin, recite Greek, and speak comfortably in German and French.

The family of the Reverend Lowell was always invited to partake in the large family gatherings held at Bromley Vale or in town at John the Rebel's grand house on Colonnade Row. But the Lowell clan never convened at Elmwood, as it was a house known for its discomforts (it had neither indoor plumbing or gas lighting); its haphazard housekeeping (bird nests and animals skulls lay on top of opened books); its unusual dining hours (a meal could be delayed for hours by the fortuitous catching of rare birdsong); and the rather intellectual conversations that took place at the dinner table, not always in the English language.

In 1823, nine-year-old Will, Charles and Harriet's son, died of a fever. His body was placed in a small coffin that rested on trestles in the large front hall of Elmwood. The family stood around the wooden box, heads bowed, as the Reverend Lowell intoned centuries-old words of comfort. *Surely goodness and mercy shall follow me all the days of my life: and I will dwell in the house of the Lord for ever.*[11] But little comfort could be found.

Will's body was interred in the Burying Ground on Boston Common, not too far from West Church but too far from Elmwood. Charles wished the boy could have been buried closer, for perhaps then Harriet might have found it easier to grieve and let go. As it was, she plunged into a deep depression. While the others returned to daily chores and pleasures, Harriet remained bound and burdened by her loss. She passed days in a stupor of listlessness, enclosed in the shuttered darkness of her room or sitting outside in the path of the sun, eyes closed against the brightness. Her days of languor were followed by days of animus spent shuttling anxiously around the house, muttering under her breath.

One evening at dusk, the Reverend Lowell went to her while she sat in the garden. He bent his head down, and whispered to her the words of a psalm: *Make me to understand the way of thy precepts: so shall I talk of thy wondrous works; My soul melteth for heaviness: strengthen thou me according unto thy word.*[12]

Harriet turned her head away.

In a repeat of history, just as his grandfather the Reverend John Lowell had lost a child and then found himself immersed in a religious controversy, now a grieving Charles found himself drawn into a battle over dogma. The trouble had begun back in 1805, when Henry Ware was appointed the new Hollis Professor of Divinity at Harvard. Hollis, a Baptist, had stipulated in his bequest to Harvard in 1721 that the only requirement for the professorship was accepting "the Bible as the only and most perfect rule of faith and practice," as understood and interpreted "according to the best light that God should give. . . ." No other religious affiliation or adherence to doctrinal orthodoxy was necessary. And yet for years the professorship had gone only to orthodox Congregationalists, traditionalists who preached about hell, damnation, and original sin.[13]

Henry Ware changed all that once and for all. He was a Unitarian who believed in the power of human agency and the all-encompassing love and forgiveness of God. Under his guidance, Harvard started a School of Divinity with an explicitly nondenominational mandate; it would be unaffiliated with any particular church but instead committed to "principles of pure, rational, and undogmatic Christianity."[14] The boys of Harvard breathed freely under the new tolerance, happy to be part of this "college where hot-gospelling was poor form, hell was not mentioned, and venerable preachers treated the students, not as limbs of Satan, but as younger brothers of their Lord and Savior."[15]

Traditional Congregationalists were outraged. Preachers took to their pulpits to voice their opposition to the new Unitarian way of doing things. Pamphlets were written, sides drawn up, battle plans made. For this was a war: conservative Congregationalists against the liberal Unitarians, with institutions as the battlefields and parishioners as the foot soldiers. Where they walked—into which church they entered—would determine the winner. The split became known as the Unitarian Controversy, and there were few in Boston who did not become embroiled, through interest or act or argument, in its unfolding.

John the Rebel could not resist marching onto the field of battle. Once more, he took up his pen and went back into the public arena, this time not for law or politics, but for freedom of religion. Urged on by his friends, including John Kirkland, president of Harvard, John churned out pamphlets criticizing the unbending dogma and rigid orthodoxy of Puritan Congregationalism. He attended the first Unitarian church in New England, King's Chapel (which had started out as the first Anglican church in New England in 1686). Having been bred on doctrines of tolerance and self-determination, tenets passed on by his father and his grandfather before him, it was natural for him to rail against the orthodoxy of the old church.

Let each man worship on his own, how he sees fit, so long as he does worship—this was John's way of thinking. In a letter to his son, John Amory, in 1819, he wrote that "religion is a thing of a private nature and belongs to every man's own conscience. . . . I know not what your practices have been but I recommend to you private prayer. It wonderfully calms the mind and fortifies our good resolutions. . . . In danger and distress it produces a serenity which nothing else can give."[16]

Charles was disgusted by the battle over dogma. There was a bigger problem facing the northern congregations. Why worry over religious doctrine when the *practice* of religion was failing? When human beings refused to treat their fellow man with the love and respect called for by God? The divisions within Protestant congregations didn't cause him any bother and the Unitarian controversy didn't rile his blood the way it did his brother's. It was the division made between men themselves that caused deep anguish for Charles. He had traveled through the southern states and seen for himself the "evils and miseries" of slavery.[17] It was an institution, he argued, that stunted all "intellectual and moral powers" and must be reviled by all who are "wise and good."[18] Slavery might be an institution upheld by the government, but that did not make it right. "We must do nothing that we believe to be wrong, though all the world should unite to do it."[19] At West Church, he offered up weekly prayers on behalf of fugitive slaves in the North and those held captive in the South.

Hanging prominently in the Reverend Lowell's dining room at Elmwood was a portrait of the British abolitionist William Wilberforce, a man Lowell had met during his student years in Scotland. He remembered the words of Wilberforce: *There is nothing more terrible than oppression and cruelty, and no duty more important than the delivery of our fellow creatures from such conditions.*[20] His father, the Old Judge, had worked to put language in the Massachusetts constitution ensuring that all men were free. Now powerful mercantile interests of the North, including members of his own family, were aligning with southern plantation owners to protect the institution of slavery and the status of slaves as property.

Susan Lowell, wife of John Amory Lowell and daughter of Francis Cabot Lowell, died in August of 1827. Anna Cabot Lowell, John Amory's sister, wrote in her diary, "Now she is gone and our eyes will never behold her like. She has left a void."[21] John Amory Lowell went to live at Bromley Vale with his father, John the Rebel. His two unmarried sisters, Anna and Amory, took over the care of his two children. Since the days when they were just teenagers, Anna and Amory had been put in charge of minding young children during Sunday services at the First Church of Roxbury. They had notebooks full of lesson plans for French, history, geography, geology, religion, and zoology. Much older now but still with high hopes, they turned to schooling their niece Susan and nephew, another John.

Rebecca Amory Lowell was a particularly prodigious reader, raking through the library at Bromley Vale and ordering in new releases every month from the Corner Bookstore, a bookshop on Washington and School streets in Boston. She kept detailed notes of all the books she read in a journal she dedicated to "the observations which I may make on the works that I shall hereafter pursue." She hoped, "by this journal, to ascertain the changes which time may make in my opinions, to record the remembrance of books that had long been forgotten, and to retrace many pleasing associations which, otherwise, would have vanished forever."[22] The books included Hayley's *Life of Cowper*; *The Curse of Hechana*, by Louthey; *The Siege of Rochelle*, by Madame de Gentis; *The Bride of Abydas*, by Lord Byron; *Letters of Madame de Maitenon*, about which Amory noted, "Ambition, no doubt, mixed with her piety but it was an ambition of no sordid kind . . . neither riches nor titles did she seek"; and Rollin's *Ancient History*—all seven volumes, and she noted, "as entertaining as it could be made." About the five volumes of Bigland's *View of the World*, she wrote, "I am consoled for the tediousness of the greater part of it, by the hope that my general history of geography and history is increased."[23]

Much as he loved Bromley Vale, John Amory needed his own place. He purchased a large home on Pemberton Square, just a short walk from King's Chapel and close to the former home of his grandfather, the Old Judge. In 1829, John remarried and brought his new wife, Elizabeth Cabot Putnam, to live in the house on Pemberton Square.[24] His sister Anna was not happy with the marriage—she wrote in her diary that she would try at friendship with the new wife "for the children's sake," but no one could ever replace her beloved Susan.[25] The rest of the Lowell clan, however, was pleased. Elizabeth was a cousin by marriage and related in some way or other to most of the people John Amory Lowell did business with. A small circle of families, a concentration of wealth. And John Amory Lowell was very good with family and with wealth.

14

1829–1840

Calamity may come upon us suddenly. A few days—nay,
even a moment—may reverse our prospects of worldly good.
—THE REVEREND CHARLES LOWELL

John Amory Lowell rose to leadership in the Whig Party of Massachusetts, together with Abbott Lawrence, one of his closest friends and most trusted business associates. The Whigs had formed in opposition to the presidency of Andrew Jackson and his Democratic Party, and took many of its members from the former Federalist Party. Like the Federalists, the Whigs believed in the importance of a mercantile and industrial economy led by a strong government.

As the years progressed, a division began within the Whigs, between those who tolerated slavery, the Cotton Whigs, and those who wished to see it abolished, the Conscience Whigs. Congress had tried to address the issue of slavery, meeting concerns of the North and the South, in creating the Compromise of 1820. The compromise offered promise to those opposed to slavery, in that the institution would not be allowed to spread throughout new territories of the United States, and by setting a line limiting slavery to the south (with the exception of the new state of Missouri). At the same time, the compromise appeased those in the South, by assuring plantation owners that slavery could continue in the southern states where it already existed.

The Conscience Whigs of the North criticized the Cotton Whigs for not pushing for an end date to slavery, condemning the largely manufacturing-class members as those who "truckled to expedience in everything for the sake of slaveholding gold."[1] The Cotton Whigs countered that slavery needed no end date: As an institution, it was unsustainable on economic terms and would die out on its own. No need to push for its abolition; no need to upset the southern growers upon whom northern manufacturing depended. So long as slavery stayed where it belonged, down south, and the cotton produced by slaves kept coming north, slavery could be tolerated and slowly deaccelerated, until a new workforce could be created. Many of the Cotton Whigs, including John Amory Lowell, founded colonization societies aimed at giving black slaves the funds to buy their freedom, thereby compensating their former owners for loss of property, and then to emigrate to Africa.

When William Lloyd Garrison gave his first public speech in Boston, at the Park Street Church on July 4, 1829, it was at an event sponsored by the American Colonization Society, of which John Amory Lowell was an active member. But Garrison was not interested in furthering the goals of the colonization societies. He described slavery as "a gangrene preying upon our vitals—an earthquake rumbling under our feet—a mine accumulating materials for a national catastrophe" and demanded that there begin immediately "a gradual abolition of slavery" to be led by the northern states. And if slavery "cannot be speedily put down—not by force, but by fair persuasion . . . if we must share in the guilt and danger of destroying the bodies and souls of men, *as the price of our Union;* if the slave States will haughtily spurn our assistance, and refuse to consult the general welfare; then the fault is not ours if a separation eventually take place . . ."[2]

John Amory Lowell and his fellow merchants, manufacturers, and bankers had no interest in separating from the South. The men who profited from booming northern economies based on cotton—manufacturing, shipping, banking—sought to execute a balancing act between what was right and what was profitable. It was not that John Amory and his Cotton Whigs liked slavery; they didn't. But they reasoned that it could be tolerated until it died out, as they claimed it would do, under the weight of its own inequity.

In March 1836, John Amory Lowell received the news that his cousin, John junior, son of Francis Cabot Lowell, had died in Bombay. For the past few years, John had been on an odyssey around the world, having fled Boston after the deaths of his younger brother Edward, his wife, Georgina, and his two daughters, Georgina and Anna, all of whom had died between November 1830 and June 1832. Anna Cabot Lowell, John Amory's sister, had been Georgina's best friend, present at the births of both her children; the second daughter had been named in her honor. After the deaths, Anna wrote in her journal of her despair over the vagaries of life and death, "all directed by an unseen hand." She wept and prayed, and then returned to her duty, to do "all that is in my power to the happiness of others."[3]

John junior could not return to his duty after the deaths of his wife and children; he chose instead to escape. He traveled through Europe and then headed east, crossing from Europe to Malta and then on to Africa, crossing the northern deserts to Cairo and the pyramids. While traveling in Africa, he dressed up in local garb, stopped shaving, and took up smoking a hookah. He traveled by Arabian horse and African camel, and met the king of Egypt, Muhammad Ali, while traversing the Nile—they met for dinner aboard the king's dahabeah. John took the king's advice and traveled across the Nubian Desert to witness "the great caravan of Darfour . . . 600 merchants and pilgrims, 4,000 slaves & 6,000 camels, laden with ivory, tamarinds, ostrich feathers. . . ."[4]

John junior fell ill in Egypt. He made camp at Luxor atop an old palace looking out over the pyramids. Contemplating his own demise and legacy against the stones of past empires, he wrote out his will, naming his cousin John Amory Lowell as executor of its provisions. He wanted to leave a legacy not of wealth but of a different sort of treasure. After recovering his strength, he continued on with his journeys. Having barely survived a shipwreck off the coast of Mocha, he made it as far as Bombay, where once again he became ill. On March 4, 1836, he died.

The instructions that John junior left in his final will were explicit; the legacy he wished implemented was laid out in every detail. An institute for lectures was to be set up in Boston for the purpose of instruction in "the truth of those moral and religious precepts, by which alone, as I believe, men can be secure of happiness in this world and that to come. . . ."[5]

The lecture courses offered would cover a range of subjects, including "physics, and chemistry, with their application to the arts; also on botany, zoology, geology, and mineralogy, connected with their particular utility to man." John Lowell, Jr., believed that "the prosperity of my native land, New England, depends on the moral qualities, and . . . the intelligence and information of its inhabitants. . . ." He was adamant that the courses be reasonably priced and open to all, regardless of race or gender, so long as attendees were "neatly dressed and of orderly behavior."[6]

Public lectures were very popular events in mid-1800s Boston and could be traced back to the Thursday sermons that the early congregations in New England were required to attend. The lecture hall, offering midweek courses on a range of subjects, had replaced the meetinghouse. Now it was John Amory's plan to have the Lowell Institute replace them all.

The first lecturer John Amory Lowell invited to speak at the new institute was Benjamin Silliman of Yale, who agreed to give a twelve-lecture course on geology. Posters went up, flyers went out, the word went round. When it came time to sell tickets, the Corner Bookstore agreed to be agents, selling from their window on Washington Street. The day that tickets went on sale, the neighborhood around Washington Street became overrun with eager attendees. The windows of the bookstore were shattered in the crush of men and women trying to buy tickets. The lectures were sold-out events. The Lowell Institute was a success.

In early 1834, the women working in the mills in Lowell went on strike. The mill town envisioned by Francis Cabot Lowell had been transformed and the workers were not happy. As more and more mills had been built along the Merrimack, more and more cloth was produced. The more cloth that was produced, the lower its value, and profits went down. The owners of the mills, including John Amory Lowell and Abbott Lawrence (who had established the mill town of Lawrence, Massachusetts) responded to the falling profits by lowering the wages of their workers and increasing the pace—required productivity—of work. Hours per week also went up, with fewer holidays offered per year.

The evening programs for self-improvement, offered first under Frances Cabot Lowell, were still available, with lectures provided at the grand Lyceum at just pennies per lecture. But the workers were too exhausted by their shifts to contemplate evening improvement classes; as one girl explained, "Who after thirteen hours of steady application to monotonous work, can sit down and apply her mind to deep and long continued thought?"[7]

Under Francis Cabot Lowell's management of the mill at Waltham, workers' hours had been long. But the wages were comparatively good, the living conditions were pleasant, and the nature of the work was generally safe. Now, in a drive to raise profits, not only were wages at the Lowell mills reduced but women were given more than one machine to operate, and more and more women and machines were brought onto the floors; working conditions deteriorated and living quarters became overcrowded. As the country edged toward a depression in the late 1830s, wages went down again, while demand for productivity went up. Workers found themselves slipping backward into poverty. Francis Cabot Lowell's dream of an educated, well-compensated, and well-cared-for class of workers had vanished.

The first walkout of Lowell mill workers lasted only a few days and most employees returned to their machines. But they sang songs of protest under their breath while they worked.

> The factory bell begins to ring,
> And we must all obey,
> And to our old employment go,
> Or else be turned away.[8]

In October 1836, the women of Lowell walked out again, this time to protest a rise in the rents charged for room and board. Not only had the rents gone up but wages had been lowered once again. Over fifteen hundred workers joined in the strike. Work at the mills dwindled; production rates slowed way down. By the end of the year, mill owners buckled to the pressure and rescinded the rent hike. They did not raise wages, however. Striking workers went back to work, but not happily. The women of Lowell had begun to feel like slaves, not the valued workers that Francis Cabot Lowell had envisioned twenty years earlier.

> Oh, isn't it a pity, such a pretty girl as I,
> Should be sent to the factory, to pine away and die?
> Oh, I cannot be a slave,
> I will not be a slave,
> For I'm so fond of liberty,
> That I cannot be a slave.[9]

The Reverend Charles Lowell despaired. Slavery, the conditions of the mills, poverty in Boston: Did the words of compassion and action that he offered up, week after week to his largely privileged congregation, make any difference at all? He was becoming worn-out. Problems at home didn't help. Harriet's health had continued to decline over the past fourteen years, her periods of lucidity and coherence giving way to longer periods of languid depression. Charles's daughter Rebecca, whom they all called "Little Bec" or "Becca," seemed to be following in the steps of her mother's mental instability, sometimes shutting herself up alone in her room for days. The Reverend Lowell decided that a trip abroad would help both mother and daughter. He would wait until spring and then go. He could just afford the expenses of such a journey by selling off some of the property left to Harriet when her father, Keith Spence, died in 1826.

Charles's daughter Mary was well settled, having married Samuel Putnam, a Boston merchant, in 1832. As for the Reverend Lowell's youngest two boys, Robert (recently graduated from Harvard) and James, called "Jamie" (still in school), they could stay home in Elmwood under the care of their older brother Charlie and his wife, Anna Cabot Jackson. Anna was the granddaughter of Jonathan Jackson and daughter of Patrick Jackson. She and Charlie had married in 1832. Their union so far had proved to be a happy one.

A new liveliness and sociability pervaded Elmwood when Charlie and Anna moved in, bringing with them their four young children, Anna, Charles, Harriet, and James. Mealtimes were normalized, the house was put in order, and, with Harriet's moodiness, Little Bec's strangeness, and the Reverend Lowell's seriousness no longer pervading the household, a lighter spirit prevailed. Anna brought two of her sisters to live with them at Elmwood, and the home became a hub of Jackson family gatherings. Robert and Jamie loved the company of the Jacksons; Jamie fell in love with Anna's sister Hannah and wiled away the hours sitting beside her and composing poetry in his head. When she decided to marry Samuel Cabot, he sank into a depression and even contemplated suicide one evening, going so far as to put a pistol to his forehead. But he put the gun away and got back to the task of living. He was a college boy and found much at Harvard to distract him from heartbreak.

Before leaving for Europe, the Reverend Lowell had left all of his finances in the care of his son Charlie. His older sister Sally followed suit, trusting her nephew with her life savings. John the Rebel had been feeling poorly and could no longer take on the management of the family fortunes. His son, John Amory, was a financial whiz but so busy with managing family business interests that to ask him to take on the additional burden of managing his uncle's money would have been an imposition. Charlie was a responsible and intelligent young man. His father-in-law, Patrick Jackson, trusted him so much that he had made his son-in-law overseer of his coal-mining operations in Pennsylvania. The Lycoming mine was a new venture for the Jacksons and held great possibilities for profit. Charlie assured his father and his aunt Sally that he could keep watch over their investments while also managing the mining and smelting operations in Lycoming.

On paper, the plans for the Lycoming mining operations looked grand but viable. Independent researchers had confirmed the quality of the coal present in the mountain, and Patrick Jackson had gotten hold of a new design for smelting iron. The coal pulled from the mountain would be sold for use domestically and also for the running of trains; a portion of coal mined would be kept on-site to fuel the company's ironworks and nail-manufacturing plant. High hopes were put into the new hot-blast furnace, designed to turn out iron of the highest quality.

The first attempt at running the hot-blast furnace failed. The machine was redesigned, tinkered with, altered, and retooled. A second attempt was made at smelting. The furnace failed. Then there were problems with the quality of the coal coming down the mountain. People complained that the coal clogged their ovens; railway operators said the coke made from the coal was too light to fuel their trains. There were problems with the nail factory: the nails were coming out defective.

Charlie was confident that pumping in more cash could solve all the problems at Lycoming. He set to work trying to find investors or banks willing to lend funds. Perhaps if the national economy had remained stable, the Lycoming operations could have been saved. But with the onset of the panic of 1837, which began as a run on banks and quickly spread to a recession that extended to all sectors of the economy, there was little that Charlie Lowell could do to stave off disaster. In the end, he used his own money, as well as the funds of his father and his aunt, to shore up the company. He crossed his fingers and hoped for the best.

But the best didn't happen. The worst did. The initial assessment of the coal had been wrong and its quality proved to be poor; the hot-blast furnace never worked; the nails never came out right. Auditors came down from Boston to look over things in Pennsylvania. What they found was a disaster. All operations at Lycoming were shut down. Charlie was forced to resign amid accusations of "lavish expenditures" and "inefficient management."[10]

On February 14, 1840, headlines in the Boston newspapers announced the bankruptcy of Charlie Lowell. The articles alluded to accusations of "financial mismanagement and moral turpitude."[11] The Lowell family name was tarnished; the savings of Charlie Lowell, the Reverend Lowell, and Aunt Sally Lowell were gone.

Anna took the four children and moved back in with her parents in Boston. Charlie was left at Elmwood with his brothers. But then they, too, took their leave of him. Robert fled Boston and traveled west to Albany, where he began to study for the Episcopal ministry. He would never return to live in Boston. Jamie, just graduated from Harvard, moved into cheap rented rooms in Cambridge and tried to become a lawyer. He had dreamed of being a poet, but there was no money left to pursue such dreams.

The Reverend Charles Lowell returned from Europe a financially ruined man. Together with his son Charlie, he made plans to shore up what little income he still had as pastor of West Church. Elmwood's fertile fields could be rented out to farmers; rooms in the house could be let to boarders. Household economies would be made. There had never been much extra money at Elmwood and now there would be no extras at all. Harriet retreated to her room; Little Bec tried to take over the role of housekeeper, but her own health was frail. The happiness and warmth that had stirred Elmwood to life while Anna Jackson Lowell and her brood lived there disappeared. Now the air went flat and cold, and the house seemed to shrink in on itself, its beams and clapboards creaking in protest. An old house, feeling its age.

The Reverend Lowell preached stoicism in the face of disaster. "No period of life, no favorable combination of circumstances in our lot, can exempt us from calamity. We are 'born to trouble.' It is an inheritance sad indeed, but one which we cannot refuse. We may be happy in our families; prosperous in our affairs; possessed of health; surrounded by friends; but all will not avail to avert the stroke. Our mountain never standeth so strong that it cannot be moved . . ."[12]

Holding strong to his faith, he bowed his head beside his son Charlie, the two of them alone at the dinner table, and prayed out loud: "Look backward now, whilst thee are yet a pilgrim on earth, and behold how much cause there is for gratitude and trust and consolation . . ."[13]

John the Rebel took his newspaper in hand on the morning of March 12, 1840. He was in town for the week, staying at his home on Colonnade Row. He had been suffering from ill health for the past few years and the news of his nephew's disgrace and his brother's poverty were not helping him to feel any better. He moved his chair closer to the fire, for the wind blew bitter against the windows of his library. He settled back into his chair to read. Suddenly, the paper slid from his hand. John the Rebel, age seventy, was dead from a stroke.

John Amory Lowell walked through the rooms of Bromley Vale. The old house still had its collection of Staffordshire, its Paul Revere silver, the miniature of the Old Judge painted by John Singleton Copley, and a portrait of John the Rebel painted by Gilbert Stuart. There were also shadow portraits of Francis Cabot Lowell and his wife, Hannah. They never had had their likenesses painted, and now all that the family had were these black silhouettes. The hallways of Bromley Vale were lined with treasures sent back from Egypt by John junior, statues and obelisks and effigies, some still in their calico and linen wrapping. The statue of a cat-headed goddess that the Lowells called Pash or Pasht (rather than the name used by Egyptians for their goddess Sekhmet) had been unpacked as soon as it arrived and stood sentry in the back garden.

John Amory's five children joined him as he toured the grounds, planning the changes he would make. He had two children by Susan—Susan and John—and three by Elizabeth—Augustus, Lissie, and Ellen. Another girl would be born soon, and they would call her Sara. John Amory wanted to make Bromley Vale a paradise for his children; he thought of adding more follies to the one built by his father, who had constructed a crenellated castle tower modeled after the Tower of London—or so his father had always teased them when they were children. John the Rebel had built greenhouses for his many specimens of flowers and the snips of fruit trees. John Amory planned a new greenhouse that would be only for pineapples; he and Elizabeth loved pineapples.

He would build a cottage for his maiden sisters, Amory and Anna. They could move with all their books and papers, the reams and reams of Sunday school lessons they'd prepared over the past twenty years. He'd let the ladies choose what furniture they wanted, and buy whatever new might be needed; he'd let them decide on a name for the new cottage and make it their own. But Bromley Vale now belonged to him.

The Reverend Charles Lowell took it upon himself to tell his older sister Sally the news of their brother John's death. Aunt Sally, the name by which all her family called her, lived close to Charles in Cambridge, having moved there from Charlestown after her stepmother, Rebecca, died. She rented rooms in a former Tory mansion down the street from Elmwood. During the Revolutionary War, Gen. George Washington had used the mansion as his headquarters. When he moved out, Andrew Craigie, one of his generals, bought the house and then died there, leaving little in the way of fortune to his widow, Elizabeth. She was a bit of an eccentric, known for quoting Spinoza and protecting tree worms. To keep her home, the widow opened Craigie house to boarders, including Aunt Sally and a young Harvard professor named Henry Wadsworth Longfellow.

Longfellow and Sally became friends. He also called her Aunt Sally and considered her to be like one of his family. He loved her energy and wit, and described her in a letter to his father as being "a good deal like a fly, brisk and buzzy. She is an excellent old lady; and does everything in the most genteel style."[14]

Sally took the news of John's death quietly, much as she had taken the news of Charlie's bankruptcy and the loss of all her savings. At the age now of sixty-nine, so many of her friends had died, as well as family members. She would mourn them, pray for them, and then go on living as best she could, until her own time came. She was the eldest living daughter of the Old Judge and proud of it. She could no longer afford the rooms at Craigie house, but she would make do, as Lowells always made do. She made plans to move.

Longfellow was distressed when she told him she was leaving Craigie House. She waved his concerns away. She had found a small cottage nearby. She would live there quite well, she assured Longfellow, with her cat, her teapot, her books. The worst part of Charlie's bankruptcy was the shame, she insisted. Charlie's ignominy was "the first stain" on the Lowell's estimable coat of arms; she explained how the honor had been granted centuries before by Queen Elizabeth. Longfellow wrote again to his father, this time to tell him about Aunt Sally's stoicism in the face of poverty; when "she finds herself alone in her cottage, I think she will suffer very much."[15]

He went to visit her in the new home, where he found she had hung his portrait on the wall and dubbed her tiny quarters "Hyperion," after the romance he had published in 1839. She recited now for him from his book: "Look not mournfully into the Past. It comes not back again. Wisely improve the Present. It is thine. Go forth to meet the shadowy Future, without fear, and with a manly heart."[16] Longfellow reached forward and took his friend's hands.

In this case, it was a womanly heart that was so brave. He squeezed her palms gently and bent his head in respect.

The Reverend Lowell bore up under Charlie's scandal and the death of his eldest brother. The losses only seemed to strengthen his resolve to make the best use of what time he had left on earth. He vowed to fight the complacency of the wealthy in his community, and the scourge of slavery upon which northern wealth fed. That his own family—the children of his brothers—were profiting from the cotton trade, building it up, relying on it to grow wealthier and wealthier, did not lessen his resolve but, instead, strengthened it. He took to his pulpit with renewed vigor. The line between Lowells widened, a rift between conscience and cotton: on one side, the poorer Lowells, protesting the institution of slavery; on the other side, the richer Lowells, profiting from it.

It would take a war to bring them back together again.

Part Five

WAR

The economy of war is to be tested by
the value of the object to be gained by it . . .

—JAMES RUSSELL LOWELL,
"THE PICKENS-AND-STEALIN'S REBELLION"

15

1842

> There came a change. They took my free,
> My careless ones, and the great sea
> Blew back their endless sighs to me . . .
> —MARIA WHITE LOWELL, "AFRICA"

U nion or disunion?"

The question rang out at a meeting of the Essex County Anti-Slavery Society. A resolution had been proposed and votes were to be tallied. William Lloyd Garrison waited expectantly, confidently. His motion would pass; he was sure of it. Northern abolitionists would demand that the states of the North separate from the South and become a new union that was pure, clean, noble. The old union was "a guilty and fatal compromise made by the people of the North with southern oppressors, by which slavery has been nourished, protected and enlarged up to the present hour, to the impoverishment and disgrace of the nation, the sacrifice of civil and religious freedom, and the crucifixion of humanity . . ."[1]

"There can be no union with slaveholders!" The call rang throughout the hall.

Of the 275 society members in attendance, 251 voted in favor of separation. In favor of taking apart the union, leaving the South to the South and making the North a model of decency and progress. Twenty-four members of the Anti-Slavery Society, however, raised their hands in dissent. They voted against separation. Included in those twenty-four were James Russell Lowell, son of the Reverend Charles Lowell, and his betrothed, Maria White. The year was 1842.

Jamie Lowell and Maria White despised slavery as much as Garrison did. But while disunion might separate North from South, abolitionists from slavers, the moral from the immoral (as Garrison would say), such separation would do nothing to end slavery itself. The North would no longer be united with evil, but evil would still flourish. Better to hold the country together and rid it completely of the plague of slavery, what Jamie called the "opiate which has made men drowsy."[2] Jamie and Maria were in agreement: The answer to slavery was to wake people up to its evils, to attack it, and to end its practice. It was the obligation of those opposed to slavery to end it for once and for all across all the states of the union.

Maria White had been schooled in obligation: obligation to morality, duty to community, sacrifice of the self for the greater good. She was taught as a girl by the Catholic Ursulines in Charlestown and she'd absorbed their vow: *Serviam* ("I will serve"). The vow made by Saint Michael in refusing Lucifer. Although never swayed to leave her Unitarian religion, Maria found in the Catholics a coloring of sweet mercy that softened her ingrained New England dictates of duty. Compassion matched with commitment, love elevating duty.

In 1834, when Maria was still a student with the Ursulines, the Catholic convent was attacked by a mob. False rumors had spread that girls were being held against their will in the convent, chained in subterranean cells. The mob was led by the Know-Nothings, members of a political party based on nativism and strongly opposed to immigration, especially to the influx of the Irish into the Northeast. The Know-Nothings played on the fears of many New Englanders: *What will these Catholics plant in Puritan ground?*

The mob arrived at the convent in the dead of night, carrying torches and screaming epithets. They banged with heavy fists against the convent's thick wooden door. Convent sisters gathered in the front hall, hugging one another, fearful and unsure. Mother Mary Edmond St. George, the leader of the convent, pushed her way through. She pulled back the dragging weight of the door slowly and steadily. Cold, damp air poured in. Mother St. George stepped through the open doorway and faced the angry crowd. Holding her head stiffly, chin up and her shoulders erect, she looked around her.

"Disperse now and leave us in peace," she commanded. "For if you don't, Bishop Fenwick has twenty-thousand of the vilest Irishmen at his command in Boston, who will whip you all into the sea."[3]

Shots rang out into the night air. Terrified, a few sisters shuffled forward to pull the Mother Superior back into the convent. The door was slammed and bolted. Maria White and the other students were awakened and told to dress quickly. They had been instructed to always leave their clothes folded neatly by their beds, and now they dressed in the dark. Students and sisters fled through the back doors of the convent, running out across the dew-wet rows of the kitchen garden. They climbed over low stone walls and hid in the yards of surrounding farmhouses. Covered by the shadows of trees, they watched as the convent was burned to the ground.

James Russell Lowell had also been schooled in obligation, but by very different teachers. He came into the world with a caul, a sign his mother read with joy in the dim light of a cold February morning. She lay in her wide bed in a second-floor bedroom at Elmwood and proclaimed that this son was special: The covering of membrane over his delicate head was a sign of great things to come. He would live his life under a cape of good luck; he would grow old but never weak; he would speak with passion and hold forth with angels as well as sprites, dance a balance of faith and fantasy. It was her blessing, and his obligation.

To preserve the proof of such fortune, Harriet had the membrane pressed onto paper and saved. A family heirloom. The paper was lost, the talisman disappeared, but the fact of it would never be changed. Harriet sought to set Jamie on a righteous path, one bathed in warm and golden light. Gold: the color of the light that streamed in the windows of Elmwood, the hue of the skin of summer peaches in the back orchards, the scent of marsh grass drying in autumn's last heated rays. Golden boy, with golden curls that would turn reddish brown as he grew, but always with streaks of pure molten warmth when the sun shone upon his head.

Harriet taught Jamie to sing at the same time as he learned to walk, taught him to run and read by the time he was three. "The brain, as well as the limbs, require exercise," she told him firmly.[4] But the heart needed exercise as well, and love was expressed in the Lowell household through storytelling. Harriet would take her little boy up onto her lap and into the warm well of her tiny arms and body and tell him fairy stories from the Orkney Islands, crooning ballads from her own childhood. His sister Mary, nine years older than Jamie and like a second mother, put him to bed every night with stories from Spenser and Shakespeare and Raleigh. Elaborate fantasy and misted history, the stories told by Harrier and Mary led little James forward, and allowed him to see himself as a mythical knight or fearless explorer or magical faun.

It was his father, the Reverend Charles Lowell, who provided the purpose in Jamie's dreams and told him the stories of his family. Percival, the Reverend John, the Old Judge. Charles Lowell steadied his son, a sturdy hand caressing the blond curls, a Bible verse recited over his head. *For ye shall go out with joy, and be led forth with peace: the mountains and the hills shall break forth before you into singing, and all the trees of the field shall clap their hands.*[5]

He reminded his son of the joys of duty. To do good for others, to care for others more than for himself, to put community before self, family before individual, sacrifice before satisfaction—therein lay happiness, his father promised. Jamie felt his first duty bound most of all to this father, this totem of goodness and grace and kindness: "My Father . . . Whom if I had not the higher privilege of revering as a parent, I should still have honored as a man and loved as a friend. . . ."[6]

Jamie was seven years old and had climbed up into the gnarled old ox-heart cherry tree in the front yard when he spotted his father coming up the path from Cambridge Village—for it was still just a village then. He could see it from his perch in the tree, spreading out before him, "tufted with elms, lindens, and horse-chestnuts . . . the noisy belfry of the college, the square, brown tower of the church, and the slim, yellow spire of the meeting house."[7]

His father walked slowly, one hand cupped in the other as if in supplication to some overpowering force. He stopped beside the tree and looked up into its branches. He felt his son's presence before actually spotting him there, a flash of red-blond curls in the green. The Reverend Lowell smiled and his sad face transformed. How nourishing it was to witness the bliss of youth when death had called close by.

He told Jamie, "John Adams is dead."[8]

Adams had been of the same generation as the Old Judge, but he had lived longer, seen more, done so much. Like Old Judge Lowell, he was part of the old world, a man of the Revolution. Part of the early days of a new country, a man of the new nation. All men must die and go to their peace, the Reverend Lowell knew, but acceptance of such passage was never easy for him, not right away. He needed time to mourn, to pray. To absorb. To believe again in life everlasting.

Jamie jumped down from the tree and landed in a somersault of limbs, raising the dust at his father's feet. Charles Lowell suspected the fall was an orchestrated one. Jamie was like a monkey, swinging from branches, shimmying up and down limbs, with just minor scrapes to show for it all. This tumble in the dust was calculated, a ploy to make his father laugh, or at least to force him to reach over and lift his son up. *Thou, which hast shewed me great and sore troubles, shalt quicken me again, and shalt bring me up again from the depths of the earth.*[9]

Thomas Jefferson had died the same day. The Reverend Lowell would not receive the news for weeks, but when he did, it bore no mentioning at all.

Jamie went to a local school run by a strict scholar and even stricter disciplinarian (always "with the book in his left hand and a rattan in his right"[10]) and then on to Harvard, entering at the age of fifteen. Harvard was still a mere gathering of seven buildings then, scattered across the scruffy Yard and enclosed by the houses, gardens, and fields of Cambridge. "During Freshman year, I did nothing, during Sophomore year, I did nothing, during Junior year, I did nothing, and during Senior year I have thus far done nothing in the way of college studies,"[11] Jamie wrote in the spring of 1838. But he did write poetry, and in his senior year, his peers voted him class poet, granting him the honor of writing the class poem for commencement exercises.

Senior year also brought dishonor: rustication. His uncle Frank had been expelled in 1792 for starting a bonfire in the yard. His cousin John Amory Lowell, son of John the Rebel, had been rusticated in 1814 for yelling out of a window to a friend passing by in Harvard Yard. Jamie was expelled now for, among other reasons, wearing a brown suit instead of a black one on Sunday, keeping his hat on while in chapel, and missing lectures and recitations. His father expressed disappointment. His aunt Sally professed disgust. She accused Jamie of giving in to the "Spence negligence" (from his mother's side of the family) and advised him to pull up his boots (of the right color) and get to work.

Jamie was ordered by the college to spend his period of rustication in the village of Concord, under the careful watch of the Reverend Barzillai Frost. Frost was old-school: formal, distant, cold. Fortunately for Jamie, Ralph Waldo Emerson lived nearby and he welcomed the young student into his home for succor against the coldness of Frost. Jamie was happy for the invitation and happier still when he discovered their common ground: Both had been rusticated from Harvard in their senior year and both had nonetheless been voted class poet by their peers. Jamie admired Emerson for his cool head and even cooler proclamations: "[the] walls of the mind's chamber are covered with scribblings, which need but the bringing of a candle to render them legible" was a favorite. Jamie scribbled it in his journal.[12] But he was unimpressed by the band of local Transcendentalists, of which Emerson was the leader. He took a special aversion to Henry David Thoreau, finding him to be a bit too dedicated to nature and less so to mankind. The wilderness was fine "for a mood or a vacation but not for a habit of life."[13]

The class poem that Jamie composed for commencement could not be recited by him during the festivities because he was still under official banishment from campus. But the forty-four-stanza poem was printed and distributed throughout the class. Congratulations rang in; Jamie swelled with pride. He thought perhaps it might be grand to become a poet, to follow his passions and write. But setbacks in the family finances brought on by his brother Charlie's bankruptcy provided no funding for his endeavors. He would have to earn his way in the world—not an easy thing to do as a poet. And always in the back of his mind, the question of duty pestered at him. Would writing poems serve the greater good?

He was interested in theology, but he had no set religious beliefs, other than his faith in his own father's abilities. Studying to become a minister wouldn't work for him. If he could not be a preacher, he would follow another family path: He would become a lawyer. There was an opportunity to enter into an apprenticeship in the offices of Charles G. Loring, a family friend. He would take the position offered and try to make it his mission: the law, the fight for justice. He didn't feel the passion that a Lowell always needed to rise to offered opportunities. The law was not his calling. But for now, it would have to do.

> They tell me I must study law.
> They say that I have dreamed, and dreamed too long;
> That I must rouse and seek for fame and gold;
> That I must scorn this idle gift of song,
> And mingle with the vain and proud and cold.
> Is, then this petty strife
> The end and aim of life . . . ?[14]

In the fall of 1839, Jamie went out to Watertown to see a Harvard classmate named William White. There he found Maria, sister to William, sitting beside their father, Abijah White, in a room with wide windows that looked out over golden meadows. The room was a tableau of country gentry, with upholstered and tufted chairs, a fine carpet across the floorboards, and silk curtains hanging at the windows, framing the harvested countryside. The Whites had been in Watertown since the late 1600s; on their mother's side, they were distantly related to the heretic Anne Hutchinson. They were Puritan stock, those who had done their duty well and prospered. Jamie later described Abijah White as "the most perfect specimen of a bluff, honest, hospitable country squire you can possibly imagine."[15] His Georgian home was his castle, his beautiful children his royalty. Maria, tall and slender and fair, smart and warmhearted and kind, was the princess and the favored daughter.

When Maria rose up from her chair to take Jamie's hand, she seemed pale and fragile. But her gaze was steady, and as she began to speak, her voice low and clear, Jamie realized she was very strong. It was a special female strength that he recognized. His mother had been like her once, his sister Mary was still, and his sister-in-law Anna, who carried all the burdens of the family after Charlie's bankruptcy and disgrace, carried such strength in spades. And now Maria: ". . . with a gentle courage she doth strive/ In thought and word and feeling so to live/ As to make earth next heaven . . ."[16]

Jamie recognized another trait in Maria, one he knew well, for he himself bore the trait with pride. It was the mark of the angels, the sign of one who spoke to the spirits, and they listened. "Not as all other women are/ Is she that

to my soul is dear;/ Her glorious fancies come from far,/ Beneath the silver evening-star. . . ."[17] A comingling of heaven and earth: "she seems half of earth and *more* than half of heaven . . ."[18]

Maria invited Jamie to a meeting of her "Band," a group of young men and women who met frequently to discuss slavery and women's rights, and to recite poetry. Some, like Maria, had been disciples of Margaret Fuller and felt no restraint in expressing their opinions about the role of women in society. Most were followers of William Lloyd Garrison and members of antislavery societies. All fancied themselves poets, but Jamie thought none so talented as Maria. She recited her poems with ease, delivering the lines in a perfect rhythm of sincerity and passion. The slight cough that sometimes took her away from the group was no reason for concern, reasoned Jamie. Such a star would burn brightly for a long time.

Maria's calm and steady manner was a perfect match to Jamie's more rambunctious demeanor. One day they were out walking in Cambridge, when suddenly he stopped, still and quiet as a statue. Maria waited. Jamie leapt in one bound to the top of the large stone column marking the edge of Harvard Yard. There he stood, tall and with his chest thrust out like a rooster. He flung back his long curls and gave out one long, low crow. Then he dropped to the ground, took Maria's arm, and took up the conversation where they had left off.

While Maria admired him for his spontaneity and quick mind, he worshipped Maria for her loving nature: "So innocently wild and free,/ Whose sad thoughts, even, leap and shine,/ Like sunny wavelets in the sea,/ Making us mindless of the brine,/ In gazing on the brilliancy."[19] But she also was practical and capable: "She has more common sense than any woman I have ever seen. Genius always has."[20] Jamie was soon declaring his everlasting love to Maria. Never mind that she was not a cousin nor in any way related to the Lowells. She was Jamie's perfect match, and no one in or out of the family disputed it.

"Suppose you did not love me and thought me moonstruck? I do love you and believe you sane. Which has the advantage? Why clearly I, in as much as to love anything is to derive an hourly revenue from it. . . ."[21]

But Maria did love Jamie: 'You may look into my naked heart, and I will not turn away and veil it."[22]

They knew within months of their meeting that they wanted to marry, but the shadow cast by brother Charlie's bankruptcy and the Lowell family's sudden poverty prevented their union. They would have to wait until Jamie could make enough money to support them. Maria had no dowry to bring to the marriage and he barely made enough money from the law to support himself.

They became engaged and then settled in to wait, patiently and steadfastly in love. Among their friends in the Band, they became known as "the King and Queen." Maria wrote to a friend, "It is easy enough to be married—the newspaper columns show us that every day; but to live and be happy as simple King and Queen without the gifts of fortune, this is, I confess, a triumph which suits my nature better."[23]

Jamie didn't enjoy being a lawyer, although in the long letters he wrote to friends he tried to convince himself that it was the best career for him, both in terms of income and of duty. He admitted that he used time spent in the office where he was apprenticed writing "the best sonnets I have yet written and one of the best (if not the best) lyrics. . . ." What relief, he wrote, to have the time to write: "I feared the law would cover all the greensward of my soul with its dust. But Maria will hinder all that."[24] A man in love with a woman will write poetry, come what may.

When the apprenticeship ended and it was time to go out on his own, Jamie hung out his shingle—J. R. LOWELL, OFFICE OF LAW—and continued with his poems, taking time away from his writing whenever a client with a legal case came in the door. A black sailor appeared one morning, asking for help securing lost wages. Jamie took on the case and, following in the footsteps of his grandfather, refused to take payment for his work. Maria understood, and his father had preached: *Give, and it shall be given unto you; good measure, pressed down, and shaken together, and running over . . .*[25] The wedding could wait; the money would come. Justice had to be served first.

Jamie won the case and the wages were restored to the sailor. The seaman headed back to sea; the poet headed back to his law books. Years later, the sailor appeared on the doorstep at Elmwood, bearing three gifts of gratitude for Jamie: a small canoe, a piece of carved ivory, and a pouch of gold dust. Jamie was happy to take the canoe and the ivory, but he advised the sailor to keep the gold for himself.

Maria had long been a member of the Boston Female Anti-Slavery Society, and in 1840 both she and Jamie joined Garrison's American Anti-Slavery Society. Together, they attended meetings throughout Massachusetts, urging others to join in the movement. They left the Band behind, discarding friendly debates and sylvan poetry for harder battles, sharper words. The line between northerners who fought to end slavery and those who tolerated its existence was becoming a gulf, a wide space that compromise could not bridge. Charles Sumner, the soon-to-be appointed senator for Massachusetts, would label those willing to tolerate slavery the "Cotton Lords" and he condemned their compact with the South as an "unholy union . . . between the cotton planters and fleshmongers of Louisiana and Mississippi and the cotton spinners and traffickers of New England—between the lords of the lash and the lords of the loom."[26]

In 1831, the year of the Nat Turner slave rebellion and its vicious aftermath,[27] William Lloyd Garrison began running his antislavery campaign out of his printing office in Merchants Hall in Boston. Nascent antislavery committees and societies organized, and their membership grew, inspired by the printed speeches of Garrison and Lewis Tappan; as the years passed, a lecture circuit was created to inform northerners about slavery, featuring speakers directly impacted by it, including former slaves, like Frederick Douglass, and former slave owners, like the Grimké sisters.

The press, politicians, and plantation owners of the South responded to the campaign of the northern abolitionists with their own program of propaganda, issuing pamphlets and statements, and burning in public the writings of the Grimké sisters and other abolitionists. They also warned the northern mill owners, bankers, and cotton traders against siding with the abolitionists: "The people of the North must go hanging these fanatical wretches if they would not lose the benefit of Southern trade."[28]

When the mill workers in Lowell held a meeting to protest slavery, a meeting that was both widely advertised and publicly reported, southern plantation owners grew apoplectic. One southern planter wrote to Amos Lawrence, business associate and close friend to John Amory Lowell, warning him that strong measures would be taken against northern manufacturers if they could not control their workers. A Baltimore newspaper printed an editorial threatening a southern boycott of all the mills in Lowell, which would cause Lowell "to wither or be forced to expel the abolitionists."[29]

Northern mills had become so dependent upon southern cotton—over 100 million pounds of it a year by 1835—that threats from the South effectively silenced their owners' opposition to slavery. In turn, the owners, merchants, and traders dependent on cotton sought to still the voices of abolitionism in the North. While walking through Boston one day, William Lloyd Garrison was attacked by "gentlemen of the city" in "broadcloth and in broad daylight."[30] The young lawyer Wendell Phillips saw these purported gentlemen throw a rope around Garrison's neck and drag him through the streets. Phillips was so outraged by the beating of Garrison that he became an abolitionist on the spot.

As the campaign against abolitionists intensified, Jamie girded himself for battle. "Are the slaves to be forever slaves because our ancestors committed a horrible crime and wrong in making them so?"[31] He thought of his own close ancestors, and took heart. His great-grandfather, the Reverend John Lowell: how optimistic he had been about human nature and how forgiving of human transgressions. "Learn those lessons of everything virtuous and praiseworthy which are taught you . . . Be ambitious of coming as near as you can . . . earnestly entreat the divine Favour and Grace. . . ."[32] The Old Judge, Jamie's grandfather, who had gone to court and argued for the inherent dignity of all mankind: "The precepts of revealed law, golden rule of the gospel are that we are not to sell our brethren, that we are to do as we would be done unto."[33] His uncle John, the Boston Rebel: "The attack on the anti-slavery society of New York, and upon the Blacks . . . prove that the first principles of social order are in jeopardy in our nation."[34]

His own father: Both in deed and in word, his father inspired him, for he wove his deeds and words together, and did good. The Reverend Charles Lowell took clothes and food to the poor of Boston, opened his pews to blacks and whites on equal footing, prayed every week for the protection of fugitive slaves and for the relief of despair. "Go then, my people, seek for the abodes of misery; bind up the broken-hearted; smooth the pillow of sickness, and bear up the departing spirit on the wings of your prayers."[35]

Now it was Jamie's turn to add his own words and his own actions to those of generations of Lowells.

When Charles Lowell asked his youngest son to move back home to help care for his mother and sister in 1842, Jamie wasted little time in complying. He could serve his father with his presence but he would also serve a greater good with his writing. He had started to earn money for poems printed in annuals and reviews, and for essays written for newspapers and periodicals; he had some confidence now in his ability to make an income from writing. More importantly, he had gained confidence that his words could further the cause of abolitionism. He would use all his skills—"God has given me powers not given to all"[36]—to attack slavery. He would make people experience and thus understand the viciousness of the institution.

The marriage with Maria would again have to wait. But she understood, as he did, what was most important: "Maria fills my ideal and I satisfy hers."[37]

16
1842–1850

There is something better than Expedience, and that is Wisdom;
something stronger than compromise, and that is Justice.
—JAMES RUSSELL LOWELL

The Reverend Charles Lowell had grown thin and spare in the years since Charlie's bankruptcy. To his parishioners at West Church, he appeared frail, and they worried for him. They urged him to lessen the workload, reduce further his duties at the church. But money was tight and his salary, meager as it was, was necessary to the Lowell household. Harriet was descending fully into madness, hastened there by Charlie's disgrace. She wandered the house at Elmwood aimlessly, alternating between brooding silence and raging bouts of anger. Her once brilliantly red hair was now completely white, turned so almost overnight. Becca, Jamie's sister, lived more and more in her own world. She stayed closed up in her dark and silent room for days on end. Charlie was living again with his wife, Anna, on Winter Place in Boston, where she had set up a school. They were surviving, but there was no extra money to help out the family at Elmwood.

Jamie moved home in May, bringing with him the few sparse contents of his law office and rented room. He hired a cart to bring his law desk and carried it up the three flights of stairs himself to the suite of rooms at the top of the house. The desk he placed in the center room; he would sleep in the room down the hall, which had been his nursery as a child. On the walls of his new office, he positioned the busts saved from his great-grandfather's study in Newbury. The fine likeness of these early purveyors of the best of human traits—intelligence, curiosity, dedication, creativity—could now inspire Jamie, as they had once inspired the Reverend John Lowell.[1] The windows of the office faced over the back gardens of Elmwood. Jamie sat in his desk chair and looked out all the way to Fresh Pond, sparkling quartz gray under the cloudy skies. He then got to work arranging his books on shelves. When he looked up again, dusk was falling and the pond now was purple against the green meadows of its banks, the sky above a blaze of silver, mauve, and pink.

Looking down into the garden one morning, Jamie spotted a chicken coop, long abandoned in a corner overgrown with weeds, briars, and twisting vines of chinaberry. The empty nesting boxes looked forlorn and the ground before them barren, with no seeds of grain left. He'd always wanted chickens of his own. Jamie resolved to spend a portion of the little that he earned to purchase chanticleer chicks. Breeding birds and writing essays, finding eggs and laying poems. Bringing light, a golden light, back to Elmwood. Jamie hung by his desk the wooden shingle he'd taken with him when he'd closed his law office. A friend offered the advice that he could simply scrub out the last three letters, and he did: J. R. LOWELL, OFF

In 1841, Jamie's first book of poetry, *A Year's Life*, had been published. The poems included were almost entirely about Maria and his love for her: "Like a lone star through riven storm-clouds seen/ By sailors, tempest-tost upon the sea,/ Telling of rest and peaceful havens nigh,/ Unto my soul her star-like soul hath been,/ Her sight as full of hope and calm to me . . ."[2]

In 1843, his second book of poetry was published, entitled *Miscellaneous Poems*. This one drew more attention, and even some critical approval and popular praise. It sold modestly. He was doing what he wanted, raising chickens and working as a writer: "My fowls still continue to be the flower of the neighborhood. There were never such strutters and crowers as my chanticleers, or such promising layers as my hens. . . . [and] my Poems will soon reach a third edition of five hundred. About eleven hundred have thus far been sold . . . So I suppose I may get something from the book yet."[3]

Although Becca seemed happier and more social now that Jamie was home, his mother, Harriet, had become manic, even violent at times. The grandchildren were kept from her, doors were locked against her, and the gates of Elmwood were closed to contain her within its world of books and flowers and trees. The Reverend Lowell refused to admit the severity of Harriet's mental illness but clung to the belief that "the aberration of mind has its origins in the stomach, and is not an affliction of the brain. I desire to trust in God."[4]

Jamie began to suffer lapses of blindness brought on by anxiety. He went to New York City for treatment, and a journal he had started, entitled *The Pioneer*, failed because of his absence. The first issue, in 1843, had been a success, publishing the debut of "The Tell-Tale Heart," by Edgar Allan Poe, and poems by Elizabeth Barrett (not yet Browning) and John S. Dwight, and there were promises from Nathaniel Hawthorne and others of submissions in further issues. But without Jamie to lead the paper, promises faltered and only debts remained. Jamie returned to Elmwood, his sight improved, and set back to work. To help the family, to earn money for his wedding, to pay the debts he owed, to fight slavery, to do his duty to the community of mankind. But also to consecrate the duty to himself: the release of his thoughts, his worries, his beliefs, and his fears. "The horror of slavery can only be appreciated by one who has felt it himself, or who has imagination enough to put himself in the place of the slave, and fancy himself not only virtually imprisoned, but forced to toil, and all this for no crime and for no reason . . ."[5]

Poetry flowed; essays coalesced. Jamie's reputation grew.

In 1841, Jamie had earned his first four hundred dollars from writing, and by 1843, he more than doubled his profits as a writer. His writings for papers and periodicals were sought out and paid for, and his poetry books were well received, although the money that he earned from them was little. Warned by concerned friends that he should temper his antislavery and antiwar sentiments (the United States was sliding toward war with Mexico over the Republic of Texas), he shrugged off the unwanted advice. For him, all that mattered was "to do something for mankind." If being an abolitionist lessened his readership, he was proud to accept "whatever odium might be attached to a complete identification with a body of heroic men and women . . . whose superiors in all that constitutes true manhood and womanhood . . . never existed."[6]

Neither his reputation nor his popularity suffered for his strong antiwar and antislavery opinions. His first book of collected essays, *Conversations on Some of the Old Poets,* would be published in 1845 and sell nicely. Maria also secured paid writing assignments. It was a good time for writers in New England, with numerous publishing houses, including Ticknor and Fields in Boston and Hudson & Goodwin in Hartford. The region boasted hundreds of newspapers, among them the *Boston Evening Transcript* and the *Daily Advertiser.*

Nearly as many weekly and monthly periodicals were published, all with their particular and sometimes peculiar point of view. The *Broadway Journal,* originally based in New York City, was purchased by Edgar Allan Poe to fulfill his dream of editorial control, and *The Dial* was started by Emerson as a vehicle for spreading Transcendentalism. Abolitionists founded a number of publications, including newspapers, periodicals, and annual books (like Maria Chapman's *The Liberty Bell*). William Lloyd Garrison had begun publishing *The Liberator* in 1831, and many more antislavery periodicals came out in the years thereafter, including *The Emancipator,* the *National Anti-Slavery Standard,* the *Pennsylvania Freeman* (Jamie served for a time as its editor), and *The National Era.**

---

* The *National Era* would come to fame in 1851 when it published in serial form Harriet Beecher Stowe's *Uncle Tom's Cabin.*

Between the two of them, Jamie and Maria would write for all the anti-slavery publications, submitting not only essays and opinion pieces but also poems. Jamie thought all of Maria's verses were wonderful: "She is quite cutting me out as a poet—though she laughs when I tell her so, God bless her!"[7] The satisfaction of doing good was multiplied when the fees they earned finally tallied enough that they could make good on their long engagement. Writing for the freedom of slaves had set them free—free to marry and create a family of two: Jamie and his Molly.

On December 26, 1844, at the White family home in Watertown, the couple was married by the Reverend Lowell. Jamie clasped Maria's hand in his, grateful beyond belief for her "gentle and holy presence" that had "set his spirit free," her "whiter and purer" soul that had enveloped him like an "all embracing hope." Maria, in turn, gathered up all "the inspiration of that beloved voice . . . its sweet accord with every true tone of my own heart."[8] The Reverend Lowell blessed their union: *Wherefore they are no more twain, but one flesh. What therefore God hath joined together, let not man put asunder.*[9]

Jamie and Maria moved to Philadelphia. They went seeking a gentler winter climate for Maria, who still suffered from a persistent cough. There they rented rooms at 127 Arch Street, on the top floor of the home of Emma Parker, a Quaker and an old friend of the White family. The view from their rooms was of redbrick buildings cloaked in grime and frost. Philadelphia, not Cambridge, would now be Jamie's inspiration. Alone in their "little room . . . with white muslin curtain trimmed with evergreen," they spent the winter contentedly reading, writing, and working.[10] They were "happy as two mortals can be," Jamie wrote in a letter to a friend.[11]

But they missed Cambridge: "the birds, the flowers, warmth, and out of door happiness. . . ." By the summer, they returned to "dear old Massachusetts"[12] and to Elmwood, where once again Jamie settled into the suite on the third floor: "Once snug in my attic, my fire in a roar, I leave the whole pack of them outside the door."[13] Maria alone was allowed entry inside the door. The third floor became her aerie as well, their shared nest in the sky. Together they worked in the rafters, and together they came down from the heavens to take their meals with the mortals of Elmwood, the Reverend Lowell and Little Bec, and guests who came by. A visitor to Elmwood wrote to a friend, "As handsome and happy young couple as one can hardly imagine . . . she as gentle, as delicate, and as fair as a lily . . . he is full of life and youthful ardor . . . Pity it is that this much-loved young wife seems to have delicate lungs. Her low, weak voice tells us of this . . ."[14]

Harriet was no longer at Elmwood. Before Jamie and Maria returned to Cambridge, she'd been committed to the McLean Asylum for the Insane, in

Somerville—just a few miles down the road by carriage but a whole world away from Elmwood. The Reverend Lowell had taken Harriet to McLean on a sunny but cool spring day. Riding along in the carriage beside his silent wife, he felt chilled, body and soul. He reached for her hand and she let him take it, but she offered no warming squeeze. She stared ahead, the gauze of a veil hiding her face. Harriet had been the love of his life, she had chosen him over all other men, and now he was taking her to a place of isolation and retreat. The Lowells had been early supporters of McLean and its policy of giving its patients a relaxed life in a pastoral setting: the "rest cure."[15] But as beautiful as the building and its surroundings were, it wasn't Elmwood.

That evening, riding home again over roads scored deep by melting winter snows, the solitary Reverend Lowell had felt an ache, the pain a deep physical pounding against his chest. He disembarked from the carriage at Elmwood and went to stand alone amid the shadows of trees and bushes, the rising moon a sliver to the east. He breathed deeply, trying to still the pounding in his chest. Harriet was still here, saved and recorded in the heartstrings of the garden. But the garden was silent that night, not even a cricket's chirp or a frog's croak to break the heavy, still air. He bent his head and prayed. *As a bird that wandereth from her nest, so is a man that wandereth from his place.*[16]

Harriet would never return to Elmwood.

In 1844, John Greenleaf Whittier had written to Jamie, asking him to write a poem to lead the antislavery movement: "Give me one that shall be to our cause what the song of Rouget de Lisle was to the French Republicans."[17] De Lisle had written "La Marseillaise." What could Lowell offer that would rouse abolitionists and goad to action those who hesitated to join the fight against slavery? He got to work writing, and rewriting. The war with Mexico was at hand and gave him plenty of inspiration. It was a war to extend the reach of slavery into the Republic of Texas and increase the power of the slaveholding states. Greed, ambition, and corruption weighed against freedom. It was a crisis of morality and decency, of good versus evil. "Once to every man and nation comes the moment to decide,/ In the strife of Truth with Falsehood, for the good or evil side/ . . . For humanity sweeps onward; where to-day the martyr stands,/ On the morrow crouches Judas with the silver in his hands . . ."[18]

Jamie's poem "The Present Crisis" was published in 1845. Within months, it had become the anthem of the antislavery movement. Garrison and other leaders quoted from it often in their speeches, and it was set to music and sung at antislavery meetings. Whittier's request for a "Marseillaise" to lead the antislavery movement had been answered with a poem that became a hymn for all time: "When a deed is done for Freedom, through the broad earth's aching breast/ Runs a thrill of joy prophetic, trembling on from east to west . . ."[19] Politicians quoted from it, mothers sang it to babes at their breasts, and students recited it at school. Even sailors learned the lines and went about their work on deck, orating to the waves.

In December 1845, a baby girl was born to Maria and Jamie. They named her Blanche, in honor of Maria's maiden name. Maria, worn out by the last months of pregnancy and the birth, took to her bed. Jamie happily assumed all the duties of little Blanche's care. His plan was to raise her to be "as independent as possible. . . . a great strong, vulgar, mud pudding–baking, tree-climbing little wench."[20] Jamie wrote little poetry but many letters during the months he spent caring for Blanche. He wrote about diapers and bedtimes, lullabies and burping. He described how when his daughter smiled, the curve "began in the dimple of her chin, and thence spread, like the circles round a pebble thrown into sunshiny water, with a golden ripple over the whole of her person, being most distinctly ecstatic in her fingers and toes."[21]

And when she laughed, he said, "she laughs all over. You can see it through her clothes. The very tips of her toes twinkle for joy."[22] As for the color of her eyes, Jamie wrote, "They are said to be like her father's—but, in my opinion, they are quite too heavenly a blue for that. . . ."[23] Her mother nicknamed her "Morning Glory," for she was "full of life and light . . . lit as with a sunrise."[24]

Between his letters extolling the many wonders of Blanche, Jamie wrote essays for the national and even international antislavery publications. He signed some of them anonymously: "for I wish Slavery to think it has as many enemies as possible."[25] In a series of articles on "Anti-Slavery in the United States" that he wrote for the *London Daily News,* he explained that "the struggle must not be between the Northern and Southern States, but between Barbarism and civilization, between cruelty and mercy, between evil and good. . . ."[26] For the American papers, he continued to push for freedom: "We cry out most loudly against slavery because that seems to be the foulest blotch. . . . Absolute freedom is what I want. . . ."[27]

He still worked at his desk on the third floor. He looked up often to take in the view over Cambridge and Fresh Pond and the gardens of Elmwood, in all its changing seasons. When the Charles River froze in winter, he marveled at "the flat marshes beyond the river, smooth and silent with glittering snow."[28] And what joy in the spring, when "the song of the bobolink comes rippling through my opening window and preaches peace. . . ."[29] He kept notes on all the birds he saw: cedarbirds in hawthorn bushes; kingbirds building their nests in the orchards; hummingbirds covering the cherry trees in full blossom; the cries of the goldfinch stealing lettuce seeds from the kitchen garden; mating songs of the indigo buntings and sparrow hawks and chickadees.

In March 1847, Blanche began to suffer from teething. The doctor was called. He prescribed purgatives and mustard baths, and applied a leech to her tender skin. Within two days, the little golden girl was dead. "As a twig trembles, which a bird/ Lights on to sing, then leaves unbent,/ So is my memory thrilled and stirred;—/ I only know she came and went."[30] Blanche had come like a promise in the cold of winter and left on the tail of a spring wind.

The Reverend Lowell broke down and cried when Blanche died. Jamie had never seen his father cry before. Charles leaned over her small body and straightened the white linen encircling her. The cloth had been placed to keep her comfortable but now would be her shroud. Through his tears, he could only repeat, over and over, "She was perfect, perfect."[31]

Then he drew himself up and turned to the task of comforting Maria and his son. The three stood together, praying for consolation. *Thy sun shall no more go down; neither shall thy moon withdraw itself: for the Lord shall be thine everlasting light, and the days of thy mourning shall be ended.*[32]

Maria, weeks later, while walking out in the garden, noticed shoots of morning glory starting to come up along the stone walls of Elmwood. She almost fell to her knees, her body trembling. But then she steadied herself against the wall, lines composing themselves in her head. "The morning-glory's blossoming will soon be coming round,/ We see their rows of heart-shaped leaves upspringing from the ground,/ The tender things the winter killed,/ Renew again their birth,/ But the glory of our morning has passed away from earth."[33]

Blanche was buried on a hill in Mount Auburn Cemetery, carried there by her father. A small stone marker, white as snow, proclaimed only her name: *Blanche.* Her tiny shoes, the only ones she had ever worn, were in Jamie's pocket, and when he returned to his study at the top of Elmwood, he hung them from a nail above his desk. There they would stay for the rest of his life.

Jamie threw himself into his work and into caring for Maria, who was pregnant again. It was time now to release what he had been tinkering with for so long: his poetry capturing the dialect, wit, and wisdom of the Yankee soul. Puritan values of common sense, common work, common good, caught in the nuance of a lilt, a saying, the line of a hymn recalled. Jamie called these new poems *The Biglow Papers* and used the characters he created—Parson Wilbur, Hosea Biglow, and Birdofredum Sawin—to expose and attack everything he despised in present-day America. The country needed saving, Jamie reckoned, and there were none who could show the way better than his three characters: the faithful parson, the simple Yankee farmer Biglow, and the immoral rascal Sawin.

The three fellows observed, opined, and condemned (or celebrated, in the case of Sawin, a southern sympathizer and warmonger) all the issues of the time: the folly and dangers of Manifest Destiny; the degradations of slavery, not only for the enslaved but the slaveholders; the hypocrisy of politicians; the prevalence of greed; and the brutal realities of war. As Biglow himself put it:

> Ez fer war, I call it murder,—
> There you hev it plain an' flat . . .
> If you take a sword an' dror it,
> An' go stick a feller thru,
> Guv'mint aint to answer for it,
> God'll send the bill to you.
>
> Wut's the use o' meetin'-goin',
> Every Sabbath, wet or dry,
> Ef it's right to go amowin'
> Feller-men like oats an' rye?[34]

The Biglow Papers were a huge success, popular with critics and readers alike. Although John Amory Lowell and his son Augustus, along with certain of their business associates, bristled at Jamie's condemnations of the wealthy, there were other "political opponents as well as friends [who] laughed loud and long."[35] Lowell had used humor, satire, and grim reality to portray his country as he saw it, and the country in return—at least in the North—lapped it up. He became one of the Fireside Poets, joining the ranks of Longfellow, Whittier, and William Cullen Bryant, all of whom wrote poetry that could be read aloud by families around the family fire. His popularity eclipsed the others: He was the most read and recited poet in the United States, and would remain at the top until Longfellow published his "Paul Revere's Ride."[36] John Amory Lowell might have been one the wealthiest men in New England, but James Russell Lowell was one of the most famous in all of the country.

Money was still and always would be tight at Elmwood. Reverend Lowell had reduced his workload even further at West Church, tired out and worn down from grief for his confined wife and his dead granddaughter. His diminished salary was scarcely enough to bring food to the table. Maria had inherited lands from her father, but it was still up to Jamie to cover all the expenses of Elmwood, to care for his sister Becca, and to pay for Harriet's upkeep at McLean. He had his wife to provide for, and now another daughter, Mabel, born in September 1847. Jamie worked harder and harder, and tried to think of ways to save a bit, spend less, make more.

But still he opened his purse to those in need. When he received a letter asking for a contribution that would go toward buying the freedom of a slave, he responded first with the official stance of the American Anti-Slavery Society: "I resolutely decline to give you anything"—the society believed that buying a person out of slavery put money into the slaveholder's pocket, he explained. But then he quickly added, "In my private capacity, I will send what I can, assuring you that if my poems were more popular, my gifts should be larger."[37]

The baby, Mabel, was a delight to all the Lowell family and her sturdiness was a relief: "her little fat arms fly like Wind Mill sails."[38] She teethed without trouble and soon began to walk, then run, then climb, much as her father had done. The gardens of Elmwood were her playground, as they had been her father's: the birds her friends, the trees her meetinghouse, the flowers her ingredients for potions and posies. She loved to spend time with her father, and while he worked in his study, she would sit on the floor beside him. She interrupted him frequently with questions. One night, she asked about the falling snow—"who makes it snow?" and Jamie answered that God in heaven, who "cares for us here below." He thought then of "a mound in sweet Auburn/ Where a little headstone stood;/ How the flakes were folding it gently,/ As did robins the babes in the wood." He stooped to kiss Mabel, "And she kissing back, could not know/ That *my* kiss was given to her sister,/ Folded close under deepening snow."[39]

Blanche was his first child and the mark that her death had scored upon him could never be erased: "Blanche still holds the first place in our hearts."[40]

More published works came out in 1848. *The Vision of Sir Launfal,* a long form poem and one of his most enduring pieces ("And what is so rare as a day in June?") had been printed in a periodical but now came out as a book, and sold out. Another volume of poems came out later in the year, along with a book-length poem entitled *A Fable for Critics.* The *Fable* was a book of satire, offering portraits, flattering and not, of fellow writers, including Emerson, Margaret Fuller, and Edgar Allan Poe ("There comes Poe with his raven, like Barnaby Rudge/ Three-fifths of him genius and two-fifths sheer fudge"), and even Lowell himself ("The top of the hill he will ne'er come nigh reaching/ Till he learns the distinction 'twixt singing and preaching").[41]

Readers and critics loved Lowell—readers for his wit and heart, and critics for his productivity and distinctly American voice; they proclaimed him "the poet of the future."[42] But Jamie did not give up his antislavery work. He was now on the executive committee of the American Anti-Slavery Society, and was as active as ever in its meetings and proclamations.

In 1849, a third child was born to Maria and Jamie—another daughter, whom they named Rose. But Rose was not as sturdy as Mabel. By February of the following year, she died from complications associated with teething, just like her eldest sister. Maria wrote to a friend, "Thank God for having blessed us with a little life rounded and perfect as a tear drop."[43] Jamie wrote, "She was very beautiful, fair with large dark gray eyes and fine features. Her smile was especially charming, and she was full of smiles till her sickness began. Dear little child! She had never spoken, only smiled."[44] Jamie refused to hold a funeral. He allowed his father to make a short prayer over her tiny casket and then he carried her up the hill to Mount Auburn. Another small white stone, marked only with a name: *Rose*.

Jamie sunk into grief after Rose's death and nothing could draw him out— not the birds outside his window nor the budding trees, not even the footsteps of Mabel coming up the stairs and her tentative knock on the office door. He continued to write for the antislavery publications—it was his duty and his conviction—but there was no joy, no satisfaction, and no relief. Sorrow dogged his every step; memories clouded his vision. Maria and his sister Becca took on the care of Mabel, for the little girl's questioning eyes brought reverbera- tions of pain to her aching father. He couldn't explain Rose's absence to Mabel, or to himself.

In March 1850, Jamie went out to McLean Hospital to see his mother. Harriet was dying. Jamie sat with her, stroked her hand. He spoke to her, but she could not hear him: "The wide chasm of reason is between us;/ Thou confutest kind- ness with a moan;/ We can speak to thee, and thou canst answer,/ Like two pris- oners through a wall of stone."[45] He stayed there with her until he could stand it no longer: her labored breathing, her pale face contorting with pain and then relaxing into a sleep like death—but not death, not yet. He rose from the chair and left to walk about the manicured grounds of McLean, the clipped bushes and tall trees, a rose garden still stark and bare from its winter pruning.

He finally rested, taking a seat on a bench that faced the windows of his mother's room. The building had been a mansion at one time, designed by Charles Bullfinch, creator of so many elegant buildings in the Boston area, in- cluding University Hall at Harvard and luxurious mansions on Beacon Hill. Jamie imagined his mother as the lady of the house, preparing herself for rest amid luxury and comfort. He prayed she would find only peace and joy in the world to come.

He waited on his bench until the shades of the windows were lowered. He knew then that his mother had died.

He went home to his aging father and newly pregnant wife, his disordered sister, his happy child, his chickens, his books and papers. Back to the desk on the third floor, Blanche's shoes hanging by a nail, and a window overlooking the spring-budding garden. Mabel had been put to bed and was supposed to be sleeping, but when she heard her father's footsteps, she called out to him. He went to her and she clasped her arms around his neck. He felt her soft breath against his cheek, smelled the warmth coming up from her, sweet and comforting.

All that was important to him now remained centered in his family. His wife, his child, his father, and his sister. The obligation was clear: to keep them all safe and sound. Nothing else mattered.

17

1850–1853

The faith of the gospel worketh by love,
and no other faith is genuine.
—THE REVEREND CHARLES LOWELL

In the fall of 1850, the Reverend Charles Lowell was invited to give the open-ing prayer at an antislavery rally to be held at Faneuil Hall. The request had come directly from the organizers, including Josiah Quincy III and Wendell Phillips. The Reverend Lowell considered who this Josiah was to him: his sister Anna's long-ago suitor (a young dandy come to court at Bromley Vale); presi-dent of Harvard when his sons Robert and James were students. Once mayor of Boston, and member of Congress, and of the Massachusetts Senate. A good man, and now an old man, even older than Charles Lowell. Lowell knew Quincy well and admired him. Phillips was a young pup in comparison, but passionate and devoted in the fight against slavery. The Reverend Lowell had heard about how Phillips refused to consume sugar or wear cotton, as both products derived from the labor of slaves. Phillips was a man committed to the cause: the end of slavery.

The rally was being held to protest the newly enacted Fugitive Slave Law. The Fugitive Slave Law, part of the Compromise of 1850, provided that of-ficers and officials of all states, free or slave, were required to assist in the seizure and return of any man or woman accused of being a runaway slave. Just days after the law had been signed by President Millard Fillmore, the brutal reality of its reach had been demonstrated in the case of James Hamlet. On the morning of September 26, Hamlet left his home in Williamsburg, Brooklyn, and traveled to Manhattan, where he worked as a porter in a store on Water Street. Little did he know that at the same time just blocks away in Foley Square, Alexander Gardiner, clerk of the federal court in Manhattan and a newly named commissioner under the Fugitive Slave Law, was consid-ering a sworn affidavit that had just been presented to him. The affidavit, signed by Mary Brown of Baltimore, Maryland, stated that James Hamlet was her property.

Commissioner Gardiner quickly scanned through the accompanying papers brought in by Brown's son Gustavus, and Gustavus's son-in-law, Thomas Clare. He noted that the affidavit of Mary Brown was signed not with her signature but merely with a mark. Presumably, the woman did not know how to write. But she did know of her rights under the new Fugitive Slave Law. She demanded the speedy return of Hamlet, a man she claimed had run away from her in 1848. Commissioner Gardiner was well acquainted with his rights under the law, as well: If he were to find that Hamlet was indeed a runaway slave, he would be awarded ten dollars. If, on the other hand, he determined Hamlet to be a free man, he would be paid only five dollars. It took no time at all for Gardiner to reach his decision. He issued a warrant for Hamlet's arrest.

A deputy from the federal marshal's office went to the store on Water Street and took Hamlet into custody, leaving him no time to send word to his wife or to inform his employer. Hamlet was brought to a second-floor room in Federal Hall, the old stone building that had served as the capital building for the country just after the Revolutionary War. There he waited, confined to a dusty and airless room, uncertain of the charges against him. It was only when Commissioner Gardiner finally arrived and read out the affidavits sworn to by the Browns that he understood he was being taken back into slavery.

Hamlet pleaded for a chance to speak, but Gardiner denied his request. The Fugitive Slave Law specifically prohibited any fugitive from offering testimony against the sworn affidavits of the aggrieved property owner. Gardiner barely took a breath before pronouncing Hamlet to be a slave. He then ordered that Hamlet be returned immediately to Baltimore. With his arms shackled together, Hamlet was taken down to the docks and loaded onto a steamship bound for Baltimore. Hope H. Slatter, a notorious slave trader, took over in Baltimore, placing Hamlet in a prison kept for runaways. Slatter wasted no time in putting Hamlet up for sale for the Browns at the price of eight hundred dollars. Hamlet was once again just a piece of merchandise to be bought and paid for.

The Reverend Lowell had heard about the seizure of Hamlet just days after it happened, the terrible news passed on to him when he walked to weekday services at West Church. Lowell's parish duties had been reduced, but evening services were a favorite of his. To leave the busy streets of Boston and enter the quiet and peaceful church was always transforming: outside, the din of commerce and pleasure; inside, the silence of the faithful. But after hearing the story of James Hamlet, the clanging of the door haunted the Reverend Lowell as he entered his church. The closing of the heavy wooden door behind him matched, in his mind and imagination, the shutting of the worm-eaten door of Hamlet's cell, four hundred miles to the south. How could things have come to this?

The plight of northern blacks was growing worse every day. Lowell had been to the South and witnessed for himself what slavery looked like, and it was ugly. Now slavers were free to come north and drag any black person they could catch back down into the "evil and miseries" of slavery.[1] Two students at Anna Jackson Lowell's school—the one she'd started after Charlie lost all their money—had been born of a black slave and her white master. Their white father paid for the two of them to live in the North and attend Anna's school. He had hoped they would be safe there, free to study and prosper. When he died, the older sister felt it was her duty to attend his funeral. While attending services for her father, her uncle had her seized and taken to the slave quarters, claiming that she was now his property, as he had inherited all the slaves and slave offspring of his brother. The young woman, despairing of her future, killed herself.

Lowell was a familiar figure in the black neighborhoods of Boston. He knew their churches, their Masonic and literary societies. In the weeks following the passage of the Fugitive Slave Law, he had seen panic spread through their West End neighborhoods. He saw it for what is was: the start of a migration. A flight away from the slavers, with the goal now to reach Canada. The Reverend Lowell understood. With the federal government committed above all else to upholding the property rights of slaveholders and ignoring the rights of free black men and women, what recourse was there but to flee? Those blacks who remained in Boston became guarded, scared beyond measure for their freedom. Warnings spread about slave hunters haunting the streets in order to seize black men and women and carry them back to slavery.

After the reenslavement of James Hamlet, a call went out across the North: *We must fight this terrible law.* In New York, over fifteen hundred people gathered at Zion Church, not far from where Hamlet had worked. Money was raised to buy Hamlet back from slavery but saving one man was not enough. Resolutions were passed, vowing noncompliance with the Fugitive Slave Law: "We will call upon all American Citizens, who have any regard for constitutional law, or any reverence for the history of our glorious past, or any pride in our national reputation abroad, to join in the cry of repeal—repeal the infamous bill, which barters the life and liberty of a freeman for the oath of any wretch who may swear that he is a slave."[2]

In Boston, heart of the northern antislavery movement, the call to fight against the Fugitive Slave Law was pitched with anger and righteousness. The entire Compromise of 1850 was engineered to ensure that slavery would continue, the abolitionists argued, and not only in the South. Under the compromise, Texas would enter the union as a slave state. The white male settlers of New Mexico and Utah were to be admitted to the union with their status—slave or free—to be determined by those who settled there.* Slavery was moving westward. It was no longer confined to the South.

Massachusetts senator Daniel Webster rose in defense of the Compromise of 1850, but antislavery activists already knew where he stood: on the side of the slavers and against the rights of blacks.† He stood with the South, and New Englanders were becoming increasingly suspicious of the South. The fear was that the slave states would soon outnumber the free and that the South would eclipse the power of the North in the running of the country.

There had been little support in Massachusetts for the Mexican-American War because of the fear that the sole purpose for fighting it was to secure more territory for the United States—territory where slavery would be allowed. The Massachusetts legislature proclaimed the war to have been "unconstitutionally commenced by the order of the President . . . with the triple object of extending slavery, of strengthening the slave power, and of obtaining the control of the Free States."3

Now the outcome of the war that northerners had feared—more slave-holding states—was coming to terrible fruition. Texas was entering as a slave state, and perhaps Utah and New Mexico would, as well. But what had not been expected was that all Americans, no matter whether they lived in free or slave states, would be required to assist in the hateful trade of slave hunting. The new Fugitive Slave Law overrode state interests, state law, and state morality.

On October 14, 1850, flyers went out throughout Boston, calling for a meeting and inviting all "Citizens of Boston without distinction of party . . . to consider the condition of the Fugitive Slaves, and the colored persons of this city, under the New Fugitive Slave Law."4 The meeting would be held at Faneuil Hall. Josiah Quincy would speak, as would Wendell Phillips, Frederick Douglass, and Theodore Parker, the Transcendentalist pastor who called the Fugitive Slave Law, "a hateful statute of kidnappers."5 The conveners of the October 14 rally intended it to be a "Rocking of the Old Cradle of Liberty."6 New England was where the fight for freedom from tyranny had begun back

---

* The compromise was offered to balance the coming in of California as a free state. California had asked to enter the union in 1849, booming as it was with settlers. Thousands were still making the trek west by land and sea in search of gold, following the gold rush of 1848.

† Webster was driven from office in July 1850; he was appointed secretary of state by President Millard Fillmore and served in that position until his death in 1852.

in 1776, and Faneuil Hall had been the site—"the Cradle of Liberty"—where the fight was debated, planned, cheered on.

New Englanders were exhorted to rise up again and join in the fight against the federal law giving slavers the right to trawl the streets of Boston. To fight against what abolitionists called "the tyranny" of southern interests over northern certainties. To declare that slavery was wrong and inhumane, and that an economy based on the degradation of another human being was immoral and unpleasing to God. "We solemnly appeal to Christians of every name, to all sober and humane men . . . to all that love man, to behold and ponder this iniquity which is done among us!"[7] Long ago, the Puritan preachers had railed, *Make yourself worthy to God. Keep our community pleasing in the eyes of the Lord.* Although New Englanders now belonged to a plethora of denominations, the men behind the October 14 rally hoped that the ingrained ideals of community and God would lead them all to agree: *Together, we must fight slavery; together, we will be pleasing in the eyes of the Lord.*

But what if the only outcome to fighting the compromise would be fighting a war between the states? As much as New Englanders despised the idea of slave hunters roaming freely through their towns and villages, they feared even more the idea of their nation cleaved in two or bound in a terrible war. It was not only economic fear that underscored the growing support for the Compromise of 1850—the need to keep the northern economy going—but fear of turmoil, uncertainty, and unrest. Rebellion against the Fugitive Slave Law could be seen as rebellion against the union—and there were many in New England who wanted to preserve the union above all else.

Already hundreds of Bostonians had signed up to help the United States marshals in their compliance with the Fugitive Slave Law, and money was pouring in to support what was deemed "the Unionist Cause."[8] Abolitionists had been attacked in the press and on the street, some dragged by their necks, punched, and kicked. Bands of poor immigrants had been hired by local cotton merchants and shippers to infiltrate antislavery gatherings, disrupt the proceedings, and inflict beatings on the abolitionists.

Josiah Quincy and his fellow organizers were desperate to prevent any outbreak of violence during the October 14 meeting. Only if they could ensure the safety of all the participants could they attract the kind of large audience that they needed. They needed the attendance of a big crowd to reassure the black population that Boston was on their side, and to marshal the forces necessary to offer them protection. So many blacks had already left the city, and the ones remaining felt vulnerable and afraid. But how to ensure a modicum of calm during a period of such strong feelings, both for and against the compromise and its Fugitive Slave Law? How to hold a meeting of rebellion in peace?

The Reverend Lowell was the answer. His attendance at the meeting would not only demonstrate the moral imperative of fighting against the Fugitive Slave Law but would also guarantee a level of respect and security. Charles Lowell had baptized generations of Beacon Hill Bostonians. He'd known as babes the men now running the state house, the countinghouses, the mills, and the docks. He was revered in the white communities as well as the black ones for his "piety, wisdom, compassion, and gentleness."[9] If ever a man could unify a crowd, it was the Reverend Lowell. And, of course, he was a *Lowell*, the name associated with mills, shipping, and banking. Uncle to John Amory Lowell, one of the most powerful of the Cotton Whigs. There was no man in Boston who would raise a hand against the Reverend Lowell, and therefore no better man to lead the October 14 rally forward in peace.

The Reverend Lowell recognized the opportunity and the mission: to call for the end of slavery, to awaken those still slumbering in inaction and acceptance. It was his duty to rally every member of his congregation to fight for the freedom of all humans, under God. For one evening, the entire city of Boston would be his congregation and he would preach to them all. He would counsel them in the ways of the Lord. He agreed to offer the opening blessing for the October 14 rally.

The evening of October 14 was a mild one for the season. The sun set in pinks and orange across a cloudless sky. A breeze blew in from Boston Harbor, cooling the crowds that had arrived early at Faneuil Hall, eager to get in. So many people had turned out for the meeting that dozens had to be turned away. There was simply no room in the four-thousand-square-foot hall to accommodate everyone who wanted to attend. The pull was magnetic: to fight for freedom. No human should ever be held in bondage, so said the state constitution and the Scriptures. So said these gathered people of New England.

The admitted crowd stood shoulder-to-shoulder, their faces lit up by the hundreds of chandelier lights. Voices were raised in agitation; feet pounded on the wooden floorboards. Over 3,500 people clapped their hands, stomped their feet, calling for meeting to begin. They were here to fight the Fugitive Slave Law, or, as Wendell Phillips would urge the eager crowd, to "trample the law under our feet."[10]

As the Reverend Lowell approached the stage erected at the far end of the hall, the jumble of raised voices stopped. The stomping feet stilled and the clapping hands now came together, clasped tightly as if in prayer. The crowd was silent and reverent, waiting. The Reverend Lowell stepped up onto the platform and took his place in the center. Took possession of the stage and of the crowd simply by standing, quiet and sure and calm. He had wizened with age; his back was stooped and his frame, spare. But his square Lowell chin was steady as he stood with his hands before him, long fingers intertwined. He raised his eyes and looked over the people. He was hoping to see the faces of two who had been beside him in the fight for freedom. Two who he loved, and who loved him and each other. A joined presence that he needed.

He saw Charlie and Anne, and their fifteen-year old son, Charles. Mary was there with Samuel, standing with Becca. But Jamie and Maria were absent; once the most ardent of abolitionists, the grieving couple had stayed away. Their hearts were too heavy, their stamina for any fight depleted: "Such enormities as the Slave Law weigh me down without rebound," Jamie wrote to a friend. He and Maria abhorred "this horrible Slave bill" but could not join the protest against it in body; only in spirit.[11] The Reverend Lowell bowed his head and invoked a private prayer on behalf of his weary son and ailing wife. *Mercy and truth are met together; righteousness and peace have kissed each other.*[12]

Then he raised his head again and began to speak.

"Assembled before Thee, as we trust and believe, for a holy purpose, we humbly and earnestly invoke Thy blessing . . . May the time shortly come, when this whole nation shall feel the injustice of making merchandise of human beings . . . God of mercy, who hath made of one blood all nations, incline the hearts of all men, everywhere, to kindness and brotherly love; hasten the time when, without violence and bloodshed, every yoke shall be broken and the oppressed go free; when none shall make merchandise of the souls of men; when all shall be made free. . . . Forgive our sins, O God; forgive the sins of the nation against our brethren, intelligent, moral and immortal like ourselves . . ."[13]

After Lowell spoke, more speakers took the stage: Wendell Phillips; Charles Francis Adams, congressman and leader of the Conscience Whigs; Thomas Parker. The keynote speaker was Frederick Douglass, whose autobiography, *Narrative of the Life of Frederick Douglass*, published in 1845, was a best-seller across the North. Douglass spoke about the fear that the new law had struck in his heart and the hearts of all other blacks in Boston, both those who were refugees from slavery and those who were free with papers, like him.

"Perhaps the hunters are even after me as I am speaking!" Douglass declared.[14]

A resolution was proposed and passed: "That we cannot believe that any citizen can be found in this city or vicinity, so destitute of love for his country and his race, and so devoid of all sense of justice, as to take part in returning a fugitive slave under the law."[15]

After the October 14 rally, membership in the Boston Vigilance Committee grew to more than two hundred members, all committed to fighting the Fugitive Slave Law. A warning system was put in place, to get the message out if and when a slave hunter seized a black man or woman, and for public protests to be mounted. A legal committee was formed to represent anyone taken under the Fugitive Slave Law and argue for their freedom under the laws of the state of Massachusetts and under God.

On February 15, 1851, Shadrach Minkins, a black man who had escaped from slavery the year before and come to Boston, was arrested by federal marshals at Taft's Cornhill Coffee House where he worked as a waiter. He was taken to the courthouse just blocks away on Court Square, to be held pending a hearing on his status as a fugitive slave. Members of the Boston Vigilance Committee received the news and spread the word. The cry went out through Boston: *Protect our own!* Within hours, the courthouse was surrounded by an angry crowd demanding that Minkins be freed. His hearing was held, with Charles G. Davis and Robert Morris, Boston's first black lawyer, defending Minkins against the fugitive slave claim.

Just as the proceedings were coming to an end, a group of black men, led by Lewis Hayden, a fugitive slave from Kentucky and ardent antislavery activist, charged into the room.* They grabbed Minkins from his seat and then ran from the courthouse. The crowd around the courthouse quickly closed around the fleeing captive and his rescuers, protecting them as they fled from their pursuers. Minkins was spirited away, hidden first in the attic of Hayden's neighbor and then taken to Cambridge. From there, he would be smuggled away via the Underground Railroad to Canada. Minkins would live there the rest of his life, a free and undisturbed man.

A few months later, in April 1851, a fugitive slave named Thomas Sims was seized off the street in Boston and, like Minkins, taken to the courthouse to be held until transport to the South could be arranged. Led by the Boston Vigilance Committee, angry crowds once again gathered around the courthouse, demanding Sims's release. But this time, President Millard Fillmore was prepared. National Guardsmen were sent to Boston. They formed a solid line of protection around the courthouse, and secured all the entrances in and out of the building with chains. The Boston Vigilance Committee came up with an escape plan to break Simms out of the courthouse through the window of the room where he was being held. But then the windows were sealed with iron bars and guards were posted outside his door.

"This is the first time hostile soldiers have been in our streets since the

---

* After the Civil War, Hayden would be elected to the Massachusetts legislature, representing Boston.

Red-Coats marched up Long Wharf," Wendell Phillips said in his speech to the over one thousand protesters gathered on the Boston Common. "May the government which sends us these [soldiers] earn the same hatred that the masters of the Red-Coats won!"[16]

The Reverend Lowell offered what help he could to the Boston Vigilance Committee in their multipronged legal fight to save Sims, including soliciting funds from his parishioners and encouraging his old friend Charles Greeley Loring (the lawyer under whom Jamie had apprenticed) when he undertook the legal defense of Sims. But despite numerous legal maneuvers, Sims was ruled a fugitive slave under federal law and ordered to be returned to the South and to slavery. In the early hours of April 12, "after the moon had gone down, in the darkest hour before daybreak," Sims, accompanied by over one hundred soldiers, was marched down to the harbor and loaded onto a ship bound for Georgia.[17] Six days later, he arrived in Savannah, where he was publicly whipped before being returned to his owner.

After Sims was taken away, the Reverend Lowell wrote to his fellow clergymen who had refused to join in the fight against the Fugitive Slave Law and scolded them: "those of your brethren and others who interpret the Scriptures as giving countenance to slavery, . . . do not understand the scriptures but wrest them to a bad purpose . . ."[18] From the pulpit, he railed against those in Boston who would ignore the condition of slaves, admonishing them to consider "the evils of slavery; a miserable inheritance to the enslaver, and a monstrous injustice and cruelty to the enslaved; an institution which disregards the tenderest charities of life; sets at nought the most sacred relationships . . . ruthlessly tears asunder husband and wife, parent and child, to be bought and sold, and driven about like the beasts of the field."[19]

Wealthy New Englanders like John Amory Lowell who supported the Compromise of 1850 were condemned in public and in the press. Emerson wrote of the "poor smell" found at the corner of Beacon and Mount Vernon streets, the neighborhood where the Cotton Lords lived. Theodore Parker vilified those who slept on "unsold bales of cotton" while slaves labored on. Wendell Phillips sarcastically noted that enforcement of the Fugitive Slave Law was a means of determining whether "the mills of Abbott Lawrence make him worth two millions or one." And Josiah Quincy wrote that "Boston has now become a mere shop—a place for buying and selling goods, and I suppose, also, of buying and selling men."[20]

One newspaper blamed a combination of "money and Websterism" (referring to the influence of Daniel Webster) for a "victory of cotton over the conscience of the people." The Massachusetts senate publicly denounced "1500 of the most wealthy and respectable citizens, merchants, bankers" for supporting the U.S. marshals who kidnapped Sims and returned him to slavery, and then passed a resolution demanding a repeal of the Fugitive Slave Law on the grounds that it was "alien to the spirit of the Constitution and abhorrent to the feelings of the people of this Commonwealth."[21]

John Amory Lowell did not respond to the attacks against him. While he did not approve of slavery, he would not fight the institution. He still clung to the hope that in time the system would come to an end. He, and others like him, believed that the Compromise of 1850 would finally end all the debates over slavery. Slavery was still confined to the South, in his view; and with California coming in as a free state, there was balance between slave and free in the union of states. The compromise brought stability—good for commerce—and if the price to be paid for such stability was the enforcement of the Fugitive Slave Law, so be it.

In July 1851, Jamie left for Europe with Maria, their daughter Mabel, and their son, Walter, just six months old. The hope was to restore Maria's health by taking her to live in a gentler climate, and to help them all by leaving a place that reminded them too often of Blanche and Rose, and of Harriet. Jamie had spent the past year putting pen to paper, out of duty and out of conviction and for the income it paid him. But nothing mattered more to him than protecting his family. He could do no more for the cause: "It seems to me as if I had said my say—for the present at least—and had better try silence for awhile. I am sick of politics and criticism . . ." But ever mindful of duty, he added in his letter to Sydney Gay, "I feel as if I could do more good by working in my own vein, however narrow."[22]

He needed to leave. To get away. He owed a duty to his family to keep them safe. He sold off lands left to Maria by her father to fund their trip. He placed his trust in God to keep them safe on their journey, and in his father to keep Elmwood safe for their return. Jamie was a man pulled between two places, one with old pleasures and painful memories, and one with nothing known and everything new to discover.

Five weeks upon a ship and yet the sights were every day unusual and exciting: "a shoal of fish through the phosphorescent water" like "the streaming of northern lights; the sails by moonlight; sunrise in mid-ocean, naked sun meets naked sea."[23] Maria rested in the cabin; Jamie took the baby and Mabel traipsing around the vessel, belowdecks ("two rats, one red and one blue"[24]) and up above, looking out over the sea, always looking for and finding something to marvel at: "the sea still rimmed our prosy lives with mystery and conjecture."[25]

Once arrived in Italy, the family moved into a villa in Florence. They were delighted with how cheap it all was. Six rooms and a kitchen, with luxury to spare: "people can live like princes . . . in Italy on fifteen hundred a year."[26] They had rented Casa Guidi, the house of Robert and Elizabeth Barrett Browning. It was close to the Pitti Palace and the Boboli Gardens, and far from Boston and the cemetery at Mount Auburn. Mabel flourished and Walter grew, and even Maria gained strength enough to walk the streets with her family, taking in all the beauty of Florence and then resting in a chair set out on a yellow stone terrace. The family steeped "themselves in the sun and ripen[ed] slowly as peaches."[27]

At the end of the year, the Reverend Charles Lowell suffered a stroke. Jamie received the news just as he and his family were leaving Florence to go south to Rome. He wanted to return to Elmwood immediately, but Maria had grown ill again and was too weak to travel back to America. Jamie took his family south to Rome and wrote often to his father, offering his love and concern. He sent a letter to his brother Charlie, asking that he and Anna look after the old man. Charlie promised that they would. In a letter to his sister Mary, Jamie complained about a new travel book that had come out, titled *Rome in Eight Days*: "soon we shall have boys put through college in six hours, washing & meals included . . ."[28] He intended to enjoy Rome slowly, in long walks and late dinners, and in the companionship of the family he was keeping safe.

As the cold and snow of winter gave way to the rain and gray of early spring, the Reverend Lowell recovered from his paralysis. He left his sickbed to sit in a chair by the window in his library. His library held thousands of books, most of which he had read, for he loved to read. Not only the Bible and its studies but also the plays of Shakespeare and the sonnets of Milton, the novels of Thackeray and the histories of Charles Rollin. He could close his eyes and recall words he'd memorized for having read them so often: "O Nightingale, that on yon bloomy spray,/ Warblest at eve, when all the woods are still,/ Thou with fresh hope the Lovers heart dost fill . . ."[29]

On days when the sun shone, Reverend Lowell looked out to see the fresh shoots in the garden, rising crowns of flowers and tiny lime green buds on the bushes. The forsythia bloomed brilliant yellow by the end of March and the grass turned from winter brown to spring green. His daughter Mary came often to visit, as did his grandsons Charles and James, sons of Charlie and Anna. Becca made sweets for her nephews and brought hard biscuits and honeyed tea for her father and sister.

In Rome, Maria was also growing stronger, finding nourishment in the southern light. Her children bloomed beside her in the heat. Jamie wrote happily to his father about the rambunctious Walter: "if he hears my voice, he immediately springs up in Mary's lap, and begins shouting lustily for me. He is the fairest boy that ever was seen, and has the bluest eyes, and is the baldest person in Rome except for two middle-aged Englishmen, who, you know, have a great knack that way . . ."[30]

But then Walter fell ill. For three weeks he lay in his cot in Rome, doctors visiting, his parents always by his side. Mabel played on her own in the courtyard just off the Piazza Barberini. She could hear the gurgle of the fountain on the square, smell the spring jasmine growing over the ancient walls of the yard. One afternoon, the nursemaid took her out for a walk through Rome. When they returned in time for dinner, Mabel reported to her mother that she had seen a man hanged in a square. Maria would not let her out walking again.

On June 9, 1852, Walter died. He was buried in Rome: "Harsh grass and weeds alone are wrought/ On his low grave's uneven swell."[31] Maria wrote to her friend Sarah Shaw, "He was just unfolding a rare and lovely nature but it is useless to think of it. I am tired of broken promises, and cannot think of a future for Mabel, she is well now, today, but I have no certainty for tomorrow."[32] Jamie wrote to his sister Mary, "How beautiful and full of promise he was . . . nobody but we will ever know . . . I cannot write about him . . ."[33] The letter broke off.

Jamie, Maria, and Mabel arrived back in Elmwood in the fall of 1852. Mabel ran through the rooms as if blessing each one with her return. She stayed close to her grandfather, hugging him around his knees and offering up her forehead for a kiss. She asked if she could bring him his lunch, for he was still too weak to go to the table; he assented. Every day after, she was the one who carried his noonday tray to him. Becca was happy that Jamie's family was back again, and she rallied herself to act as Mabel's teacher. She gave her little niece lessons in sewing and reading, and told her stories by the glow of the library fire.

Jamie went to visit his sister Mary and her husband, Samuel Putnam, soon after returning to Cambridge. The Putnams traveled often, but when they were home, their house on Beacon Hill was a meeting place for New England abolitionists. Mary had written a novel, plays, and poems against slavery; her *Record of an Obscure Man,* highly praised by William Lloyd Garrison, contained arguments against slavery and prejudice that were used by abolitionists around the country. Jamie was eager to once again become involved in the cause, but Maria was too weak to join in the fight. Closer to Elmwood, Henry and Fanny Longfellow invited Jamie and Maria for evenings of good food, company, and late-night conversations. Whenever he visited, Jamie went out to the back gardens at Craigie House to inspect the hens and roosters. Their crowing and cooing reassured him. He had long ago recommended that Longfellow take up chickens and was pleased that his friend's brood was doing so well.

Both Henry and Fanny Longfellow noticed how pale Maria looked, and how often she coughed. She tried hard to be discreet, but the cough had become an echo after every word she said. Jamie refused to admit how ill his wife really was. He knew she went through cycles of wellness and illness, and wanted to believe that she would recover her strength now that they were home at Elmwood: "It is very slow and tedious work getting up her strength, especially to a person of her energetic temperament but she bears it beautifully . . ."[34]

His hopes were rewarded with the coming of spring, and the settling in of warm summer months. Maria grew stronger. She and Mabel were often in the garden together, Maria seated under an arbor of wisteria while Mabel played in the grass. Family came to visit, Maria's sister Lois and Jamie's sister Mary. Jamie's nephews, Will, James, and Charles, all of them growing up. Charles was at Harvard, and Jimmy and Will would soon follow him there. Dinner parties were held outdoors, a table from the kitchen brought out and a comfortable chair set at the head for the old minister. The assembled party, the Longfellows, the Lowells, the Putnams, would sit under the stars and talk about politics and poetry and religion. A moonflower grew amid the vines of wisteria, and in the dark, its heavy, heady scent colored their visions. All could be made right in the world, they decided, and they fixed problems one by one. Mabel slept in her mother's lap, Becca teased her nephews, and the Reverend Lowell dozed off. Jamie relaxed beside his sister, feeling settled and happy and hopeful.

A cold fall set in that year. Over one night of hard frost, the vines on the arbor froze, turned brown, and shriveled away. The last of the tomatoes and cucumbers in the kitchen garden puckered up and fell, unripe, to the ground. Only the chrysanthemums remained, their buds tightly held, for they were stingy with their color and would wait as long as possible before blooming. October arrived wet, and the weeks that followed were damp and gray. Maria took to her bed, for her cough had returned. The Reverend Lowell spent his afternoons seated beside her, holding her hand while she slept. Mabel played on the floor and sang to her mother, and even Rebecca joined in the care of her sister-in-law, reading aloud from Hawthorne's *Twice-Told Tales*. Jamie, who had raised funds to help Hawthorne when he'd lost his job at the U.S. Custom House in Salem in 1848, liked his writing well enough. Maria found his stories charming; Becca loved them all.

One afternoon, Becca read aloud the story about the New Year, dressed as a young maiden, coming into a party to bid farewell to the Old Year: "A few dismal characters there may be, here and there about the world, who have so often been trifled with by young maidens as promising as she, that they have now ceased to pin any faith upon the skirts of the New Year. But, for my own part, I have great faith in her . . ."

Becca paused and looked over at Maria, who was smiling. Becca took a deep breath and then continued: "And should I live to see fifty more such, still, from each of those successive sisters, I shall reckon upon receiving something that will be worth living for."[35]

At night, it was Jamie who kept watch over Maria. In letters to friends, he began to admit that he feared for her health, that this time she would not be able to recover from her illness. "I cannot bear to write about it but she is very dangerously ill—growing weaker and weaker . . . It is only within the last week that I have realized the danger. She has been so often ill and rallied from it that I supposed she would soon begin to get better. But there seems to be no force left now . . . I understand now what is meant by 'the waters have gone over me.' Such a sorrow opens a door clear down into one's deepest nature . . ."[36] Lying with Maria at night, wide-awake beside her as she fitfully slept, Jamie saw visions: "a crescent of angels standing and shining silently." He knew the end of Maria's life was near.[37]

On October 27, 1853, Maria died. Fanny Longfellow had just given birth to a daughter: "Two angels, one of Life and one of Death,/ Passed over our village as the morning broke . . ." Henry Longfellow wrote in a poem he dedicated to Maria.[38] An abundance of joy, and an abundance of sorrow. The Reverend Lowell prayed, knowing that for both, thanks were due to God. *Blessed are they that mourn, for they shall be comforted.*[39]

The day Maria White Lowell was buried, the sky was clear. All the rain and clouds of the past days had been swept away on high winds. The procession of mourners and the casket reached Mount Auburn late in the afternoon, just as the sun was setting. The western horizon blazed red and orange; the leafless trees of the cemetery were black outlines against the vivid color. Mabel stood, her grandfather by her side, close to the casket. It was opened one last time. The little girl, just six years old, bent close to her mother and said goodbye. She turned to look for her father and saw him, hunched against a tree and crying. When she looked back at the coffin, the lid had closed. Her mother was gone.

The chrysanthemums in the garden bloomed the next week, but it was too late. No one noticed their brilliant splashes of orange and yellow and purple and pink. More rain came and the stalks bent under the weight, then laid their heads of color on the ground. The next frost sealed them to the soil, and then the snow came.

To her father-in-law, Maria left her "cloak lined with fur to wrap around his knees. . . ."[40] For her daughter, she asked that Jamie find a suitable tutor because Rebecca exhibited too many "queerities."[41] And for her beloved husband, she left a promise. She would always be there, looking after him: "For I should weary of the endless blue,/ Should weary of my ever-growing light,/ If that one soul, so beautiful and true,/ Were hidden by earth's vapors from my sight . . ."[42]

Jamie sat alone at his desk in the still and quiet house: "For it died that autumn morning/ when she, its soul, was borne/ To lie all dark on the hillside . . ."[43] He stopped the pen's passage across the paper. He could write nothing more of poetry. Instead, he opened his journal and added to the scrawl he had started days before and would continue on with for months. Two letters, two initials, one after the other. In small letters, whispering from thin, angry scratches across the ivory page. Or in thick scrawls, almost tearing through the paper.

M.L. M.L. M.L.

There was no mission left to him, no opportunity to recognize and to seize. There was only grief.

18

1853–1861

Though the cause of Evil prosper, yet 'tis Truth alone is strong,
And, albeit she wander outcast now, I see around her throng
Troops of beautiful, tall angels, to enshield her from all wrong.
—JAMES RUSSELL LOWELL, "THE PRESENT CRISIS"

Before Maria Lowell died, James Russell Lowell had been invited by his cousin John Amory Lowell to prepare a series of lectures for the Lowell Institute. Over the past thirteen years the institute had grown, gathering fame and reputation not only for audiences eager to learn from a wide array of speakers but also for lecturers keen to be invited to appear. Evenings at Marlboro Chapel on Washington Street, where the lectures were held, most often sold out (tickets were free but had to be reserved) due to the astute planning of the institute's sole trustee, John Amory. He provided lecturers that were well known in their field, and he ensured a broad range of fields were represented: Thomas Nuttall on botany, Jospeh Lovering on electricity and electromagnetism, Jared Sparks on American history, Orville Dewey on the "Problem of Human Destiny."

Having managed the endowment of the institute as well as he managed his own money, John Amory Lowell had plenty of funds to pay for eminent speakers to come from far away, and to pay them well enough to make the visit attractive. Often, the guest lecturers were invited to stay out at Bromley Vale as guests of John and his wife, Elizabeth. Louis Agassiz, the Swiss biologist who gave his first lectures at the institute in 1846 and then became a professor at Harvard, was so frequent a visitor that he became quite at home at Bromley Vale. He used the maids' "pincushions as butterfly mats," requisitioned household water jugs to hold his newly picked specimens of local ferns, and claimed dresser drawers as temporary homes for what the servants called "the professor's little beasts." One morning, the household came to a standstill when they heard Mrs. Agassiz shrieking, "Louis, there is a snake in my shoe!" He answered calmly, although setting off panic in all listeners, "Only one snake, my dear? Why, where's the other? There were two!"[1]

After Maria died, John Amory again urged Jamie to work on lectures for the institute. Jamie's situation—losing his children and his wife—mirrored the situation of their cousin John junior—the son of Francis Cabot Lowell—who had lost his daughters and wife in a relatively short period of time. No one in the family wanted Jamie running away to Egypt as John junior had done or rotting away on his own in the attic at Elmwood. It was up to John Amory Lowell to offer his cousin a new opportunity, and all the Lowell family prayed that he would take it.

Jamie felt "very unhappy," and very lonely, living with his father—"perfectly deaf"—and his sister—"who never speaks for a week together." He found joy in the presence of Mabel—"my nature is naturally joyous and susceptible of all happy impressions"—and yet still the tears came: "I have found the secret of them and something seems to catch in my throat as I am writing."[2] In search of solace and company, he often went to visit his sister Mary Putnam in Boston and his sister-in-law Anna Lowell in Cambridge. He loved his nephews, Mary's son Will and Anna's sons, Charles and Jimmy. He found in the three boys a wonderful semblance to the youth he had once been. The boys were full of life, certain of themselves and their causes (they were antislavery all the way), but also happy just to have fun: They enjoyed coming up with puns with their uncle Jamie, and tramping around in the woods after him as he pointed out the more subtle points of nature. Jamie counseled his nephews to study hard, not only books but the world around them: "a person with eyes in his head cannot look even into a pigsty without learning something that will be useful to him."[3] The purpose of study? To gain knowledge and then to use that knowledge "to benefit others and to pay our way honourably in life by being of use."[4]

Anthony Burns arrived in Boston in the spring of 1854. He was a fugitive, having run away from his southern master and stowed aboard a merchant ship heading north. He found a place to live in Boston, and then a job. He felt as if fate had smiled upon him. He wrote to his brother, still enslaved in Virginia, to tell him of his good fortune. The letter was confiscated by his old owner, Charles Suttle, who then traveled straight to Boston to reclaim his property under the Fugitive Slave Law. On May 24, Anthony Burns was arrested and taken to the federal courthouse, to be held there under armed guard until transportation could be arranged to take him back south, much as Minkins and then Sims had been held three years before. As crowds had gathered for Minkins and Sims, so they gathered now for Burns. An escape plan was hatched, only to be foiled: The rescuers, led by the radical minister Thomas Wentworth Higginson, made it as far as the hallway of the federal courthouse before they were beaten back into the street.

A hearing was held to adjudicate Burns's status, and Judge Edward G. Loring, a county probate judge and U.S. commissioner under the Fugitive Slave Act, ruled that Burns was a slave. To ensure that Burns would make it down to the pier, where a ship awaited to take him south, President Franklin Pierce ordered more and then more federal troops to Boston. When Burns was taken from the courthouse, he was bound in shackles and then escorted through town by one thousand guards, including federal soldiers, county militia, and Boston police. Close to fifty thousand angry New Englanders surged through the streets, calling and hooting in protest against the seizure of Burns. Office buildings were draped in black bunting; flags were hung upside down; church bells tolled; men and women hissed, hooted, and cried out, "Kidnappers! Kidnappers!"[5] The crowds were pushed back by soldiers brandishing bayonets and lances, and Burns was hustled down to Long Wharf, loaded onto the waiting ship, and taken away.

Charles Lowell, Jamie's nephew, was in the crowd watching as the boat left the harbor. With him was his Harvard friend Henry Higginson. Higginson turned to Charles, his face pale with emotion. "Charlie," he said, "it will come to us to make this right."[6]

On May 30, 1854, in the midst of Burns's trial, President Pierce signed into law the Kansas-Nebraska Act. Northerners were stunned. The act opened wide the door to slavery in new territories, an issue that most thought had been laid to rest with the Compromise of 1850 and the Missouri Compromise of 1820, which had established the line above which slavery could not exist (in response to concerns of how to deal with territories secured in the Louisiana Purchase). Now the vast territories of Nebraska and Kansas—north of that line—were thrown wide open to the possibility of slavery: all white male settlers of the regions would be allowed to vote on the question of slave or free, deciding the status of their territories for themselves.

The seizure of Anthony Burns and the passage of the Kansas-Nebraska Act together formed a turning point. The reality that slavery could not be contained in the Deep South finally penetrated the ranks of northern bankers, manufacturers, and merchants. The compromise they had committed themselves to in 1850 had failed. Congress, led by pro-slavery forces, had betrayed them with a new compromise, one that virtually guaranteed the spread of slavery and the repeat of scenes such as the taking of Minkins, Sims, and Burns from the streets of Boston, where they had lived as freemen, and returning them to the South to be slaves.

As Amos A. Lawrence, nephew of John Amory Lowell's close friend Abbott Lawrence and son of Amos Lawrence, wrote in a letter the day after President Pierce signed the act, the Cotton Whigs of the North "went to bed one night old

fashioned, conservative, Compromise Union Whigs & waked up stark mad Abolitionists."[7] Even John Amory Lowell agreed: Enough was enough. When
Amos A. Lawrence asked for help in planning a mass exodus of emigrants to
Kansas, John Amory Lowell signed on. The Lawrences and the Lowells hoped
that "by establishing emigrants in large numbers in the Territories, it will give
them the power of using at once those social influences which radiate from the
church, the school, and the press, in the organization of a community."[8] A bold
but simple plan: populate the territory and thereby guarantee that when it joined
the United States, its voters would mandate that it entered as a free state.

John Amory agreed to help not only because of his outrage over the Kansas-
Nebraska Act, and not only because the Lawrences were old friends and business partners. Katharine Lawrence, daughter of Abbott Lawrence, had just
married his son Augustus. The Lawrence family, like the Lowells, had come
to New England in the 1600s, settling in Groton. Amos Lawrence had come to
Boston as a young man, taking over a merchant's shop. In a few years his brother
Abbott joined him in Boston and together the two created one of the largest
mercantile trading firms in the United States. Trading cotton and woolen products, they became interested in manufacturing. Abbott was an early investor in
the mills at Lowell and later at Lawrence, the town named for him. By the year
1850, the two brothers were among the wealthiest men in New England.

The merging of the Lowell family with the Lawrence family cemented the
ties built on commerce and accumulation of wealth; now they would also be
joined by a commitment to contain slavery to the southern states, where John
Amory Lowell, his son Augustus, and Abbott Lawrence believed it belonged.
It would be up to Amos A. Lawrence to convince all of them that to contain it
was not enough. Slavery had to be abolished.

The Massachusetts Emigrant Aid Company (later called the New England Aid Company), was formed, with Amos A. Lawrence as its treasurer and
John Amory Lowell as a director and member of its executive committee.
With such prominent names at the helm, money came in from wealthy families across Boston to fund the wave of emigrants to Kansas. Hundreds of so-
called Free-Soilers set off for the territory. By the winter of 1854, six hundred
settlers had formed towns, set up local governments, and were prepared to
form a new state. The town of Lawrence was founded in honor of Amos A.
Lawrence, and its settlers were devout in their purpose: to create this new
state as one without slaves, now or ever.

Abbott Lawrence, who had served two terms in the U.S. House of Representatives and was well connected in Congress, asked President Pierce to recognize
the New England settlers as the legally constituted government of Kansas. But
opposition came from pro-slavery settlers in Missouri, to the north, who had

sent their own groups down to Kansas to stake claims. Pierce refused to accept Kansas as a free state. Towns and villages throughout the territory, on both sides of the free-or-slave referendum, began to take matters into their own hands.

James Russell Lowell set to writing again, intent on creating another caustic Biglow poem, this time focused on the Kansas-Nebraska Act. He was still on the executive committee of the American Anti-Slavery Society and wanted to contribute more than just his name and presence to the society's work; he wrote a friend of his "shame" in failing to work for the cause: every man who hadn't "passed his Master's Degree in Black-guardism ought to speak out" against this act, which was such a terrible "swindle."[9] But the inspiration for Biglow failed—he could write only four lines reviving Parson Wilbur and Hosea Biglow—and Jamie threw himself into preparing the twelve lectures that would make up his course for the Lowell Institute. He had to be of some use, somehow, to someone. Jamie would get to back to Biglow, publishing his "Biglow Papers, the Second Series" in *The Atlantic Monthly* in the early 1860s. But for now, he put everything he had into his Lowell Institute lectures.

The lecture series, titled "The English Poet," was advertised in the fall of 1855. It quickly sold out, even with two seatings of each lecture offered, one in the afternoon and one in the evening. Bostonians were eager to hear what Jamie had to say about Chaucer and Spenser, about Milton, Butler, and Pope. And not only Bostonians were enthusiastic: *The Boston Daily Advertiser* arranged to reprint each lecture day by day, and to distribute them around the country. Senator Charles Sumner, an antislavery politician elected to the United States Senate from Massachusetts, taking the seat previously held by Daniel Webster, wrote from Washington, D.C., that he'd read "with delight every word" of Jamie's lectures.[10] Already famous as a poet and essayist, now Jamie was finding fame as a teacher.

Within the year, Jamie was asked to join the faculty at Harvard as professor of modern languages, a position long held by Henry Longfellow, who had decided to retire. "He has won his spurs and will give the college just what it needs," Longfellow wrote in his diary.[11] He was pleased that his old friend was taking on his position at the college.

In the year after Maria's death, Jamie had moved with his daughter Mabel to the Cambridge home of Maria's sister Lois Howe and her husband, Dr. Estes Howe, just down the street from Elmwood. The painful memories evoked by Elmwood were too much for him to bear and he left for a time its gardens, his chickens, and Blanche's tiny shoes hanging from a nail on the third floor. But on the day Jamie accepted his Harvard appointment, he ran all the way up Brattle Street and along the path of elms to reach his father's door. He had such good news to share. He had found his new mission, his new duty. He was coming back to life. In 1857, after a yearlong trip to Europe to prepare for his Harvard teaching, he would remarry, taking as his wife Frances Dunlap, the governess of his daughter Mabel. Jamie knew he would never love anyone as he had loved Maria, but Frances suited him just fine: "I am going to put myself wholly in Franny's hands," he wrote.[12] On her part, Frances was devoted to Jamie and convinced that she had found her duty in him, for he was "a sensitive and superior being to care for."[13]

John Amory Lowell and Amos A. Lawrence were facing a serious problem in Kansas. Pro-slavery forces from Missouri, heavily armed and aggressive, were flooding into the territory, not only creating their own settlements but also attacking the Free-Soil settlements in violent confrontations. The Free-Soilers from New England had for the most part come to Kansas without guns or weapons of any kind. They sent desperate appeals back to the New England Emigrant Aid Company asking for guns with which to protect themselves. Amos A. Lawrence acquiesced, and John Amory Lowell agreed: "when farmers turn soldiers, they must have arms."[14] By May 1855, large shipments of the very latest in guns (the breech-loading Sharps rifle) began arriving in the territory from supporters back east, hidden in boxes labeled "primers" and "books."[15] The nickname for these rifles were "Beecher's Bibles," drawn from a comment made by the preacher Henry Ward Beecher that a rifle might be "a more powerful moral agent on the Kansas plains than a Bible."[16]

Among the settlers receiving weapons was John Brown. Brown had left New England for Kansas with his four sons, their passage funded by the New England Emigrant Aid Company. Amos A. Lawrence had approved of his migration, despite some misgivings. Lawrence knew Brown from Brown's days as a wool merchant and was well aware of Brown's conversion to ardent abolitionism. Brown had loudly and publicly consecrated his life to ending slavery back in 1837, after Elijah Lovejoy, a Presbyterian minister and antislavery activist in Illinois, was murdered by pro-slavery activists. If violence was the only means to ending slavery, Brown would not flinch from it, for slavery was a "state of war to which the slaves were unwilling parties . . . they have a right to anything necessary to their peace and freedom . . . No people could have self-respect or be respected who would not fight for their freedom."[17] Lawrence advised Charles Robinson, an agent of the New England Emigrant Aid Company in Kansas, to make sure that "some controlling power" kept close watch on Brown.[18]

On May 19, 1856, Senator Charles Sumner began a speech to his fellow congressmen denouncing the Kansas-Nebraska Act and deriding pro-slavery forces for their violence in trying to make Kansas a slave state. He quoted lines from Jamie's poem "The Present Crisis," to dramatic effect:

> For Humanity sweeps onward: where to-day the martyr
>   stands,
> On the morrow crouches Judas with the silver in his hands;
> Far in front the cross stands ready and the crackling
>   faggots burn,
> While the hooting mob of yesterday in silent awe return
> To glean up the scattered ashes in History's golden urn.

Sumner then went on to criticize those senators who would allow slavery to spread throughout the union. He directed his venom at two in particular, James Murry Mason of Virginia, a man of "inhumanity and tyranny" (he had drafted the Fugitive Slave Law) and Senator Andrew Butler of South Carolina— "he has chosen a mistress to whom he has made his vows . . . I mean the harlot, slavery."[19] Sumner's speech was so long, he had to present it in two parts. When he finally sat down, on May 20, he had no idea of the conflagration he had started. He'd wanted to light a fire under his fellow congressmen, but the flames would reach further than he could have imagined.

Two days after he finished his speech, Sumner was physically attacked on the floor of the Senate chamber by Preston Brooks, a Congressman from South Carolina and the cousin of Senator Butler. The chamber was deserted but for the two men, and Brooks took the opportunity to repeatedly strike Sumner with a cane. Even when Sumner fell to the floor and tried to crawl away under the protection of a desk, blood streaming into his eyes, Brooks continued to beat him. Only when Brooks's cane broke into pieces did he cease his attack; he strode off, leaving Sumner prone on the floor. The injuries suffered by Sumner were so severe that three years would pass before he returned to take his place in the Senate.

News of Sumner's beating reached John Brown at his settlement of Osawatomie in Kansas. He seethed over the brutality of the attack; the violence of slavery was now playing out on the floor of the U.S. Congress. But he would hold himself in check, for now. Then pro-slavery settlers attacked the Free-Soil settlement at Lawrence, Kansas. They blew up the Free State Hotel in a barrage of cannon fire, threatened and terrified the settlers, burned and looted homes and shops, and dumped the printing presses from the Free-Soil newspaper into the river. John Brown could no longer contain his rage. Vowing revenge, he led an attack against a settlement of pro-slavery Missouri farmers, killing and mutilating five settlers. In retaliation, proslavery settlers went after Brown's band; they killed his son Frederick and burned down the settlement at Osawatomie. In the North and the South, Americans reeled in the wake of what the press called "Bleeding Kansas." Leaders of Emigrant Aid Company back in Massachusetts worried they might be blamed. The company had supported Brown and surreptitiously supplied him with guns. They held their breath and wondered, *What will Brown do next?*

James Russell Lowell was asked by the publisher F. H. Underwood to take on the editorship of a new magazine. Underwood wanted the proposed magazine to publish literature with a distinctly American voice, along with essays about current issues, including the crusade against slavery. Underwood, along with Ralph Waldo Emerson and Oliver Wendell Holmes, considered Jamie to be the perfect man to head up the new venture. Despite the workload imposed by teaching at Harvard, Jamie took the job. It was Jamie, throwing ideas around with Holmes, who came up with the title of the new periodical: *The Atlantic Monthly*. In its pages, Jamie would find a new and powerful venue in which to not only promote fellow writers but perhaps even more important, to condemn the institution of slavery.

In March 1857, the Supreme Court made its decision in the case of *Dred Scott v. Sanford*. Dred Scott was a black man born in slavery but who had lived for a period of years in places where slavery was illegal (Illinois and the territory of Wisconsin). Scott argued that because he had lived free for a period of time, he was a freedman and a citizen with rights under the Constitution of the United States: "once free, always free."[20] But the Supreme Court held that because of his race, Scott was not a citizen of the United States and had no protection under the Constitution. The justices then went further and declared the Missouri Compromise of 1820 invalid for setting limits on how far slavery could be allowed to spread.

Abolitionists were outraged, while slave owners rejoiced. Jamie wrote in *The Atlantic Monthly*: "We have been asked to admit, first, that slavery was a necessary evil; then that it was a good both to master and slave; then that it was the corner-stone of free institutions; then that it was a system divinely instituted under the Old Law and sanctioned under the New. . . . the South turns upon us and insists our acknowledging that slaves are things. . . . through the Supreme Court of the United States, that negroes are not men in the ordinary meaning of the word. . . . The slaveholding interest has gone step by step, forcing concession after concession, till it needs but little to secure it forever in the political supremacy of the country."[21]

———————

Lowell Coat of Arms.

Reverend John Lowell (1704–1767).
(Harvard University Portrait Collection, Gift of the Estate of Ralph Lowell, 1978, H646)

Reverend John Lowell, seated at head of table.

Judge John Lowell (1743–1802). *(Harvard University Portrait Collection, Gift of the Estate of Abbott Lawrence Lowell, 1943, H513)*

John the Rebel Lowell (1769–1840). *(Harvard University Portrait Collection, Gift of the Estate of Ralph Lowell, 1978, H648)*

Anna Cabot Lowell, "Nancy" (1768–1810).

Reverend Charles Lowell (1782–1861). *(Collections of the Massachusetts Historical Society)*

Harriet Brackett Spence Lowell (1783–1850).

Elmwood. *(Courtesy of Historic New England)*

Maria White Lowell (1821–1853).
(MS Am 1054.5 Daguerreotype of Maria White Lowell, Houghton Library, Harvard University)

Elmwood Library.
(Courtesy of Historic New England)

James Russell Lowell (1819–1891). *(Image on right Courtesy of Library of Congress Prints and Photographs Division, Theodore Roosevelt Digital Library, Dickinson State University)*

John Amory Lowell (1798–
1881). *(Harvard University
Portrait Collection, Gift of the
Estate of Ralph Lowell, 1978,
H649)*

John Lowell, Jr. (1799–1836).
*(Portrait of John Lowell, Jr., painted by
Charles Gleyre, courtesy of The Lowell
Institute)*

Anna Cabot Lowell (1808–
1894). *(Courtesy of Historic
New England)*

William Lowell Putnam (1840–1861).
(Collection of the Massachusetts Historical Society)

James Alfred Roosevelt (1885–1919).
(Courtesy of Harvard University Archives)

James Jackson Lowell (1837–1862).
(Courtesy of Special Collections, Fine Arts Library, Harvard University)

Charles R. Lowell, Jr. (1835–1864).
(Courtesy of Special Collections, Fine Arts Library, Harvard University)

Charles Russell Lowell, Senior (1807–1870) with Charles Russell Lowell Junior (1835–1864).

Mabel Lowell Burnett (1847–1898).
(Smith College Museum of Art, Northampton, Massachusetts)

Augustus Lowell (1830–1900).
(Courtesy of the American Textile History Museum)

A. Lawrence (1856–1943) and Percy Lowell (1855–1916). *(Courtesy of the Lowell Observatory Archives)*

Katherine Bigelow Lowell (1832–1895) with son Percy. *(Courtesy of the Lowell Observatory Archives)*

Percy Lowell in Korea. *(Courtesy of the Lowell Observatory Archives)*

Percy Lowell on Mars Hill. *(Courtesy of the Lowell Observatory Archives)*

Percy Lowell and his wife, Constance Savage Keith Lowell (1863–1954). *(Courtesy of the Lowell Observatory Archives)*

Wrexie Louise Leonard (1867–1937). *(Courtesy of the Lowell Observatory Archives)*

Percy Lowell playing Santa. *(Courtesy of the Lowell Observatory Archives)*

Portrait of A. Lawrence Lowell. *(Harvard University Portrait Collection, Bequest of Abbott Lawrence Lowell, 1943, H515.A)*

A. Lawrence Lowell.

Anna Parker Lowell (1856–1930). *(Harvard University Portrait Collection, Bequest of Abbott Lawrence Lowell, 1943, H515)*

View of Cotuit, painted by Anna Parker Lowell. *(Harvard Art Museums/Fogg Museum, Gift of Mrs. Ralph Lowell, 1949.45.5)*

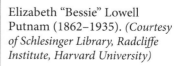

Elizabeth "Bessie" Lowell Putnam (1862–1935). *(Courtesy of Schlesinger Library, Radcliffe Institute, Harvard University)*

Bessie Lowell reading to Amy Lowell. *(Courtesy of Schlesinger Library, Radcliffe Institute, Harvard University)*

William Lowell Putnam (1861–1923). *(Courtesy of Schlesinger Library, Radcliffe Institute, Harvard University)*

Amy Lowell (1874–1925) as a young girl with sheepdog. *(MS Lowell 62 f.1, Houghton Library, Harvard University)*

Amy Lowell as a young
woman with hat. *(MS 62 f.2,
Houghton Library, Harvard
University)*

Amy Lowell in third-floor suite at Sevenels. *(MS Am 2088 34,
Houghton Library, Harvard University)*

Amy Lowell. *(2004M–47 Photo of Amy Lowell with book on
lap, by Moffet, Houghton Library, Harvard University)*

Amy Lowell in garden at Sevenels. *(MS Am 2088 14, Houghton Library, Harvard University)*

Amy Lowell receiving honorary degree from Baylor University.

Ada Dwyer Russell (1863–1952).

Alfred Roosevelt (1856–1891) with Elfrida (1883–1963), Kate (1887–1961), and James (1885–1919). *(Alfred Roosevelt and his children. [1889–1891?]. Prints and Photographs Division. Library of Congress. Theodore Roosevelt Digital Library. Dickinson State University)*

Entrance to Sevenels. *(Courtesy of Historic New England)*

Library at Sevenels. *(MS Am 2088 20, Houghton Library, Harvard University)*

Amy's third-floor suite at Sevenels. *(MS Am 2088 32, Houghton Library, Harvard University)*

Sevenels. *(MS Am 2088 9, Houghton Library, Harvard University)*

Elmwood.

Entrance to Sevenels. *(Courtesy of Historic New England)*

Library at Sevenels. *(MS Am 2088 20, Houghton Library, Harvard University)*

Amy's third-floor suite at Sevenels. *(MS Am 2088 32, Houghton Library, Harvard University)*

Sevenels. *(MS Am 2088 9, Houghton Library, Harvard University)*

Elmwood.

In 1857, the nation suffered a financial panic when the unstable and unregulated national and local banking systems faltered, suddenly leaving overblown railroad building, manufacturing, and real estate development unsupported. Banks and insurance companies collapsed; northern manufacturing slowed down; unemployment spiked. Amos A. Lawrence wrote to Robinson in Kansas that "we have been so distressed as hardly to be able to consider anything deliberately, but how to save ourselves from total prostration."[22] The fight for Kansas would have to wait, now that northern businessmen were intent on saving themselves.

John Amory Lowell struggled to keep his mills and related businesses profitable. Workers demanding reduced working hours and raised wages were rebuffed. Instead, production demands were increased and wages stagnated. Mill owners like Lowell ignored the overcrowding of working and living spaces and the increasingly dangerous working conditions. With profits faltering, the owners no longer felt the paternal interest manifested by Francis Cabot Lowell for his mill workers. The type of worker had also changed after many New England farmers and their families headed west following the discovery of gold in California. Daughters and wives of newly arrived immigrants, mostly from Ireland, were hired to work the looms, while their fathers and brothers were hired for laying new roads in the towns, digging railroad lines, and working construction on expanding mills. These new workers were less interested in evening improvement classes and matron-supervised dorms, and more interested in a living wage and decent working hours. Unions began making inroads and the mill owners were put on notice. The balancing act between North and South had a new weight on the scales: the interests of workers.

Every year, Jamie went on a hiking trip to the Adirondacks. He tried to go after the first frost, when the blackflies had gone and the air was fresh and cool. Some years, he took friends along, including Estes Howe, his sister-in-law's husband, and W. J. Stillman, journalist and painter. One year, he invited Longfellow to join him, but upon hearing that Emerson was going and taking a gun with him, Longfellow begged off, saying, "No, I'm staying home. Somebody will be shot."[23]

Other years, Jamie took along his nephews Charles and Jimmy, the sons of Charlie and Anna. At night, Jamie and the boys camped out, building large fires and then settling down to sleep under a huge expanse of glittering darkness. They pulled constellations from the sky and took turns naming them. ". . . Night brings more companions than the day/ new constellations burn, and fairer stars . . ."[24] Jamie woke early every morning, as was his habit. He watched the boys sleeping and thought, *My boys.* His boy, Walter, had never

had the chance to grow up. But these boys were his boys, too, and he prayed
that they would grow up to be men.

Five mills along the Merrimack River shut their doors by the end of 1857, done
in by the financial crisis. John Amory Lowell managed to keep his mills operating, but at a high cost. In the fall of 1857, he suffered a stroke, which left his
right hand paralyzed. His son Augustus took over more responsibilities in the
family businesses. Along with other northern manufacturers and bankers,
Augustus realized that the only way to weather the financial crisis was to ca-
ter to the South. The South had the money and goods to help out the North, as
their cotton-based economy had not been so hard hit as the banking, trading,
and manufacturing economies of the North. But southern plantation owners
would only help if concessions were made, not only in terms of better lending
agreements from northern banks and more lucrative mercantile contracts
but also in political matters: Southern leaders demanded that northern agitation against slavery had to stop. Bankers and manufacturers made financial
concessions, and promises were made about silencing the abolitionists. Gloat-
ing over the northern compromises, Senator James Hammond, a wealthy slave
owner from South Carolina, proclaimed, "Cotton is King!"[25]

On October 16, 1859, John Brown led a band of eighteen armed men in an attack on the U.S. arsenal at Harper's Ferry, Virginia. His plan was to foment a
massive slave rebellion by supplying weapons to surrounding populations of
runaway and liberated slaves. However, before the plan could be implemented,
the arsenal was surrounded by government troops, and Brown and his band
were captured and imprisoned. On December 2, John Brown was hanged.

   Despite all the concessions made by northern businessmen toward the
South, Brown's raid reignited southern suspicions of northern treachery. Many
in the South saw a connection between northern money and John Brown's wild
scheme. There was no doubt as to Brown's ties to the Kansas Aid Committee, a
radical offshoot of the New England Emigrant Aid Company. Theodore Parker,
Thomas Wentworth Higginson, and Frank Sanborn were all New Englanders
tied to Brown—and to the Lowell family. Higginson's wife lived with Anna and
Charlie Lowell on Quincy Street in Cambridge.* Sanborn was good friends
with Anna and Charlie's son Charles. Jamie had had frequent exchanges with
both Parker and Higginson and printed works by both in *The Atlantic Monthly.*

---

* Old Aunt Sally had lived there for a while as well. When she could no longer live
alone, Anna had taken her in. Sally had forgiven Charlie for losing all her money in
1837. She died in 1851.

And all the Lowell children and grandchildren of the Old Judge were connected to Higginson by virtue of the fact that the judge's first wife had been Sarah Higginson, Thomas's great-aunt. New England family connections went deep, and many in the South were certain that such connections mattered more than commerce. Southern plantation owners grew increasingly certain that all northerners were in on a conspiracy to foment rebellion among southern slaves. "Defend yourselves!" cautioned Georgia senator Robert Toombs, soon to be a leading secessionist. "The enemy is at your door!"[26]

James Russell Lowell was asked to write an essay explaining and justifying the raid on Harper's Ferry, but he declined. "I am a little afraid of John Brown," he explained.[27] But he did write essays for *The Atlantic Monthly* about the upcoming presidential election. For Jamie, there just one issue at stake—slavery—and just one man willing to end it without compromise—Lincoln. "The slaveholding interest has gone on step by step ... Yield to its latest demand,—let it mould the evil destiny of the Territories,—and the thing is done past recall. The next Presidential Election is to say Yes or No."[28]

Abraham Lincoln was elected president of the United States in November 1860. In December, South Carolina seceded from the Union. Trade between the North and the South came to a grinding halt and the impact on the North was immediate. Workers were laid off, businesses closed, mills went silent, and stocks fell. Anxious crowds gathered in the streets of Boston, denouncing the abolitionists and blaming them for the economic crisis. Wendell Phillips derided the gathered crowd as "snobbish sons of fathers lately rich, anxious to show themselves rotten before they are ripe."[29] The rotten ones took him by the neck and almost lynched him in the street.

In early January, Mississippi seceded from the Union, followed by Florida, Alabama, and Georgia. The crisis, economic and political, deepened.

The Reverend Charles Lowell became ill and took to his bed. Jamie returned to Elmwood and did his best to make his father comfortable. He helped the old man write a missive to the parish of West Church, asking them all to "love one another."[30] On January 20, 1861, at the age of seventy-eight, the Reverend Lowell died. "I am going now" were his last words.[31] Charles had once written to Jamie, "That you may live as long as is best for you ... and at the end of life, having the testimony of your conscience that in simplicity and godly sincerity you can say 'Well done,'" is the fervent hope and prayer of your truly loving father ..."[32] A prayer enforced by example, for Jamie had seen his father live well. He had been a good man.

Four days later, funeral services for Charles Lowell were held at West Church, the church he had led for fifty-five years. Charles G. Loring spoke at the service, barely holding back his tears: "I passed from childhood, through youth and manhood, to old age, under the ministry of our deceased pastor; my joys have been augmented by his congratulations, and my griefs were assuaged by his sympathy and counsel; I have counted his friendship and his example among the choicest of treasures . . ."[33]

The coffin was carried to Mount Auburn Cemetery. There, laid deep in the earth, he rested beside his wife, Harriet, and close to his grandchildren Blanche and Rose, and their mother, Maria. Jamie bent his head and prayed in gratitude for such a father. A man who had worked hard, held his faith close and his family closer, and loved everyone and everything in abundance. "Yet after he was dead and gone,/ And e'en his memory dim,/ Earth seemed more sweet to live upon,/ More full of love, because of him."[34]

After his father's death, Jamie returned to live again at Elmwood, along with his second wife, Frances, and daughter Mabel, bringing company to his sister Becca and new life to the old house. "I am sitting in my old garret, at my old desk, smoking my old pipe, and loving my old friends," he wrote to his friend Charles F. Briggs.[35] He was once more at home, and there he would remain.

William Appleton was, along with his father, Nathan Appleton, a longtime business partner of the Lowells. In the spring of 1861, he was aboard a steamer held at anchor outside Charleston Harbor. There were some who surmised he had gone south in an effort to negotiate a peace between North and South, but if that was his intention, he failed. In the early hours of the morning of April 12, 1861, long before daybreak, Appleton was awakened by the sound of cannon fire. He rushed from his cabin, dressed only in woolen socks and a long linen nightshirt closed at the neck with a silk ribbon. From the deck, he could see the flare of Confederate guns against the dark sky and hear the pounding, boom after deafening boom, as they fired upon the federal garrison of Fort Sumter. "Every flash we could see, then the smoke; then followed the report; the bombshells we saw ascend and would anxiously watch whether they fell in Fort Sumter," he wrote to friends back north.[36]

The Civil War had begun.

The Lowells of Massachusetts supported the Union cause, from John Amory Lowell and his son Augustus, who had sought compromise with the South, to Charlie Lowell and his wife, Anna, who, along with Charlie's brother Jamie and sister Mary, had sought to end slavery without conditions. All were united now in their hopes to preserve the union of American states, and everything such a union stood for. In their minds, New England had been the birthplace of liberty and the foundation of American constitutional government. Now New England would fight for her country. "No price is high at which the social and political unity of this entire continent can be purchased," Jamie wrote.[37] But the price would be higher than any of the Lowells could imagine.

19

1861–1864

In these brave ranks I only see the gaps,
Thinking of dear ones whom the dumb turf wraps.
Dark to the triumph which they died to gain . . .
—JAMES RUSSELL LOWELL,
"ODE RECITED AT THE HARVARD COMMEMORATION"

Mary Lowell Putnam sat back in her chair, her breath caught in her chest. She was seated at the dining room table in her house on Beacon Street in Boston, a table where so many family meals had taken place, so many events celebrated or mourned, as the occasion called for. And what did this occasion call for? There was no meal on the table, only the rich tapestry cloth hung with brightly colored tassels that protected the dark mahogany below. Mary clutched at a tassel now, her grip so tight, she almost pulled the covering from the table. Her son William Lowell Putnam stood before her, standing in front of an open window. The sunlight blazed up behind him and his face appeared to float before her, solitary and framed like a portrait of a dead relative. Or like a saint in the paintings she'd seen on the many trips through Italy she'd made: a halo of light around his head. Then she banished the thought. Her son would not be a martyr.

Mary had married Samuel Putnam on April 25, 1832, a marriage encouraged by her cousin John Amory Lowell. Samuel was the older brother of John's second wife, Elizabeth Cabot Putnam, and an established Boston merchant. Samuel had given Mary the gift of the world—they'd lived abroad for long stretches, making homes in France and Germany, and traveling throughout Europe—and Mary had given Samuel the gift of conscience. Mary converted Sam to the cause of her family—the eradication of slavery— and together Mary and Sam had invited into their home antislavery families, including Jamie and Maria; Jamie's old friends, Francis and Sarah Shaw; and the Reverend James Freeman Clarke, an ardent activist not only against slavery but for the rights of women. It should have come as no surprise to Mary that when the war to end slavery began, her son William would join up.

But now her breath had stopped in her throat, held so hard that she could barely think or talk. Will was going to war.

Will was their third child and second son. Mary and Samuel had had four children, three boys and a girl. Their youngest child died when he was two years old. Mary and Samuel left Boston then, moving to Europe to live. Mary, who read as voraciously as her father, the Reverend Charles Lowell, and spoke all the modern languages of Europe and more than a few of the ancient ones as well, took over the schooling of her young children: geography, languages, history.

Young Will took to history with a passion. He read his books, listened to lectures, and then found proof of the past: the story of Hadrian in the fallen palaces and temples of Rome; the march of Hannibal as his family traveled the mountain passes between Switzerland and France. In the hills south of Florence, he found the markers of even more ancient civilizations, risen and fallen centuries ago. Willy found lessons in history that went beyond dates and facts. He discovered what he saw as the duty handed down by its scholarship: not to repeat the sins of the past, but to make the world anew, always better than before. After his older brother Alfred died of cholera in 1855 while the family was living in Italy, Will took this duty even more seriously. He had just turned fifteen years old and was now the only surviving son. The family returned to Boston and Will entered Harvard College, planning to study history and law.

And now war had begun between the states.

Will Lowell stood before his mother, his long hair brushed back, curling around and under his ears, his eyes wide with concern. Mary reached up from her chair to touch his chin, a strong Lowell chin. Will was prone to smiling, but now all humor was erased from his face. He was serious and calm, and the gravity made him seem older than his twenty years. He lowered himself down to one knee beside his mother and took her hands in his.

"People say this war will not last more than six months and they are wrong . . . It will go on for nearer six years," he told her, "but when it is over slavery will have been abolished."[1] How confident he was, kneeling before his mother, sunlight dappling their intertwined hands. That confidence would last until his very last letter home: "Human beings never drew sword in a better cause than ours."[2]

Charles Lowell, cousin to Will Putnam and the eldest son of Charlie Lowell and Anna Cabot Jackson Lowell, had been uncertain of what to do when the war started. He was living in Maryland, a state populated by pro-Confederate supporters, and working at the Mount Savage Iron Mines. Having graduated from Harvard in 1854, valedictorian of his class, he had set to learning the business of mining. The family fortunes had never recovered after his father Charlie's bankruptcy. His mother had closed her school and now took in boarders at their house on Quincy Street in Cambridge. His father worked at the Harvard Athenaeum, a job secured for him through John Amory Lowell: he was kept busy cataloging the Athenaeum's thousands upon thousands of books. Charles was determined to support himself and bring new stability and honor to the family name. By 1861, he had worked himself up to the position of ironmaster at Mount Savage, managing the works of the large mine. The position was a good one, and he was loath to leave it. But should he now return to Massachusetts? Join the North in the fight to save the union? He wrote to his mother, "this war news is so startling that I do not quite know where I am."[3]

Charles traveled to Baltimore for business in April 1861. He decided to stay on for a few days when he heard that the Sixth Massachusetts Volunteer Infantry would be passing through Baltimore on their way to Washington, D.C. Within days of Lincoln's request for soldiers following the attack on Fort Sumter, the Sixth Massachusetts was on their way south; it was the first volunteer militia unit to answer the president's call. They were ready to fight because they had been training since January. John Albion Andrew, the new governor of Massachusetts, had anticipated that war was coming. Now his foresight paid off.

The new militia units of Massachusetts were spurred on not only by their governor but also by the man who would become their de facto regimental poet, Henry Wadsworth Longfellow, whose poem "Paul Revere's Ride" had taken the North by storm. Since its publication earlier in the year, Longfellow had become the hero poet of New England. His poem celebrating the bravery of the Revolutionary patriots roused a patriotic fervor in those anxious to fight for the Union, and lent a mythical quality to their quest:

> For, borne on the night-wind of the Past,
> Through all our history, to the last
> In the hour of darkness and peril and need,
> The people will waken and listen to hear
> The hurrying hoof-beats of that steed,
> And the midnight-message of Paul Revere.[4]

Volunteers in the Sixth Massachusetts included men from the mill towns of Lowell and Lawrence. Mill owners like John Amory Lowell, Augustus Lowell, and Amos A. Lawrence supported the enlistment of their workers. When the troops came to Boston before heading south, Augustus and his sons,

Percy and Lawrence, and even baby Kate (held tightly in her father's arms), took their place along the street, joining the crowds that cheered the regiment on. "The city is completely filled with enthusiasm," wrote one volunteer soldier, "gray-haired old men, young boys, old women and young are alike wild with patriotism."[5] Financially and politically, the Lowells and the Lawrences, along with other wealthy New Englanders, would support the Massachusetts regiments to the end. There was complete agreement among the wealthy bankers and industrialists of New England: "the Union must be saved."[6]

With mill workers leaving to fight, and cotton supplies from the South cut off, John Amory Lowell and other manufacturers had to come up with new ways of doing business. Over the years of the war, there would be desperate scrambling to mechanize the manufacturing industry in order to reduce the need for workers. The workers remaining in the cotton and woolen mills would be pushed harder; legislation calling for a reduction in the workday from twelve hours to ten would languish—fought by the mill owners—until long after the end of the war. Securing cotton for the mills along the Merrimack during these years would take ingenuity. Diversification of manufacturing interests beyond cotton would have to grow. Guns, railroads, leather goods—all would be needed in the war effort, and the lords of the loom would now have to become lords of the ironmongers, of the railroads, and of the factories.

Already well positioned as the director of the Suffolk Bank, John Amory Lowell, aided by his son Augustus Lowell, would facilitate over the next few years the financing needed for the war. Funding was funneled through the banks, as the federal government issued treasury notes, printed new money, and created new regulations that would create a strong national banking structure. National debt grew, but instead of crippling the economy, debt spurred economic growth during the war, and would continue to do so for a period of time afterward. John Amory Lowell and his son Augustus would ride that wave of potential and, in helping fight the war for the Union, seal their own fortunes in new opportunities seized.

Charles Lowell, having concluded his business in Baltimore, waited with growing excitement for the Sixth Massachusetts to appear. He'd heard of their reception in the Northern towns, for the newspapers had been full of reports: flags, banners, cheering crowds in Springfield, Hartford, Trenton, and Philadelphia. Thousands of well-wishers, waving white handkerchiefs and blue scarves, had cheered them through New York City, accompanying them on the march from the railroad station down Broadway to the piers to catch the ferry to New Jersey: "immense crowds, immense cheering," noted one observer. "God be praised for the unity of feeling here! If it only lasts, we are safe."[7]

The first large horse-drawn cart carrying soldiers was due to pass by Charles Lowell soon. He had positioned himself on Pratt Street, the street that led from the northern railroad terminal at President Street Station to the southern one at Camden Station. Charles stood with other Northerners eager to see the soldiers, but a distinctly Southern crowd had begun to form around their little group. Lowell overheard the grumblings—*dirty abolitionists*. The crowds were turning into a mob, a pro-Confederate mob. Charlie raised a cheer when the cart carrying the first of the Massachusetts men appeared rumbling down the street. But all around him, men and women jeered and booed the passing soldiers seated humbly in their wagons.

Cart by cart passed. Each one was jeered and the crowd seemed ready to attack, but then each was finally allowed to continue on. Then suddenly the mob surged forward and surrounded one of the last passing carts. The cart was pulled over and surrounded by hundreds of screaming Southerners. The soldiers from Massachusetts jumped down from their wagon seats and tried to form orderly lines. They proceeded down the street, marching in a huddled formation, waving a white flag before them. Rocks, paving stones, and bricks were hurled at the Northern soldiers. George William Brown, the mayor of Baltimore, ran to the front of the line to march as its leader, trying to calm the crowd and impose order.

Then shots rang out, fired out over the crowd. Smoke from guns filled the air. Gangs of men began to grab for the upheld muskets of soldiers. One Northern soldier, frightened for his life, lowered his gun and fired over the crowd; soldiers alongside him followed suit. The mayor began waving his arms and screaming, "For God's sake, don't shoot!"[8]

By the time the last of the Massachusetts troops were loaded onto the southbound trains, four Northern soldiers had been killed—all of them men from Lowell or Lawrence—and more than thirty-five had been wounded. Twelve citizens of Maryland lay dead on the streets, and many more were injured. By order of Mayor Brown, all city bridges serving trains going north, including those of the Philadelphia Railroad and the North Central Railroad, were burned down. All the telegraph poles communicating to the North were torn to the ground. Baltimore had cut itself off from the North and aligned with the South.

Charles Lowell decided on the spot, with dust and smoke still rising from the pounded streets all around him, that he would join the Union army and fight. Fight until the end. He wrote to his mother that evening, "I want to see the

Baltimore traitors put on trial at once and armed rebellion everywhere crushed out." Rebellion crushed, and the union restored. On the back of the envelope he addressed to Quincy Street, Cambridge, he added, "Henceforth I will always hail from Massachusetts."[9]

Charles arrived the next day in an unsettled Washington, D.C. The terrible melee in Baltimore had been just one more incident underlining the ever-widening divide between North and South. The capital was on edge, its citizens nervous about an attack from Virginia rebels. It was as if the city were under a siege that had not yet been declared. Charles managed to find a place to sleep in the home of an old friend of his aunt Mary Putnam and his uncle Jamie, a one-eyed Polish count named Adam Gurowski. Gurowksi was a member of the Clay Guards, a group of armed volunteers put together by Senator Cassius Clay. Clay was a southern planter from Kentucky and also an avid abolitionist. His Clay Guards patrolled the uneasy streets of Washington and promised to protect the White House from what many thought was an imminent attack.

Charles wrote to Massachusetts senator Sumner asking for his help in securing a commission in the army. In his letter, he listed his qualifications, including "enough mathematics to put me at the head of my class at Harvard" and the ability to "ride a horse as far and bring him in as fresh as any man." He then asked to be given a place as an artillery officer: "I believe, within a week or two of preparation, I could pass the examinations."[10] By the end of May, Charles got his commission as a captain in the Third U.S. Cavalry. His close friends and Harvard classmates Robert Shaw and Henry Higginson were also in Washington and had received their orders, as well. They were to be officers in the Second Massachusetts Volunteer Infantry.

Mary and Samuel Putnam resigned themselves to Will's enlistment. Mary even wrote a recommendation for her son and sent it directly to Governor Andrew, who was responsible for delivering commissions to volunteer officers: "He is our only son but we know that, in desiring to enter the army, he is actuated by a deep and ardent feeling of patriotism, and by a sincere conviction of the justice of the cause to which he would devote himself."[11] On July 10, 1861, one day after his twenty-first birthday, Will received his commission as second lieutenant in the Twentieth Massachusetts Volunteer Infantry. His cousin James Jackson Lowell, brother to Charles, was given the commission as first lieutenant in the same regiment. Jimmy was three years older than Will, and one of his favorite cousins. Charles, Jimmy's older brother, had always been serious and a bit forbidding with his stern face, short hair, and trim mustache; his longhaired, always smiling brother, Jimmy, was much more approachable.

Jimmy was known as the fellow who would "walk a dozen miles for wild flowers, skate all day and dance as long as the band would play."[12] But like his cousin Will and his brother, Charles, Jimmy took his responsibilities as a Lowell seriously. He'd graduated first in his class at Harvard in 1858 and just begun his studies at the law school when the war began. Those studies would have to wait, he decided, until the war had been fought and slavery had been abolished. When he made his announcement of enlistment to his parents at their home on Quincy Street, Anna and Charlie Lowell accepted the news calmly. Their son Charles was already in Washington, securing his position in the army. Anna, their eldest daughter, was studying to be a nurse so that she could care for injured soldiers.

Only Jimmy's sister Harriet, pregnant with her first child, felt a chill of premonition. Her husband, George Putnam, suffered from ill health and could not go to war. Would the wages be exacted from her brothers instead?

Will and Jimmy found many friends among the officers of the Twentieth Massachusetts Volunteer Infantry, all Harvard graduates like them. Jimmy Lowell's old German instructor, George Schmitt, was a captain; so were Jimmy's friends Caspar Crowninshield and Charles Folsom Cabot; Henry Howard Sturgis and Oliver Wendell Holmes, Jr., were second lieutenants; Paul Revere was a major, while his brother Edward was an assistant surgeon (the Reveres were direct descendants of the midnight rider). Not only were these boys friends themselves but their families were all friends and business associates. Most of them were also related, and able to trace kin—cousins, uncles, nephews—going way back. The close connections of the Boston elite carried over to the war: The boys were not alone, and the parents were not alone. Mary Putnam took some comfort in knowing that news, arriving in late-night letters and scribbled notes from the camps and battlegrounds, would be shared between families. Good or bad, it would be shared and it would be borne.

The Twentieth Massachusetts left the training camp at Readville, outside of Boston, on September 4, 1861. They took the train to Groton, Connecticut, and then went by ferry all the way down Long Island Sound to New York City. They had an evening stopover in New York on the way to Washington, and a group of them, Will and Jimmy included, took the opportunity to escape for a couple hours to Delmonico's for one last steak dinner together before reporting to duty. *Occassionem Cognosce*, of a different kind.

After a few days in Washington, D.C., the Twentieth Massachusetts was sent to Poolesville, Maryland. There they waited for battle orders. They sat through long, hot, humid days and restless nights, holed up in their damp campgrounds close to the Potomac River. Finally, in October, the call to battle came. The Twentieth was ordered to cross the Potomac into Virginia, climb the ridge at Ball's Bluff, and carry the day against the unsuspecting rebel forces stationed there. It was to be an easy assignment, and the soldiers set off confidently.

Will Putnam and Oliver Wendell Holmes, Jr., were among the first lines of troops to climb up the bluff. Jimmy Lowell and others came up behind them. But instead of finding a clear path to an easy victory, the soldiers of the Twentieth found themselves in hell. Confederate soldiers had been lying in wait for them. As the first coats of blue appeared, they raised their guns and fired. Men fell, screams rang out; then another line of bluecoats appeared, up and over. Another volley of shots, more falling men, more screaming. Birds flew out from the trees, racing to get away from the noise, the smoke, the acrid, terrible smell.

The adjutant for the Twentieth Massachusetts, Charles Peirson, was shot in the torso. He staggered to the ground, and Will Lowell ran to help him. A volley of bullets: Will was shot straight through the lower abdomen. A gaping hole, searing pain, then the fall to the dirt and leaves and grass. Jimmy, coming up behind, ran to help his cousin and was shot in the thigh. Their captain, George Schmitt, was shot in the head. Holmes waved his sword, crying out, "Will no one follow me?"[13] A bullet hit him directly in the chest. He fell to the ground on his back. Above him, he could see only a faint smudging of blue behind clouds of gray and brown smoke. A tight black formation of fleeing birds. And then the fading of light.

Will ordered the men who had come to help him to leave him be. He knew the wound was mortal and told them that any help they had to offer should go to someone who could be saved. As one of Will's fellow officers wrote to Mary Putnam, "The men were so accustomed to obeying him that I could hardly persuade them . . . after he told them to leave him and help someone else . . ."[14] Fellow officer and Harvard classmate Henry Howard Sturgis dragged Will onto his back and carried him down the bluff to a boat. They crossed to an island in the river where a field hospital had been set up. Will was given morphine for the pain, then left alone while others were treated.

Jimmy Lowell was brought in later to be treated for his leg wound. As he lay on the table, after the bullet had been excised and the wound bandaged, he looked around him. Men screamed and moaned, cried out, and then went horribly silent. Doctors worked in a panic to aid the wounded, and for those soldiers too broken to fix, doses of morphine were given to ease the pain. Jimmy trembled and shook, then closed his eyes against the horror around him. But with his eyes closed, the battle loomed up, terrifying and real. He saw men shot as they crossed up and over the bluff, falling to join a host of corpses on the ground; men scrambling back down the bluff and then diving into the water, trying to escape but collapsing under musket fire; boats hit and sinking down into the river; drowning men, everyone clutching and clawing, dragging one another down in desperation.

But the worst vision of all was of his cousin Will, lying on the ground while blood spread around him, his bowels splayed, his eyes gripped with pain. Jimmy had left Will while he stumbled forward, trying to fight on even with his injured leg. He'd left Will for dead. But had his cousin survived?

The time had come to move. The battle was over and now the goal was to get wounded soldiers to the regimental hospital back at camp. Jimmy went on one cart, ignorant of the fact that his cousin Will Lowell, still alive, was being loaded upon a cart with Oliver Wendell Holmes, Jr. The long line of carts headed out slowly, a bone-cracking ride over uneven grass and dirt. Jimmy cried out in protest. Beside a heavily drugged Will, Holmes passed out from the pain. When he came to, his cart had stopped. He heard the words *beautiful boy* murmured tearfully and felt hands reaching across him. He turned to see the hands pass over Will's face, closing his friend's eyes. Mary Lowell Putnam's son had died.

Jimmy Lowell stayed in the regimental hospital, his leg wound healing but still painful. When his brother, Charles, visited him in Poolesville, he broke down in tears, sobbing. *Will is dead*, he said. Charles nodded. The news was already on the way to Boston.

Mary Lowell Putnam met the train carrying her son's body. He was in a wooden box, his body and face still covered in dirt and blood. She touched his sullied hand, then leaned over and cleared the matted hair back from her son's forehead. Underneath, the skin was clean, unlined. Smooth, like a child's. Words came to her then: *Peace I leave unto you—with you, my peace I give unto you.*[15] Words she had heard her father repeat many times, in sermons and in family prayers at Elmwood. Words that for the first time in her life she understood.

Mary gathered all her strength and arranged to have her son taken home. Governor Andrew accompanied her back to the family's house on Beacon Street. Upon arriving at the front door, Georgina Putnam, Will's sister, opened the door and stepped forward to greet the governor.

"Governor Andrew, we thanked you when we got Willy's commission and we thank you now."

Governor Andrew leaned hard against the doorway. Tears rolled down his cheeks and his shoulders shook. Mary stood beside him, resting one hand on his back.[16]

Mary bathed her son one last time, then dressed him in the clothes he'd left behind when he went to join the Twentieth Massachusetts. She planned a funeral for him and sat straight and tall through the readings and the address. Then she and Samuel, Georgina, and all the cousins and aunts and uncles followed the procession that carried the body of William Lowell Putnam across the Charles and down Brattle Street to Mount Auburn cemetery. Will was buried amid the grass and fallen leaves, one pale stone on a hillside dotted with the stones of cousins and uncles and aunts. Mary remembered how as a boy Will had loved to sled down the long hill of Boston Common. As a student, he'd loved the sonnets of Shakespeare, quoting lines to his mother over dinner. *Thy eternal summer shall not fade . . . / Nor shall death brag thou wander'st in his shade . . . / So long as men can breathe, and eyes can see,/ So long lives this, and this gives life to thee.*[17]

In a memorial essay Mary composed for Will, she wrote about "the sunshine in his light locks and the warm hue of his hazel eyes. . . . so much greatness and beauty inhabiting a mortal form should [not] fade from earth and leave no record of its passage . . . If we may ask his country to hold him in her memory . . . it must be not only because he laid down for her an almost untasted existence, but because he gave up with it projects of great and noble accomplishment."[18]

She asked his female cousins, including Jimmy and Charles's sister Harriet, to work together sewing and embroidering a banner in his honor. The ensign was made of silk and embroidered on one side with an image taken from the Lowell family coat of arms: an arm with its hand grasping an upward-held sword. On the other side of the banner, a pine tree, the symbol of freedom since the days of the American Revolution. The phrase *Stand in the Evil Day* was stitched in below the tree. The words came from the Bible: *Wherefore take unto you the whole armour of God, that ye may be able to withstand in the evil day, and having done all, to stand.*[19] The banner would take its place on the fields of battle, where Will Putnam no longer could.

In November, Harriet gave birth to a baby boy. She named him after her slain cousin: William Lowell Putnam.

Jimmy Lowell convalesced in Boston through the fall and winter, but by February 1862, he was back with his regiment, again at camp in Poolesville. His father wrote to him encouragingly: "I never doubted your courage . . . I have never . . . had a moment's anxiety about your principles, your conduct, or your doing your duty on all occasion and under all circumstances . . . My darling boy, from the time you entered the world until now you have been nothing but a source of unmingled pleasure and joy to your mother and me."[20]

In early spring, the Twentieth Massachusetts was sent to fight in the Peninsula Campaign, an operation devised by General McClellan to capture the Confederate capital of Richmond, Virginia. The Twentieth and other regiments were ferried down to Fort Monroe; they would then work their way back up the peninsula between the York and James rivers, arriving at Richmond from the south, its most vulnerable point. Charles Lowell was at Fort Monroe with his cavalry division when Jimmy and his regiment arrived from Poolesville. He was able to see his brother for a few moments before the Twentieth moved out to begin the march north. The brothers clasped hands, and then Jimmy was off.

The hike north was long and miserable. The troops had to walk through marshy ground and then cross over the Chickahominy River to arrive in position to lay siege on Richmond. Mosquitoes swarmed and the air was heavy with humidity, heat, and churned-up clouds of swollen pollen. Dr. Nathan Hayward, another Harvard man and surgeon with the Twentieth, wrote home that the Chickahominy was as "an alligator, rattlesnake, diabolical looking swamp as ever I saw. . . . Dante would have introduced it into his Inferno."[21]

The fighting outside of Richmond was intermittent but rough: "Three a.m. always finds us in line of battle."[22] The conditions were terrible, with heavy rains creating muddy roads. The heat was oppressive, and biting gnats and flies joined the legions of mosquitoes. There was an increasing lack of basic necessities, including fresh water. Jimmy came down with dysentery and suffered from diarrhea. He grew thin, his rib bones sharp and jutting, and he often felt weak and tired. But when the time came to fight, to again lay siege against Richmond, in skirmishes up and down hillsides and in meadows and fields, Jimmy rallied his strength. He gathered his men around him, encouraged them with a few words, and then led them forward, all fatigue and illness and uncertainty hidden in a tunic of bravery and confidence. It was what his men needed, Jimmy knew: to believe that victory in the siege against Richmond was possible. Jimmy hid his own doubts about the campaign. But, tightening the belt around his thin waist, he carried on.

Anna Lowell, Jimmy's older sister, had trained as a nurse and was now stationed close by the fighting on the peninsula. She'd been assigned to work on the *Daniel Webster,* an old ocean steamship converted into a floating hospital for the Union army. The ship was anchored at Harrison's Landing on the James River, where its nurses and doctors would take on wounded soldiers, care for them, and then carry them north to hospitals and rest. Anna knew both her brothers were nearby her somewhere, but she had no idea how to reach them. When she saw a familiar face from Boston, she asked after them. In this way, news was shared. She learned that Jimmy was in the thick of the siege against Richmond. The fighting was bad and the number of dead and wounded on both sides rose daily. When the rebels were driven back from a held position, they burned all the supplies left behind, poisoned wells, and destroyed fields. Food grew ever more scarce for the Union soldiers and fresh water was impossible to find. Men died not only from the battles but also from diseases, the result of drinking bad water and living in unhealthy conditions.

Anna wondered, *Are my brothers safe?* But she heard no news to the contrary, and so she allowed herself to hope.

By the end of June, Jimmy's company fell into a battle at Glendale, close to Richmond. The Union forces were pulling out of the peninsula. General McClellan's planned siege against Richmond had failed. Oliver Wendell Holmes, Jr., recovered from his wound at Ball's Bluff, was on the line with Jimmy when the fight at Glendale began. He looked over to his cousin and Jimmy nodded. Holmes nodded back, and then the two began the charge, trying to hold off the Confederates while the Union army behind them retreated. When Holmes looked again for Jimmy, he had vanished from sight. That last image of his cousin nodding to him across the line would haunt Holmes for the rest of his life.

Jimmy had taken a hit to the abdomen, much like the shot that had felled Will Putnam. He tried to stand but couldn't rise to his knees. He asked his men to go on without him; then he ordered them to: "Don't mind me, men, go forward."[23] An orderly carried him to the field hospital set up in the house just beyond the woods, in a place called Nelson's Farm. Dr. Hayward of the Twentieth gave Jimmy one look and dosed him with morphine.

The order to retreat came in and was repeated up and down the Union line. Jimmy refused to be moved; his wound was too terrible, the outcome too certain. He told his men to leave him behind at Nelson's Farm. Giving his sword to one of his fellow officers, he asked that his father be told of how his son had been "dressing his line when he fell."[24] He then asked to be laid down beside a wounded man from his own company. He wanted to die beside a man who had fought under his command. Darkness came quickly after the sun set, the heavily leafed trees hiding any last remaining light of day. The officers and men of the Twentieth Massachusetts, those still standing, knew it was time to leave. As soon as they retreated into the shadows of the trees, rebel forces surrounded the farm.

When the Twentieth Massachusetts arrived back at Harrison's Landing two days later, they were met by Anna Lowell, desperately searching for Jimmy.

News of the defeat at Glendale had reached her. Officers from Jimmy's company told Anna how he had been wounded, and that he lay in a farmhouse now behind enemy lines. Anna tried desperately to get passage through to Jimmy, but all routes were closed to her. She was given her brother's sword to take home to her family. She accepted it as a last memento, for she had been advised against hoping that he might have survived his injury. Anna returned to the boat on the river, worn-out and in despair. A few days later, the boat set sail for Boston.

It was not until weeks later that Charles Lowell was able to find the Confederate doctor who had treated his brother at Nelson's Farm. He learned that James Jackson Lowell had survived four days and died on the Fourth of July. He had been buried at the farm, under a tree behind the house. Charles vowed that after the war his brother's body would be retrieved and reinterred in the family plot at Mount Auburn. He wrote to his mother, "I am glad the little fellow was not moved to Richmond, merely to die and be buried where we could never find him."[25]

Charlie and Anna Lowell gathered with family in their home on Quincy Street. They had no body yet to bury but a terrible loss to grieve over. Anna hung black bunting at the windows and stopped all the clocks in the house. Black armbands had been ordered and would be delivered soon. Jamie Lowell came to offer what he could. He had buried children of his own and knew there was little comfort to be given, but he tried. He stood beside his brother Charlie as Charlie waited at the window for a visit from his daughter Harriet. Her little baby William, nicknamed the "beautiful Bunch," with his beaming smile and dimpled cheeks, would bring some solace. But the grief would remain.

More deaths in the family. Warren Dutton Russell was the grandson of Elizabeth Cutts Lowell, daughter of the Old Judge, who had married her brother's law clerk, Warren Dutton, in 1806. In the spring of 1861, at the age of sixteen, Warren's little brother Francis joined the Artillery Unit of the Regular Army. Four months later, he was back home again, recovering from wounds received while fighting in Virginia. Warren, his older brother by four years, saw his injured little brother and decided it was time now for him to go and fight. He signed up with the Eighteenth Massachusetts Volunteer Infantry. On August 30, 1862, he was killed during the Second Battle of Bull Run. Warren had been "standing close by the colors of his regiment, waving his sword and cheering on his men in a charge" when "grape-shot struck him in the neck and killed him instantly."[26] He was buried where he fell, and a small monument was erected, made of fieldstone and cannonballs. Francis died on May 11, 1864, from disease contracted in camp. He was nineteen years old.

On January 1, 1863, President Lincoln signed the Emancipation Proclamation. Thousands gathered at the Tremont Temple in Boston to celebrate. Hundreds more gathered at the Music Hall, including James Russell Lowell, his close friends Charles Eliot Norton and Henry Longfellow, and his old friends Ralph Waldo Emerson and John Greenleaf Whittier, the man who so many years before had asked Jamie to write an ode for the antislavery movement. Now the blessings promised had come true: Jamie wrote to a friend that finally the country was "on the side of freedom, justice, and sound policy."[27] Emerson read aloud to the gathered crowd his poem entitled "The Boston Hymn:"

> To-day unbind the captive,
> So only are ye unbound;
> Lift up a people from the dust,
> Trump of their rescue, sound![28]

Slavery was no more, on paper and in the law. But the war to end it in practice was still on.

Governor Andrew sought out Charles Lowell's help. The time had come to put together a new regiment, a unit made up entirely of volunteer black soldiers. Andrew needed Lowell's assistance in recruiting white officers for the regiment. The man to lead the group had already been chosen: Charles Lowell's good friend Col. Robert Shaw, the son of Francis and Sarah Shaw. Shaw seconded Andrew's call for help, and Lowell responded with enthusiasm. This had been a dream of his ever since the day he'd witnessed, along with Henry Higginson, the sight of Anthony Burns being taken back into slavery from Boston. Lincoln had made all blacks free; now Charles Lowell would help them organize to fight with honor and dignity.

Many young men, well known to Charles and well regarded, had applied for a position in his cavalry unit. Charles went through the list and chose those men whom he thought would be good candidates for Shaw's regiment—all fair-minded abolitionists—and then he wrote to them, suggesting that instead of joining the cavalry, they might like to become part of the Fifty-fourth Massachusetts, a regiment sure to make history. Wilky James, the younger brother of William and Henry James, joined up to fight with the Fifty-fourth, and Lowell recruited his young cousin Cabot Russel to come along, as well. Wilky and Cabot had been students of Frank Sanborn, one of John Brown's chief New England supporters. They were devoted to the cause of black freedom,

proud to lead the black soldiers who volunteered for the regiment, and pleased
to be serving with Robert Shaw.

But the father of Cabot Jackson Russel was not pleased. William Russel
had tried hard to keep his only son out of the war. After Cabot was suspended from Harvard in the fall of 1861 (for failure "to attend to his studies"[29]),
his father sent him on a trip out west. William knew that Cabot was a committed abolitionist—he had a portrait of John Brown hanging over his bed
at home—and feared that his son would join the army now that he had been
expelled from college. Cabot Russel had already told his father that if anything happened to his Lowell cousins, he would "want to enlist."[30] Russel
senior hoped that a western adventure would cool Cabot's ardor and settle
him out of harm's way. As soon as Cabot heard of Jimmy Lowell's death,
however, he wrote immediately to his father, "Now I shall certainly go."[31]
He returned east, and by September, he had joined up. When the Fifty-
fourth Massachusetts regiment was formed in the spring of 1863, he applied
to join and was brought in as a second lieutenant. He was eighteen years
old.

Charles Lowell and Robert Shaw's sister Josephine (called "Effie") met in the
early months of 1863, when Charles was home recruiting officers for his regiment and helping Shaw recruit for the Fifty-fourth. Many parties were held in
Boston that winter, not only to rouse support for the Union efforts (the Union
Club was formed, with headquarters located in the former mansion of Abbott
Lawrence) but also to give the young soldiers a chance—for just an evening or
two—to forget the savagery of war. Charles met Effie at one of these evening
balls. By March, he and Effie Shaw were engaged to be married. James Russell
Lowell, who had known both Charles and Effie all their lives (he and Maria
had been good friends of her parents, Sarah and Frank), now wrote to Sarah
Shaw about "this good luck of Charlie's" and that Effie's "force of character &
good sense" would "assure both to herself & Charlie a happy life." He ended
the letter with hope: "I believe it is one of the most happy things in the world,
as we grow older, to have as many ties as possible with whatever is best in our
own past, and to be pledged as deeply as may be to our own youth. . . ."[32]

The Fifty-fourth Massachusetts was honored with a parade through
Boston before heading south to war. The streets thronged with well-wishers
and the city was decorated with banners and flags. Colonel Shaw, on horseback,
led his 1,007 enlisted men and 39 officers around the Boston Common and
then down Tremont Street to the state house. Finally, they paraded through
Beacon Hill. At the home belonging to Mary and Samuel Putnam, the entire
company paused. Colonel Shaw raised his hat from his head and offered it in

salute to Mary, in remembrance of her son Will and in thanks for her gift to
the regiment of a splendid blue banner, inscribed with the words *In Hoc Signo
Vinces.*[33] "By this sign you shall conquer": used by the Emperor Constantine
in his fourth-century battles and adopted by the Christian crusaders in the
Middle Ages. Now raised by a black regiment headed to war.

Robert Shaw later wrote in a letter to his wife, Annie, "The more I think
of the passage of the Fifty-fourth through Boston, the more wonderful it seems
to me. Just remember our own doubts and fears, and other people's sneering
and pitying remarks, when we began last winter, and then look at the perfect
triumph of last Thursday. We have gone quietly along, forming the regiment,
and at last left Boston amidst a greater enthusiasm than has been seen since
the first three-months troops left for the war. . . . Truly, I ought to be thankful
for all my happiness . . . and if the raising of coloured troops prove such a benefit to the country, and to the blacks, as many people think it will, I shall
thank God a thousand times that I was led to take my share in it."[34]

On July 18, 1863, the Fifty-fourth Massachusetts was sent to attack Fort Wagner on South Carolina's Morris Island. As the sun lowered in the western sky,
Colonel Shaw led his men up and onto the parapet of the fort, scaling its
earthen walls to arrive at the top. Upon sighting the Union soldiers, Confederates holed up inside the fort let loose a torrent of hand grenades, exploding
shells, and bullets. Shaw was hit in the chest and fell forward into the fort. The
soldiers of the Fifty-fourth did not hesitate, but continued their climb up and
across the parapet. There they raised the Union flag, waving it high overhead.
Then they clambered down into the fort to fight. Cabot Russel was hit and
ordered his men to carry on: "Do not touch me; move on men! Follow your
colors."[35] When his friend Captain Simpkins attempted to pick Cabot up
and carry him back to safety, Simpkins was hit by a bullet. He fell dead across
Cabot. The battle turned in favor of the Confederates, and two hours later, it
was over. By day's end, with at least two hundred forty-six Union soldiers
killed and eight hundred wounded, and fewer than one hundred eighty Confederate casualties (thirty-six dead), the Confederate army still held the fort.

News of the disastrous battle traveled back to Boston. Shaw and more
than half of his officers were dead. Cabot Russel's father raced down to South
Carolina in search of his son, but there was no injured man in the hospitals,
no dead body accounted for. The Confederate commander, Brigadier General
Hagood, confirmed that Robert Shaw had died in the assault on Fort Wagner
and had been buried with his black soldiers in a mass grave. Cabot Russel's
body was never recovered and the Lowells and Russels presumed that the
eighteen-year-old—a few days shy of his nineteenth birthday—had also been

killed and then buried alongside the slain black soldiers of the Fifty-fourth Massachusetts. The mass burial was intended by the Confederates to be seen as a degradation of the white officers, but the families refused to let it be seen in that way. Frank Shaw, Robert's father, instead demanded that the black men of the Fifty-fourth and their white officers, equal in death as in life, be allowed to rest there always, buried side by side at Fort Wagner, joined for all time.

Charles Lowell felt a heavy burden as the friends of his youth and his family members fell all around him. He wrote to Effie, "I am under very sacred bonds to be good and gentle and noble—to my Aunt Mary, I must be Willy—to my mother and father, Jim, and now to your Mother, as far as I can, Rob."[36] He would fight now not only for those slain in Baltimore back in '61; not only to free the blacks from southern chains; and not only for the duty he owed to world as a Lowell. He wrote to Effie, "I wish the President had said a rebel soldier shall die for every Negro soldier sold into slavery. He ought to have said so."[37] The fight was still about slavery, but it was also about the love he had felt for his friends and cousins, and the need to assuage his grief over their deaths. To right the imbalance made by their sacrifices. To tip the scales to justice.

In the fall of 1863, Charles married Effie Shaw. A year later, awaiting battle orders in the Shenandoah Valley, he wrote her one of the few letters in which he revealed a fear of being killed. Effie was pregnant with their first child and Charles was anxious to see his wife, and to be there when the baby was born: "I don't want to be shot until I've had a chance to come home. I have no idea that I shall be hit, but I want so much not to now, that sometimes it frightens me."[38]

But by mid-October, Charles wrote to Effie that he was safe—"so safe do I feel tonight"—and then to his mother, he wrote, "We are in a glorious country, with fine air to breathe and fine views to enjoy; we are kept very active, and have done a good deal of work. I have done my share, I think—but there's nothing to make a letter of . . . I only write this to make you write to me. Isn't it lucky that I keep always well and hearty?"[39]

Three days later, he was dead.

The Battle of Cedar Creek began early on the morning of October 19. Charles was shot twice during the battle, the first time when a ball launched by a Confederate soldier ricocheted off a stone wall, pierced the sleeve of his coat, and traveled up along his body, striking him hard in the chest and becoming embedded in the muscle there. Charles found it suddenly hard to breathe; he felt clammy and ill, and when he tried to speak, he found that he could not; he had lost the use of his voice. He was certain that his wound was mortal, but he refused to leave the field. There was still work to be done. He asked his men to place him on a horse so that he could lead his soldiers forward. Strapped into the saddle and with his officer's staff at his side, he rode up to the front of the Second Massachusetts Cavalry unit. He gave the order to charge in a hush, for he could only whisper; then an aide called it out, loud and clear. Three thousand mounted cavalry men responded, with Charles leading the way forward into a "living wall of the enemy . . . a leaden sheet of fire . . . [shots falling] in perfect showers. . . ."[40]

Charles was hit again, this time by a bullet that severed his spinal cord and left him paralyzed. As he fell from his horse, his adjutant, Henry Alvord, reached to catch him and lower him to the ground. As the Union troops continued forward toward victory, Charles was carried back to the field hospital. He was placed on a narrow table. All around him on the floor lay the wounded and the dying. Capt. Rufus Smith was one of these men. He had been shot through the stomach and had no chance of surviving the injury. He had been given morphine for the pain but still cried out in misery. He did not want to die.

"I have always been able to count on you," Charles now told Smith. "You were the bravest of the brave; now you must be strong, you must meet this as you have other trials. Be steady, I count on you."[41]

As the day passed into night, Charles called the attending doctor, Oscar DeWolf, to his side. He told the doctor that he had no pain but only wanted to talk a bit. He told DeWolf about his parents, his wife, their coming child, and his impending death. About Effie, he said, "She will bear it, Doctor, better than you and I think . . ."[42] He dictated a letter to Effie, then managed to write a few words of his own. He left orders for Henry Alvord, detailed directions for their unit to follow in the coming day. Late in the evening, he and DeWolf fell asleep side by side.

DeWolf was awakened in the early hours of the morning by Lowell's hand on his head. "Well, doctor, you and I have had a little nap," Lowell told him.[43]

As dawn broke, Charles Lowell's fellow officers gathered at the door to his room. One by one, they were allowed in to see him one last time. Lowell took each of their hands in good-bye. Caspar Crowninshield, who had served with Will Putnam and Jimmy Lowell in the Twentieth Massachusetts, began to cry when Lowell reached for him. He fell to his knees, covering Charles's hands with his own and dropping his head forward, as if asking for penance: penance for living on. Then Lowell's men came through, one after the other. After taking his leave of each of them, Lowell laid back on his table to rest. His breath was labored, his face pale. At nine in the morning, he died. The sergeant who had been charged with keeping an eye on Lowell came to find DeWolf, his voice breaking as he reported the news: "The Colonel does not breathe."[44]

Two days later, the letter announcing Charles Russell Lowell's promotion to brigadier general, signed by President Lincoln, arrived at camp. Along with it came the promotion of Gen. Wesley Merritt to major general. Merritt took his letter and that of Charles Lowell and, shaking his head sadly, said, "I would gladly give up this if he could only take that."[45]

Before they were married, Charles had written a letter to Effie confiding his belief in the beauty of the world: "Everything is ours to enjoy, nothing is ours to encage; open, we are as wide as nature; closed, we are too narrow to enjoy a sea-shell's beauty . . ."[46] Effie could only pray now that heaven was as bountiful and full of wonder for her husband as earth had been.

The funeral service for Charles Lowell was held on October 28, 1864, in the newly built Appleton Chapel of Harvard College. His body was carried the two blocks from Anna and Charles Lowell's house on Quincy Street to the church through a cold drizzle of rain. Edward Waldo Emerson, son of Ralph Waldo Emerson and a student at Harvard, watched in the rain as the coffin was carried up the steps of the chapel; he would always remember, "when the sudden gusts blew the yellow leaves in showers from the college elms, hearing the beautiful notes of Pleyel's Hymn, the tune to which soldiers were borne to burial. . . ."[47]

Once inside the chapel, the coffin was placed upon the communion table. It was draped in the Union flag, then Lowell's sword, hilt, and scabbard were laid on top, beside his cap and gauntlets. The altar behind was buried beneath flowers and branches that had come from all over New England: scented geraniums, Cape jasmine, and camellias mixed with forest fern and pine. Their combined perfume of earth and rain wafted across the coffin and down through the rows of pews. Vines of ivy and myrtle wound around the pulpit; pots of chrysanthemums, purple and peach and gold, lined the chancel.

All the connected families were there, Lowells and Putnams and Jacksons. Mary Lowell Putnam sat beside her brother Charlie and sister-in-law Anna.* James Russell Lowell was accompanied by his second wife, Frances, and daughter Mabel; John Amory Lowell by his wife, Elizabeth. Rows of females stretched out behind John Amory, sisters and cousins, daughters and aunts: Harriet, Anna, Georgina, Ellen, Elizabeth, Sara, Caroline; the old aunts, Anna and Amory and Becca. Old Dr. James Jackson, who long ago had been helped by Frances Cabot Lowell to pursue his medical studies, was there. The Lawrences, including Amos A. Lawrence, also attended, as did the Appletons, including Fanny and her husband, Henry Wadsworth Longfellow. Other mourners included Senator Sumner. Frank Sanborn, Thomas Wentworth Higginson, the Shaws, the Crown-

---

* Mary's husband Samuel Putnam had died in December 1861.

inshields, and the Perkins. Alongside the men and women of Beacon Hill were Charles's classmates from Harvard, some of them on crutches, others leaning heavily on one another, worn-out by war and by sorrow.

The Reverend George Putnam gave the funeral address. He was the father of Harriet's husband, George, and longtime Unitarian minister of the First Church of Roxbury. He began his address by listing the men and boys who had already died in the war, brothers, near and far cousins, and friends: James Jackson Lowell, William Lowell Putnam, Robert Shaw and Cabot Russel, James Savage and Stephen Perkins, Warren Dutton Russell, Francis Dutton Russell. He told the gathered mourners that if Charles could speak, he "would bid us couple their name and memory with his. And they . . . would gladly have his funeral rites made theirs, and their only ones, by any thought or mention of their names with his. They loved him so much, and looked up to him with such ardor of admiration and affection!"

The Reverend Putnam spoke about Charles's life, his education and work and then his decision to join the army: "He would live for his country, and die for it, if so ordered." He concluded his address by addressing the matter that weighed so heavily upon the hearts and minds of those gathered: the toll of death and blood exacted by the War Between the States.

"This mighty mother of us all, our country, . . . steeps her soil in her children's most precious blood. . . . she does it not in cruelty, but in love, that she may preserve her own glorious life, her own imperial sovereignty, and her benignant power to bless her children, and fold them under her brooding wings, to nourish and keep them, as she only can, in freedom, in honor, and in peace . . . The young life which so lately animated the form that lies shrouded there . . . she has paid for it,—paid *him* . . . paid him in the splendid sphere of duty and sacrifice she opened to him . . . in the loftier spirit she breathed into him, whereby to do valiantly, to live greatly, to die willingly."[48]

He was silent for a moment, his prepared address completed. Then he walked to the coffin. Holding his arms out before him, he said in a low voice, "Are we paying too heavy a price for our country's freedom?"[49]

There was no answer.

Henry Lee Higginson and Henry Alvord, along with four other pallbearers, moved forward to lift the coffin onto their shoulders and carry their fallen friend from the chapel. Rain poured down on the procession that wound its way to Mount Auburn Cemetery. As the coffin of Charles Russell Lowell was lowered into the ground, the band played "The Dead March" by Handel. Charles was interred beside his brother, James, and his cousin Will. Their uncle Jamie stood by, shoulders bowed. Grief for the three boys formed verses in his brain: "Is earth too poor to give us/ Something to live for here that shall outlive us?"[50]

Part Six

REINVENTION

A poet is the most contradictory creature imaginable, he respects
nothing and reveres everything, but what he loves he makes his own.
And this then is just the touchstone of the true legend, it can be
made over in any image, but always remains itself.

—AMY LOWELL,
PREFACE TO *LEGENDS*

20

June 9, 1888

Every thing is happy now,
Every thing is upward striving;
'Tis as easy now for the heart to be true
As for the grass to be green or skies to be blue . . .
—JAMES RUSSELL LOWELL, *THE VISION OF SIR LAUNFAL*

A light breeze skimmed over the front steps of St. Paul's Church in Brookline, Massachusetts, stirring the lace-trimmed hem of Elizabeth Lowell's dress. She stood at the open doorway but turned for just a moment to look back at the coachman. Patrick Burns had been with the family for years and had taught Bessie all she knew of horses, and more. Burns nodded at her now and she took her father's arm. The two of them, father and daughter, proceeded forward through the door and into the church.

Inside, William Lowell Putnam waited for Bessie. Will was her cousin, and as such, she had been aware of him most of her life. But awareness had grown to something more over the past few years, to interest, then affection, then love. All her family trusted Will, but no one trusted him more than Bessie. For Will, she would give up her role as stand-in mother for her little sister and manager of the family home, called Sevenels. For him, she would start a family of her own, manage a house of her own. With him, she would create a new branch of the Lowells and the Putnams, adding to an already-outstretched tree.

A family tree of Lowells and Putnams, to whom so much had been granted: That was the lesson taught to Bessie by her mother. And to whom so many choices had been given: That was the lesson from her father; to which he added the obligation to choose well—not only for oneself but for the family and the community. *Occasionem Cognosce.* Recognize opportunity, seize your chance, make your choice. Bessie had chosen Will, and he, in turn, had chosen her.

She was twenty-six years old, sturdy and sober and sure of herself. Her hair was thick and brown, and her eyes were hazel. She had the soft Lawrence chin of her mother and the broad forehead of a Lowell. Her thin lips were usually drawn tight in a line of determination, but today they were shaped into irrepressible satisfaction. Will, twenty-seven years old, had been named for Will Putnam, who died in the Civil War just a month before he was born. It was Will's smile—he'd been nicknamed "the beautiful Bunch" as a baby—that had saved his grandparents, his aunts and uncles, and his mother, Harriet, from all-consuming grief after the deaths of Willy, then Jimmy, then Charles. Little Will had brought assurance of life everlasting; the souls of lost sons appearing in the face, the gestures, the laugh of a baby.

Even as a grown man, Will laughed and smiled easily, and his friendliness was infectious; it was returned. He was not a handsome man, for he looked like a walrus, with his bristling whiskers and bulging eyes. But he had that smile, and he was kind and smart. Across the lines of Brahmin families, he was trusted not only with money, for he invested for many of them, but with their confidences. He kept secrets well, and money grew under his care.

Fourteen-year old Amy, Bessie's younger sister, had prepared for days for the wedding. How to greet guests, how to sit still in church, how to eat daintily, and not too much. At an engagement party for her elder sister, Katie, Amy had eaten so many plates of rice that at the end of the evening she could not button her coat. She never wore that coat again. In a self-portrait she drew just days before Bessie's wedding, she'd sketched herself in profile: sweet smile, straight nose, hair worn in a single braided plait down her back—and a belly that looked as if she carried a large parcel beneath her dress, bound across her middle. Today, she wore a dress of pale green silk over white muslin that billowed when she walked and hid her girth. A silver ribbon held back her hair, combed smooth for the day.

Katie had come up from New York City, where she lived with her husband, Alfred Roosevelt, first cousin of Teddy. Her two eldest children were with her, Elfrida and James, but baby Katharine, not even a year old, had been left at home with her nurse. Katie had dressed for the wedding in the sober colors of gray and lilac befitting a society mother. Her hair was neatly piled under a voluminous hat of soft felt decorated with white ostrich feathers and silk ribbons; around her neck she wore a silk scarf. Her gloves were white satin, with pale violet stitching at the wrist. She sat upright in the second-row pew, her children quiet beside her.

Percy, Bessie's eldest brother, had been standing by the doorway, greeting guests as they arrived at St. Paul's, serving as head usher for his sister and Will. With his claret necktie and striped flannel suit, he stood out from most of the Brahmin men, but of course he would. His choice had been made six years earlier. He'd been back to Boston occasionally since then, checking in with family and coming back to serve as best man at the wedding of Teddy Wharton and Edith Jones. Now he was home again, this time to stand for Bessie. He had walked away from his own engagement to a Brahmin woman when he decided to leave Boston and the family business to travel far away. Augustus had always told his sons they should do what they want, but he'd cautioned them, "Whatever your hand finds to do, do it with all your might."[1] Percival chose to travel, and he was covering as much ground as he could.

He ended up, again and again, in the Far East, Japan and Korea. Using charm and persistence, he'd been granted permission to travel in remote areas where Westerners were seldom allowed. He stayed in local inns (using two futons as a mattress and rolling up another as a pillow) and ate local delicacies, although he noted later, "We are not inwardly contrived to thrive solely on rice and pickles."[2] While in Japan, he climbed to the top of Mounts Fuji and Ontake, and scaled three active volcanoes, Shirane, Asama, and Bandai. Wherever he went, he carried his journal, his camera, and his telescope. Using his journals and photos for inspiration, he decided to write travel books. He published one about Korea, *Choson: The Land of the Morning Calm*, in 1885, and another about Japan, *The Soul of the Far East*, which had just come out. Two more books, *Noto: An Unexplored Corner of Japan* and *Occult Japan*, would come out in the next few years. The books sold well, and started a Far East travel trend among New Englanders.

No matter how far away he traveled, Percy stayed close to his family, especially his mother and his sisters Bessie and Amy. He sent long letters to his mother, Katharine, describing surroundings she would never see for herself: "my garden is a miniature range of hills on one side, a pond on the other. One plum tree is blooming now, another comes along shortly, and a cherry tree will peep into my bedroom window all ablush toward the beginning of April. . . ."[3] To his sisters, he wrote letters of advice, taking his role as eldest brother seriously. "And after all, life itself is but one long journey which is not only misspent but an unhappy one if one does not interest oneself in whatever one encounters," he wrote to Bessie. He ended by reminding her, "You are fortunate in having a family who care for what is worth caring for . . . Good-bye, sweet puss."[4]

Bessie's brother Lawrence sat in a pew with his wife, Anna, on one side and his mother on the other. Anna was the great-granddaughter of Francis Cabot Lowell, and Lawrence's third cousin. Anna's brother, also named Francis Cabot Lowell, had been Lawrence's good friend at Harvard. Francis introduced his sister to his friend, and in the summer of 1876, with still one year left to go at Harvard, Lawrence escorted Anna down to Boston Harbor to see her off on the steamer ship *China,* bound for Europe. When she returned eight months later, Lawrence was there at the docks, waiting for her. Two years later, they were married at King's Chapel in Boston.

They lived now at the foot of Beacon Hill, just a stroll away from Lawrence's fledgling law practice on State Street. But Lawrence never strolled; he walked with impatience, never fast enough for his own desires. As a college student, he had simply run everywhere he wanted to go. Even dressed up in evening clothes, coming to and from a Harvard dance, he would run, mile after mile. He set college records in distance running: it was his nature to move and to move fast. As a lawyer and a husband, it was more proper to walk. So he walked fast. Now he sat, his body still but for the tapping of one foot, up and down, insistent on the flagstone floor of the church.

Katharine Lowell reached over to set a quieting hand on her son's shaking leg. Lawrence took his mother's hand and gave it a gentle squeeze. He noticed how thin his mother's hand was, how dry the skin. His mother had been a beautiful woman, but illness—and the treatment for it—had sapped her vitality. She suffered from Bright's disease, the same kidney disease that had killed Teddy Roosevelt's wife after giving birth to daughter Alice. Similar to Mrs. Roosevelt, it was childbirth that had brought on Katharine's illness. The disease had started with the birth of Bessie and her twin brother, Roger. When Roger died a year later, in 1863, Katharine succumbed further. The symptoms of the disease, including back pain, swelling of the face and hands, and nausea and fever, were bad enough. But the treatment included bloodletting and diuretics, which left Katharine weak and listless. Augustus took her and the children off to Europe, hoping that the more temperate conditions there, along with long sojourns at mountain spas and a careful diet, would help his wife.

During the journey to Europe, Katharine stayed in her stateroom, leaving Augustus to care not only for their own children, two boys and two girls under the age of nine, but also for three young Gardner cousins they were shepherding over to waiting parents. Nannies were brought along but proved to be of little help. The older nanny was seasick the entire voyage. The younger one, of sound stomach but with little sense, allowed the children to play wherever they wanted to, a dangerous choice when traveling aboard a 2,500-ton paddle steamer. Lawrence, eight years old at the time, remembered one afternoon spent playing out on the open roof of the deckhouse. Somehow he ended up hanging by his hands from the side of the roof, his legs dangling over open sea. His father arrived just in time to rescue him, pulling him up to safety. What Augustus remembered of the voyage were all the buttons he had to do up, morning after morning, dressing his boatload of children.

The boys were left to study in Paris while Katharine, Augustus, and the girls spent the next two years traveling from spa to spa. During their voyage back to Boston in 1866, Katharine felt so much stronger that she was able to help out with the children. She spent her afternoons above deck with them, and was enchanted by the pod of dolphins that seemed to want to accompany them all the way home. Lawrence wrote a letter to his tutor back in Paris: "we sore the spouting of wales and percy and I sore some porposis . . ."[5]

Now, on this perfect day in June 1888, Katharine Lowell could forget the recurring bouts of illness. The disease still flared up again and again, but the past year had been an easy one. Although she had been subjected to debilitating treatments, she felt stronger just sitting in church, her family around her. She watched as Bessie was escorted by Augustus down the aisle to meet a beaming Will. The young couple then turned to face the Reverend L. K. Storrs and the ceremony began. Katharine and Augustus had been married on a June day as lovely as this one: blue skies, soft breeze, petals of apple blossoms and pear floating in the air, scenting it with hope and joy. Then, as now, there had been a gathering of old New England families on a sun-blessed summer day. The future and the past joined together.

Katharine had received many offers of marriage as a young woman. Not only was her father, Abbott Lawrence, one of the wealthiest men in Boston but Katharine was well educated and lively. She spoke French, Italian, and German; she sang like a lark and played piano like a prodigy. She loved to dance, and she recorded the details of the many dances, hops, and balls she attended—and what she wore to them—in the diaries she kept throughout her teens. "A pink bodice with a pink silk shirt very short, worn over a white muslin dress. A fall of wide black lace went round the waist. White satin shoes with pink rosettes, a hat trimmed with pink satin ribbon, black mitts with pink bows, two pearl bracelets, the skirt looped up over the white of the sides with large pink rosettes . . ."[6]

Louis-Napoléon Bonaparte, soon to be Emperor Napoléon III, noticed Katharine at the Opera House in Paris when she was eighteen years old. The forty-two-year-old traveled to England, where Katharine was living then with her parents. Her father was serving as United States ambassador to Great Britain under President Zachary Taylor. Taylor had wanted Abbott to be his vice president, but Abbott had declined, asking instead for the posting to England.

Bonaparte asked Abbott for his daughter's hand in marriage—as Katharine noted in her diary, "if agreeable the Prince would come over and the negotiation would be made"—but Abbott said no. He wanted his daughter "to marry an American."[7] And she did: Augustus Lowell was an eighth-generation American and a New Englander to boot. She first met him at a dance in

Newport in 1848, but it took time for the attraction to develop and the liaison to take. When they finally did marry on June 1, 1854, the joining was momentous. Their marriage consolidated control over an extended empire of mills, railroads, banks, and trading houses. Two Massachusetts towns had been named for the families—Lowell and Lawrence—and the marriage made the geography complete.

Before the Civil War, Katharine and Augustus had lived both at Bromley Vale in Roxbury and in Boston, where they rented a town house for the winter months. When the family returned to America in 1866, Augustus discovered that the lands of Bromley Vale were going to be bisected by a new train line. His father, John Amory Lowell, had moved almost full-time to the city by then, living at number 7 Park Street, but his two older aunts, Anna and Amory, daughters of John the Rebel, still lived in their small cottage on the grounds; they had named it "Bromley Side."[8] Augustus reassured the two old ladies they could stay as long as they wished, and he secured their rights in the house and the property around it. But he sold the rest of the land and Bromley Vale with it, and began looking for a new country place for his wife and children.

A daughter was born to Augustus and Katharine in May 1870 and died the same day; they gave her the name of May and buried her beside Roger. In 1874, their last child was born, a girl. Augustus had wanted to name her Amory after his father, John Amory, and his aunt Amory, but Katharine protested the masculine nature of the name and insisted on Amy. They were now seven in the family, two parents and five children. In honor of them all, Augustus decided to call the estate he had just purchased in Brookline Sevenels. Seven L's. A place named just for them, and hidden away from the world behind high stone walls and waving pines. The entrance to Sevenels was marked by thick pillars; between them began a long graveled path that led up the hill, winding between towering elms and then emerging from the shadows to reach long terraced lawns, bordered in redbud and hawthorn bushes. At the top of the lawns stood the house.

The house could have been ugly. It was tall and square and mud brown. But the bright green leaves of lilacs and the dark green of rhododendrons pressed up beside the house, and Boston ivy climbed along its edges all the way to the roofline. When the bushes bloomed in springtime, it was as if the house were alive, breathing out in exhalations of purple and fuchsia, and taking in gulps of green. In the fall, the ivy burned red, setting the house aglow against crisp blue skies.

To the side of the house, a sunken garden with multiple beds had been laid out. Two greenhouses stood at the far end, where lilies grew in winter and grapes grew year-round. There was an open arbor, heavy with wisteria and clematis, and a hidden path bordered in yews that led to ordered groves of fruit trees. Beyond the apples and pears lay a wide plantation of pines and, farther on, long meadows and a pond. A barn for the horses, a cobblestoned stable yard, and copper beeches standing guard. For the children, Sevenels was "paradise."[9]

In November of 1872, a terrible fire had broken out in Boston. It burned for over two days and consumed entire blocks of warehouses. Sixty-five acres in total burned to the ground, and the glow created in the sky could be seen as far away as New Hampshire. The Great Boston Fire came in second in destructiveness only to the Great Chicago Fire of 1871, and like that one, it left thousands homeless and many more jobless. Businesses shut down and insurance companies went bankrupt trying to meet the damage claims. Combined with the losses from the Great Chicago Fire and the steady rise of inflation nationwide, along with massive failures in railroad speculating, the United States was hit with what came to be known as the panic of 1873. There were runs on banks and foreclosures on properties; over fifty railroad companies went out of business, tens of thousands of people lost their jobs, and banks and even the New York Stock Exchange closed their doors for a short period of time.

Augustus Lowell stayed steady and confident through the ensuing years of depression. New avenues for moneymaking would open up, and Augustus was ready. *Occasionem Cognosce.* Copper mines, telephones (the first telephone was demonstrated in Boston: "Mr. Watson—come here—I want to see you"), and electricity. Iron companies, clothing mills, and machine shops. Augustus invested in them all, while also keeping a steady hand over the dozens of manufacturing and trading firms that he had helped found or had invested in: the Cranberry Iron Company, the Plymouth Cordage Company, the Merrimack Manufacturing Company, the Massachusetts Cotton Mills, the Lowell Bleachery, the Lowell Machine Shop, and the Glendon Iron Company. There were some who called him hard in business but no one who denied that he was honest.[10] He was vigilant in his goal to increase profits and dividends, to make money and more money. John Amory Lowell had been a rich man, increasing the holdings passed on by his father, John, and father-in-law, Francis, many times over. His son Augustus took things even further, increasing the family fortunes by a factor of seven.

On Bessie's wedding day, the magnificent horse chestnut on the front lawn was in full bloom with pink-and-white cone-shaped flowers; it hummed like a hive, bees dipping in and out. In the formal garden, a profusion of early-summer flowers grew in the beds. Columbines and winged sweet peas preened alongside orange pansies and pink foxglove; coreopsis sprung bright as bananas, ice blue heliotrope spiked forward with its sticky leaves, and mignonette rested in its fragrance, strong in morning dew but fading now in the sun. Early roses grew everywhere, faintly colored but deeply scented.

Of all the flowers Augustus Lowell grew in his garden—and it was his garden, his domain, as the gardens at Bromley Vale had been his father's before him—those he loved best were his roses. So many roses, of every color and size. For every child, a different variety had been planted; for his wife, dozens of bushes, and all tended by him. He went out early in the morning to cut fresh bouquets, which were then placed in silver pitchers all around the house. During one particularly florid summer, Augustus cut one thousand roses over a three-day period—an abundance of scent for his seven Lowells.

Guests gathered on the lawn and waited for the newly married couple to emerge from the house. When Bessie and Will finally came out on the front step, with beaming smiles and clasped hands, a cheer rose up to greet them. Their marriage had at its heart, love. But the joining was more than just a mingling of hearts. It was a declaration of position, a tightening of relations, a manifestation of survival: the Lawrences, the Putnams, the Bigelows, the Holmes, the Jacksons, the Crowninshields, the Lymans, the Bathchelders, the Sohiers, the Cabots. They had sent their representatives to the memorial services for William Lowell Putnam twenty-seven years earlier; now they had come together to celebrate the wedding of the man named for him. A drum circle of generations, a repeating of names, a sharing of history. Joined together on this perfect day in June.

21

1891–1897

No dread of failure found a place in him.
Whose soul was full of youth's consuming fire . . .
—A. LAWRENCE LOWELL, MARCH 1892

Katie Roosevelt and her husband, Alfred, rented a house in Mamaroneck, a shore town not far from New York City, for the summer of 1891. They had moved into their new home on Fifth Avenue just months earlier. Designed to remind Katie of Boston, the Fifth Avenue house had tall, broad windows and a high stoop lined with black wrought-iron railings, and was built of red brick and limestone. But with summer coming, escape from the city seemed wise. The already-potent smells of New York City—rot and waste, human and animal—would intensify, along with the grime on the streets, the heavy air, and the heat of the sun. Retreating into heavily shaded rooms or the leafy green of Central Park wouldn't be enough, and although the Roosevelt estate in Oyster Bay was always open to them, the young family wanted a summer place of their own.

It seemed, at the time, the right choice: to settle for a few months in a house by the sea. The air would be clean, the open window views lovely, the smells that wafted about, sharp and fresh. Salt water and sea grass and plum roses. Alfred planned on docking his sailboat in Mamaroneck harbor so that he could go out on the water any evening he pleased and still make it down-town in the mornings to the offices of Roosevelt & Son on Wall Street. The children—Elfrida, age seven; James, age six; and Katharine, age three—would spend their days outdoors, splashing around in the shallows by the rocks be-yond the house or playing in the oak-shaded yard, overseen by their nanny. Katie told friends later that she had looked forward to entertaining all the summer visitors they were sure to have.

Katie had married Alfred in December 1882. He was not the first man to propose to her, but he was the only one whose proposal she'd prayed for, and her parents agreed with her choice. It was a bold move, venturing beyond the Boston circle of friends and family to marry a man from New York. A Roosevelt, yes, but still a New Yorker. But then, Boston wasn't the same the same place in 1882 as it had been in 1854, when her mother had married her father, joining two prominent Brahmin families. The war had changed everything.

Katie was just a child when the Civil War ended, but she listened to the stories her father told, and she knew how different things had been before. The Lowells had made their money for decades on the manufacturing and trading of cloth. Whole towns had grown up around their mills: schools and churches, libraries and banks. The Lowell name stood for so much: prosperity, opportunity, community. After the war, the measures taken to keep the mills running and profitable had grown even harsher than just before the war. Was it any surprise that strikes had been organized, walkouts threatened, legislation on working hours and pay fought for—and won? Katie felt the injustice of it; years later, she would write that "the most valuable and inspiring thing is the spirit . . . the spirit of a living Democracy—the feeling of a great, abiding, human fellowship—a oneness among all women—in which there are no districts, and no localities, no race, or creed, or anything that separates—only one great city, that women are trying to make into a home. . . ."[1] But she was unsure of what she could do to help the women less privileged than she. And so she chose to leave Boston. What her father did was his business.

The business of Augustus was making money. But he never intended to pass the mantle of business on to his own children. As Lawrence recalled many years later, "Somehow he made us feel that every self-respecting man must work hard at something that is worthwhile, and do it very hard. . . . In our case, it need not be remunerative, for he had enough to provide for that; but it must be of real significance."[2]

On the morning of July 2, 1891, Alfred Roosevelt set out as usual for the train station at Mamaroneck. His driver took the horses at a leisurely pace, certain there was time enough to get Mr. Roosevelt on the 8:14 train into the city. The two men chatted, Alfred in a good mood under the bright sun. As the carriage drew closer to the station, the train was just pulling in. The driver whipped the horses to go faster and the carriage moved quickly under and beyond the railroad's iron bridge, then stopped just at the lower end of the station. Alfred jumped down from the carriage and leapt up the stairs to the platform, where the train was already in motion, leaving the station. Alfred ran forward and caught the handrail on one of the cars. He struggled to pull himself up and onto the train. He was still clinging to the car as the train rushed toward the railing of the road bridge. He held on tightly to the car door, but his body slammed against the iron railing and he lost his grip. He fell and rolled back beneath the train.

A trainman who had witnessed the fall yanked frantically on the bell cord, signaling the emergency. The train wheezed to a stop. Conductors in coveralls and men in suits ran up the platform toward the bridge, rushing to Alfred's side. The train wheels had passed right over Alfred's leg, just above his ankle. Now blood oozed from the jagged wound, pooling on the wooden slats and dripping down between the boards onto the gravel below.

Alfred was taken back to his summer place, carried in the same carriage he had so cheerfully boarded less than an hour before. He was laid down upon a bed made of strangers' coats, his wounded leg held stable by a pale and shaking passerby who had witnessed the accident and come to help. Katie rushed from the house to meet the carriage on the grassy drive. A phone call had told her of the accident and warned her of Alfred's injuries. Telegrams were sent out immediately: Doctors were called; his father was summoned. Alfred lapsed into a state of shock. By the afternoon, the condition of his leg had grown so dangerous that an amputation was performed in an effort to save his life. His right foot was cut off a few inches above the ankle. Morphine was given to kill the pain, and Alfred fell into an uneasy sleep. In the early-morning hours of July 3, Alfred died.

Katie left the house by the sea. She closed up the home on Fifth Avenue. After Alfred's funeral in New York, she went up to Boston with the children. When she left again to settle the estate, the two elder children remained behind to live at Sevenels with Aunt Amy and their grandparents. Katie couldn't care for them; she could barely tend to the youngest girl, or herself. The world she had chosen, a life with Alfred, was gone.

Amy was nine years older than her niece Elfrida, eleven years older than her nephew James. When Amy was a child, her mother had often been ill and Bessie had taken over her care. Now Amy took over the care of Katie's two children at Sevenels. Together with the cook, Amy planned meals that were sure to whet their appetites: buttery mashed potatoes and creamed chicken; peach pie made with fruit from the trees at Sevenels; cheese from Vermont and maple candies from New Hampshire, and eggs from chickens hatched just down the road. The children rode out with Amy in the morning to fetch the eggs. Amy promised James she would teach him to drive the pony himself. She played games with the children during the day, and took them on outings to Cambridge and Charlestown; she read to them at night from her favorite childhood books, the stories of Rollo and the adventures of Marco Polo. Those volumes were treasures to her, and she had never let anyone borrow them from the bookcase where they were kept in her third-floor suite. But for her niece and nephew, the case was thrown wide open: they could take any book they liked, and she would read to them such passages as this one from *Rollo on the Atlantic*: "When Rollo was about twelve years of age, he made a voyage to Europe under rather extraordinary circumstances. He went alone; that is, he had no one to take care of him. In fact, in addition to being obliged to take care of himself, he also had his little sister Jane to take care of, for she went with him."[3]

Amy taught Elfrida poems and lured her into contests of memorization. Elfrida won every time. One afternoon, she recited Poe's "The Raven," with every word perfect and every intonation correct, having committed the entire poem to memory within just a day: "And my soul from out that shadow that lies floating on the floor/Shall be lifted—nevermore!"[4] Amy rewarded her niece with colored pencils and a sketchbook lined in cardboard and velvet; a long satin cord dangled to mark the chosen page.

The only way Amy could distract James was to take him out riding in the pony cart, and so she took him driving every day, rain or shine, giving him his lessons in driving as promised. She herself had learned to ride as a very young girl. Patrick Burns, the Lowell coachman, had taught her. He had been a jockey at Haymarket in England as a young man, and "knew more about horses than any man alive."[5] When Amy was only two years old, Burns allowed her to drive a pony cart to church, with him seated beside her, the reins she proudly held looped quietly over his own little finger. By the age of five, she was driving out on her own, but always under the coachman's strict direction. "Burns was born to command," Amy said.[6]

One afternoon, Amy decided to take James out to Fresh Pond in Cambridge. The gloomy October skies had given way to sun and light, although the weather was chilly. The trees that circled the pond would be a brilliant red and orange, the last vestige of color before winter settled in. From Fresh Pond, they could pay an easy visit to Elmwood. Becca had died in 1872, and cousin Jamie had died just a month after Alfred Roosevelt. Both were buried at Mount Auburn.

Even with the ghosts that flitted among the tall elm trees, the unswept walks and the forsaken chicken house, Elmwood was a lovely spot to visit. Young James Roosevelt could hunt for treasures in the garden, much as Jamie and his brothers and sisters had decades earlier. Amy planned on sitting out in the sun, swathed in blankets, while James played. She packed a picnic for when James grew hungry. She loaded the basket up into the cart, and then her nephew climbed up. Amy settled him in beside her and went to gather up the reins. The mare harnessed to the cart was restless. Amy spoke to her in soothing tones, then clucked softly to get the horse moving forward.

All of a sudden, the mare bolted. The cart was dragged off at a gallop, careening across the cobblestones and barreling straight toward the stone walls that marked the boundaries of Sevenels. Within moments, the horse, cart, and its occupants would crash into the walls. Amy had only one thought in her head: *Katie has lost her husband and now I am killing her boy.*[7]

Lawrence was just that moment coming into the stable yard. He quickly assessed what he saw—bolting horse, flying reins, sister and nephew in a runaway cart—and without second thought, he stepped forward into the path of the horse. He grabbed her bridle and gave a sharp pull to the bit. Feeling the firm grip, the mare settled down, the cart swinging behind her. She jerked to a stop, panting and blowing through her wide nostrils. Her flanks shook; the sweat on her muscles foamed. The cart listed to one side, then righted itself. James remained seated, trembling and wide-eyed, while Amy leapt down from the cart. She threw her arms around her older brother. She would later tell every member of the family, "Lawrence saved our lives."[8]

Lawrence appreciated the praise. For months now, he had been feeling weighed down by what he thought of as the stultifying employment of law. He and Francis Cabot Lowell III, his cousin, brother-in-law, and good friend, barely made enough money to justify the existence of their law practice. Frederic Stimson, a close friend of Percy, joined their firm as a partner, but things didn't improve. The work generated by the firm was not only nonremunerative but, worst of all, intolerably boring. The cases that came in the door were dull, the tasks of everyday lawyering were monotonous, and there was no end in sight to the tedium.

"I was a failure at the practice of law," Lawrence later declared, and the failure weighed heavily upon him.[9] He had thought the law was worthwhile, but now he questioned his choice. He missed the life he'd had at Harvard, his friends and his classes, his clubs and his professors. As college days receded and old friends scattered, Lawrence wrote to these friends often. He wrote of how much he missed "the old times" and despaired of losing "the ties that bound us together in college." He tried to start up a dinner club, as a "very agreeable way of keeping us from drifting apart as our paths diverge." He loved his wife, Anna, but he missed the friendships that had grown so easily and been forged so deeply within the halls of Harvard.[10]

In 1892, Lawrence wrote a poem and saved it in a notebook he marked *Private*. The poem tells of a young man buoyed by high hopes and with a "dreaming of what his life should be,/ He sailed o'er distant seas in quest of fame/ Or planning great deeds beyond the mountain . . ." But then long years pass: "An old man worn and pale/ Still climbed the crags, though gone all hope to scale/ The Peak that cold and lovely mocked his pain." The boy has become an old man, unsatisfied and unfulfilled; he wonders if "this our gloomy tale/ Of hope and strife and failure marks the end/ Of human life . . ." Having tried all his life to achieve something, in the end his "dreams . . . alone are true, and all the rest in vain."[11] Long on dreams but short on fulfillment: Lawrence worried about the trajectory of his life.

He appreciated the freedom from financial worries granted to him by his father, but he fell short of the conditions Augustus had placed on such freedom: *Do something worthwhile and with all your might*. Lawrence didn't possess the imagination or courage of his elder brother, Percy. His strength had always been in his convictions: of right and wrong, worth and insignificance, valor and cowardice. He valued above all the imperative of duty in his Boston Brahmin world. He needed to do *something* with all his might. But what?

One of Percy's earliest memories was of watching Donati's Comet, which crossed the evening sky for 112 straight days in 1858, when he was just three years old: "I can see yet a small boy half-way up a turning staircase gazing with all his soul into the evening sky where the stranger stood."[12] His father gave him a 2.5 inch refractor when he was twelve, and he used it to observe the heavens, dreaming and speculating about what was up there. For his seventeenth Christmas, his mother gave him a copy of Richard Proctor's *Other Worlds Than Ours,* and in 1893, his great-aunt Mary (mother of William Lowell Putnam, who had died in the Civil War, and sister of James Russell Lowell) gave him a copy of Camille Flammarion's *La Planète Mars.* It was this book perhaps more than any other that would launch him into space.

Percy carried a telescope with him to college and then took it with him on all his travels. He'd written his Harvard graduation treatise on the nebular hypothesis, explaining the origin of the solar system as the collision of two stellar bodies resulting in the formation of a nebula, around which the entire planetary system developed. When he visited Isabella Stewart Gardner (married to a Lowell cousin) in her magnificent home on Beacon Street, he listed his home address as he best understood it: "Cosmos."[13]

While on what would prove to be his final trip to Japan, in 1893, Percy received news that an astronomer he admired, the Italian Giovanni Virginio Schiaparelli, was suffering from deteriorating eyesight. Schiaparelli had become famous for documenting in 1877 what he called "canali" on the surface of Mars. He plotted the canals onto a map of Mars, and astronomers around the world took notice. In 1879, Schiaparelli observed the canali again, and even suggested the possibility of double channels existing on the planet. Percy found the possibility of the canals exciting—but if the great astronomer could no longer look up to Mars, then who would follow up on his findings?

Percy decided it would be he himself who would take up the work Schiaparelli had begun. Percy was convinced that the "canali" were true canals, not just channels (the word has both meanings in Italian). Even more, Percy believed, the canali were evidence of life on Mars. There might not be life there now, but there had been once. It all made sense, given the nebular hypothesis: The universe was in a state of evolution, and Mars had evolved faster than Earth and was now approaching the end of its existence. Mars might be the map to Earth's future: what had happened to the Red Planet might happen to Earth. Percy wanted to discover more, and Schiaparelli was the man to show him the way.

Percy left Japan by the end of the summer of 1893, traveling to Italy to find Schiaparelli. At his observatory outside of Milan, Schiaparelli shared with Percy all of his drawings and maps of the canali. He warned Percy not to see things that could not be verified by others. But Percy was already convinced that Schiaparelli's canals demonstrated Mars had once harbored intelligent life. He found an ally in a French astronomer named Camille Flammarion, the author of the book that Great-Aunt Mary had given him years ago. Flammarion, like Percy, believed that Mars was capable of hosting life; he went so far as to say in 1892, "the present inhabitation of Mars by a race superior to ours is very probable."[14]

Percy traveled to Paris to see Flammarion, where he lived in a magnificent apartment close to the National Observatory and the Luxembourg Gardens. The apartment was decorated with images of planets and constellations: antique paintings, engravings, and prints; planetary globes, astronomical charts, and even furniture carvings. As Percy would later write to his father, he was invited to dine with the French astronomer, where they "sat in chairs of the zodiac under a ceiling of pale, blue sky appropriately dotted with fleecy clouds, and indeed most prettily painted. Flammarion is nothing if not astronomical."[15] From the dining room table, Percy could see the sun setting behind the National Observatory. As night fell, thousands of stars came out, and Flammarion invited Percy to take a look from any one of his many telescopes.

Two men from different continents, Flammarion thirteen years older and a bit bolder, with bushy whiskers, wild hair, and a bow tie always askew; Percival, tall and elegant, always in a perfectly pressed jacket and crimson tie knotted just so, and more temperate in his pronouncements—and both enchanted by the possibilities hidden in the skies above. Was there life up there somewhere? Flammarion agreed to help Percy any way that he could in furthering research that would buttress their shared belief that there was, or had been, life on Mars. They were already certain that conditions existed on Mars such that life could have flourished there; now they just had to convince the world.

To obtain the proof they needed, Percy wanted to establish his own observatory, located somewhere with optimal conditions for sky viewing. After sending scouts out to numerous sites and visiting himself, Percy chose the top of a flat pine-covered hill close to the small town of Flagstaff in the territory of Arizona. The site was rustic and quiet; the atmosphere around Flagstaff was clear and clean; and the weather patterns, stable. It was perfect. The town fathers of Flagstaff volunteered to build a road up the hill to make it easy to deliver the supplies necessary for building and outfitting an observatory. At the time, the only building on the hill was a two-man warming hut that had been built for hikers. Percy drew up his plans to expand the hut and build another structure—an observatory—to house the twelve-inch and eighteen-inch refractor telescopes he would be borrowing for the 1894 opposition (a period when the Sun and the Earth are on the opposite sides of Mars). Within a few years, he'd buy another and larger telescope, a twenty-four-inch refractor. Seated below it, Percy felt both dwarfed by its size and enlarged by its scope, for it brought the universe as close as the palm of his hand.

On the very first night that he claimed the flat-topped hill as his own—it would come to be known as "Mars Hill"—Percy camped out in the open under the stars. He wrote later of the deep pleasure and satisfaction he found there: "To sally forth into the untrod wilderness in the cold and dark of a winter's small hours of the morning, with . . . the frosty stars for mute companionship, is almost to forget one's self a man for the solemn awe of one's surroundings. . . . [It is] a fitting portal to communion with another world. . . . where the common and familiar no longer jostle the unknown and the strange."[16] Unlike his father, Percy did not believe in God. But he did believe in the universe and felt a deep reverence for it. And now, thanks in part to the money that Augustus had promised (and Percy had wisely invested), he had found his place and his space. His choice had been made: to enter the universe and find answers for the people on Earth.

The best time to see Mars and gather information as to its surface and its atmosphere was during a time of opposition. It was during an opposition in 1877 that Schiaparelli had first noted the canali, and it was during another in 1879 when he saw them again. With an opposition coming up in 1894, Percy threw heart, soul, and a lot of money into getting his Flagstaff observatory ready in time to get good views of Mars.

Against all odds, the new observatory and its telescopes were up and running in time to watch the opposition that began in June 1894. For two months, Percy barely moved from his perch atop Mars Hill, where he watched the sky. He took notes, made sketches, returned his eye to the telescope. Based on what he saw, he sketched out a map indicating hundreds of canals; some of these canals appeared to connect to dark circles, which Percy drew onto the maps as well, labeling them "oases." He began work on a book to be titled, simply, *Mars*. He also wrote articles and prepared for lectures he'd arranged to give at the Massachusetts Institute of Technology (where he had been appointed a nonresident professor of astronomy). The topic of his lectures: Mars and its potential for life. After just a summer of observations, Percy felt confident in his claim that Mars had been a habitable planet in its past. He would not go as far as Flammarion, who proclaimed "Mars was most likely currently inhabited."[17] Flammarion also speculated that "Martians are winged creatures, but whether bats, birds or butterflies," he remained uncertain.[18] Percy consistently held that Mars had the atmosphere and history to have *at one time* fostered life, that the construction of canals would have required intelligence and thus proved life had existed, and that "any Martian life must differ markedly from our own."[19] He went on to emphasize that Martians would not look like man: "Man is merely this earth's highest production to date. That he in any sense gauges the possibilities of the universe is humorous."[20]

The lectures that Percy gave at MIT were a huge success. His audience found the arguments he made about Mars both simple to understand and very persuasive. He began by stating that in order to prove the possible existence of intelligent life on a planet, it was necessary to demonstrate both that the planet had the atmosphere necessary to support life (water, oxygen) and that proof of such life, in the form of artificial markings or debris left on the planet, be evident to observers. Percy then showed that his own findings indicated that Mars had the atmospheric indicators that would allow life, and that the channels he saw were proof of intelligent Martian life. Faced with an increasingly hot planet, Martians had created an elaborate canal system to move water from its poles, where water was abundant, to the drought-ravaged areas around the equator, where it was needed.

Katharine Lowell died on April 1, 1895. She was buried a few days later on the family slope in Mount Auburn Cemetery. The ground was spongy from weeks of rain, and the gravel paths between the graves were pitted with puddles. The gathered Lowells, Putnams, and Lawrences were dressed in black: black dresses, suits, armbands, veils, and hats. The skies overhead were silver and the stones of the neighboring graves were gray. But there was color, too, that cold spring day. Purple crocus bloomed along the paths, and carpets of blue scilla spread over the grass. Branches of early-blooming witch hazel were yellow against the brown hollows of Mount Auburn's low hills.

Percy, of all the Lowell siblings, was the one most shaken by his mother's death. Throughout all his travels, a "daily stream of letters" had passed between them, to and from "My darling Percy" and "Dearest Mother."[21] In 1894, Katharine had written to Percy, "I watched you till you had quite gone last evening and my heart was in my throat. I love you so my darling that I could only commend you to his care who loves you more dearly . . . I leave you in perfect faith that he will do everything for you the person I love best on earth."[22] She always kept with her a small prayer book that bore the imprints of teeth marks made by Percy when he was a baby.

Percy asked that all of his mother's personal belongings be given to him for safekeeping. No one in the family objected. The prayer book, her brushes and combs, her writing sets, the letters shared between them—all of it now belonged to Percy.

Throughout that spring and summer of 1895, Mars mania took hold of the public, fed by Percy's highly readable book, his popular lectures, and his willingness to be interviewed. Newspapers published question-and-answer sessions with Percy, printed alongside his illustrated maps of the canals and oases. Accompanying stories told of reported signals sent from the distant planet and other sightings of alien communications in the night sky. Fiction writers used Percy's ideas on how Martians might look—"gills, for example"[23]—or why Martians had died out (the extreme heat) to write fantasies about Mars. One young man who fell under Percy's influence was H. G. Wells. Relying on Percy's theories of the warming planet and its inhabitants' efforts to find water, Wells wrote *War of the Worlds,* first published in 1897 in serial form. Wells's novel tells the story of a band of Martians leaving their planet in a desperate search for water. They arrive on Earth intent on securing what they need to stay alive. A massive invasion begins, setting off a war between humans and Martians.

Astronomers and astrophysicists from the more established observatories grew disgruntled with Percy's celebrity; they worried that his popularity might undermine the respect accorded to the science of astronomy. They began to attack Percy and his ideas about life on Mars, portraying him as a fantasist, and implying that he was not a real scientist, but a man bent on proving things he already believed to be true. Edward S. Holden, director of the renowned Lick Observatory in California, wrote, "It is a point to be noted that the conclusions reached by Mr. Lowell at the end of his work agree remarkably with the facts he set out to prove before his observatory was established at all."[24] There was some support for Percy from the community of astronomers—those who praised him for his skillful writing, his collection of facts, and the importance of other observational work being carried out at his privately funded observatory—but few went so far as to support the contention of intelligent life on Mars.

Percy was also criticized by many religious leaders. In their view, God had created life on Earth, and on Earth alone. Percy wrapped himself in the mantles of Copernicus and Galileo, and proclaimed, "Just as [Earth] is now known to be but one of many bodies revolving around the sun, so, doubtless, it is but one of many worlds evolving in due course the phenomenon of intelligent life."[25]

The attacks from other astronomers, the intense interest of the press and public, and the demand for more proof from everybody added to the pressures of Percy's already overburdened work schedule. He had worked hard to get the observatory at Flagstaff up and running in record time, and he was now managing its operations as well as planning for its expansion. He was writing for *The Atlantic Monthly* and *Popular Astronomer,* and more publications wanted contributions. In 1895, he finished writing *Mars,* just a year after finishing and publishing his last book on Japan, *Occult Japan.* Almost immediately, he began work on his next book, *Mars and Its Canals.* Invitations to lecture kept arriving at Flagstaff, asking Percy to speak not only about Mars and his findings but also about his travels in Japan and Korea.

In addition to planning a trip to both Mexico (to make astronomical observations) and to Europe (to consult with astronomers there), Percy traveled back and forth between Flagstaff and Boston, where he was consumed with settling his mother's estate and working with his publishers. While in Flagstaff, he lived on little sleep, spending day and night at his observation post: "Night is not at all necessary for astronomical research—the planets—the inner ones, including our friend Mars, can almost and in some instances much better be observed by day . . . I am now thinking of going up the hill at sunrise, taking Mars till 9:30 and Venus and Mercury the rest of the day . . ."[26] Nothing made him happier than looking up at the heavens and observing their rhythms and changes, much as an ancient shepherd might have: "With the stars for sole companions while his sheep slept, he watched the stars night after night . . . [it was] the birth of our acquaintance with the rest of the universe . . ."[27]

In the spring of 1897, Percy collapsed while on a trip to Boston. The doctors who were called in to treat him diagnosed his condition as neurasthenia. Dr. George Beard, an expert in the affliction, considered it to be part of a "large family of functional nervous disorders that are increasingly frequent among the indoor classes of civilized countries, and that are especially frequent in the northern and eastern parts of the United States." Percy was a perfect example of this "essentially American disease" that was particularly prevalent in "brain-working" households.[28] In other words, his relentless ambition and productivity had taken their toll.

The treatment of neurasthenia centered around keeping a patient quiet and calm. Bed rest was prescribed, along with a healthy diet and little agitation or mental activity. Percy was told to stay away from his books, especially those relating to the universe, constellations, Mars, or math. He was ordered to leave all business of the observatory in Flagstaff to local staff; he turned over all the financial operations to Will Putnam, his brother-in-law. He returned to his old rooms at Sevenels and withdrew from the world, submitting himself to the careful watch of his father and his youngest sister, Amy. The man who fell to Earth returned now to his childhood home.

22

1897–1900

> . . . I live a thrall
> With all my outer life, a clipped, square hole,
> Rectangular; a fraction of a scroll
> Unwound and winding like a worsted ball.
> —AMY LOWELL, "THE STARLING"

Amy Lowell was up in her third-floor rooms at Sevenels, surrounded by the family dogs. The sheepdogs jostled over each other, around and around, until, as if held up by strings and then suddenly released, they dropped to the floor and rested on their haunches. Heads cocked, ears pitched forward, they watched their mistress as she sat very still and silent on her bed.

Bessie had come from Boston to look in on her little sister—having received the message from her father that all was not well—but Amy would not even open the door of her bedroom. Bessie retreated down the stairs and went to sit with Augustus in the library. Heartbreak was a terrible thing, or so she had heard. Bessie had never experienced it herself. Her first and last suitor had been Will Putnam. Even as a young debutante, she'd shown as little interest in the men at the balls as they had in her. No time for nonsense; Bessie had been a serious girl, unflappable and certain. Now she was a mother with children of her own, but no one frustrated her more than her little sister.

As Augustus and Bessie sat down to dinner, Percy joined them. He was feeling well enough these days to sit at the table for meals, although he spent most of the rest of the day in bed. And then Amy appeared in the back doorway, coming in from the kitchen. Her face was freshly scrubbed, but the signs of crying could be seen in the redness of her eyes, and in their puffiness. She sat down next to her father and waited quietly for the soup to be brought in. She wanted her dinner. But she didn't want to talk. The family knew why she was upset, and talking about things wouldn't change the facts. When her father reached over to touch her hand, Amy gave him a sad smile. He had always been so tender with her, and she knew it wasn't that way with her siblings. The older ones thought of their father as severe but fair; by the time Amy was born, Augustus had mellowed beyond fairness to delight. And she returned the love tenfold.

Many were the evenings Augustus and Amy had spent together in the garden. The first business to tend to was the feeding of Augustus's pet mockingbird, kept in a cage swinging on a tree. Next, it was the gardens that needed their attention. Augustus taught Amy everything he knew, knowledge he'd gathered working side by side with his father, passed down to John Amory from his father, John the Rebel, "the Roxbury Farmer." John the Rebel had learned at the side of his father, the Old Judge, who had first transformed the gardens at Bromley Vale from strictly kitchen gardens—vegetables, herbs, fruit—to flower gardens. Roses, lilies, morning glory, and evening primrose. Lessons passed down: how to harvest seeds from pods and store them away for the next season; when to prune roses, when to feed them; how to divide lilies, coreopsis, mums; when to cut back delphinium, and how to spur asters to a profusion of blooms.

Augustus preferred to spend his time with Amy teaching her about plants and trees, rather than lecturing her about self-control and restraint. Bessie made no secret of her opinion that Amy needed more guidance: "Almost the only discipline Amy got was what I gave her when we happened to be alone together at home."[1] Augustus allowed his youngest the run of the gardens and the rooms of Sevenels, and rarely restrained her interests and enthusiasms. Amy was allowed to choose everything, from the type of cakes served at tea to the names for the dogs and horses to what books would be purchased for the library, upstairs or down (although her father refused to have any Shelley in the house, because the Englishman was an atheist). Reading was the only sedentary activity she liked, for she didn't consider it sedentary: It was exercise of the imagination and adventure for the heart and soul. When asked in school what was her favorite exercise, she'd replied, "Reading."[2]

On her third-floor library shelves, Amy kept her books neat and dusted: *Moonfolk: A True Account of the Home of the Fairy Tales,* by Jane G. Austin; *At the Back of the North Wind,* by George MacDonald; *Little Women,* by Louisa May Alcott; the novels of Thackeray and Sir Walter Scott, Dickens and Jules Verne; the poetry of Keats, including the "Faery Songs": *Shed no tear! O shed no tear! The flower will bloom another year. Weep no more! O weep no more! Young buds sleep in the root's white core . . .*[3]

Amy wrote her own books, which she cared for as lovingly as those she collected in her bookcase. One of her first stories was about a horse that was good and a cat that was bad. They had a fight. "The horse beet. That is all."[4] Her stories evolved into longer plots, with colored illustrations, richer characterization; these she bound in cardboard and paste and then sold to raise funds for the Perkins Institution for the Blind (it was her mother's idea).

Augustus gave Amy books from his own childhood to add to the collection she had growing on the third floor. She noticed that they were all inscribed to him, gifts from aunts and cousins. One inscription read, "J. Augustus Peabody Lowell, a new year's present from his aunt Amory, January 1, 1836." She asked her father about the New Years' presents and he explained that in his youth, gifts were presented a week after Christmas, in deference to the Puritan prohibition of Christmas celebrations. "I was sent to school on Christmas Day," he told her. "It was seen as an ordinary day of work and duty." He'd been at Boston Latin School, an institution founded by Puritan ministers in 1635, a year before the founding of Harvard College.[5]

When Amy was sent off to Miss Bridge's School at 57 Chestnut Street, she attempted to exercise the same dominion over her classmates that she enjoyed at home. Girls were grilled with three questions: How old are you? What are you reading? What time do you go to bed? If the answers pleased Amy, the girl would become a friend. But unlike at home, her dominion at school was not absolute. When she became too overbearing, her chosen friends would yell at her, "Shut up, Amy Lowell!"[6] Amy was good-natured enough to smile—and to stop ordering the other girls around, at least for the moment.

At those times when her mother was feeling strong, Katharine wrested authority from her youngest child and disciplined her, forcing her to practice her French grammar and her handwriting. When Amy got the role of Tony Lumpkin in the school play, *She Stoops to Conquer,* Katharine stepped in and said no: Her daughter would not play a man onstage. Amy was a small girl in height, only five feet, two inches, and had dainty feet and hands, but she was large in girth. Katharine may have been concerned that the only reason her daughter got the role was because she was fat—and no Lowell would be shamed in such a way.

One day, Amy wrote a note to her mother. Her father looked the note over and saw how Amy had signed it.

"But why did you sign it, 'Your loving son, Amy'?" he asked her.

"Why of course Mamma will know, and I couldn't spell 'daughter,'" Amy replied.[7]

When Amy came out as a debutante in the fall of 1891, her season was a success. She was invited to two balls at Copley Hall and dozens of dances, including the Bachelor's Ball, the Cinderellas, which ended just short of midnight, and the Cheap and Hungries, where few refreshments were offered for the carousing dancers. Sixty dinners were held in her honor, and invitations to sleighing parties and evening assemblies poured in.

Amy liked the dancing parties best of all. Despite her weight, she was a great dancer. She attended Papanti's Dance Studio on Scollway Square, a school started by Lorenzo Papanti in 1827. A slim and handsome Italian, always dressed impeccably in patent-leather dancing shoes and a brushed dinner jacket, Papanti was the dance teacher of choice for generations of Boston Brahmins. In 1834, Papanti had introduced a new dance, called "the waltz," to Boston society, launching it to American ballrooms everywhere. By the time Amy was a student, Papanti had passed away, but his studio kept going. Amy was an excellent and enthusiastic pupil, unlike her sister Bessie, who had to be coaxed by Percy to attend her lessons: He told her the lessons were absolutely necessary "before coming out in society."[8]

By the end of Amy's debutante season, it appeared as if she had formed an attachment with a Boston boy. The years passed; Amy continued to see her young man. Marriage was proposed and accepted. But then in the summer of 1897, Amy's purported fiancé became "entangled elsewhere." The engagement was called off and the Lowell family never mentioned the young man's name—or existence—ever again.[9]

Augustus did not like to see his daughter so brokenhearted, so quiet and solemn at the dinner table. He missed her laughter and her conversation, even her boldly stated opinions, often contrary to his own. He missed her theatricality. When the Italian actress Eleonora Duse had come to town the year before, playing the character of Santuzza in Pietro Mascagni's *Cavalleria Rusticana*, Amy had become infatuated with the role. She walked up and down the hallways of Sevenels, imitating the gestures and talk of a woman full of wrath. A woman who had been seduced, then set aside. A woman who sought vengeance. The play ended in tragedy, with the lover killed in a duel and the woman left forever bereft and alone. How augurous a performance it had turned out to be. All of Amy's easy gaiety and carefree confidence had been destroyed by the thoughtless machinations of a boy. Without Katharine to guide him, Augustus had turned to Bessie for help. Percy, tending his own wounds of despair, had little to offer. But Bessie also floundered against the wall of silence that was the heartbroken Amy.

And then Amy came to Augustus one evening in the fall of 1897 with a proposal. She wanted to go on the Banting diet. William Banting was a prominent undertaker in London. His family's firm had overseen the funerals of George III in 1820, George IV in 1830, the Duke of Wellington in 1852, Prince Albert in 1861, and would bury Queen Victoria in 1901. But William Banting's fame had nothing do with his funereal services. He had become known for the enormous amount of weight he had lost following a diet he devised himself. He wrote up the details of his diet in a pamphlet that was distributed widely and for free in London, then throughout England and the Continent, and had now made its way to the United States.

Banting had gone from obese to statuesque on a regimen of vegetables, fruits, and simply prepared meats. By the time his diet reached the States, it had become limited to asparagus and tomatoes and fish (very similar to the diet Amy's mother had followed as part of the treatment for her kidney disease). Banting's diet had been further refined by the advice that it should be followed while partaking of a journey through a hot climate, such as that found in Africa. The idea was that excessive heat would sweat out the fat, assisted by the diuretic effect resulting from the consumption of so many vegetables.

The plan that Amy proposed to her father was that she follow the Banting diet while traveling on a dahabeah up the Nile River. After only a tiny bit of haggling, during which Amy agreed to take on an approved group of friends to serve as chaperones, Augustus gave his approval. Amy enlisted four women to accompany her, Polly Cabot and her nurse, and Frances and Ellen Dabney. In late December 1897, the women arrived in Egypt, where a boat, hired by Amy through Cook's travel agency, waited for them. The women spent Christmas Day sightseeing, visiting the Sphinx at Giza and the surrounding pyramids. The next day, Amy and her friends boarded the boat and began their journey on the Nile.

The *Chonsu* ("God of the Rising Moon") was an elegant vessel with solid brass fittings and two slender white sails. On board, the furnishings were luxurious and ample: "sofas and long chairs and Turkish rugs and plants."[10] There was room enough for Amy and her four friends (three single staterooms and one double in the stern), and for the crew of seventeen, including a chef and chef's assistant. Amy wrote to her father of her satisfaction: "Cook is most liberal in the way in which he fits up his boats, there is nothing that one could possibly want that is left out . . ."[11] Small as it was, at just seventy-five feet long, the *Chonsu* was sturdy enough to make it through the cataracts of the Nile, or so Amy had been assured. She was warned to keep the crew in hand and not to hand over a single penny more than what had already been paid.

Amy quickly tired of the Banting diet, but the Nile provided her with endless fascination. She wrote to her father and sister about the pink cast of the river at sunset, the purple glaze of sunrise, the night sky studded with stars—"I have never seen the stars so brilliant anywhere else."[12] She marveled at the towering scale of the ancient monuments she visited, traveling inland from the river by donkey. The temple at Karnak "impressed me more than any building I ever saw in my life . . . built of all kinds of materials, pink and blue granite, sandstone, etc., and all this with the intense blue of the African sky above it, & flooded by the more than intense African sun."[13]

Amy took photograph after photograph, having hauled her Kodak camera along. When she returned home, she would ask the artist Joseph Lindon

Smith to paint a landscape based on photographs she'd taken of the rock temples at Abu Simbel in Nubia: "Never shall I forget Aboo Simbel as our dabaheah swung around the curve in the river and those four colossal figures sat gazing calmly down upon the blue river with that bright orange tumble of sand beside them."[14]

The border of Lower Nubia was marked by the first cataract of the Nile, an ascent of three miles upriver through a treacherous run of pools and rapids. The *Chonsu* had to be lifted from pool to pool, then navigated through the rapids, then lifted again—an arduous passage, and one about which Amy had been warned. But she was not prepared for the mutiny of the crew as the final stretch of the cataract was reached. The crew, amassed all together on deck, began swaggering about, complaining about the hard work of navigating the last run of rapids and wringing their hands and thumping their chests. They demanded that more money be paid to them or they would leave the boat to capsize, plunging the women to their deaths in the swirling waters.

Five American women alone on the Nile, and four of them were growing increasingly hysterical. Amy alone stayed calm, determined to figure out a way to bend the mutinous men to her will. She had noticed that the crew seemed fascinated by her fountain pen whenever she took it out to jot something down in her journal. They leaned over her shoulder to watch as the pen, with no need for filling from an ink pot, left a trail of words across a page. What else might it be able to do? Amy decided to wield her pen as a weapon. Rising up to her full five feet, two inches and still carrying ample weight despite the diet, she charged toward the crewmen, holding the gold enameled writing instrument boldly before her.

She never knew whether it was her size or her pen that cowed the crew, but the men immediately backed down. They went back to their duties and the boat was carried successfully over the cataracts. When they balked again at having to navigate the *Chonsu* across the channel to the island of Philae, Amy had had enough. She herself navigated the boat, and the crew fell in line behind her, assisting her as best they could.

For another six weeks, Amy journeyed along the Nile, eating her fish and tomatoes, and taking copious notes of all she saw. When the light was right, with the sun high and shadows sharp, she took photos: leaning palm trees on the shoreline, flat boats on the Nile, carved stone rising majestically from circles of sand. At night, she and her friends lounged on pillows and rugs, gazing out across the water: "moonlight on the Nile is even more beautiful than I have ever seen it anywhere else."[15]

Amy, her companions, and the crew traveled peaceably together until "the wind began to blow, and wind on Land in Egypt means unbearable, blinding, dust. We stood it as long as we could, but at last it became intolerable and we had to give up and come home . . ."[16] It was not only the wind but also world events that sent Amy home. The battleship the USS *Maine* had just exploded in the harbor of Havana, Cuba. The ship had been sent to Cuba to protect U.S. interests during the Cuban revolt against Spanish rule, and the American government assumed the Spanish were behind its destruction. Within weeks, the cry heard around the States was "Remember the Maine, to hell with Spain!" By the end of April, war had been declared between the United States and Spain. It was time for Amy to go home.

Amy hurried back to Brookline. When she arrived at Sevenels, her family was surprised to see her thinner than she had been in years. She also seemed happy, and she had nice color from being out under the sun for so long. But within days, Amy's energy flagged. During her months away, everything had been so lovely and new: "I never imagined anything so beautiful as it is. It is just as everyone had always said it was . . . Perfectly wonderful."[17] But now she was home again, with her father and her dogs, and nothing had changed. No marriage offer seemed imminent, and her family frowned upon the notion of a woman attending college. Amy decided to go west to California to warm up on a friend's farm in the Jamacha Valley, just outside of San Diego. There she regained her weight and resolved never to diet again. But all other resolutions seemed beyond her.

In March 1900, Harriet Lowell sat at the breakfast table of her family's home on Beacon Street. She was the youngest daughter of Bessie and Will Putnam, one of the five children born since the wedding twelve years earlier. George was the eldest boy, born in 1889 and named for his grandfather and his great-grandfather, the Reverend George Putnam who gave the funeral address for Charles Russell Lowell in 1864. Katharine, named for Bessie's mother, was born in 1890, followed by Roger, named for Bessie's lost twin, born in 1893; Harriet, named for Will's mother, was born in 1897; and Augustus, named for Bessie's father, arrived in 1899.

Bessie was a hands-on mother, nursing her children and schooling them, feeding them, disciplining them, and putting them to bed every night. Will was good help to her, at her side through the births and landmark events—the first word, first step, first skip down the paths of the Boston Garden—but he was also the family treasurer for the Putnams and the Lowells, and money manager for the sprawling collection of brothers, sisters, cousins, uncles, and aunts. Percy had turned over the running of the observatory in Flagstaff to Will following his breakdown; Augustus turned increasingly to Will for counsel in where to invest his money; and it is likely that Katie Lowell Roosevelt also relied on Will as she implemented her plan of returning to Boston to live in the Back Bay with her three children.

Bessie gave to two-year old Harriet her usual glass of morning milk, along with a plate of buttered toast. Little Gus sat in his high chair, a scramble of eggs before him. Harriet dawdled over breakfast, laughing at her brother as he plastered egg into his hair. Her mother instructed her to finish up her milk, and she did, gulping it down, then letting out a burp, which made the baby and Bessie laugh.

By midmorning, Harriet had become ill. Not long after breakfast, she'd climbed into her mother's lap, complaining of stomach pains. Now she was lying in her mother's bed, alternating between vomiting and diarrhea. Bessie worked to keep her clean, washing her face and changing her into clean nightdresses. Harriet's face was white, the pallor a contrast to the dark circles that appeared under her eyes. Bessie washed her forehead with a cool cloth. She urged her daughter to sip from a glass of water. The doctor, who promised to be on his way as soon as he could, had told Bessie to keep Harriet hydrated. Harriet's eyes became glazed, her face paled even more, and her breaths grew shallow. Again and again, Bessie cleaned her child; the housemaid took the soiled sheets and brought fresh ones, white and cool and crisp. But within minutes, Harriet was sick again.

The doctor diagnosed an infection brought on by drinking unclean milk. He had seen the same symptoms too many times: stomach cramps leading to nausea, diarrhea, vomiting. He advised Bessie and Will, who had come home as soon as he received Bessie's message, to keep Harriet clean and comfortable. But the most important thing was to give her water, little sip after little sip; severe dehydration brought on by the diarrhea and vomiting was the danger. As the day wore on, Harriet became listless. Her breath came low and fast; her eyes were half-closed. Will tenderly lifted her to a sitting position and Bessie dribbled water into her mouth.

Please, Bessie prayed, *please.*

In the dark hours before midnight, little Harriet died in her father's arms.

Although the dangers of drinking impure milk had been understood for years, and the city of Boston had put in place strict pasteurization regulations for milk produced within the city, there was no controls over the milk that was brought into Boston each day from outlying farms. Cities and towns and villages had varying standards for purity; some had no regulations at all. Harriet was a victim of the patchwork of laws governing milk. Bessie, devastated by the death, lamented both its cause and its preventability.

In early June 1900, Augustus Lowell underwent an operation for his gallbladder. The surgery went as well as could be expected and Augustus returned home to Sevenels. On the night of June 19, he complained of pain. His strength lapsed, and he returned to bed weak and pale. Amy became alarmed and the doctor was called. On June 22, Augustus Lowell died.

Augustus's coffin was placed in the library at Sevenels. White lilies were arranged at the head and foot of the casket, forming a sweet-smelling cushion, a curtain to decay. Black bunting hung from the windows and was draped in a swath over the front door. On the evening of June 24, the five Lowell siblings gathered in the library. They sat in hard chairs placed alongside the coffin of their father: Percy, in recovery from his mental and physical exhaustion; Lawrence in a funk of malaise and worry; Katie, a widow with three young children; Bessie, a grieving mother; and Amy, mistress now of Sevenels but with little idea of what to do with the life that lay before her. They sat together, but each was isolated in his or her own cocoon of misery or frustration or despair.

At the funeral service the next day, the minister from King's Chapel read from Corinthians, common enough at such services. *Beareth all things, believeth all things, hopeth all things, endureth all things . . .*

Hope and endurance. Faith and forbearance. The five Lowells had all heard the family history growing up, told by their father and their grandfather, and by their old aunts Amory and Anna. Now the aunts were dead, and their grandfather, and their father. But the stories remained, especially that of a Lowell who had come across an ocean, already an old man but determined to start over in the New World. A world where he could make his own choices and build a future for his family. Where he could make a change, make a difference, build something new. The duty of the Lowells in the New World.

Every generation faced a new world. No voyage across an ocean was required; time alone was enough to make the challenges unexpected and the opportunities unforeseen. And always, always: the chance to start over. To start fresh. To reinvent oneself, and one's place in the world. The Lowell siblings had been raised on the possibilities of reinvention: the old English merchant who became a colonial farmer; the preacher who became a community leader; the loyalist who became a revolutionary; the trader who became a manufacturer; the lawyer who became a pamphleteer; another preacher, transformed into an abolitionist, his son a poet who became a professor. Boys who had been students became soldiers, and heroes.

Believeth all things, hopeth all things. The twentieth century had begun, and it was time for the Lowells to start over again. A new century, with new worlds, new hopes, and new opportunities to be seized.

23

1901–1913

> Only to the accustomed and the commonplace
> do men take kindly at once. The strange terrifies them.
> It is with ideas in men as with unfamiliar sights in beasts.
> Both shy at first at what they have never seen before.
> —PERCY LOWELL, "THE LOWELL OBSERVATORY AND ITS WORK"

By the spring of 1901, Percy was back in Flagstaff. He had not been at the observatory in Arizona for four years, but now it would once again become his home base, his bit of paradise under the stars. ". . . I sit in my silent dome/ Wharf of this my island home/ Whence only thought may take passage to that other island across the blue . . ."[1] A crossing from one world to the next, one planet to another. Percy was on his way back to Mars.

The wooden warming hut on Mars Hill had been expanded, and now Percy set about making his "Baronial Manor" as he called it, it even more comfortable, commodious, luxurious. The rustic house spread out under Percy's guiding hand, a maze of open rooms under beamed ceilings, with large stone fireplaces in the common areas and wide windows throughout. By the time Percy was finished adding on to the house, it would have over twenty rooms and even a garage for a big red automobile. But not yet. That was still in the future.

A library held Percy's always-growing collection of books. He telephoned his book orders to Boston on a regular basis: novels, mysteries, scientific treatises. *Send me full set of James Fenimore Cooper. The Malvern Murders. Savante's Theories of Chemistry.* The requested books were sent out on the next westbound Limited.[2]

There were staff rooms for meeting in and guest rooms for sleeping in, and a dark-room for developing film. The dining room, with its views over mountain peaks, could seat dozens at its huge table; the kitchen was supplied with a large stove and walk-in larder to keep the food coming. There was a master bedroom for Percival and one equal in size for his secretary, Louise Leonard. Louise had been with Percival from the very beginning of the search for life on Mars, hired as his secretary in 1893. She was prim and pretty, with large brown eyes, a generous bosom, and an easy smile. Percy called her "Wrexie." She'd gone scouting with him to Africa in his search to find the perfect spot for an observatory. When he settled on Arizona, she headed west from Boston to move in. She left Mars Hill when Percy needed her (which was often) and was at his side whenever he returned to the renovated hut on the hill.

Along the back of the building ran a porch with wide boards and split-log railings. It was decorated with rattan chairs and Navajo rugs, and in a corner, there was a table for Percy's very first telescope, a 2.25-inch refractor, a gift from Augustus back in 1870. Young Percy had climbed out through a window and set the telescope up on the flat roof of Sevenels to observe the skies all night long. Now he used the childhood refractor to look at the same skies but through a new atmosphere: the clean, crisp skies of Arizona.

Like all the Lowell ancestors before him, Percy also tilled the ground around his home, creating flower beds resplendent with hollyhocks, zinnias, and lilies, and a fenced vegetable garden that specialized in gourds, squashes, watermelon, and pumpkins. Louise helped him in the garden, keeping watch when he was traveling: "Am fresh in from gardening—8 pm and as I turned to lock the gates who should I see but our tame friend: Jack Rabbit Esqr . . . I wanted you then, to see him too! . . . The gourds and pumpkins are doing as well as can be expected . . . I covered them all for fear of frost as I don't want anything to happen to them while you are away . . ."[3] Percy had a barn built to hold cows and horses; the matriarch of the cow family was named Venus, and one of her children was called Satellite.

When Percy returned to the observatory after his breakdown, one of his first priorities was to bring in more professional staff. Vesto Melvin Slipher was hired as an assistant astronomer; a few months later, Carl Otto Lampland joined the team. Slipher was hired as temporary help but stayed on at the Lowell Observatory for fifty-three years. Lampland stayed for forty-nine years, until his death in 1951.* Under Percival's leadership, the men got to work on proving life could exist on Mars. Water was the linchpin: Prove that the canals were real, that water had been carried via the canals, and then it would follow that life on Mars, past or present, was a possibility.[4] Observations would have to be made, photos taken, measurements drawn, maps created. There was an opposition coming up on March 23, 1903, another in 1905, and another in 1907. Percy wanted his observatory to be ready for all of them.

To buttress Percy's claims about past life potential on Mars, not only was

---

* In 1906, Vesto Slipher's younger brother, Earl C. Slipher, began working at the observatory, and he stayed for fifty-seven years.

more evidence needed but the evidence needed to be synthesized into a demonstrable theory of planetary evolution. Percival saw that synthesis as his mission, and his alone. "No great man ever cooperated with another in the idea that made him great; the thing is unthinkable . . ."[5] He would take the data collected by his scientists and turn it into proof that the atmosphere of Mars had not only fostered life but flourished with it. Astronomy, geology, evolution, climate, gravity, math, engineering—everything Percy knew had to come together, for "the genius is the man who not only has the requisite ideas but who contrives to combine them."[6] Years later, he would lecture a group of students, saying, "For all great work imagination is vital . . . Imagination harnessed to reason is the force that pulls an idea through."[7]

Percy wrote in a letter to his friend and Lawrence's old law partner, Frederic Stimson, "true seeing is done with the mind from the comparatively meager material supplied us by the eye."[8] Day after day, night after night, Percy himself went out to the wood-slatted dome built on the plateau of Mars Hill, towering pines all around. Seated below the huge refractor telescope, he kept watch, night and day, for activities in the heavens: "though parted by a gulf more impassable than any sea, the telescope lets us traverse what otherwise had been barred and lands us at last above the shores we went forth to seek . . ."[9]

He took notes of what he saw, created drawings and charts and maps. He gathered up the data collected by Lampland and the Slipher brothers. Then he went back down the hill to his desk in the library and got to work writing. He sought to arrange his observations and charts and maps into relatable, readable treatises on Mars and space: "the whole object of Science is to synthesize and so simplify; and did we but know the uttermost of a subject we could make it singularly clear."[10]

Percy wanted the entire world to see Mars as he did, as a premonition for Earth, for "in Mars we are able to glimpse, in some sort, our future. Different as the course of life on the two planets undoubtedly has been, the one helps, however imperfectly, to better understanding of the other."[11]

In the spring of 1906, Percy put the final touches to his book *Mars and Its Canals*. All of the data gathered by him and his staff, all the theories he'd been collating in his head, all the conversations he'd had, his dreams, the words he'd read and absorbed—everything came together now in his second book on Mars. It was published in the fall of 1906 and the reaction was immediate. The book was greeted with acclaim, excitement, and enthusiasm. Fans had been waiting since 1895 for more of Mr. Lowell on Mars, and he gave them what they wanted: additional proof of the potential for life having existed on Mars, with some pondering over what it could all mean for humans on Earth.

Percy wrote in the book's concluding chapter, "By studying others we learn about ourselves, and though from the remote we learn less easily, we eventually learn the more."[12] He was intent on spreading all that he had learned, and as soon as the book came out, he began an eight-part lecture series for the Lowell Institute. The lectures were to be given twice weekly, on Mondays and Thursdays, for a month. The lectures were so popular that Percy agreed to repeat them on Tuesday and Friday nights. The streets on those evenings were filled with motors and carriages dropping off lucky audience members "as if it were a grand opera night."[13] Four nights straight of lectures, for one month. Percy's energy was equal to the tasks he demanded of himself. But for how long?

Lawrence Lowell sat at his desk in Harvard's Sever Hall, reading the *Boston Evening Transcript*'s report: "Lowell's lectures on Mars are among the most memorable ever delivered at that Institute . . . Mr. Lowell's wisdom in concentrating on Mars is justified the more and the thanks of the world have been well earned by his devotion to it."[14] The report went on to assure readers that the entire lecture series would be reprinted in *The Century* for all those who had wanted to get into the one thousand-seat lecture hall but had been denied entry. The lectures were sold out, Lawrence read, not even any room to stand.

Lawrence was now a professor at Harvard, and had been for the last five years, teaching classes in the science of government. He had written numerous essays and articles on government, and published three books: *Essays on Government, Governments and Parties in Continental Europe*, and *Colonial Civil Service*. A fourth book, entitled *The Government of England*, was coming out in 1908. Was the teaching of government to be his place, his mission? Lawrence wanted more. Now he rose and went to stand by the high window looking out over Harvard Yard.

All the leaves on the towering elms were gone, fallen and raked away. Lawrence could see clearly down to the students walking along the gravel paths. In groups large and small, they scurried to and from classes, their heads tucked into coat collars against the chill of an early dusk. The steps of Memorial Hall had been swept clean by the wind and lay now in shadow as the sun set behind University Hall, its gray marble walls like a mausoleum. Winter was coming. Lawrence had been up at Cotuit, on Cape Cod, the weekend before. He'd gone into the woods near his house and felled trees, as the stand needed culling. Logs from those trees would be delivered to his house at 132 Marlborough by the end of the week. Firewood to get him and Anna through the coldest months of the year. Nothing warmed like a real wood fire.

Happy as Lawrence was to be back in the universe of Harvard, circulating among students and faculty with the vocation of learning at their core, he saw where improvements could be made. Harvard could be so much better, stronger, brighter. Standards tightened, scholarship furthered, laziness banished and, in its stead, a resurgence of vitality. A stronger community sprouting forth from the old traditions. There were changes Lawrence wanted to make at Harvard, changes he needed to make. But as a mere professor, he was limited in what he could do. He needed to move on. He needed to move up. The sacred office in University Hall—the office of the president—was the place he coveted.

MARS INHABITED, SAYS PROFESSOR LOWELL, proclaimed *The New York Times*.[15] Percy was hailed as "the foremost living authority on the most interesting of planets"; "our greatest Martian student"; and, in a reference to the current president of the United States, "the Roosevelt of Astronomy."[16] Invitations poured in for him to give lectures, receive honorary degrees, and to write more and more articles; requests for interviews from newspapers around the world arrived; letters and telegrams came in by the bushel, congratulating Percy on his "magnificent work" and praising him for his "clearness and eloquence of expression and convincingness of argument." Even a minister wrote to Percy, praising him for having written "among the greatest books I have read in the past five years . . . some day theology will be shaken out of its seed-pod present of earth-centrocism and egotism by the study of soul-life on this brother planet."[17]

At the end of 1907, *The Wall Street Journal* wrote, "Think back on the year. . . . What has been in your opinion the most extraordinary event of the twelve months?" The *Journal* answered its own question: Certainly it is "not the financial panic which is occupying our minds to the exclusion of most other thoughts . . . but the proof afforded by astronomical observations that conscious, intelligent human life exists upon the planet Mars."[18]

But once again, astronomers and astrophysicists from the more established observatories, most of them graduates of rigorous doctoral programs, did not appreciate Percy's literary expositions on Mars and the nature of the universe. Percy was vilified both privately, in letters circulated among all the major observatories—William Wallace Campbell of the Lick Observatory leading the charge—and publicly, in a six-month series of letters published in the journal *Science*. Campbell called Percy "a trial to sane astronomers,"[19] and most scientists in the field tended to agree with him. Alfred Russel Wallace, former colleague of Charles Darwin and respected throughout scientific communities, wrote a book refuting Percy's observations and conclusions, and Eliot Blackwelder, a well-known geologist from the University of Wisconsin, questioned whether Lowell deserved the title of "scientist" at all.

In the spring of 1908, Katie Roosevelt—now Katie Bowlker—called the meeting in her Beacon Street drawing room to order. Those seated around the opulently decorated room included Katie's closest friends, along with her sister Bessie and a large number of assorted Lowell, Putnam, and Jackson cousins. The women were all from Katie's social circle, Brahmin to the core and with pedigrees going back to the Puritans. Katie had called them to her house with the purpose of organizing their combined talents for the good of Boston. She was ready now to fight against the inequities of the world she lived in, in her own way, by forming the Women's Municipal League of Boston. For the next ten years, she would be the organization's president and guiding light.

The town she had been born in had become once again the town she belonged to. And she wanted to give back to this city, make it a better place for all who lived here. Not just for the elite, the Brahmins who enjoyed the Boston Symphony and the Athenaeum, took daily strolls through the Boston Garden and down Commonwealth Avenue, dined at two and took tea at six, married their daughters to cousins, sent their sons to Harvard, and buried their dead at Mount Auburn. She wanted to help all the women out there, the ones she saw on the street, serious and pale-faced as they headed to jobs in offices and on manufacturing floors. Or the mothers who looked overwhelmed as they ferried their swarms of children through the streets. Women who had not had her good luck. Katie knew her good position was due to the family to which she had been born; her marriage to her first husband, who had loved her so much and provided for her, and now to her second husband, a fine man.

Katie had met Thomas J. Bowlker in England the year after Augustus died, when she was on a trip abroad with her children. Bowlker was an Englishman, a graduate of Cambridge, and an ordained minister in the Anglican Church. At the time Bowlker and Katie met, he was assistant headmaster at a boys school outside of London. He fell madly in love with Katie and proposed marriage soon after their first meeting. Katie was happy to marry Bowlker but explained that she would never leave Boston for good ever again. Bowlker gave up his career in England to follow Katie back to the United States. He moved into the house on Beacon Street, intent on forming a new life around her and her three children, Elfrida, James, and Kate.

By 1908, the children had grown into adults. James had just graduated from Harvard College and was working in New York City. Elfrida had married Sir Orme Clarke of England in 1905. She lived with her husband and her son, Humphrey, on a grand estate outside of London. Kate was soon to be married to Josiah Stanley Reeve, a nice young man from a prominent Pennsylvania family. Katie and Thomas had become an old and settled couple. Settled, but not complacent. Katie's experience with the death of her first husband, Alfred, had schooled her against complacency. The question before her now was, How to translate her desire to change Boston for the better into action?

Katie reasoned that the sphere of women was the home. But her vision of home had expanded beyond the walls of her Beacon Street mansion. She saw the entire city of Boston as her larger home. It was the duty of privileged women like herself to keep not only their own house in order but the large house—Boston—as well. Katie wanted to institute what she called "municipal housekeeping": "what is that part of the city's work that women can best take for their share? . . . They are better fitted than men, by their training, to understand, and therefore to improve city conditions, in those directions which we have grouped under the general name of municipal house-cleaning, and municipal home-making, using these words with their largest meaning . . ."[20]

The health and welfare problems of Boston would be addressed head-on, not by supplanting the efforts of men but by harnessing the power of women. The women of Boston, she explained, "had a keen sense of their individual duties and responsibilities to their homes, their charities, their hospitals, their various organizations." They were "awaking more and more to a sense of communal consciousness" and the "time seems ripe now when all women can unite together to form an intelligent, concerted body of public opinion, which shall be so representative, and so influential, that no public official can disregard its desires."[21] Katie's strategy was threefold: first, to educate women of her social class on the workings of local and state government, and so empower them to influence the workings of government; second, to launch women-led volunteer programs aimed at improving the sanitary, religious, and family conditions of all classes of Boston women; and third, to institute experimental programs aimed at improving health and welfare that would be so successful, the city itself would be inspired to take over the experiments and implement them citywide.

In 1902, Katie's sister Amy had spoken up at a meeting of the Brookline school board, protesting the reappointment of an aged and ineffective teacher. While speaking, Amy was booed and hissed by the audience, but she continued on nonetheless, and in the end, her position was adopted by the board and the man was not reappointed. But when Amy finally descended from the dais, the women of her family surrounded her, chastising her audacity at speaking out as a woman. Now just six years later, Katie felt certain that asserting herself as a woman in the public sphere was the only way to effect change in Boston—and she was more than willing to do it. She adapted the definition of Brahmin duty to suit herself and further her goals.

Bessie was emboldened by her sister's reinvention of proper female

Brahmin activity. No longer were women to be limited to behind-the-scenes philanthropic work. Bessie charged to center stage, taking on leadership of the Department of Public Health created under Katie's Municipal League. Bessie also founded and led a Committee on Milk, joining forces with the Massachusetts Milk Consumers' Association. Her home on Beacon Street, just down the street from her sister's, became headquarters for both the Department of Public Health and the Committee on Milk, with Bessie sending out a battalion of females to work on improving milk inspection in Boston and the environs, and lobbying for legislatively mandated statewide and national purity standards. Bessie wrote to President Taft, urging him to join national efforts with local programs; "by cooperating they could do much more than is present possible to purify Boston's milk supply . . ."[22] Taft sent her request over to the Pure Food Commission and the Public Health Service. It would not be until 1924 that national standards for milk hygiene, milk grading, and pasteurization were set and regulated. But Bessie couldn't and didn't wait. She went about haranguing and harassing suppliers, local legislators, and anyone who could help at all to ensure that safe milk was available now for all the children of Boston.

On June 10, 1908, an announcement appeared in the *Boston Herald*. Percival Lowell had been married that afternoon to Constance Savage Keith at St. Bartholomew's Church in New York City. The announcement stated that "the bride, who was unattended, wore a frock of white Liberty satin, trimmed with Brussels point and a white Tulle veil. She carried a shower bouquet of sweet peas." The announcement went on: "Few intimates in Boston knew of [their] intention to marry. . . ."[23] And no one on Mars Hill had known of it, least of all Louise Leonard. A year earlier, on June 23, 1907, Louise had written to Percy about the garden the two of them had always tilled together: "Two morning glories were out this morning and the sweet pea under the servant's window has put forth a beautiful pink flower . . . how we did miss your face . . ."[24] Now Percy's next-door neighbor in Boston had carried a bouquet of sweet peas down the aisle of a New York City church and married the man Louise had worked beside for years. A man she was devoted to and most probably loved— had loved for years. Louise may have blanched at the news of Percy's wedding, but she did not falter. She knew she was integral to the work of the Lowell Observatory and she soldiered on, buttoning up her emotions for another day.

Constance Savage Keith was forty-four years old, eight years younger than Percy. She had never been married and supported herself by selling commercial and residential real estate in Boston. By no one's account was she an attractive or nice woman. There were some who rumored that Constance had somehow "blackmailed Percival into matrimony."[25] While in Korea, Percy had had a relationship with a Korean woman that an American diplomat claimed resulted in a child; while traveling in Europe in 1904, Percy kept a travel diary in which naked photos of one paramour were posted, while details of sex with another were recorded ("I liked it when suddenly she knelt between my knees . . ."[26]). There was certainly fodder to sully the reputation of Percy; after his death, Bessie admitted, "my brother was a brilliant man, but not a good one."[27] But did Constance wield such a weapon to secure her marriage? According to her own memoirs, she was devoted to him and to life on Mars Hill, where she would "live in the atmosphere of such men accomplishing great things. . . ."[28]

After marrying, Percy and Constance traveled to London, where they made news by flying over Hyde Park in a hot-air balloon. Percy wanted to know what the Earth looked like from the sky. To be five thousand feet above the ground, the smog of London swirling all around, might not be like soaring through space but the balloon afforded a bit of an aerial view. With the inventiveness that Percy was so proud of exercising, he imagined what the Green Planet would look like from the heavens. A still young planet, with time on its side. What did Constance see? The tops of trees, leaves turning yellow and brown; the murky blue ribbon of the Serpentine; and slashes of gray that marked the way in and out of the park.

Thousands of people gathered in the Old Yard at Harvard on the morning of October 6, 1909. A. Lawrence Lowell was to be inaugurated president of Harvard. Charles W. Eliot was retiring after forty years. In the seats arranged before the platform that had been erected in front of University Hall, delegates from around the country and the world sat dressed in their scholarly robes: President Hadley from Yale, Franklin Carter, former president of Williams, Frederick Jackson Turner from the University of Wisconsin, Horace Davis from Stanford, James Bryce from Oxford, Eduard Meyer and Otto von Gierke from the University of Berlin, the mayors of Cambridge and of Boston, the ministers from the old churches of Cambridge and the preachers of the college, the United States senator from Massachusetts, and the state's congressmen. Every hue of blue, gold, maroon, purple, and orange was represented in the clothes the men wore, in silks and satins and wools.

Above the seated rows of men, on gleaming white staffs topped with golden eagles, flew the colorful seals of America's oldest universities: William and Mary, Yale, the University of Pennsylvania, Princeton, Washington and Lee, Columbia, Dartmouth, and Brown. The seal of Harvard was affixed to a staff borne by the sheriff of Middlesex County, who stood in the center of the platform. He waited patiently for the crowd to settle. Into the farthest reaches of the Yard, men and women had gathered, standing room only, to witness the celebration. Finally, the sheriff moved to the center of the platform and struck his staff against the wooden floor.

"The meeting will be in order!" he cried out in a loud voice.

The president of the Board of Overseers, John D. Long, moved to the front of the platform, carrying with him the Harvard College charter, seal, and keys. He proffered them to Lawrence, who stepped forward and, with a grave face, accepted his new role as president of Harvard College. It was only when he turned to sit in the presidential chair that he allowed himself to smile. He continued to smile as the alumni chorus sang a celebratory hymn. The opportunity he had been hoping for, for so many years, had finally presented itself. Lawrence would seize that opportunity and never look back.

In his first statement as president, he made his intentions clear:

> Aristotle remarked that man is by nature a social animal; and it is in order to develop his powers as a social being that American colleges exist. The object of the undergraduate department is not to produce hermits, each imprisoned in the cell of his own intellectual pursuits, but men fitted to take their places in the community and live in contact with their fellow men. . . . The task before us is to frame a system . . . which shall produce an intellectual and social cohesion, at least among large groups of students and points of contact among them all.[29]

He went on to set out his plans for creating a community of scholars, joined together socially and academically. To bring this new "cohesion" to social life, Lowell proposed establishing freshman "dormitories and dining halls, under the comradeship of older men, who appreciated the possibilities of a college life, and took a keen interest in work and their pleasures." Academically, cohesion would be achieved by organizing students' scholarship in a system of concentration and electives, with classes chosen to fulfill a specific course of study and filled in with a selection across fields: "the best type of liberal education in our complex world aims at producing men who know a little of everything and something well." To encourage academic excellence, Harvard would confer honors degrees based on class work and the completion of an honors thesis.

He finished his speech with a flourish: "It is said that if the temperature of the ocean were raised the water would expand until floods covered the dry land; and if we can increase the intellectual ambition of college students the whole face of our country will be changed. When the young men shall see visions the dreams of old men will come true."[30]

It was unusual for an inaugural address to establish in such detail the plans of the incoming president. But Lawrence had been waiting for over ten years for the chance to remake Harvard and he knew exactly what he wanted to do.

On the following evening, a dinner was held to welcome Lawrence Lowell as president. Lawrence sat with his wife, Anna, at a table adorned with ancient college silver, rarely taken out but now shining in splendor: the Great Salt given to Harvard in 1644; two large silver loving cups, a gift dating to the 1700s; a silver bowl that had belonged to President Holyoke, the ninth president of the college. Tradition lay upon the table, and upon the shoulders of the newly installed president. Not all the old college customs would make it into the new century. Lawrence was ready to remake the institution of Harvard and create new, and what would prove to be lasting, college traditions. But although he would work to revitalize the academics of the college and forge a new cohesion among its students, he would balk at widening its embrace. Lawrence had a firm idea of what made the ideal college man, and he had no intention of taking in those who could not assimilate to the ideal.

In the spring of 1913, ground was broken in Harvard Yard to begin construction of two freshman dorms, Smith Hall and Standish Hall. Lawrence had raised the funds, sending out appeals that explained how freshman dormitories "would give far greater opportunity for men from different schools and from different parts of the country, to mix together and find their natural affinities unfettered by the associations of early education, of locality, and of wealth."[31] For years, the rich students rented out rooms on the "Gold Coast" of Mount Auburn Street. Poorer students had spread out through houses and apartments in the dowdier of Cambridge neighborhoods, sharing rooms with others or squeezing themselves into closets, cellars, and garrets they could call their own.

Now all students would be housed together in a layout designed by President Lowell himself: a series of suites, floor by floor. The center room of each suite would be a study, and every study would have its own fireplace, because Lawrence remembered with fondness his own student years on Linden Street, spent studying by a fire. Around the study, five or six single bedrooms would offer privacy for each student. Lowell redesigned the Faculty Room chairs from time immemorial, the black slat-backed chairs not known for their comfort. He made them comfortable, kept them painted black, and added a golden insignia, each unique to the freshman house for which the chairs, one for each student, were destined.

The freshman dorms were the start of a larger plan to create housing for all the students, dorms in which they would be required to reside. A commingling of classes and backgrounds, all for one purpose: "to make the college truly national in spirit."[32] For Lowell, a resilient social group was one that blended together; differences were assimilated to a core cohesion, and from there, strength and effectiveness flourished. Years earlier, during the agitations of the Boston Irish on behalf of the nationalist movement in Ireland, Lawrence had written how important it was to make "naturalized foreigners Americans, and nothing but Americans . . . We want them to become rich, and send their sons to our colleges, to share our prosperity and our sentiments. We do not want to feel that they are among us and yet not really a part of us."[33]

The type of community that Lawrence wanted to create mirrored in many ways the one Percival Lowle had joined in 1639, when he asked for entry to Newbury and was welcomed in. A unity of purpose and a paring away of differences: *We are all equal before God.* But just as in the Congregational towns of centuries earlier, those who differed from the norm would be thrust out. Then as now, those not adhering to the communal dictates of acceptable behavior "shall have the liberty to keep away from us, and such as will come will be gone as fast as they can, the sooner the better."[34] For Lawrence, assimilation was the core of community. For those who separated themselves by religion or sexuality, or those who were separated by virtue of race, acceptance in the community would not be granted. Lawrence simply could not see any value in allowing deviations from the norm, only danger.

24

1913–1917

On and on, from bough to bough,
The leaves are thick, but I push my way through;
Before, I have always had to stop,
But to-day I am sure I will reach the top.
—AMY LOWELL, "CLIMBING"

On a cold, wet day in March 1915, Amy Lowell stepped up on the dais in the large meeting room of the National Arts Club on Gramercy Park in New York City. She was there to address the Poetry Society of America, and the room was filled with poets and poetry lovers, literary critics and publishers. Amy felt nervous but betrayed no sign of it as she settled her notes on the podium, then straightened the pince-nez on her nose. She raised her eyes and looked out over the rows of filled seats. She been allocated five minutes to speak. Time constraints meant nothing to Amy. She was certain that once she began to talk, the audience would become so enthralled that all sense of time would slip away.

Her companion, Ada Dwyer Russell, was in the audience, seated toward the back. Even across the wide stretch of seats, Amy could feel the older woman's encouragement. She had met Ada in 1912, at a luncheon held in the actress's honor. Ada was in Boston performing in the play *The Deep Purple* at the St. James Theatre. Amy had seen the play three times and was looking forward to meeting the famous actress in person. For the first time ever, Amy arrived on time at the home of Elizabeth Ward Bruen on Louisburg Square. Many of her friends were there, including Annie Endicott Nourse, founder of the South End Music School, a music school for the impoverished; Mary Hill, wife of the impressionist and jazz composer Edward Burlingame Hill; and Methyl Palfrey, married to lawyer John Gorham Palfrey, grandson of John Amory Lowell's college roommate of the same name.*

---

* Methyl was pregnant at the time with her daughter Susan, who would go on to win sixteen grand-slam tennis titles and was the only woman to play in a men's tennis match (during World War II, when men were not to be found and her husband needed

Amy's friends surged forward to greet her in a commotion of exclama-
tions and waving hands, but Amy ignored them and made straight for the
guest of honor. For the next two hours, she monopolized all conversation with
the actress and by the end of the afternoon, she had invited Ada for dinner at
Sevenels. Over the next two years, the women saw each other as often as they
could manage, in between Ada's theater tours and Amy's traveling. By the
summer of 1914, Ada agreed to move in with Amy and manage her household.
But the two women were more than friends, more than business associates.
They had become lovers. The proof would come out in Amy's work, not only
in how productive she would become over the coming years but also in the
nature of what she wrote. Amy Lowell would step out from under the conceal-
ing cloak of Boston Brahmin womanhood and bare herself—and her lover—
before the reading public. And it would all begin that day at the National Arts
Club.

Amy's first book of poetry, mostly composed of poems written before she
met Ada, came out in the fall of 1912. Entitled *A Dome of Many-Coloured
Glass*, it contained poems that traveled along lines of traditional verse, following a formulaic and formal style of rhymes and meter and couplets. Amy had
decided to become a poet after attending a number of performances by the
actress Eleonara Duse in the fall of 1902. As she herself remembered it, she
saw Duse onstage and, upon returning home, immediately "sat down, and
wrote [a] poem." It had "every cliché and every technical error which a poem
can have, but it loosed a bolt in my brain and I found out where my true function lay."[1] She set to work, writing poem after poem for *A Dome of Many-
Coloured Glass*. What heartache ensued when, after publication, the book was
widely panned by critic after critic. Louis Untermeyer, writing for *The Chicago
Evening Post*, cast the worst insult of all: "to be brief, [the book], in spite of its
lifeless classicism, can never rouse one's anger. But to be briefer still, it cannot
rouse one at all."[2] Amy Lowell had been called boring. In despair over the bad
reviews, she took to her bed for weeks.

She emerged in the early days of 1913, determined to turn herself around.
Having discovered a new kind of poetry called Imagism, Amy wanted to find
out more. The new movement was promoted by Ezra Pound and included a
number of poets living in London, including some expat Americans. When
Pound published an essay listing the essentials of Imagism in the March 1913
issue of *Poetry* magazine, Amy read it with avid interest. But there was a se-

---

a doubles partner). In 1950, Susan successfully lobbied on behalf of Althea Gibson
to allow Gibson to play in previously all-white tournaments. Susan's brother, John,
also a great tennis player, married the daughter of Kermit Roosevelt, Teddy's son.

cret at the heart of Imagism, Pound wrote; he referred to it as "the Doctrine of the Image," a mystery whose solution would not be revealed to the general public.[3]

Amy was intrigued, and then more than intrigued: She was angry. How dare such a secret be kept from aspiring poets! Who was this Pound, so arrogant and sure of himself, and so determined to bar the gates to the garden in which he himself frolicked? Amy decided she would hunt down Pound and demand from him the hidden ingredient that might open up her poetry. In the spring of 1913, Amy loaded herself onto a steamer bound for England and went in search of Pound and his circle of poets.

When Amy finally met Pound and his band of writers in London, it became clear that there were no secrets to be revealed. Imagism was a movement, but it was also a scheme devised by Pound as a way to get noticed. Amy tucked that bit of news away—publicity would become one of her strong suits—and went out to visit Henry James in East Sussex. James was an old friend of her cousin James Russell Lowell. Henry and Amy talked a long while about books and writing and the literary life. When Amy left James's house, she cut a sprig of lavender from his garden. She would keep that sprig always, saved between the pages of a book. It would be a reminder of what she now understood. There was no secret ingredient to writing, whether it was fiction or essays or poetry. The formula was simple: hard work matched by inspiration. Hard work, she was capable of, she knew, and inspiration was everywhere—in her garden, in conversations, in travels, in history, in love and in friendship. All would serve to guide her over the years to come.

On the ocean liner home to Boston, Amy sneaked out on deck most evenings to smoke cigars. She'd picked up the habit after her father died—it helped her concentrate—but she dared not smoke during the day, for fear that as a woman, she would be castigated for smoking. One night, someone spotted her puffing out below the stars, and when Amy disembarked on the wharves of Boston, she was greeted by hordes of reporters, crying out questions about her smoking habits. Newspapers from Boston to Los Angeles blared the headline: THE SISTER OF PRESIDENT LOWELL OF HARVARD SMOKES CIGARS.[4] From that point on, Amy never tried to hide her smoking. What bothered her most about the press coverage was not the revealed habit, but the manner in which she had been named: *sister of President Lowell.*

The next summer, Amy went back again to London, this time with Ada. They sailed on the *Laconia* on June 23, 1914. On the journey over, the women heard the news that Archduke Ferdinand of Austria had been shot in Sarajevo. But they had no idea of what the assassination would lead to. Shipboard jollity went on as usual, with dinner parties and dances and afternoon teas. Even over the weeks that followed, as news of war filtered through—Austria-Hungary's declaration of war against Serbia, and then Germany's declaration against Russia—the idea of a world war seemed impossible. England had never seen such beautiful weather, day after day of sunshine and warmth, and evenings clear and soft, every star in the night sky visible.

Amy and Ada took advantage of the weather to take excursions into the English countryside, ferried about in Amy's Pierce-Arrow convertible. The car had been shipped over on the same transatlantic liner they'd traveled on, along with Amy's chauffeur, George, and two sets of his livery. His driving suits matched the color of the Pierce-Arrow: a deep, gorgeous maroon. One morning in late July, the couple set out for Max Gate, home of the writer Thomas Hardy. Only a few clouds lurked on the horizon, but George had been warned that nasty weather was coming. He tried to convince Amy that it would be unwise to remove the top of the Pierce-Arrow for the long drive to Dorset. Amy was adamant: The top must be removed. She wanted a full and open view of the hills of Surrey passing by in all their glory, while she afforded a full and open view of herself in all her glory. She had purchased a special hat for the occasion, trimmed with white-and-blue feathers and a stuffed yellow bird.

Amy placed the hat on her head, tying it securely under her chin. The ladies and their chauffeur set off. Less than an hour into their journey, the clouds moved in en masse and opened up, letting loose a steady downpour of rain. By the time Amy and Ada arrived at Hardy's door, the two women and their driver were soaked to the bone. As Hardy told the story, he opened the door to "two very bedraggled ladies."[5] The tiny yellow bird hung off Amy's hat by a thread, and the feathers lay slivered and flat along the wet felt. Hardy and his wife, Florence, welcomed the women and their driver into the house to dry out by the fire. The trio stayed all afternoon, George cozy in the kitchen and Ada and Amy ensconced with their host in his sitting room.

Hardy's sitting room was a calm sea of books, neatly stacked on tables or arranged in bookcases that wrapped around the room. Pen-and-ink sketches of Dorchester were lined up above the fireplace, and large windows gave out on a stretch of rocky meadows and fields. The room reminded Amy of her own library, but on a smaller scale. She had renovated the front and rear parlors of Sevenels after her father's death, converting the two rooms into one long space with a fireplace at either end. Shelves lined an entire wall, filled from floor to ceiling with books. On the wall opposite, large windows let in splendid southern light during the day; two chandeliers and lamps provided light by night. Paintings hung above the two fireplaces: at the eastern end, the painting of Amun Ra in Egypt that Amy had commissioned from Joseph Lindon Smith, and at the western end, two paintings of stormy skies by Constable and a mellow river scene by Whistler.

Amy had all of Hardy's books in her library, but of his novels, she liked *Jude the Obscure* best; of his poetry collections, her favorite was *Poems of the Past and Present,* especially the poems Hardy had written about the Boer War: "O it was sad enough, weak enough, mad enough— / Light in their loving as soldiers can be—/ First to risk choosing them, leave alone losing them/ Now, in far battle, beyond the South Sea!"[6]

The two authors, one successful and one hopeful, sat side by side. One was traditional and the other was thrusting forward in a new style, and yet their sensibilities meshed. They talked easily together while their two mates, Florence and Ada, sat quietly by. Only with the subject of war now raised did Ada chime in. She and Amy had seen soldiers parading through the English countryside as they drove from London, and when they came through Salisbury, they had been shocked to see the marketplace lined with cannons. Was war imminent? The couples seated around a warm fire in Dorchester, and George chatting with the cook in the kitchen—all hoped that Germany could be stopped and that Great Britain could be saved from sending its boys to war. But Hardy was pessimistic. The women shook their heads as he told them of messages he'd received from friends in London. England was preparing for war. The decision of Prime Minister Asquith was imminent.

On the evening of August 4, Amy and Ada stood on the balcony of their suite at the Berkeley Hotel, overlooking Piccadilly Circus below. As Amy wrote later, "A great crowd of people with flags marched down Piccadilly, shouting *We want war! We want war!* They sang the Marseillaise, and it sounded savage, abominable. The blood-lust was coming back, which we had hoped was gone forever . . ."[7] By midnight, the announcement was made: Great Britain had declared war against Germany.

Amy and Ada found themselves stranded in England. There were no berths available on ships going to the United States. All spots had been taken as Americans from all over Europe streamed into London, looking for a way home, joined by hundreds of Europeans eager to escape the theater of war. Refugees from the Continent streamed in while trainloads of British soldiers steamed out. Amy went to the train station one afternoon seeking news of friends abroad; when she saw the English boys heading off to war, she stopped dead in her tracks. Small groups of children sang to their departing fathers and brothers. Their voices were strained but clear, bells of light in the darkness of the station.

Here's the dawn coming on won't be long,/ Then the sun will come shining through,/ To show me the place I once knew./ Fare thee well,/ Fare thee well and adieu,/ Fare thee well,/ With this song I'll be gone,/ Fare thee well.

It was an old English song and it reminded Amy of Hardy's sad poems of war. He had been right after all.

Percy was in London at the time and managed to secure a place back to America on the *Mauretania;* he helped Amy to find space for her car and chauffeur, but there were no suites available for Amy and Ada. He wished the women the best of luck and left Amy waving good-bye to him from her balcony at the Berkeley.

Herbert Hoover, still a private citizen at the time, albeit a wealthy one, had set up a volunteer program at the Savoy Hotel to help stranded Americans. Amy went to see him, and admired how quickly Hoover got things done; his committee "cashes cheques, gets steamship bookings, suggests hotels and lodgings, provides clothes, meets trains."[8] She offered Hoover a gift of ten thousand dollars to help with his work and asked what else she could do. Within days, Hoover had her pacing back and forth along the tracks of Victoria Station carrying a giant placard with directions to aid stations.

Amy and Ada finally secured berths on the *Laconia,* the same ship they had come over on in June. They returned to the United States in late September, just in time for the release of Amy's second book of poetry, titled *Sword Blades and Poppy Seed.* This book, along with the seven more books of verse that Amy would publish over the next fifteen years, would follow a design created by Amy, with the help of the printer Daniel Berkeley Updike: small enough to fit in a lady's pocket and sturdy enough to bear carrying around; the title boldly printed in black lettering along the spine; and inside, poems printed in Merrymount font, created especially by Updike and named for Mount Wollaston in Quincy, Massachusetts.

Although most of the poems in *Sword Blades and Poppy Seed* had already been published in magazines, the combined impact of the collected volume launched Amy as a star. The collection, with so many of the poems dealing with war, loss, and sorrow, seemed perfectly timed. The new style of poetry that she used—impressionist observations set in free verse—made her poetry accessible and yet also very current in a way that her first book of poems had not. The public bought it up; Hardy wrote from England to congratulate Amy; and even Louis Untermeyer, who had so panned her first book, proclaimed her to be "a whole new poet."[9] She was boring no longer.

Amy had become the American voice for Imagism, and a new voice for poetry in America. Having secured her own lucrative deal for a third, then a fourth book of poetry, she set out to secure contracts for a series of Imagist anthologies to be published by Houghton Mifflin. In those books, she would promote not only her own career but also the careers of fellow poets, including D. H. Lawrence, Hilda Doolittle, James Joyce, and William Carlos Williams. She felt a special affinity for David Herbert Lawrence, whom she had spent much time with in England, including a wonderful day visiting Lawrence and his wife, Frieda, in the cottage they shared in the low hills of Buckinghamshire.

The cottage rented by the newlyweds was old and weathered, its stones pocked with scars and its shutters worn and unpainted. Cracked pots of fuchsia stood beside the low front door. Later, Amy would recall the afternoon as a sensory delight: the deep sweet smell of the tawny roses twining over golden stone walls; the sharp taste of ramps and onion in the salad; the sparks of light that seemed to shoot off Lawrence's red hair in sunlight; the touch of Frieda's hand, rough from working in the garden. It was obvious to Amy that David and Frieda were wanting for money. She couldn't send David cash—she didn't believe in charity—but she could make sure his poems were published in the United States. And there was more she could do: Once she had returned to the United States, she packed up her typewriter and sent it off to David. She knew he had no extra money to buy one for himself and that it would help his work tremendously, especially his novel writing. When the typewriter finally arrived, David wrote to Amy right away. "The typewriter has come and it is splendid. Why did you give it away? I am sure you must have wanted to keep it. But it goes like a bubbling pot, frightfully jolly."[10]

In December 1914, Amy gave the first public reading of her poetry, at Steinert Hall in Boston. The reading was a fund-raiser for Belgian war refugees, an offshoot of the work she had done in London. Hans Ebell, a pianist from the conservatory in Kraków, would play a few selections after Amy and the poet Josephine Peabody each recited a selection of poems. Peabody had been educated at Radcliffe and had taught at Wellesley; her style of poetry was more in line with the nineteenth century than the twentieth, but she and Amy were great friends.

Ada had been a renowned actress of the London and New York stage before she gave it all up to live at Sevenels. She now used her considerable skills to coach Amy as the poet rehearsed her readings through the cold, wet days of November 1914. Amy also enlisted the help of Carl Engel, a close friend and talented musician. Her grand finale would be a performance of the poem, "Bombardment," which gave a visceral rendering of the bombing of a church. The manner in which Amy read the poem, in cadences fast and slow, and the words she'd chosen would convey the drama of the bombing. But Amy had more in mind than just words to convey the experience depicted in her poem.

Together with Carl Engel, she planned how he would position himself backstage, out of sight of the audience. And when the time was right, he would be ready to perform.

Steinert Hall had been built in 1896 in a subterranean space carved out beneath the Steinert piano store at 162 Boylston Street, just steps from the Boston Garden. It was not a large space, but the interior proportions were pleasing and elegant, and the dome-shaped ellipse was designed for perfect acoustics. The walls and ceiling were burnished yellow, with beveled borders of apricot and red. On the night of Amy's performance, light from the sconces and the center chandelier shimmered off the golden walls and soaring white columns. A perfect half-moon stage glowed under a wide arch. Rows of red velvet seats spread out like an opened fan. Voices buzzed; there was a stirring of skirts as women and men took their seats, and the rustle of paper as programs were opened.

Amy made her way to the stage, taking her time as she moved smoothly down the aisle and then walked up the steps to one side. She was dressed in a silk dress of deep burgundy, and wore a magnificent hat the color of dusky rose, with a large diamond pin shot through on the side, shining now under the lights. She waited for the audience to settle and quiet. Then she began her program, fourteen poems in all.

Thirteen completed, and it was time for the last one—"Bombardment." She glanced backstage to make sure Engel was ready. He was. And so she began to recite.

> Boom! The Cathedral is a torch, and the houses next to it
>   begin to scorch. Boom! The Bohemian glass on the
>   *étagère* is no longer there. Boom! A stalk of flame sways
>   against the red damask curtains. The old lady cannot
>   walk. She watches the creeping stalk and counts.
>   Boom!—Boom!—Boom!
> The poet rushes into the street, and the rain wraps him in a
>   sheet of silver. But it is threaded with gold and powdered
>   with scarlet beads. The city burns. . . .
> And the steeple crashes down among the people. Boom!
>   Boom, again! The water rushes along the gutters. The
>   fire roars and mutters. Boom![11]

With each "Boom!" Carl Engel crashed on the timpani before him. The huge kettledrums produced a resounding crash to underscore the spoken word: "Boom!" Crash. "Boom!" Crash. The audience was stunned, and then awed. When Amy finished her recitation, they rose to their feet as one and applauded loud and long. It was no easy task for Josephine Peabody to climb up those stairs and begin her own recitation. Later, all anyone could remember of the evening were the drums, banging home the terror of the *bombardment*.

Robert Frost came to see Amy on a snowy evening a few months later, in February 1915. The month had started with a blizzard, four days of unrelenting snow that paralyzed the city, closing down everything and anyone. What a terrible turn of fortune it was that those four days included the three days scheduled for the Boston Women's Municipal League Benefit. For weeks, Amy and her sister Katie worked on the event, organizing and planning and arranging. The program would include three French operas altogether new to the United States (and translated by Amy). The operas were sure to be popular with Boston's wealthy and elite, and the renowned soprano Maggie Teyte, along with tenors John Campbell and George Mitchell, provided additional star power to the draw of the evening.

Amy organized musicians for the thirty-five-piece orchestra (most on loan from the Boston Opera) and cajoled the composer Arthur Shepherd to offer his services as conductor. Livingston Platt, Broadway genius, created the set and costumes, and Daniel Berkeley Updike, designer of Amy's books, took care of the tickets and invitations. The costs of the production were tremendous but Amy didn't care. She spent the thousands of dollars for Katie, because for Katie she would do anything. Both sisters were sure their program would be the charity event of the season and that all costs would be recouped, with ample funds left to further the lofty goals of the Municipal League.

Then the snow began to fall. For the first evening, an audience did manage to struggle through the streets to arrive at the Castle Square Theatre on Tremont Street. The theater was not filled to capacity, but there were enough people there for it to count as a real performance. But the snow continued. By the next day, February 3, the streets and gardens of Boston and Brookline had become buried in drifts. There was no distinguishing where grass started and asphalt left off. All that could be seen from Amy's third-floor aerie was a blanket of white, surrounding the house on all sides. Snow on the ground, on the bushes, on the trees, and still tumbling flakes kept coming down, as if in a god-driven fury. Amy imagined Zeus in the skies above, hurling his fists this way and that, and from those fists came ever-larger balls of snow, balls that broke up and multiplied into trillions of flakes, turning over and over and over as they fell to earth. There was nothing for it but to cancel the remaining performances.

On another snowy morning three weeks later, the maid, Elizabeth Henry, came into the library, announcing that there was a phone call for Amy from a man by the name of Frost. Amy went out to the hall to take the call.

The voice on the phone was deep and hoarse. "*I am Robert Frost, I want to see you, and I have read your review . . .*"[12]

Amy had discovered Frost's poetry in a bookshop in London in the summer of 1914 and had fallen in love with his verses. She and Ada had taken turns reading his poems aloud in their room at the Berkeley. After returning home to Boston, Amy tried to convince Houghton Mifflin to publish *North of Boston* in America. They were not interested, and so Amy turned to *The New Republic* and demanded that they allow her to review Frost's book. Now Amy invited him to dinner.

At dinner that evening, Frost told Ada and Amy how he happened to find Amy's review of *North of Boston*. He'd just arrived from England with his family and the group of them were trudging uptown from the landing wharf in New York. Frost came upon a newsstand, purchased a copy of *The New Republic*, along with a few newspapers, and then went with his wife, Elinor, and their four girls to enjoy a cup of coffee and apple pie at a corner restaurant. He sat back in his booth, opened up *The New Republic*, and discovered Amy's review. "Not only is his work New England in subject, it is so in technique. . . . Mr. Frost has reproduced both people and scenery with a vividness which is extraordinary . . . Mr. Frost has chosen his medium with an unerring sense of fitness. . . . He goes his own way, regardless of anyone else's rules, and the result is a book of unusual power and sincerity."[13] Frost read the review through twice and then showed it to his wife.

That evening at Sevenels, Frost leaned close to Amy across the dinner table and told her that the review had been "like a welcome to his native land."[14] Amy clasped his hand in hers and smiled. The two poets would remain friends until the end of Amy's life.

For her talk before the Poetry Society of America in March 1915, Amy dressed in more sober clothing than she had worn for the Steinert Hall fund-raiser. The gray silk suit she wore artfully covered her large bulk, and the white collar of her shirtwaist framed and emphasized her more delicate face: pink lips, straight nose, large blue eyes. Amy's thin hair had been augmented with a postiche (a wig of braided hair) and was arranged into a wrapped bun. A long pin of plain polished silver was stuck in her lapel. The only color was on her fingers, rings studded with semiprecious stones: garnet, opal, and tourmaline. The colors of blood, starlight, forest leaves.

Amy began her talk. She briefly described the tenets of Imagism and what the movement could mean for American poets. By using common words and language, and writing in free verse, a poet could express things in a new and creative way, and in a way that drew the audience into the experience. The use of images was crucial to creating that immersive experience. Any topic could be explored, with no subject forbidden. The poem itself should be focused, definite, and clear. No fuzzy edges: All was crystalline, sharp, and vivid.

To illustrate her points, Amy began to recite her poem "Spring Day." The gathered crowd grew increasingly uncomfortable as a vivid image came alive, invoked by Amy's words. Her conservative and elegant clothing seemed to be falling away before their eyes, to be replaced by a naked Amy, frolicking lazily in a bath: "Little spots of sunshine lie on the surface of the water and dance, dance, and their reflections wobble deliciously over the ceiling; a stir of my finger sets them whirring, reeling. I move a foot, and the planes of light in the water jar."

Discomfort gave rise to snickers; then a kind of meanness took over the crowd and the audience gave vent to laughter tinged with nasty disdain. Amy did not falter. She continued on reciting, her voice clear and steady, her words evocative yet innocent:

I lie back and laugh, and let the green-white water, the sun-flawed beryl water, flow over me. The day is almost too bright to bear, the green water covers me from the too bright day. I will lie here awhile and play with the water and the sun spots.

The sky is blue and high. A crow flaps by the window, and there is a whiff of tulips and narcissus in the air.[15]

By the time Amy finished reciting, the crowd was howling. But then their howls of laughter turned to howls of derision. Amy Lowell, all two hundred or so pounds of her, had had the audacity to speak of nakedness and bathing and narcissus—symbol of vanity—all in what she presumed to call "a poem."

"That's not poetry," came the angry cries from the audience.[16]

Amy Lowell was unfazed. Her words most certainly were poetry and she would keep on writing it and performing it, and writing about it. No one could stop her now. As she would explain later, "Personally, I believe in the motto live and let live . . . But it has been made evident to me that the large majority of people do not share my tolerance . . . [A poet who] points out the beautiful effects of a light striking the water in a bathtub . . . is taken as a personal affront. . . ."[17]

At the Harvard commencement in the spring of 1915, graduating senior Edward Estlin Cummings, who would become known as e.e. cummings, gave an address entitled "The New Art." He alluded to a new form of poetry being created in the United States, and then quoted from a poem by Amy Lowell, *Grotesque*: "Why do the lilies goggle their tongues at me/ When I pluck them;/ And writhe and twist,/ And strangle themselves against my fingers . . ."[18] He described the poem as demonstrating "a clear development from the ordinary to the abnormal." The next day, the *Boston Transcript* proclaimed in a head-line, HARVARD ORATOR CALLS PRESIDENT LOWELL'S SISTER ABNORMAL.[19]

For Amy, her new poetry was a perfect expression of who she was, where she lived, and the times in which she lived. The face of America was changing, and as it changed, the cultural identity of the country grew stronger, richer, deeper. The poetry Amy espoused belonged to her not only as an American but as a Lowell: "We of the pure Anglo-Saxon stock are constantly coming into contact with people of other nationalities, and consciously or unconsciously are being modified by them. We may not realize it, but slowly before our eyes, the American race is being born. And one of the evidences of it is that we are beginning to hew new pathways for ourselves in this most intimate thing—Poetry. . . ."[20]

Amy herself was forging new paths for poetry. She wrote erotic works: "when you come, it brims/ Red and trembling with blood,/Heart's blood for your drinking;/ To fill your mouth with love/ And the bitter-sweet taste of a soul."[21] And: "As I would free the white almond from the green husk/ So would I strip your trappings off,/Beloved,/ And fingering the smooth and polished kernel/ I should see that in my hands glittered a gem beyond counting."[22]

She experimented with poems that reflected music, such as her poem about Stravinsky: "Sabots slapping the worn, old stones,/ And a shaking and cracking of dancing bones . . ."[23] She wrote free verse and rhymed verse and soon would start on her historic epics, tracking ancient stories to seduce mod-ern audiences. And seduced they were. Amy Lowell was becoming known not for her cigars and "Boston marriage" (living with another woman), but for her poetry. At Lawrence's inauguration in 1909, Amy had told a friend of her de-sire to avoid being known as "the sister of Harvard's president." She wished, instead, that Lawrence might become known as "Amy Lowell's brother."[24] Her wish seemed close to coming true.

Percy was barely aware of his sister Amy's growing fame. His own work con-sumed him. Having weathered the worst of the criticism over his speculations on Mars, he was now intent on making a new discovery in the universe: a dis-covery that would need only *seeing* to be believed. Scientists might debate what the lines on Mars actually were, but a new orb—a newly discovered planet—once observed and documented, could not be disputed. For those who had been listening carefully, Percy had been asserting for years that there was a ninth planet in the universe. In his book *The Solar System*, published in 1903 and based on a series of lectures he had given at MIT, he observed, "It may seem to you strange to speak thus confidently of what no mortal eye has seen, but the finger of the signboard of phenomena points so clearly as to justify the definite article. The eye of analysis has already suspected the invisible."[25] Putting the Mars controversy firmly behind him, Percy set out now to find this "invisible" planet, and to make everyone see it.

Percival's plan was to first calculate, using his prodigious mathematical skills, the specific area in the sky where the planet might be, and then to direct his team of Lowell Observatory photographers to try to capture photographic proof of its existence. The math involved in calculating the location of the planet was complex, time-consuming, and very, very difficult, involving computational analysis that utilized theories of celestial mechanics. Percival described the work, in a massive understatement, as "rigorous mathematical investigation."[26]

Percival did not work alone on his calculations. He put together in Boston a team of mathematicians, led by a young woman named Elizabeth Williams. The team always worked under Percy's guidance; as he wrote in a letter back to Carl Lampland in Flagstaff, "Miss Williams and I have been pegging away at it. . . ."[27] And a year later, in a telegram: "Hope to wire position in a few days. Calculations tremendously long."[28] A letter from Louise Leonard to staff at the Observatory confirmed this: "It has been a long computation, and Dr. Lowell and Miss Williams have been faithful to it all winter. We feel rather heavy with it but when [the planet] is found it will brighten our hearts and make us glad. I am sure you appreciate what the work has meant. . . ."[29]

Math was an area where critics could not assail him, Percival knew, and he was going to use his mathematical abilities to prove, once and for all, that his science was sound and his astronomical predictions were accurate. The search for the ninth planet would redeem his reputation and "improve his credibility among other astronomers."[30] But once again, his health dogged him. He missed weeks in the office in Boston, laid up with a terrible case of shingles and then with exhaustion. "It is nervous exhaustion," Leonard wrote to Vesto Slipher at the observatory, "and he is up and down. Some days he cannot even telephone. He gets nervous about the work. . . ."[31]

By January 1913, Percy was back at his desk, reworking calculations and sending tweaked coordinates to photographers in Flagstaff. He spent hours poring over negatives of their captured images, trying to spot what he called "Planet X." Months of winters turned into springs, then summers into falls, and he traveled back and forth between Boston and Flagstaff, making a quick trip to Europe in the summer of 1914 to consult with Flammarion and other astronomers. Then back to Boston, and on to Flagstaff, and back again to Boston. He and his staff worked long, hard hours, but what was there to show for it?

Percy agonized over not finding the planet that he knew was out there in space. Perhaps the telescopic camera back in Flagstaff was not strong enough to reach where he had directed it; perhaps he and the photographers had missed seeing the planet even as it passed fleetingly before them. Percy decided he could wait no longer for photographic proof; he would publish his calculations and lay open his suppositions. Unlike the works he had published on Mars, this one made no bold declarations of a discovery, but instead proffered his work as a first step in finding a new planet in the universe.

He laid out in exhausting detail the calculations he and his team had undertaken to ascertain where the ninth planet might be found. Even though he and his team had failed in finding Planet X, such failure did not mean that he would stop searching: "to learn of the general solution and the limitations of a problem is really as instructive and important as if it permitted specifically of exact prediction . . . that, too, means advance."[32]

When spirits lagged, Percy consoled his staff in Boston and in Flagstaff with assurances that their hard work would eventually pay off. As he said in a lecture that he gave in August 1916, "Gauge your work by its truth to nature, not by the plaudits it receives from man. In the end truth will prevail and though you may never live to see it, your work will be recognized after you are gone."[33]

On a cold day in late January 1909, Bessie Lowell Putnam made her way through the damp streets of the North End, walking toward the Boston Common. The skies overhead were gray and heavy, and Bessie was cold through to her bones. She looked forward to the warm fire that was sure to be crackling away in her drawing room on the other side of the common. She only hoped to arrive before Will did. She liked to be there when he came home, to be the first one he saw when he came in the door. Often he arrived with a forehead tight with worry, eyes bagged with fatigue. But when he saw her, his face always brightened. His straw brown hair in wisps that never laid flat, his walrus mustache, his red-rimmed eyes under hedgerow eyebrows—all the discordant pieces fell away, for he had a beautiful smile and he always had one for her.

Will continued to smile even as Bessie turned their Beacon Street home into headquarters for the all the commissions and committees and organizations she headed up. Working for clean milk, clean markets, safe food, healthy children; working against the suffragists, because Bessie believed that women's best influence was not in the voting booth, but in the community. The house on Beacon Street became her war room, her citadel for strategy and planning and implementation. Two secretaries called the downstairs library their office, and papers and pamphlets were set in towering piles around the front parlor. Posters lined the ample hallway, obscuring family portraits. Wigged and powdered Lowells and Putnams, their faces now covered by large white placards: CLEAN MARKET DIRTY MARKET WHICH DO YOU PREFER TO BUY AT?[34]

Bessie had promised Will that her work would never invade their other home in Manchester-by-the-Sea, on Boston's North Shore. And she kept that promise, because she knew Smith Point was Will's sanctuary. He loved nothing more than to sit at the windows of the large frame house on the rocky coast. From there, seated in an overstuffed chair that cushioned his back and embraced his aching legs, he could look out over the calm waters of the harbor; leaning forward to open the window, he would take in deep breaths, filling himself with the scents of the coast—the sea, the waving stands of bee balm, bluebells, and tickseed, the low pines that grew from the cliffs—and then sit back again to catch the cries of gulls calling across the wind. Smith Point was his favorite place, a wild space that he and Bessie had tamed together: "Together we discovered our wilderness, together we have made it our garden, together we have loved it, and together found much happiness in it."[35]

Having crossed the gravel paths of the common, Bessie now made her way down the last stretch to home. Her feet ached after a day spent walking through the streets of the North and West Ends of Boston, making visits to local milk stations, trying to gauge their effectiveness throughout the poorer neighborhoods of Boston. The stations were clean—there was no question of that—and they provided safe milk for the children of Boston at a low price. But the neighborhoods themselves were so unsanitary: small, unkempt stores lined the sidewalks, dirty and ill-lit, with refuse strewn about and listing doors left open to flies and street dust. The windows of the tenements above were black with grime, the steps to the apartments unswept, and the smell of sewage and rot was everywhere. Bessie knew the subcommittees of the Municipal League—for Immigrants, for Housing, for Sanitation, for Streets and Alleys, City Waste Disposal and Smoke Nuisance—had programs in place to clean up the stores, the sidewalks, and the streets and alleys. But it wasn't enough.

Bessie was starting to think that more work had to be done beyond the providing of safe milk and food, and sanitary living conditions. Through her work with various committees of the Municipal League, she had come to know many mothers from the lower classes of Boston. She was horrified by the lack of support these women received when pregnant and after giving birth. What they didn't know about the state in which they found themselves was shocking; what they didn't know about childbirth was even worse. Bessie had been haunted through her own pregnancies by what she had witnessed and heard about her mother's period of confinement. Katharine had suffered a lifelong illness due to problems incurred during pregnancy, her Bright's disease having been brought on by childbirth and what Bessie now was certain was related to eclampsia.

When she found herself pregnant for the first time, Bessie faced her doctor straight on and demanded to know what could be done to avoid eclampsia. The word came from the Greek and meant a sudden flash. Eclampsia caused sudden convulsions and seizures during childbirth, often leading to coma and death. One terrible flash of pain and a woman's life ended. Bessie wanted none of it. And so she had learned what she could do to avoid it. She learned the symptoms, which included headaches, swelling of the feet, and muddled thinking and vision. She took control of her first pregnancy, and it had gone well, as did the next four. Bessie had been lucky but also smart. Eclampsia was avoidable; her mother's years of suffering from kidney problems could have been avoided, as well. Certainly Bessie was concerned with the next generation—"to improve the efficiency of future citizens by beginning with the health of babies"[36]—but as a mother who had borne five children of her own, she was just as concerned with the present generation: the mothers of Boston. How could she help them?

She and Will talked late into the night that cold winter evening, and for many evenings afterward. As spring approached, Bessie came up with her solution. With the help of her sister Katie and under the umbrella of the Women's Municipal League, she set up the first ever prenatal clinic in the United States. It was a small clinic, located adjacent to the Peter Bent Brigham Hospital on Francis Street. Women who registered their pregnancy with the hospital would be directed to the clinic and then put on a rotation of weekly visits from a nurse, along with in-clinic care when necessary. There would be outreach to bring other expectant mothers in; there would be follow-up through the months of pregnancy and up until birthing day.

It was Bessie who insisted that visits from the nurse be frequent—"the intervals between visits should not exceed ten days"[37]—with tests taken including urine sampling; she was one of the first laymen to recognize the value of testing for protein in the urine and she insisted that such sampling be a part of prenatal care. (Such routine urine testing is now common in prenatal care). In its scope and its purpose, Bessie's prenatal clinic was exactly the kind of experiment that Katie had had in mind for the Municipal League: a model for improving public health that could be re-created by local and state government. Bessie did not want the clinic to be free. Every mother who wished to participate in the program was required to pay a small fee: "we believe that self-supporting work is of far more value than that supported by charity—for not only is there no limit to growth, but it is much more appreciated by those who benefit from it."[38] She also believed that a strong sense of community could be created through such self-paying clinics: When women pay for the clinic, it allows them to "feel that in so doing they are making it possible to help more women as they themselves are being helped, calling out in them the spirit of sisterhood, the united effort to better conditions for every one in the whole city."[39]

This was also in line with Katie's overriding goal: "women of every occupation, of every interest, of every degree of poverty and wealth . . . [can] gain the stimulus and uplift that comes from feeling themselves members of the great municipal body of women, who are all striving together for one common end—the making of the city in which they live a cleaner, healthier, and a happier place for its citizens."[40]

But while Katie wanted to build community, Bessie was always more motivated by what she wanted to avoid: the misery of mothers and the death of little children. The clinics for expectant mothers were expanded to provide infant care. "I well remember how, when carrying on a healthy-baby clinic . . . I used to take up to town a large box of flowers in the summer time. The clinic was held in a very slummy part of the city and long before I could get inside I was always surrounded by children of the neighborhood . . . each clamoring for a flower. . . ."[41] Bessie brought flowers to beautify the decrepit environments of the women she helped, but while the flowers faded in their jugs, the clinics provided real and lasting change for the women of Boston. During the first year of the clinic, not one woman treated died of childbirth, although three had suffered from preeclampsia—and were successfully treated for it. And out of the 205 babies cared for in the first year of the baby clinic, only 4 of those babies died.

By 1915, the Municipal League had opened two more self-sustaining prenatal and baby clinics. Bessie worked toward training and licensing midwives and social workers to help out with the work of the clinics. Within a few years, Brigham Hospital and Boston Lying-In Hospital would take over the clinics, but Bessie remained the go-to expert on prenatal care. Letters and requests for information, along with invitations to lecture, arrived from all over the world: even as far away as New Zealand, Bessie was known as the mother- and baby-care queen.

Storm clouds loomed over Mount Monadnock, but bright beams of sun still shot through the gray, illuminating the pines and lighting up patches of meadow and grass. Amy Lowell, who had purchased a country house nestled in the valley below, held her hand over her eyes and surveyed the horizon. She had named her home "Bromley Lacey" in honor of her grandfather's old place in Roxbury. It was a wooden farmhouse, so old and brown that it faded into the background of the mountain. Amy had planted a vegetable garden in the sunny corner of the yard and mowed down some of the meadowlands for laundry lines and a croquet field, but for the most part she kept Bromley Lacey as wild and untamed as the woods that loomed above her on the mountainside. In addition to the house, there was a barn for the horses, the carts, and the dogs. All seven of her sheepdogs came out with her for long summer weekends. When the days grew too hot, Amy hosed them off, one by one, with cold water from the tap.

Her third book of poetry, entitled *Men, Women and Ghosts*, was due to come out in just a few months, in the fall of 1916. *Sword Blades and Poppy Seed* was in its second printing, and her edited collection of Imagist poems, with submissions from H.D. (Hilda Doolittle), D. H. Lawrence, and Richard Aldington, had also been published and was selling well. Amy shared all the proceeds equally among the artists. Amy had also published a book of essays, entitled *Six French Poets*, which proved to be hugely popular. A lecture tour had been planned for the winter and spring. More poems were flowing from her pen every day. Visitors from nearby Loon Point, in Dublin, New Hampshire, the location of Joseph Lindon Smith's artist colony, often came by the farmhouse in the evenings for dinner and drinks. All seemed to be going as well as things could be. And then Amy looked up into the clouds coming over the mountain and decided to go on a buggy ride.

Back in Cambridge, Lawrence Lowell was facing an obstacle. His plans for freshman housing were coming to fruition, buildings popping up all around the Harvard Yard. The next step would be constructing four-year housing—living arrangements that would be mandatory for all students. But now, a flaw in the plan: Black students wanted to be a part of it, and Lawrence did not know what to do. Since the mid-1800s, Harvard had had black students enrolled in the college. They usually found rooms off campus in which to live. But with the construction of the new freshmen halls, restrictions against blacks living and eating with the white students had been called into question. All eyes turned to Lawrence. Would he prohibit black students from living beside their white cohorts?

Lawrence wrote to his good friend and a faculty member at Harvard, Barrett Wendell, "My own feeling is that we owe to the Negro just as good an education as to the white man, but that he has no right to expect social advantages which he would not get in the world outside."[42] Lawrence wanted to build the perfect college community, but not a utopian one. Blacks could study at Harvard but they could not live within the community he was trying so hard to create: The dream of "intellectual and social cohesion"[43] was not a dream to be shared by all. Lawrence had made up his mind. But the matter wouldn't end there, or then. Other students, from other backgrounds and other persuasions, would seek their place in the Harvard community, and Lawrence would once again have to consider just what he wanted his beloved community to look like.

When Amy and Ada set out on their buggy ride through the lower reaches of Mount Monadnock, the weather had been fine. Dark clouds were gathering in the west, but above them, only soft white clouds cluttered against a blue sky. As they began their descent, however, the wind picked up, bringing the dark clouds closer. All birdsong ceased, and then suddenly a storm broke across the valley, riding fast on the wind toward the mountain. Thunder clapped, lightning skidded across the sky, rain began to fall hard and fast. The mare pulling Amy's cart grew nervous. She pulled anxiously against the reins in Amy's hands, skittering up and then shuffling backward along the trail. The thunder kept booming overhead, and lightning kept cracking. Amy tried to calm the horse, speaking to her in a soft voice. But when lightning came again, so close that they could smell the wave of phosphorus, the mare heaved up on her rear legs and then fell forward, lurching sideways. The pony cart was jerked off the trail and landed with its back wheels hanging over a ditch to the side. Rain poured down, the wind howled all around, and the wheels spun in the void. Amy climbed down from the cart, calling to Ada to take the reins. She made her way carefully down to the edge of the ditch. She bent over to grab the cart from underneath its back end, then heaved with all her might. The buggy came up into the lane, all four wheels now level and even. Amy gave out a groan of pain and fell heavily against the side of the cart. She was doubled over and could not stand up straight. She shuffled over to the step of the cart and threw her arms up toward Ada. It took all of Ada's strength to drag Amy up and onto the seat. Then Ada turned the mare toward home.

By ten o'clock that evening, Amy could barely move. Her abdomen ached and a sharp pain wrenched her body whenever she changed position in her chair. Even when she kept still, the pain persisted, insistent and dull. Ada put her to bed and sat beside her, placing cold compresses across her sweating forehead and sweeping the damp hair from her face. She instructed the maid,

Elizabeth Henry, to call for the doctor. He came before midnight and examined Amy carefully. He diagnosed a tear of the abdominal muscle. Amy was dosed with opium and told to stay in bed, resting. It might be a hernia, he warned, and Amy must lie still, or the tear could get worse.

When Ada and Amy returned to Brookline a few weeks later, it should have been in celebration. The book *Men, Women and Ghosts* had sold out in eight days and a second printing was ordered, in time for holiday sales. But Amy barely took notice. The pain in her abdomen was constant, a dull ache that with the slightest movement became sharp as a knife. Once helped to her third-floor suite at Sevenels, Amy did not venture downstairs for days.

Early in November 1916, Percy went out to his garden to plant squill bulbs. He worked in the little bed of dirt under an old oak tree near the entrance drive to the observatory. The flowers would come out in April, bright shoots of purple and blue coming from the warming ground after a cold, white winter. It wasn't hard work, being out on his hands and knees and digging into the rocky soil, then planting the bulbs. But that evening, Percy complained of fatigue and an aching across his back. When Constance offered him a nightcap, he shook his head. There was plenty to choose from for a late-night drink, as Percy had laid in twelve cases of wine, along with boxes of scotch, beer, and sherry, filling the cellars of the Baronial Manor in anticipation of the impending restrictions of Prohibition, currently being debated in Congress. Percy had little doubt that a national prohibition would come to pass and he wanted to be prepared. But tonight, he declined a drink and went to bed early.

The next day, November 12, 1916, Percy suffered a massive stroke. He looked up at Constance, then over to Louise, the loyal secretary hovering behind his wife. "I always knew it would be like this," he said. "But not so soon."[44] He died that night.

Percy had left explicit instructions for his funeral. He wanted to be buried on Mars Hill after a simple ceremony. The Lowell Observatory was his chosen home; the community of astronomers, his chosen community. A mausoleum would be built on the hill, but for now, a funeral mound was prepared. The service was conducted by local Episcopal and Catholic priests, with friends and colleagues serving as pallbearers. Will and Bessie Putnam came from Boston to attend the funeral; Lawrence Lowell did not. Back in Boston, Amy was still too ill to bear the bad news of her brother's death. It must have been Katie who arranged for a log of petrified wood to be impaled into the ground of the family plot in Mount Auburn Cemetery. Percy may have settled his bones for good in the West, but he was a Boston boy and a Lowell: There would always be a place for him at Mount Auburn.

Constance fired Louise within two weeks of Percy's death and told her to leave Mars Hill. Louise left without a fuss, but she would have her revenge. In 1921, she published a memoir entitled *Percival Lowell: An Afterglow*. It told the story of her life with Percy, and of the discoveries they had made together. Louise included in the book complete texts of affectionate letters Percy had written to her over the years. There was no mention of Constance anywhere in the book. During the latter years of Louise's life, she suffered a financial downturn and Lawrence quietly paid her a monthly stipend. She would be cared for into old age.

The tear in Amy's abdomen became infected in the last weeks of October 1916. She nevertheless insisted on driving into Boston to see her book *Men, Women and Ghosts* on display in the windows of the Old Corner Bookstore on the corner of Washington Street. But when she arrived at the store, she was too weak to get out of the Pierce-Arrow and had to be driven home again. By mid-November, she was so ill that she was not told of her brother's death for days, for fear of what such a blow would do to her. When she was finally given the news, she turned on her bed and wept into the sixteen pillows she always kept there, one after another becoming damp with her tears.

On an unseasonably pleasant day in February 1917, Katie joined her husband, Thomas Bowlker, for a walk on Commonwealth Avenue. The sun was out, and the piles of snow left over from a severe storm just days before were now melting into puddles. On such a balmy day, it would have been easy for any passersby to imagine—indeed hope for—crocuses and daffodils coming up along the green-bordered path running down the center of the avenue. But Katie's mind was on rats and filth.

As president of the Women's Municipal League, Katie had made it a priority to vanquish, once and for all, the legions of vermin that called Boston home. The city's Department of Health estimated that over 750,000 rats dwelled in the cellars, sewers, and alleys of the city. With bubonic plague having broken out in San Francisco in 1907 and in New Orleans in 1914, the women of the Municipal League feared that it was only a matter of time before Boston, being the second great Atlantic port of entry, would be invaded by the dreaded disease.

Katie and her Committee on Rats and Flies had been educating the public for weeks on rat eradication. Rat clubs were formed throughout the city to teach members about rat habits and habitats, and to give instruction as to the proper methods for trapping, hunting, and poisoning rats. Posters and flyers in a variety of languages were distributed, and all the local newspapers ran articles. The efforts of the committee were to culminate in "Rat Day": an all-out effort to capture and kill as many rats as possible in a massive one-day hunt. Every citizen was encouraged to participate: Find a rat, catch it, and take the carcass to a collection point. Cash prizes would be awarded to the ones who caught the most rats. Only a few days to go and Rat Day would finally arrive.

The day before the big event, the temperatures in Boston plummeted. For four consecutive days, frigid cold kept not only potential rat hunters indoors but all the rats stayed hidden away as well, deep in their nests and burrows. Fewer than one thousand carcasses were collected on Rat Day. Only a "foreign born resident, unable to read or write the English language, who would have known nothing of the movement save for the printing of the circular in Polish, exert[ed] himself to trap nearly three hundred rats in spite of the weather and the difficulty of getting at the rodents," reported the local papers.[45] This intrepid soul, Mr. B. Rymkus of Brighton, won both cash prizes for rat catching, one hundred dollars for the greatest number caught overall, and fifty dollars for the greatest number brought to one particular sanitation yard.

The Boston Board of Health offered to carry on the rat-catching campaign, and promised Katie and her Municipal League that the rat population would be conquered. Katie accepted the promise. She counted her campaign a success: although the actual extermination rates were slight, the impact of the far-reaching education campaign would lead to eventual eradication.

Now another war loomed before her. She feared it was one not to be fought by her and her community of women, but by her son and all the sons of Boston. On April 6, 1917, America declared war on Germany. The United States had entered the Great War.

25

1917–1919

For the man who should loose me is dead,
Fighting with the Duke in Flanders,
In a pattern called war.
—AMY LOWELL, "PATTERNS"

Lawrence walked the curving path from Quincy Street across Harvard Yard. His steps were slow and measured. He stopped every few feet and turned to look around. The Yard was quiet, too quiet. On this fall afternoon in 1917, with a brilliant blue sky overhead and the air so crisp that it snapped, there should have been clusters of students passing by. Lawrence longed to see young men laughing and talking and turning their faces upward to the mellowing trees, the warming sun, the tall spire of Appleton Chapel.

But only a few groups of students passed under the trees. They shuffled their feet through fallen leaves as they walked, heads down. Out of the entire student body of fifteen hundred, more than four hundred seniors had not returned to Cambridge in the fall. They were now soldiers, not students. As of early September, the Selective Service Act had lowered the age of the military draft to eighteen years old. But the hundreds of Harvard students who had gone to war over the summer were all volunteers. The football season was canceled, for the seventy football players were off at war, along with their longtime coach, Percy Houghton, and most of his coaching staff. Two-thirds of the students from Harvard Law School had enlisted; Lawrence was surprised at what a difference their absence made.

James Roosevelt, Katie's son, who was working in New York City as a banker, had also signed up for the war effort over the summer. He was commissioned a captain and put in command of C Company, 302nd Ammunition Train, Seventy-seventh Division. Once in France, he would become the supply officer of the famous 308th Infantry, the so-called Lost Battalion, which became surrounded by German forces in the fall of 1918 deep in the forests of the Argonne; subjected to stealth and overt attacks, they had to survive for six days without food or supplies before they were rescued. Of the 550 men who went on the mission, only 194 men came back. It was up to Captain Roosevelt to make sure that those survivors had food and water waiting for them when they finally returned to camp.

Katie traveled to London in the summer of 1917 to be close to James before he shipped out to France. For the next year and a half, she would remain in England, taking advantage of James's army leaves to spend time with him, and devoting herself to war relief efforts in England. Her husband, Thomas, had died in April and she went alone; she had it in her mind that she might move to England full-time after the war. But events would transpire to bring her back to the United States, and keep her there.

Amy had slowly recovered from the injury she'd sustained on Mount Monadnock. Her abdomen still bothered her, but she could move easily now. She got to work, shutting away her grief for Percy and driving herself to complete a series of essays in which she critically examined the works of contemporary poets, including Robert Frost, Edgar Lee Masters, H.D., and Carl Sandburg. In October 1917, the essays were published in a book entitled *Tendencies in Modern American Poetry*. The book sold well, garnering new fans for Frost, Sandburg, and the other poets, and for Amy, as well. *Sword Blade and Poppy Seed* continued to sell, and her most recent book of poems, *Men, Women and Ghosts*, still in the window at the Old Corner Book Shop, was in its second edition. Now she prepared for a flurry of scheduled readings and lectures up and down the East Coast. Amy considered her readings to be performances—theater pieces that would draw on the imagery of the words and the intonation of her delivery to captivate and transport her audiences. If she garnered no initial response from her audience, she did not hold back from chiding them for their reticence.

"Well?" she would demand. "Clap or hiss, I don't care which, but do something!"[1]

Her weight was noted by her audiences but rarely criticized. That was left to her fellow writers, who could be cruel. Fanny Butcher, writer and literary critic, called Amy "the grand panjandrum of free verse," who "was so fat she literally waddled."[2] The poet Witter Bynner called her a "hippopoetess,"[3] a pejorative that Ezra Pound gleefully took up. Pound also insulted Amy by describing her as a "fleshpot," and worse: "Poor Amy, poor Amy. It is all very distressing and my Arm Chair has never been the same since she bounced with glee over some witticism. No upholsterer can do anything with it, the springs still do *such* funny things."[4]

Pound didn't go after Amy just for her weight. He attacked her as a writer, calling her poetry "perfumed [and] . . . putrid"[5] and her prose "slop."[6] He ridiculed the work she did to promote Imagism in the Unites States, describing it derisively as "Amygism." He refused to acknowledge that the Imagist writers she promoted had talent—"you tried to stampede me into accepting as my artistic equal various people whom it would have been rank hypocrisy for me to accept"—and claimed that her poets had been spoiled by Amy's "flow-contamination."[7] He was happy to use her—"I would be right glad to see her milked of her money"[8]—but denied that "autochthonous Amy"[9] had anything of merit to add to American poetry.

Amy was hurt by Pound's disparaging remarks over her weight. She was already sensitive about her looks; when she took over a hotel suite, one of the first things she did was put cloths over the mirrors to thwart the unexpected viewing. *Who could that be, that giantess in the mirror?* Pound had called her a hippo more than once, and what she saw in the mirror confirmed his condemnation. Ada consoled her, and even scolded her, telling her that girth did not define her; her contributions to the world did. Amy rallied then, for when it came to her work, she was confident of her own talents and of the talents of the poets whose careers she promoted. She went on the attack against Pound, questioning his vitality as a poet: Pound "has ceased to be a youthful phenomenon . . . he finds himself falling back at every step, and this naturally makes him exceedingly bitter." Pound's greatest fault, Amy wrote, was that "his work lacks quality of soul, which I am more and more fain to believe, no great work can ever be without."[10] Poor man, Amy pitied him: "he got everything out of books . . . I never knew him to call your attention to a tree or a sunset or the roofs of the city or anything like that."[11]

When Pound threatened to sue her for using the term *Imagism* without his permission, she had laughed. How dare he lay claim to a literary term? She consulted with her fellow poets on the Imagist collections they were putting together for Houghton Mifflin. Should they take out the term *Imagism* just to please Pound? Amy argued against it but would let the group decide. Richard Aldington, Hilda Doolittle, D. H. Lawrence, and Frank Stuart Flint all sided with Amy and pledged her their support. After all, Amy was introducing them to audiences in America and ensuring they got paid for writing poetry. What better patron and friend could they have?

Amy revised the introduction to the first collection of *Some Imagist Poets,* leaving the term but taking Pound's name out of her history of Imagism entirely. She then left it to readers to decide, explaining, "We wish it to be clearly understood that we do not represent an exclusive artistic sect; we publish our work together because of mutual artistic sympathy and we propose to bring out our cooperative volume each year for a short term of years, until we have made a place for ourselves and our principles . . ."[12]

The public responded by making Amy Lowell a superstar. Her books sold well, the books of her friends sold well, thanks to her promotions of them, and poetry as a whole was resurging in popularity, harking back to the days of her cousin James Russell Lowell and his contemporary Henry Wadsworth Long-fellow. Then, as now, there was a growing audience for poetry—in part due to the hard work of Amy Lowell. In 1916, 663 books of poetry and theater were published in the United States, "a number exceeding all other classifications except fiction, which had only seventy-more titles." It was true: "the poetry movement had saturated the country . . ."[13]

But there was a new audience Amy had not considered, and it would fall to her to fill their needs. Soldiers, it turned out, were hungry for words.

Herbert Hoover, who had been appointed head of the U.S. Food Administra-tion by President Woodrow Wilson, promoted war rationing. "Food will win the war," he insisted: "Unless we can feed both our own people and the men who are fighting for us across the water, the great cause which we have joined will be lost."[14] The farmers of the United States could feed the world, but Americans would have to help out by conserving what they ate, so that all sur-pluses could go overseas. The "Meatless Mondays" and "Wheatless Wednes-days" that Hoover instituted were voluntary, but the Lowells complied willingly. Even the dogs of Sevenels had to suffer. After living on prime beef their whole lives, they now had to make do with horse meat.

As for Amy, she could cut back on bread and meat, but no war would im-pede her right to smoke. She ordered a delivery of ten thousand of her little Manila cigars to be stored away in closets and cupboards throughout the house.

Over in England, Katie welcomed Hoover's ambitious plan. She saw first-hand the hardships suffered by the English and she knew that any supplies sent by the Americans would help stave off the growing threat of widespread malnutrition. She urged the Women's Municipal League back in Boston to publish and promote Hoover's goals of limiting consumption and waste: "Last-ing disgrace will fall upon us if lack of self-restraint should prevent us from taking our proper part in this great conflict . . . The waste of a single slice of bread each day in every home means the daily waste of a million loaves of bread. The thousand million dollars of needless waste which thus takes place can and should be stopped."[15]

Katie believed, as Hoover did, that "the outcome of the world war is in the hands of the women no less than in the hands of the men."[16] She would do what she could in England, while back in Boston, her Muncipal League sisters would do what they could in New England. Not only was the cause good, but hard work kept Katie from worrying about James. Every day the English newspapers blared out headlines of defeats and losses in Passchendaele, Ypres, Cambrai. Katie turned the pages over and refused to read the stories. Even the story of Mata Hari, a Dutch dancer turned spy for the Germans, who was executed by a French firing squad on October 15, failed to stay her hand; the page was turned and no attention paid.

Winter came early and hard in 1917. Snow fell before Thanksgiving and stayed, frozen in drifts across the lawn. There was a shortage of coal throughout the Northeast and all the Lowells shivered through the days and weeks, Bessie and Katie in the Back Bay, where the winds came off the Charles in shards of cold; Amy with Ada in the drafty, high-ceiling rooms of Sevenels; and even Lawrence and Anna in the new President's House built at 17 Quincy Street. Lawrence had commissioned and paid for the house himself. It was designed by his cousin Guy Lowell, architect of Lowell Lecture Hall and Emerson Hall at Harvard, as well as the Boston Museum of Fine Arts and the New York State Supreme Courthouse. But even the brand-new house couldn't create heat out of air. There was simply no fuel available.

As the long cold winter dragged on, students at Harvard organized themselves into chopping groups (harking back to the chopping bees of the 1600s) and went into the woods surrounding Cambridge, searching for timber. Cords of fresh-hewn wood arrived at the back door on Quincy Street. Amy and Ada signed up for deliveries for the library fireplaces at Sevenels, and the logs came late at night, the bells on the horse-drawn sleigh alerting them that more fuel had arrived. They closed off rooms at Sevenels they didn't really need; why heat the rooms no one used?

Amy's local paper, the *Brookline Chronicle*, ran a notice in early December 1917 that caught her eye. U.S. Army training camps were in need of books for their libraries. Amy called up Miss Louisa M. Hooper of the Brookline Public Library and offered to help. The two women worked to put together collections of poetry books, funded by Amy, to be sent to the six army camps set up in Massachusetts. A few weeks later, when the Poetry Society of America's monthly bulletin included a notice that the librarian at Camp Sherman, in Ohio, was asking for poetry books, Amy knew just what to do. She wrote to him immediately, including a list of the books she had provided to all of the camps in Massachusetts.

She went further: She offered to outfit not only Camp Sherman but any other camp that might be in need of poetry books. In the end, Amy sent poetry libraries to thirty-four army camps around the United States. When military hospitals contacted her for books, she was just as eager to help and sent packets of books to hospitals around the country. By the summer of 1918, Amy Lowell had placed poetry in the hands of just about any United States soldier asking for it. Modern or classics: They wanted poems and she answered their need.

Letters from the men fed by her libraries began to trickle in. Then the stream turned to a flood, a steady flow of gratitude and praise. As Amy described it, "the doughboys have had the poetry to their hands, and from the letters I have received, they seem to have made use of it."[17] Amy was even presented with the gift of original poems written by soldiers who were aspiring poets. A staff sergeant named George Gordon Ladds sent in one that Amy had framed and then hung on the wall of the kitchen at Sevenels:

> This custard of ice
> Is full of mice
> Bubbles that blink
> Bubbles that wink
> And are of blue
> Seen water through
> To rigidness of a staring cow.[18]

A letter came from Donald Evans, a published poet and the founder, along with poet Max Bodenheim, of the Claire Marie Press in New York City. The tagline for the Claire Marie Press was "New Books for Exotic Tastes." The two men believed that "there are in America seven hundred civilized people only. Claire Marie publishes books for civilized people only. Claire Marie's aim, it follows from the premises, is not even secondarily commercial."[19] In early 1917, Evans had written to Amy, asking her for an autographed poem that they could use for needed fund-raising. Amy willingly supplied the signed poem.

Now Donald wrote again, this time not as a publisher, but as an enlisted man. He had joined the army and was posted at Camp Crane, in Allentown, Pennsylvania. He wrote to tell Amy that he had received four of her books as a birthday present; for two months, those books had been all he had to read. Inspired by her works, he had begun writing poetry again.

Amy wrote back to him: "Of course we need more beauty in the world; of course that is what we are all fighting for; and of course that is what we must make the world safe for. . . . You can be soldier and poet, as we poets can do everything in the world better and at the same time. . . ."[20] More beauty in the world. Amy was bringing everything she could to the world, and now the world was answering back with joy—even in the midst of war.

"The war is for a long time," Donald wrote to Amy. "The opportunity for me will doubtless come. I shall be ready. In the meantime, . . . my mind is fresher, younger, freer. . . ."[21] All thanks to her work. Donald became another poet won to the side of Amy Lowell, joining a growing cadre of devoted friends, a swelling community of writers and artists. In June 1918, D. H. Lawrence told Amy his book *New Poems* would be dedicated to her, and in 1919, Evans published *Ironica* and dedicated the poem "Before the Curtain" "to Amy Lowell":

> Perhaps you now have made me one of you.
> And I may read my name blazing at night
> In two-foot letters over the theatre.[22]

Amy's sheepdogs—her "children," as she called them[23]—suffered from their wartime diet. They became skin and bones, their fur thin and matted, their noses not pink, but a dull beige. Guests from before the war would never recognize them now. The dogs had once been exuberant animals, sleek and confident, the most pampered of princes. When visitors came to Sevenels, the dogs had not been shut away; it was the guests who had to accommodate the dogs, not the other way around. Guests were given large canvas cloths to place over their laps to protect their clothing from the dogs' lapping affections of ample drool. If one of the dogs were to reach out and nip a bit of material from a suited thigh or bottom, Amy was prepared to pay out ten dollars, saying, "that is all I ever give for one rip."[24]

But now the dogs didn't nip and could barely drool. Their health had deteriorated under the food restrictions necessitated by the war and they often succumbed to food poisoning, what was understood to be "ptomaine poisoning." (At the time, it was thought that food poisoning was caused by consuming ptomaines, the substance released by putrefying animal or plant protein.)

Amy hated to see her dogs suffer. On a cold gloomy night in February 1918, she had all the dogs except one euthanized. They were then buried in the meadow out beyond the elm trees. The dogs used to hurtle past the trees when chasing down to the gate to greet visitors; now they were laid to rest beneath the snow-laden grasses. Amy couldn't bear to part with Prue, her oldest dog and most constant companion, a sheepdog like the others but a dog like no other. Prue could sense Amy's mood and knew when to lie still, when to growl, when to coax. And when to comfort: Through the cold nights of that long winter, Prue lay at the foot of Amy's bed, in constant vigil while the black cat, Winky, slept curled beside the pillows at the head.

When spring finally came, the flowers in the garden at Sevenels dislodged all memories of sleet and snow, and instigated instead anticipation of summer.

The war in Europe still raged, the stories in the papers were still grim, every day more men dead, more surges ahead curtailed by defeats back across the muddy trenches. But in Boston, shoots came up from the ground, bushes swelled with blossoms, and the air became soft, fragrant, kind. Amy took to her gardens every afternoon, a respite from work. A poem titled "Madonna of the Evening Flowers" was published in the *North American Review*. The poem celebrated what she found there in her gardens—and who.

> Where are you?
> I go about searching.
>
> Then I see you,
> Standing under a spire of pale blue larkspur,
> With a basket of roses on your arm.
> You are cool, like silver,
> And you smile. . . .
> But I look at you, heart of silver,
> White heart-flame of polished silver,
> Burning beneath the blue steeples of the larkspur,
> And I long to kneel instantly at your feet . . .[25]

John Livingston Lowes, an English professor at Harvard and lecturer at the Lowell Institute, sent Amy a note after he read the poem. He had liked it very much, and he asked Amy if "the Madonna in the poem was not Mrs. Russell?"

Amy wrote back to him: "How could so exact a portrait remain unrecognized?"[26]

When Amy asked Ada if she could dedicate a book of poetry to the woman she loved, Ada said no. It would be two more years before she agreed to be acknowledged as Amy's muse. But she did allow Amy to call her "Peter," both privately and in public, a nickname that was never explained. Perhaps it alluded to the apostle Peter, the rock to the mission of the Catholic Church, as Ada was the rock to the ambitions of Amy Lowell.

In the summer of 1918, the Spanish flu arrived in Boston aboard ships coming from Europe. Sailors stationed at Commonwealth Pier were the first to succumb. Within two weeks, over two thousand soldiers and sailors came down with the influenza. By the end of August, the disease had spread quickly into the civilian population of the city and beyond. Thousands became ill and hundreds died; during the last week of September alone, three hundred people died of the flu. By the middle of October, the figures were up to thousands dead. Some towns in Massachusetts had only one or two cases; other towns were decimated by loss. Everywhere schools were closed down and public gatherings banned. Morgues became overrun with the dead. Convicts were let out of prison and put to work digging graves.

Lawrence had to decide: close down Harvard or quarantine those students who posed a risk? The U.S. Naval Radio School was located on Harvard's campus. Its five thousand trainees had already undergone quarantine in September by order of the navy because of the large number of infected sailors. The danger of infection was everywhere. The question was, Who could keep the boys safe, their parents at home or Lawrence at school?

Lawrence decided to keep the boys at school. He ordered that any Harvard students who became infected be quarantined. For the time being, he suspended large classes or other forums where sizable groups of people might meet. Dr. George Minot of Harvard Medical School* and a team of medical students, along with local doctors, treated almost three hundred cases of influenza at the university's Stillman Infirmary that fall. There were weeks when both buildings of the infirmary were filled beyond capacity, but by late October, the worst of it was over. Only six Harvard students had died of the flu. Their loss was grievous, but the number of dead could have been considerably higher. Lawrence's community of scholars had been well protected, and also very lucky.

Amy was ill at home, but not from flu. During the summer, she and Ada had gone to New York so that Amy could give a lecture at the Brooklyn Institute of Arts and Sciences, a venue where she often gave talks. The night before the lecture, Amy tossed and turned in her overheated hotel room, unable to sleep. She liked to get a good night's rest before a performance and felt frustrated and helpless by her insomnia. Finally, she had climbed down from her bed. She strode over to the large-paned window and with all her might heaved it upward. A cool breeze came through and Amy smiled. She then turned to her bed, contemplating its size. If she could just maneuver it closer to the window, she would be able to fall asleep, buoyed by the fresh night air. Amy took hold of the heavy iron bedstead and gave it a pull. Instantly, a sharp pain stabbed her lower stomach, cutting across her abdomen. She sank to the ground in agony and called out for Ada.

Swaddled with bandages and dosed with a tincture of opium, Amy was able to deliver her lecture the next day. But when she returned home to

---

* Minot would win a Nobel Prize in 1934 for his work on pernicious anemia.

Sevenels, a close examination by her doctor revealed that she had reinjured herself, further inflaming and possibly tearing the abdominal muscle she had so severely strained before. In September, she underwent an operation to stitch together what had been torn apart. The operation went well, but Amy was laid up for weeks. When she began to feel better, she still kept to the house, frightened of coming down with the flu. She kept on working through it all, writing poems for the new collection (her latest, *Can Grande's Castle*, had just been published), submitting works to various magazines and periodicals, and preparing for the spring lecture season. Ada tried to restrain her from overexertion, encouraging her to rest and convalesce, but Amy shrugged her off. There was too much to do, and she was haunted by a feeling that there was too little time to accomplish all her plans.

Amy and Ada were in New York when the armistice was proclaimed on November 11, 1918. From their hotel room, the two women could hear the bugle notes that blared at exactly eleven o'clock that morning, heralding the end of the war. Amy sank back onto a chair with a sudden swelling of relief. James Roosevelt would be coming home. His months at war had been grueling and terrible, but he had persevered, and been promoted to major for his gallantry in carrying ammunition to the front under heavy fire. Now all danger had passed for him. All that waited was one long boat ride across the Atlantic and then his life as father, husband, son, and nephew could resume.

The mayor of New York, John Hylan, called for a grand holiday in the city, and he got it. A parade of joy pounded along Broadway. Confetti and streamers flew in the sky; the Flatiron building on Twenty-third Street and Broadway appeared out of the swirling mist of white-and-pink flakes of paper like a ship coming safely into port. Bands played; women sang; men clapped their hands and whooped; flags flew from every window.

For Amy, the spectacle was the harbinger of a new world. A world in which America was a leader not just in terms of soldiers and battles, farmers and food, or negotiations and peace accords but also in art, music, poetry, and theater. She had written in 1917, "We are no longer colonies of this or that land, but ourselves, different from all other peoples whatsoever."[27] In a speech she gave to the MacDowell Club in New York, she proclaimed that "the New Poetry is blazing a trail toward Nationality far more subtle and intense than any settlement houses and waving the American flag in schools can ever achieve." She believed with all her heart that "the most national things we have are skyscrapers, ice water, and the New Poetry."[28]

Now was the chance for her to prove it all to be true. With the war over, American creativity and ingenuity could flourish. Her hard work and her talent could be recognized. Every artist must work alone—Amy believed that— but every lone person needs a framework of support: "the experience of the world goes to prove that there must be a certain amount of banding together to make life possible. Alone, the individual is too weak to protect himself."[29] She wanted to protect the writers she had taken under her wing, the readers she had brought to the love of poetry. But she also craved it for herself. Approval and opprobrium.

Walking down Broadway arm in arm with Ada, amid a crowd delirious with relief and joy, Amy could feel her future unfolding like a wave. A giant blue wave that had come up behind her and now carried her along. The future rode on its white cusp, unfurled, clear and glittering. Time now opened up before her, full of possibilities. *Occasionem Cognosce.* And Amy would.

On March 3, 1919, Amy Lowell took the stage of Paine Hall on the Harvard campus. She had been invited to give a lecture by the Music Department. A dream come true: She was to be the first woman ever to lecture under the auspices of Harvard University. No longer would she be known only as Amy Lowell, sister of the president; now Lawrence would become known as Lawrence, brother to the poet. But only if the performance went well; only if the audience applauded for her. Amy and Ada spent days preparing for her presentation. Now Ada sat in the fifth row and prayed that all would go as the two women had planned.

On the ground floor and in the mezzanine, every row was full; people stood along the sides of the hall and were packed into the narrow band of space at the back. Amy waited for quiet in the hall before beginning her talk. She looked confident and sturdy behind the shortened podium, her hair done up in a neat bun, her blue eyes shining above her indigo-colored suit. Running along the ceiling above the stage, etched into the frieze, were the names of composers: Bach, Haydn, Mozart, Beethoven, Schubert, Chopin, Wagner. Seven imposing classical composers. But Amy's lecture would be about the modernists, in music and in poetry. The music of Stravinsky, Ravel, Scott Joplin. And the poetry of Amy Lowell.

Lawrence and his wife, Anna, were in the hall, along with Bessie and Will. Amy had sent out invitations to everyone she knew within a fifty-mile radius of Cambridge. Dozens of people, from librarians in Brookline to matrons on Beacon Hill, had been invited to come hear Amy Lowell lecture at Harvard. Now they waited for her to begin. The minutes passed.

Amy stood on the stage, suddenly ill at ease. She preferred to sit for her readings, especially now with her abdominal problems. But the only concession that could be made for her at Paine Hall was the somewhat shortened lectern. She rested her arms on it, then pulled them back to her side. She drew in her breath and thought back to the hours she had spent going over the musical pieces she wanted to discuss in her lecture; she would explain how the pieces all tied in with her own poetry. Edward Burlingame Hill, her old friend, who was now head of the Harvard Music Department, and Heinrich Gebhard, pianist and composer (and teacher of Leonard Bernstein), had helped her prepare. Together, the three of them had run through again and again the musical compositions Amy would be talking about in her lecture: Stravinsky's "Grotesques," Ravel's "Noctuelles," the ragtime of Scott Joplin.

It was Stravinsky who first gave Amy the key of how to reproduce the sound of music in the medium of poetry. Amy wanted to explain to her audience in Paine Hall how that came to be; how she used movements, as composers do, as well as rhythms and meters, and other sorts of musical compositional elements. After she spoke about musical components and poetry, she planned to recite some of her own poems. She had chosen works from her latest book. That couldn't have been a bad idea, could it? she wondered now. After all, *Can Grande's Castle*, a collection of prose poems, had been her biggest hit yet. The first printing, released in September of 1918, had sold out in three weeks, and the second by the end of the year. The reviews of the poems had been overwhelmingly good, with one critic calling Amy "the biggest thing since Whitman"[30] and another stating that Amy Lowell had replaced Edgar Allan Poe as the great American poet.

Finally, Amy began her lecture.

The audience listened raptly to every word, from the opening lines about Stravinsky to the final recited poem about the horses of Venice.

Great gold horses, quietly stepping above the little mandarin figures, strong horses above the whirling porcelain figures, are the pigeons the only birds in Venice? Have the swallows told you nothing, flying from the West?

The bells of St. Mark's ring midnight. The carnival is over.

In the deserted square, the pavement is littered with feathers, *confetti*, orange-peel, and pumpkin-seeds. But the golden horses on the balcony over the high door trot forward, without moving, and the shadow of the arch above them is thrown farther and farther forward as the moon drops toward the Lagoon.[31]

When she finished, everyone in the hall applauded. Some people stood and cheered; others stayed seated but clapped loudly and for a long time. The first lecture given by a woman at Harvard had been a huge success. Amy would return again to give readings and lectures at Harvard, but this first triumph would be a night she would never forget.

Within days of the lecture at Paine Hall, Ada and Amy were on their way to New York with Katie, who had returned from England at the beginning of the year. James's transport ship, the USS *Great Northern,* would be arriving any day now. Together with James's wife and children, the women waited for news of the ship's approach. And then word was sent. James Roosevelt had died aboard the ship after contracting spinal meningitis. The ship had already been within sight of land and James had asked to be carried to the deck so that he could see the coastline of America one last time. On March 26, 1919, he died.

The funeral for James A. Roosevelt was held in New York City on March 29. Maj. Charles Whittlesey of the Lost Battalion, who had become virtually mute upon his return from war, broke his silence to utter tribute to Roosevelt. He praised him for his "kindly human spirit" and described him as "a man to whom war was a bright and fine adventure. . . ."[32] Now the adventure was over. James was buried in the Roosevelt family plot in Green-Wood Cemetery in Brooklyn.

Katie returned to Boston. She resigned her leadership of the Municipal League, canceled all plans to move to England, and retired to the house on Beacon Street. It would be five years before she would return to public duty, taking over the helm of the Municipal League once again. For now, she could only retreat from the world. Amy canceled all her engagements. She did what she could to soothe her sister's pain and silence her own aching grief.

26
≈ 1919–1922 ≈

Freighted with hope,
Crimsoned with joy,
We scatter the leaves of our opening rose . . .
—AMY LOWELL, "PETALS"

In the fall of 1919, the policemen of Boston went out on strike. Nights of chaos ensued, with gangs of troublemakers and criminals roving the streets and causing trouble—grabbing women's purses, turning over street carts, throwing rocks at streetcars and lanterns, and breaking into stores and looting goods. A riot broke out on Scollay Square and one person was killed. Amy took to sleeping with a revolver under her pillow and Lawrence called for students to volunteer as peacekeepers on the streets of Boston. When a Harvard tutor by the name of Harold Laski let it be known that he supported the striking police officers and all striking workers wherever they might be, alumni of the college rose up in protest. Harvard's Board of Overseers demanded that Laski be fired immediately. But Lawrence refused to do it. "If the Overseers ask for Laski's resignation, they'll get mine!"[1]

It wasn't that Lawrence joined Laski in his support of the striking policemen. Lawrence was more likely to consider the strikers dangerous Bolsheviks than heroes. But he believed that on his campus there was nothing more important than freedom of speech; as he had said in 1915, when anti-German agitation roiled the campus, "We have endeavored to maintain the right of all members of the University to express themselves freely, without censorship of supervision by the authorities of the university. . . ."[2] In 1920, law professor Zechariah Chafee would publish a book on free speech in America, and dedicate it to Lawrence, whose "wisdom and courage in the face of uneasy fears and stormy criticism made it unmistakably plain that so long as he was president no one could breathe the air of Harvard and not be free." Chafee might have qualified his statement had he known just how viciously Lawrence would constrain the rights of one group on campus to express themselves freely and without censor. But only a small group of people would know about his actions, and Lawrence's secret would remain hidden for as long as he lived.

In August 1920, the Nineteenth Amendment was ratified, granting the vote to all women of the United States. Of all the Lowell women, Bessie had been most adamantly against women's suffrage. Katie had skirted the issue, officially stating as president of the Municipal League that "if the suffrage shall eventually come . . . the League will have proved its usefulness in serving as the best possible means of educating people to vote intelligently. If the suffrage shall never come, we believe that the League will equally have proved its value in showing how great is the work that women can do, without the vote."[3]

Amy had also demurred from out-and-out opposition to having the vote, especially when offered the opportunity to publish her works in the suffragist paper the *New Freewoman*. But Bessie actively campaigned against passage of the Nineteenth Amendment. She was a leader in the Massachusetts Association Opposed to the Further Extension of Suffrage to Women. She joined the campaign to convert college girls to antisuffragists, utilizing the help of alumni from Smith, Vassar, Radcliffe, Bryn Mawr, and Wellesley. She supported the *Anti-Suffragist,* a periodical of the movement, and contributed an essay entitled "Suffrage and the Sex Problem" to the 1916 publication *Anti-Suffrage Essays by Massachusetts Women.*

In the essay, she argued that "there is no greater sophistry than that women need the vote to protect themselves and one another from evil men." She went on to explain that "were most men libertines today, no law could be enforced against them. Were all men self-controlled and pure in heart, no law would be required. The failure of the women . . . to bring up their sons to be such men cannot be corrected by [suffragism] . . . Women have failed to do their duty, and the only way to prevent further evil is to do that duty now."[4] In her opinion, the answer was better mothering, not the right to vote.

Once women got the vote, however, Bessie threw herself into the arena, feetfirst and all the way. She got herself elected as president of the Massachusetts Electoral College, becoming the first woman ever to preside over a state electoral college. She served as national president of the Coolidge Women's Club of America and founded state branches from coast to coast. In 1924, she would be nominated as a delegate-at-large to the Republican Convention, but she gave her seat up to a war veteran and went instead as an alternate to Senator Henry Cabot Lodge. In a newspaper interview, Bessie chided women for not taking their new right seriously: "the 19th Amendment has called on us to stand before the men and help for the betterment of the country. Tell the women, they should all vote and do their part. They aren't turning out the vote as they should at all. We have a job to do—let's do it!"[5] For Bessie, the duty of women had expanded beyond teaching sons the proper way to treat women. Now it was up to women to vote, and to vote responsibly.

Late in the afternoon of May 22, 1920, Chester Noyes Greenough, acting dean for Harvard, burst into the office of Lawrence Lowell. He told Lawrence that a Harvard student had committed suicide. Lester Wilcox, brother of the dead student, Cyril Wilcox, had just been to see Greenough. Days before he died, Cyril had told his older brother Lester about a homosexual affair that he'd had; after he died, Lester found letters sent to Cyril detailing gay parties at Harvard and alluding to homosexual acts among students. A few days later, another letter arrived, this one also filled with more details of homosexual activity at Harvard. Wilcox had tracked down the writer of the letter and put together a list of homosexual students at Harvard. He then approached Greenough and demanded that something be done.

Homosexual acts were criminal in Massachusetts in 1920; those found guilty of sodomy and other "unnatural and lascivious acts"[6] could be fined and imprisoned for up to twenty years. Those found to be assisting, soliciting, allowing or providing venue for homosexual activity could also be prosecuted under various state laws. To have Harvard embroiled in criminal, and what Greenough considered to be immoral, behavior could have lasting implications for the college, not only legally but also in terms of reputation. A homosexual scandal would tarnish Harvard's image, in Greenough's opinion, and upset many alumni as well as parents entrusting their boys to Harvard's care. Greenough told Lawrence about Wilcox's demands and made his own plea for prompt action.

Lawrence found the information about campus homosexuals to be an affront to everything he was trying to build at Harvard: a community of scholars and friends, close-knit, wholesome, and honorable, forming "an intellectual and social cohesion."[7] After the end of the war, he had spoken widely about the dangers of "the intense condition of moral lassitude" descending upon a nation following the fighting of a great war. "Whose duty is it to keep the ideals of men alive, the ideals of men fresh, if not ours at the universities?"[8] Lawrence had spoken of the creep of materialism and immorality—and now such threats had presented themselves on his campus. He agreed with Greenough that immediate action was required to hunt down and remove the perpetrators of homosexual activity at Harvard.

Within days, a tribunal was convened to investigate the students and others named by Lester Wilcox. By the end of spring term, thirty people, including students, instructors, and tutors had been interrogated. Eight students were expelled from Harvard and one instructor fired, with one tutor told to leave. Permanent notice of their behavior was placed in the records of all those found guilty by the court, and only two students were ever allowed to return.[9]

Upon hearing of his expulsion, Eugene Cummings, a dental student who was just one week away from completing his five years of studies, committed suicide. The *Boston American* printed a story on June 19, with the headline, TWO HARVARD MEN DIE SUDDENLY. The story alluded to "an alleged inquisition" that Cummings had told his friends about: "he said that he was taken into the office, which was shrouded in gloom but one light dimly burning, and there questioned exhaustively." But the story also included a flat denial by the Harvard administration that any such proceedings had been conducted. As for Cummings, he was dismissed by Harvard authorities as being "unbalanced" and suffering from a "disordered mind."[10]

Under Lawrence's explicit orders, all records of the tribunal were to be locked away, and the nature and actions of the Secret Court were to be kept secret. Lawrence never alluded to the tribunal or to homosexual activity anywhere on campus or in Cambridge in any letters, speeches, or memos; nor is there any indication that he ever spoke to his wife or family members about what had occurred during those weeks of inquisition.

For Lawrence, the overriding goal of college was to create a community where young men from various backgrounds joined together to form a cohesive, coherent unit—and coherence could only be achieved through a homogeneity of values, desires, and goals. When writing about immigrants, he declared that if they could become "an indistinguishable part of the population, well and good;" otherwise, they endangered democratic institutions.[11] The same went for the college population: "There is happily in this country a tendency towards social solidarity and social service"—but only where thorough mixing and assimilation could be achieved.[12]

Lawrence's sister Amy, on the other hand, celebrated the creation of a new "American race."[13] For her diversity meant enrichment. But Lawrence could not see beyond the Brahmin traditions based on the superiority of the Anglo-Saxon way, and as the obituary written in memoriam of Lawrence noted in 1943, "when he had made up his mind, it was hard to shake him and hard even to make him listen."[14] In the years to come, Jewish students and more black students would come to him, asking for admission into the sacred halls of Harvard. But Lawrence laid down quotas limiting the number of Jewish students to be admitted (stating that "the main problem caused by the number of Jews comes . . . from the fact that they form a very distinct body, and cling, or are driven, together, apart from the great mass of undergraduates"[15]) and refused housing and dining accommodations to black students ("to compel white men and negroes to live in the same building and eat at the same table . . . would cause reprisals against them"[16]). The topic of homosexual students was not raised again during his presidency.

As far as his own sister's sexuality, Lawrence said nothing against her. Ada and Amy were invited often to the house of Anna and Lawrence, and also to the Boston and summer homes of Katie and Bessie. Ada's family in Utah, long-settled Mormons, also seemed to accept Ada and Amy's situation, although it might have been easy to ignore the nature of their relationship, especially if Amy's rather confessional poetry—". . . How have you come to dwell with me,/ Compassing me with the four circles of your mystic lightness,/ So that I say 'Glory! Glory!' and bow before you/ As to a shrine?"[17]—was never read.

Ada had been married as a young woman and had a daughter named Lorna, who was married herself now to a Utah businessman and had two children, Ted and baby Alan. Lorna and her children visited Amy and Ada often, staying with the couple both in Brookline and at Bromley Lacey, their New Hampshire home. Amy treated Lorna's children as if they were her own grandchildren, spoiling them with treats and gifts. She especially doted on Teddy, whom she called "Sonny."[18]

In the summer of 1920, as Lawrence headed off to England to receive honorary degrees from Oxford and Cambridge, Amy headed down to Texas to receive her own honorary degree from Baylor University—and to make public her love for and devotion to Ada. She had been invited to Baylor as part of its Diamond Jubilee celebration. Thousands of people were expected to attend the huge celebration. An immense program had been printed up, with three pages devoted to each honoree receiving a degree. When asked what she would like to have included on those pages, Amy had been adamant about only one item: She wanted the complete text of "Madonna of the Evening Flowers" to be printed in the program. She would not hide Ada away: "And I long to kneel instantly at your feet. . . ."[19]

Ada no longer demurred from receiving Amy's accolades in public. Many of the poets Amy supported and promoted were homosexual or bisexual, including Siegfried Sassoon, Annie Winifred Ellerman, known as "Bryher," and Hilda Doolittle (Amy introduced H.D. and Bryher to each other, the start of a long relationship). Although Amy did not proclaim her homosexuality, she did not attempt to hide it. She wrote freely of female erotic experiences. She once explained to poet John Farrar that his verses "could never equal the poetry of a young girl's naked body";[20] Amy herself wrote of the beauty of the female body and her love for it. She would never learn of her brother's condemnation and expulsion of homosexual Harvard students.

On October 29, 1920, Amy underwent a fourth operation for complications arising from her original abdominal injury. The operation, involving five doctors and three nurses, took place in a second-floor bedroom at Sevenels. Ada had been told the procedure would be a lengthy one, and its outcome was uncertain. Not only did the doctors have to address the hernia in her abdomen but Amy had other health issues that would complicate the operation. For years she had suffered from high blood pressure. Sometimes her blood pressure was so elevated that she lost her vision. She was also obese, and the extra weight caused great strain on her heart.

Ada knew that Amy had a big heart. Now she prayed that it would be strong enough to pull her through this operation. Ada waited in the library while the operation took place on the floor above. She would have preferred to be out in the garden, waiting to hear the news of the outcome, but the day was too wet and cold for it. The last mums and zinnias of the year drooped under the intermittent downpours, and collected piles of leaves shone black under a leaden sky.

A week earlier, Amy had given a lecture for the Harvard Poetry Club: "Miss Amy Lowell . . . will include remarks as she reads in such a manner as to illustrate her peculiar contribution to modern poetry."[21] The students of the Poetry Club had promised Amy could have Paine Hall for the night, and they delivered it. Every seat was taken and people stood five deep against the walls and in the aisles. At the Harvard Union that same evening, a rally was being held for the presidential candidate James M. Cox, governor of Ohio. More than a few stodgy fellows had skipped the rally and walked across the Yard to Paine Hall, hoping to get into the poetry reading and perhaps expecting a hoot. After all, it was Amy Lowell on the dais.

But when she recited "Lilacs," there was not a hoot or holler to be heard. The entire audience, old and young, clapped as if their lives depended on it. Malcolm Vaughan, a member of the society (who had been with Amy's nephew James in the ambulance service in the Meuse-Argonne), wrote to her the next day of how she had swept the "entire audience off their feet: fellows have been running to my room ever since—waving their arms, gesticulating, shouting a paean for you. None of us had ever before been present when a speaker so held his audience that the crowd sat still and would not budge until the speaker had to dismiss them . . . And you did fill the hall against the opposition of Governor Cox . . . a victory to begin with!"[22]

The poem "Lilacs" had been published in the *New York Post* in September 1919, but it was not until Amy began to recite it at readings that the beauty of it caught hold. Amy recited the poem to a crowd of twelve hundred in the Leon Mandel Hall at the University of Chicago in July, where the hall was so jammed that there were people standing in the aisles. It was a long poem, but Amy's voice remained strong through the final lines.

> Lilacs,
> false blue,
> white,
> purple,
> Color of lilac.
> Heart-leaves of lilac all over New England,
> Roots of lilac under all the soil of New England,
> Lilac in me because I am New England,
> Because my roots are in it,
> Because my leaves are of it,
> Because my flowers are for it,
> Because it is my country
> And I speak to it of itself
> And sing of it with my own voice
> Since certainly it is mine.[23]

Concluding the reading, she looked out to her audience in expectation. Those seated rose as one body, roaring in approval, and joined the standing hordes in an ovation that went on and on. Amy beamed, triumphant. This was no fluke: The audience was for her, not against her.

In Philadelphia, when she had just begun a reading at the Philomusian Club, she asked a woman in the front row if the light from her lamp shone in the woman's eyes. "No, something else shines," the woman replied, adoration in her voice.[24] Amy was met with huge and enthusiastic crowds at Brown and at Yale, where the students stormed the stage "with books for me to sign."[25] At the Brooklyn Institute of Arts and Sciences, she finished a performance and stood still, amazed, as the crowd stood up for her and clapped for seven straight minutes. Seven minutes: Amy had risen to her own feet, from the chair she had asked to be placed onstage, and stood nodding her head in gracious thanks. What happiness she had known then, in an auditorium full of poetry lovers, who loved her.

And yet there were still those who did what they could to denigrate her. Pound, Ford Madox Ford, and others in the literary elite continued to attack her looks and her poems. Ada thought it was because they were sure Amy's money shielded her from pain; Ada considered them all fools. Harriet Monroe, a poet, critic, and editor of *Poetry* magazine, had been on uneasy terms with Amy for years. Ever since Amy first appeared on the poetry scene and demanded that Harriet publish her pieces in *Poetry,* Harriet had been jealous of Amy's persuasiveness (she did publish the proffered pieces) but cognizant of her popularity and what it could do for poetry.

"She has genius," Harriet wrote about Amy, "only not of the kind we usually imply when we talk of the few fortunate poets who possess it." In other words, Harriet did not consider Amy a poet. But she was a good businesswoman: "Her genius is that of the commander, the organizer; and she has chosen to organize herself as well as the world, and bring to bear all the resources of her imagination, temperament, and scholarship in the service of a varied and practicable talent."[26]

Amy grew frustrated with the critics who disparaged her. "The more successful I am, the more I am hated . . . Meanwhile, my books increase their sales."[27] Not only did Amy work harder than anyone, sell out more readings, sell out more *books,* but also she helped other writers. If she was the magnet around which poetry swirled, she pulled other writers into the field, as well. She encouraged publishers to take a chance with new poets and new styles of poetry, as when she convinced Houghton Mifflin to put out the Imagist series as well as eight volumes of a New Poetry series, all featuring up-and-coming poets found by Amy and promoted by her. She supported periodicals that took on new poets, like Monroe's *Poetry,* Margaret Andersen's *Little Review,* Donald Evans's *Claire Marie,* and the short-lived *Others,* through which she first discovered the poems of Wallace Stevens and William Carlos Williams.

Amy sought out lecture opportunities for her fellow writers and sponsored them when they needed help, as when the young English poet Rupert Brooke came to Cambridge before the war and needed a place to stay (and impressed Amy's chauffeur, George, with how very big his feet were) or when the antiwar poet Siegfried Sassoon came to the United States on a lecture tour. Amy, who called Sassoon "the first important voice to protest against the sentimental glorification of war,"[28] helped pay his costs, sharing them with Harvard, and she invited Sassoon to dinner while he was in town; he was staying with Harold Laski but went to Amy for food, drinks, and conversation.

She had created a community of poets and of poetry lovers—a large, encompassing, growing community. Thousands of people applauded her; hundreds wrote to her. But no one loved her as Ada did. Now Ada waited for the terrible operation going on to come to an end and for the doctor to come downstairs and tell her everything would be all right.

Late that afternoon, the door to the library opened and Dr. Andrews came in. The doctor looked tired, his eyes rimmed in red, with dark bruising underneath. He no longer wore his lab coat, but there were stains on his trousers that made Ada catch her breath and look away. She felt faint. She had not eaten all day but had just sat in the library, waiting for news, looking out at the rain, and thinking about the past.

The doctor smiled then and sank down into the sofa before the low fire. Amy had survived the operation. She was resting; the group of nurses had managed to move her back up to the third floor and she was in her bed under the eaves. Ada let out a huge sigh and then a gulp of tears. She steadied herself, closed her eyes, and took a deep breath. Then she opened her eyes and offered Dr. Andrews a cup of tea.

Three weeks would pass before Amy could leave her bed and then only to go to Ada's room for a change of view. It was Christmas before Amy made it all the way to the library. A tree waited for her there, adorned with baubles and strings of beads and spun glass that glittered under the lights of the chandeliers. Piles of presents were under the tree, left by friends over the past weeks of Amy's recovery: elegantly wrapped boxes and packages; stacks of books—mysteries, for Amy loved a good mystery—tied with colored ribbons; and tins of candies and chocolates from Lewis Confectionary and Louis Sherry on Fifth Avenue.

The worst part of Amy's recovery had been the tending of the wound. It was huge, eight inches across her belly, with thirty stitches that had to be kept clean and sterilized to prevent infection. The only effective sterilizer was alcohol, but alcohol was hard to find. Prohibition was in full swing. The substitutes supplied by the doctors only irritated Amy's skin. Finally, bottles were obtained from a local bootlegger and Amy's recovering wound was effectively treated.

Bessie went on the record against Prohibition. "To my mind it is an impertinence to the Almighty to consider it wicked to use the good things the Lord has given us . . . The Lord has given us many beautiful and useful things in life which, if used to excess, injure us, but that does not mean that we should not use them in moderation." When asked if she was a "wet," a person who willingly broke the Eighteenth Amendment's proscriptions, Bessie shook her head vigorously. Breaking the law was not an option: "I do not think that anyone can feel that the breaking of a law and the encouragement to do so can be a desirable thing even in moderation. . . . I have never employed a bootlegger and I never intend to and when the prohibition amendment came I had no 'cellar' installed. I laid in only three bottles of brandy . . . to be used in case of sickness."[29]

Muriel Caswall, a Boston reporter, came to Bessie's home on Beacon Street for an arranged interview. Bessie welcomed her in and led her to the drawing room. It was a bright and cold January morning. Sunlight came in through the eastern windows, but the warmth in the room came from a fire burning in the grate. Bessie's graying hair had been arranged, as every morning, in a neat bun. She wore a brown dress with a white collar, spectacles high on her nose, and a simple gold band on her ring finger. She sat in a chair beside the fire and gestured for Caswall to sit on the other side. Caswall looked around at the posters stacked against the wall, the books piled high alongside orderly stacks of paper, and the row after row of cardboard boxes filled with pamphlets. Then she turned to Bessie and asked "about the jams and jellies she surely must have put up for the winter."

Bessie's eyes narrowed. She took a measured breath before answering and forced a smile onto her face. "I haven't put up any. To tell the truth, I feel I am a greater credit to my family as a public worker than as a jam maker. I love my home and spend all the time I can in it, but I really feel that I am of more use working for all the women of my State than in cooking things for my family. . . ."[30]

Amy and Ada arrived in Ann Arbor early in the month of May 1922. Robert Frost, poet in residence at the University of Michigan, had put together a program of poetry readings and invited Amy to participate. Carl Sandburg was invited, along with Padraic Colum, Louis Untermeyer, and Vachel Lindsay. Having arrived the day before her scheduled talk, as usual, Amy and Ada settled into the nicest hotel in Ann Arbor. That evening while preparing for bed, Amy turned and saw herself displayed in a mirror. The question suddenly came: When had she stopped putting cloths over mirrors when she traveled? For now there it was, a large mirror over the bureau, and there she was, dressed in her simple blue nightshirt, her thin hair loose around her shoulders. There she was. Large as life. And what a life it was.

Amy smiled at the vision in the mirror and then turned away.

When asked about her ancestor Percival Lowle, Amy always told the story that he had left England to escape taxes. But she knew there was more to it than that. He had left uncertainty, traveled across a wondrous but terrifying ocean, and come to a place that was a refuge for him. Safe to port. A journey, pushed by mission, ending in community. The undertaking of duty for the sake of community.

What followed was hard work and ambition, and succeeding generations of Lowells making history. History that became legend. "As a man learns, he becomes conscious, first of an immense curiosity, and then of a measure of understanding, and immediately after, of a desire to express both . . . Hence, legends; they are bits of fact, or guesses of fact, pressed into the form of a story and flung out into the world as markers of how much ground has been travelled . . ."[31] So Amy explained her own story: history wound into the skein of family and of place. Amy could trace the family line back and see how she had become who she was. An abundance of opportunities understood and undertaken.

Amy decided to begin her reading the next evening with a recitation of one of her most popular poems, "Appuldurcombe Park." She would follow up with pieces from her book *Can Grande's Castle,* and then recite one of the longer poems from *Legends.* Maybe "Before the Storm," about Peter Rugg, the New Englander cursed to drive about in his carriage until the end of time. Or maybe the "Witch-Woman," about a naked enchantress roaming the Yucatán. She would have to think about that. But there was no doubt in her mind as to what poem she would save for last.

Amy and Ada arrived at Hill Auditorium in plenty of time before the scheduled reading, only to find that no arrangements had been made for Amy's usual requests. There was no chair for her to sit in, no table on which she could place her papers, and no reading lamp. Amy abhorred the overhead lighting in these huge auditoriums and usually traveled with her own reading lamp. But to carry one all the way to Michigan? It had not even occurred to her. Now she and Ada scurried about, trying to locate a lamp, a chair, a table.

By the time all the requisite items were located, the auditorium was full. Over four thousand seats in the hall and every one taken. Amy clomped down the aisle with a found lamp in one hand and a satchel of papers and books in the other. She huffed her way up the stairs and set down her lamp. Then she looked around for an outlet in which to plug it. A janitor appeared from the wings and informed her, first, that she would need an extension cord for her lamp, and, second, that in all likelihood if she were to plug the lamp in, the fuse box would overload. Amy shook her head, not understanding. She demanded a cord and the man shuffled away to find her one. Amy set her papers down on the table that had been brought for her. A comfortable-looking chair had been set beside the table; on top of the table sat a pitcher of water and a glass. Robert Frost appeared onstage, stepping in from the wings, ready to introduce Amy to the crowd. Dressed in a pressed suit and tie, he looked as patrician and confident as ever. Amy, with her steel-framed pince-nez trailing by its gold chain down the front of her maidenly blue dress, felt like a frump beside him.

But then she remembered how she'd seen herself in the mirror the night before. She smiled at Frost now as she had smiled at herself then. Frost grinned right back at her. And then the janitor plugged in Amy's lamp and the entire theater went dark.

For the next fifteen minutes, Amy and Robert carried on a running banter that had the blind audience rolling in their seats. The high point came when Frost suggested that Amy light up a cigar and read by the light of that. Although accounts vary as to whether Amy took Frost's suggestion or not, at least one guest that evening recalled that "when she lighted up a very long and very black cigar, she presented a spectacle such as Ann Arbor had never seen."[32]

The lights came back on and it seemed as if the reading could finally commence. But then Frost tripped over the extension cord and fell against the table, which caused the water pitcher to go flying across the stage. More hilarity from the audience, more playing along from Robert and Amy, and then the moment had come. The broken pitcher was cleared away, the water mopped up. Frost retreated to the wings.

Amy sat in her chair and looked out. A sea of faces floated in the dark. She could just make out white ovals and the shadows of smiles, smudges of hands held up to hide the last exhalations of laughter. There was a chance, she knew, that they were laughing *at* her, not with her. She was a sight to see, no doubt about that. But she also knew, based on what was now years of experience, that when she began to speak, to perform, the crowd would settle down. They would listen to her and become caught up in the words. They did, every time.

> I am a woman, sick for passion.
> Sitting under the golden beech trees.
> I am a woman, sick for passion,
> Crumbling the beech-leaves to powder in my fingers. . . .

Isolated titters from the crowd. Amy went on.

> I am a woman, sick—sick—
> Sick of the touch of cold paper,
> Poisoned with the bitterness of ink. . . .[33]

The poems went on and the crowd sat still and attentive, listening. Amy could hear them breathing along with her, following her voice up and down. Last week, in Charleston, South Carolina, Amy had spoken to a group of college students: "Had I followed my inclination, I should have burst into tears when the audience stood up that night. One goes on writing and writing and writing, and wears one's self out trying to give one's visions to the world but it is only occasionally that one realizes that other people have seen those visions and have understood what one was trying to do."[34] Frost, standing in the wings, could see tonight the hold Amy had on the audience. He had seen it before and understood its power: "how often have I heard it in the voice and seen it in the eyes of this generation that Amy Lowell had lodged poetry with them to stay. . . ."[35]

Amy began her final poem, a reading of "Lilacs." Her voice remained strong through the long poem and her audience stayed with her. They followed as she led them along paths brightened by the flash of birds—"orange orioles hop like music-box birds and sing/ Their little weak soft songs"—and beside "the green sea" and up "stone hills which reach a long distance. . . ."; through "elm-shaded streets with little shops where they sell kites and marbles" and "great parks where every one walks and nobody is at home. . . ."

On and on, Amy led her listeners on a journey, guiding them across busy streets and then along quiet lanes that led to the bottom of a low hill. The spires of Boston could just be glimpsed in the distance beyond. She beckoned them to follow her up the hill through two stone pillars and along a gravel path lined with old elms. There were bodies of dogs buried on the other side of those elms; their ghosts rambled in the fields beyond. She took a detour through fields—"soft earth, and apple-blossoms"—lined with rows of gnarled fruit trees and then farther on to a house, brown and square, that sat amid a bower of blossoms.

Amy looked down for a moment through the low beam of light cast by her lamp. She saw Ada, sitting calmly on a wooden seat. Ada was nodding. She understood. Amy was taking the audience home. Taking them to Massachusetts. To the Massachusetts of the Lowells.

"Lilacs in dooryards/ Holding quiet conversations with an early moon;/ Lilacs watching a deserted house/ Settling sideways into the grass of an old road;/ Lilacs, wind-beaten, staggering under a lopsided shock of bloom/ Above a cellar dug into a hill. . . ."

Amy carried the audience back to where her history began.

"Because my roots are in it,/ Because my leaves are of it,/ Because my flowers are for it,/ Because it is my country . . ."

Percival Lowle and his wife Rebecca digging deep into the soil, planting the first seeds, slips, and bare roots. Praying for winter to pass and for their presence in the new world to settle in and flourish. Soil over clay, green shoots from dirt, petals on grass, blossoms on stone. Stones on a hill, walls following the landscape, winding round and round. A journey from there to here. Here the roots are laid, the seeds are furrowed, the bones are buried.

Generation after generation of Lowells. They came to New England, planted and harvested, sowed and reaped. They tended flocks, crafted and protected rights, created economies, and clamored for more. They fought for justice and died for what they believed in. They hoped and dreamed, built and rebuilt. They invented and then reinvented.

"And I speak to it of itself/ and sing of it with my own voice/ Since certainly it is mine."[36] Amy finished the poem, and kept her head bowed as the audience roared and clapped. It was all hers, stretching back to Percival Lowle and forward as far as she could take it.

It was the story of a family: the Lowells of Massachusetts.

Afterword

You will sit here, some quiet Summer night . . .
But you will not be lonely,
For these things are a part of me,
And my love will go on speaking to you . . .
—AMY LOWELL, "PENUMBRA"

Amy Lowell spent most of the next two years of her life at home at Sevenels, writing a biography of the poet John Keats. She took time out to go on short lecture tours and she continued to write and promote poetry. One more poetry collection was published before 1925, in addition to the six already published and her two books of criticism and her Imagist series. But it was Keats who dominated her thoughts and dreams from 1922 through the end of 1924, and taxed her energy to the state of exhaustion. She endured one more grueling surgery on her abdomen (kangaroo gut was used for the stitches, in the hopes that it would be strong enough to hold). She continued to suffer from high blood pressure, vision problems, headaches, and fatigue. Yet still she worked on, following the advice she had once given to an aspiring writer: "the object of life is work and not amusement . . . the way to get ahead is to be jealous of your hours of work, not jealous of your hours of leisure . . . no man ever succeeds on eight hours a day . . ."[1]

Part of her motivation was the long-held but never fulfilled ambition of James Russell Lowell to write a biography of the great English poet: "I like to imagine that the task has been deputed to me in his stead."[2] On November 15, 1924, Amy's chauffeur, George, drove the completed manuscript of *John Keats* down to New York City to place it, under Amy's orders, directly into the hands of Ferris Greenslet, her editor at the New York offices of Houghton Mifflin. When she went down a few weeks later to meet with Greenslet, she refused most of his edits (aimed at bringing the 1,160 page book down in size), telling him, "Ferris, you are a dear good boy but you don't know a thing about biography, not a damned thing!"[3] Finally, Ferris agreed: No cuts would be made.

A week before the February 10, 1925, release of *John Keats*, Katie fell from the window of her room at the Hotel Vendome in New York City. She had been attending a meeting in her role as the newly reinstated head of the Women's Municipal League of Boston. She died instantly upon hitting the ground.

Three months later, on May 12, 1925, Amy Lowell died of a stroke at home. Ada was by her side when she died. *Keats* was a best-seller and Ada would see to it that three more books of Amy's poetry were published after her death, *What's O'Clock, East Wind,* and *Ballads for Sale*. In 1926, Amy was posthumously awarded the Pulitzer Prize for *What's O'Clock*.

Ada sold Sevenels in the summer of 1926 and moved to a smaller house close by on Chestnut Hill. She died in 1952, at the age of eighty-nine, and was buried in Salt Lake City beside the graves of her parents.

In 1924, Will Putnam died of a heart attack while swimming in the sea at Cotuit, where Lawrence and Anna had their summer house. Bessie was heartbroken, but she soldiered on with her political and volunteer work. In 1927, in her husband's memory, she founded the William Lowell Putnam Mathematical Competition, known today as the Putnam Competition. In 1928, she founded the Fearing Research Laboratory for research on toxemia (preeclampsia) and eclampsia. Bessie died in 1935, at the age of seventy-three.

On February 18, 1930, exactly one month before Percival's birthday, the planet Percy had been looking for was found. Clyde Tombaugh, assistant to Vesto Slipher at the Lowell Observatory, found it using a new refracting telescope and astrograph (camera) paid for by Lawrence Lowell. On May 30, 1930, the planet was named Pluto to honor the man who said it was out there, the *P* and *l* of Pluto the initials of his name: Percival Lowell.

Anna Lawrence Lowell died on March 23, 1930. Her funeral was held in Appleton Chapel; university classes were suspended so that all Harvard students and professors could attend. Lawrence and Anna never had children. When asked years later by a friend who had just lost his wife when the grief would end, Lawrence replied, "Never."[4] He remained president of Harvard until 1933. Due to his committing a large amount of his own money, fifty-six buildings were constructed on the Harvard campus during his tenure, thirteen of which were for undergraduate housing. The present-day campus of Harvard exists largely within his blueprint for a unified plan of academic buildings and undergraduate housing creating a cohesive community.

Lawrence also instituted the current academic system of concentrations, electives, tutorials, Reading Period, and the presentation of academic honors for course work in a concentration. He believed that the purpose of a college education was not to train for a specific career, but to create "men intellectually well rounded, with wide sympathies and unfettered judgment . . . trained to hard and accurate thought . . . the solidity of thought that begets sound thinking . . . In short, he ought, so far as in him lies, to be both broad and profound."[5]

Lawrence died in 1943, at the age of eighty-six. He was buried in Mount Auburn Cemetery alongside his wife, Anna; siblings Amy, Katharine, May, and Roger; and his parents, Augustus and Katharine. Just across the way can be found the graves of the Reverend Charles Lowell and his wife, Harriet; his daughter Mary and her husband, Samuel Putnam, and their son William; the Reverend Lowell's son Charles, and Charles's wife, Anna Cabot Jackson Lowell, and their children, Harriet, James, and Charles, and Charles's wife, Josephine, and daughter Carlotta; the Reverend Lowell's daughter Rebecca and his son James, James's wife, Maria, and his daughters Blanche, Rose, and Mabel.

After Amy died, Ada found in the locked vault that was hidden behind a panel of books in the library at Sevenels explicit instructions for her funeral service along with a design for her gravestone. Amy wished to be cremated, with only a small group of family and friends in attendance, and then for her ashes to be interred at Mount Auburn. The headstone was to be simple, hewn from dark stone and with no ornamentation whatsoever.

Amy couldn't have planned for the time of her death. Was it fate or fortune that she died in May, when every lilac bush at Sevenels was in full bloom? A multitude of branches were cut after she died and then set out in pitchers and vases all around the house, filling the air with the heady aroma of their white, pink, and purple blossoms.

Acknowledgments

The wonderful Esther Newberg believed in the Lowells from the very start and found me the best home ever for the book I finally wrote. I am so thrilled to be part of St. Martin's Press. The whole team at the Flatiron Building is incredible to work with, including Michael Flamini, supportive and insightful and awesome; Vicki Lame, patient and kind and fabulous; the careful and determined copyeditor, Carol Edwards, and the designers who made the book look beautiful, James Iacobelli and Donna Sinsgalli Noetzel.

This book could not have been written without the help of the staff at the Pusey, Houghton, and Schlesinger libraries at Harvard University; and the assistance of Sabina Beauchard and the rest of the crew at the Massachusetts Historical Society.

I owe so much to Gerald R. Gill, professor of American History at Tufts University, who passed away in 2007. He was a great teacher and friend, and I miss him. He fostered my love of history, a passion instilled by my high school teachers Archibald Bryant and Vivian Schurfranz of Evanston Township High School.

My love of history is shared with and fed by my sisters-in-law, Joan Batten and Kathy Woodard, and my mother-in-law, Patricia Menz; they have always shown unflagging interest in and support of my work.

My parents, Tilde and Anatole Sankovitch, and my sister, Natasha Sankovitch, are integral to everything I do, with their endless encouragement and faith (and reading what I write over and over). And my sister, Anne-Marie Sankovitch, is always with me: "For these things are a part of me, and my love will go on speaking to you . . ."

My children, George, Martin, Meredith, Michael, and Peter Menz, have listened to my countless stories about the Lowells and provided a few new ones (Peter also secured a Lowell sweatshirt for me—my necessary uniform for writing on cold mornings). They are the best kids ever. The best. Even though they are no longer kids, they are still the best to me.

My husband, Jack Menz, insists that I write. And then rewrite. And then check everything one more time. He is with me through it all, in every word.

Notes

Prelude: Writing a Family's History

1. Jean Gould, *Amy: The World of Amy Lowell and the Imagist Movement* (New York: Dodd, Mead, 1975), p. 346.
2. Joshua Coffin, *A Sketch of the History of Newbury, Newburyport, and West Newbury, from 1635 to 1835* (Boston: Samuel G. Drake, 1845), Appendix A.

1. 1638–1639

1. John Latimer, *The Annals of Bristol in the Seventeenth Century* (Bristol: William George's Sons, 1900), pp. 20–22.
2. Amount equals 5,200 gallons of wine. See ibid., p. 48.
3. See http://www.seacoastnh.com/history/as-i-please/what-martin-pring-was -really-after/.
4. Francis J. Bremer, *John Winthrop: America's Forgotten Founding Father* (New York: Oxford University Press, 2003), p. 179.

2. 1639

1. John Josselyn, *An Account of Two Voyages to New England, Made During the Years 1638, 1663* (Boston: Riverside Press, 1865). All information about the Lowles' sea voyage is taken from these daily notes kept by traveler John Josselyn about the voyage he took from England to America in 1638.
2. Ibid., pp. 10–13.
3. Ibid., p. 7.

3. 1639–1665

1. Zephine Humphrey, *A Book of New England* (New York: Howell, Soskin, 1947), p. 45.
2. John Winthrop, "A Modell of Christian Charity," quoted in Robert C. Winthrop, *Life and Letters of John Winthrop*, vol. 2 (Boston: Little, Brown, 1869), p. 19.
3. John Wycliffe, a late (undated) sermon, cited at http://www.cqod.com/index-12 -31-09.html.
4. Harry S. Stout, *The New England Soul: Preaching and Religious Culture in Colonial New England* (New York: Oxford University Press, 1986), p. 17.
5. Nathaniel Ward, *The Simple Cobler of Aggawam in America* (London: Stephen Bowtell, 1647), p. 6.
6. Alice Morse Earle, *Customs and Fashions in Old New England* (New York: Charles Scribner's Sons, 1893), p. 224.

7   John Mayo, sermon on 2 Timothy 4:5, quoted in Stout, *The New England Soul*, p. 47. John Mayo was the minister of a church in Eastham, Massachusetts, from 1646 until 1655; in 1655, he became the minster of the Old North Church in Boston, where he remained until 1673.

8   John Winthrop to "Brethren of the Church of England," April 7, 1630, Robert C. Winthrop, *Life and Letters of John Winthrop*, vol. 2, p. 11.

9   Delmar Lowell, *The Historic Genealogy of the Lowells of America* (Rutland, VT: Tuttle Company, 1899), citing will of John Lowle, pp. 736–38.

10 Ibid., pp. 738–40.

11 Earle, *Customs and Fashions in Old New England*, p. 316.

12 John J. Currier, *Ould Newbury: Historical and Biographical Sketches* (Boston: Damrell and Upham, 1896), pp. 3, 175.

13 Ibid., p. 108.

14 Frances Hill, *A Delusion of Satan: The Full Story of the Salem Witch Trials* (New York: Da Capo Press, 2002), p. 196.

15 Scott Weidensaul, *The First Frontier: The Forgotten History of Struggle, Savagery, and Endurance in Early America* (New York: Houghton Mifflin Harcourt, 2012), p. 166.

16 Jill Lepore, *The Name of War: King Philip's War and the Origins of American Identity* (New York: Vintage, 1999), p. xiii.

17 Lowell, *The Historic Genealogy of the Lowells of America*, p. 6.

18 Ibid., p. 9.

19 Earle, *Customs and Fashions in Old New England*, p. 371.

20 Christina Tree, *How New England Happened: A Guide to New England Through Its History* (Boston: Little, Brown, 1976), p. 43.

21 Ibid.

22 Ibid., p. 45.

23 Thomas Gage, *A New Survey of the West-Indies* (London: E. Cotes, 1655), p. 204.

4. 1724–1738

1   Samuel Sewall, *The Selling of Joseph: A Memorial*, ed. Sidney Kaplan (Amherst: University of Massachusetts Press, 1969), p. 32.

2   John Lowell, *The advantages of God's presence with His people in an expedition against their enemies: A sermon preached at Newbury, May 22, 1755* (Boston: J. Draper, 1755), p. 21.

3   Argument of John Lowell, Esq., son of Reverend Lowell, in case of *Caesar Hendricks v. Richard Greenleaf*, Essex Inferior Court, October 1773, cited in L. Kinvin Wroth and Hiller B. Zobel, eds., *Legal Papers of John Adams*, vol. 2 (Cambridge: Harvard University Press, 1965), p. 65.

4   The furnishings associated with funerals grew to be so excessive that in 1741 a law was passed curtailing the giving of mourning gloves and rings except to those directly involved in the service, such as pallbearers and ministers. See Alice Morse Earle, *Customs and Fashions in Old New England* (New York: Charles Scribner's Sons, 1893), pp. 368, 376–77.

5   John J. Currier, *Ould Newbury: Historical and Biographical Sketches* (Boston: Damrell and Upham, 1896), pp. 432–39, 450.

6   Samuel Eliot Morison, *Three Centuries of Harvard, 1636–1936* (Cambridge: Harvard University Press, 1946), pp. 59–75.

7   Louis B. Wright, *The Cultural Life of the American Colonies*, (New York: Dover, 2002), p. 25.

8   See http://www.harvard.edu/about-harvard/harvard-glance/history-presidency /john-leverett.

9   Ebenezer Turrell, *Some account of a paper call'd the Telltale, begun in colledge Sept 1721*, Harvard University Archives, Cambridge, MA; see also "Early Extra-curriculars," *New York Times*, November 2, 2010.

10 John Lowell, *Ministers of the gospel to be cautious of giving offence, and concerned to preserve their character as ministers of God : A sermon preach'd at the ordination of Mr. Thomas Barnard, to the pastoral office of a church in Newbury, January 31, 1738,9* (Boston: J. Draper, 1739), p. 27.

11 Jonathan Edwards, "The Eternity of Hell Torments," April 1739, in *The Works of Jonathan Edwards, A. M.*, vol. 2 (London: Ball, Arnold, and Co., 1840), p. 88.

12 Jonathan Edwards, *Thoughts on the Revival in New England, 1740: To Which Is Prefixed a Narrative of the Surprising Work of God in Northampton, Mass. 1735* (New York: American Tract Society, 1845), p. 246.

13 George M. Marsden, *Jonathan Edwards: A Life* (New Haven: Yale University Press, 2003), p. 160.

14 Ibid., p.. 163.

15 Ibid., p. 165.

16 Ibid., p. 167.

17 John Lowell, *Laudable character of a woman: A sermon preached at Newbury, March 26, 1758, Occassioned by the death of Mrs. Hannah Kent, relict of the late Col. Richard Kent* (Boston: Green and Russell, 1758), p. 23, Massachusetts Historical Society, Boston.

5. 1740–1754

1   George Leon Walker, *Some Aspects of the Religious Life of New England* (New York: Silver Burdett and Company, 1897), p. 91.

2   George Whitefield, "The Righteousness of Christ, an Everlasting Righteousness," cited at http://www.reformed.org/documents/index.html?mainframe=http://www .reformed.org/documents/Whitefield.html.

3   Louis B. Wright, *The Cultural Life of the American Colonies* (1957; reprint, New York: Dover, 2002), p. 94.

4   Arnold Dallimore, *George Whitefield: God's Annointed Servant in the Great Revival of the Eighteenth Century* (Wheaton, IL: Crossway Books, 1990), p. 76.

5   *The Autobiography of Benjamin Franklin with Illustrations* (Boston and New York: Houghton Mifflin & Company, 1906), pp. 135–36.

6   George M. Marsden, *Jonathan Edwards: A Life* (New Haven: Yale University Press, 2003), pp. 231–32.

7   John Lowell, *Ministers of the gospel to be cautious of giving offence, and concerned to preserve their character as ministers of God: A sermon preach'd at the ordination of Mr. Thomas Barnard, to the pastoral office of a church in Newbury, January 31, 1738* (Boston: J. Draper, 1739), pp. 26, 13, 37.

8 Ibid., pp. 27, 35.
9 John Howard Smith, *The First Great Awakening: Redefining Religion in British America, 1725–1775* (Lanham, MD: Rowman & Littlefield, 2014), p. 149.
10 Marsden, *Jonathan Edwards*, p. 269.
11 Erik R. Seeman, *Pious Persuasions* (Baltimore: Johns Hopkins University Press, 1999), pp. 169–71.
12 John Lowell, *Laudable character of a woman: A sermon preached at Newbury, March 26, 1758, Occassioned by the death of Mrs. Hannah Kent, relict of the late Col. Richard Kent* (Boston: Green and Russell, 1758), pp. 17–18, Massachusetts Historical Society, Boston.
13 Ferris Greenslet, *The Lowells and Their Seven Worlds* (Boston: Houghton Mifflin, 1946), p. 34.
14 Lowell, *Ministers of the gospel to be cautious of giving offence*, p. 32.
15 Samuel Eliot Morison, *Three Centuries of Harvard, 1636–1936* (Cambridge: Harvard University Press, 1946), p. 87.
16 Dallimore, *George Whitefield*, p. 197.

6. 1755–1759
1 Ezekiel 33:6, King James Version.
2 Deuteronomy 20:1, King James Version.
3 John Lowell, *The advantages of God's presence with His people in an expedition against their enemies: A sermon preached at Newbury, May 22, 1755, at the desire, and in the audience of Col. Moses Titcomb, and many others inlisted under him, and going with him in an expedition against the French* (Newburyport, MA: E. W. Allen, 1806), pp. 3, 20, 23; Massachusetts Historical Society, Boston.
4 Isaac Watts, hymn "Behold the Glories of the Lamb."
5 Ferris Greenslett, *The Lowells and Their Seven Worlds* (Boston: Houghton Mifflin, 1946), p. 38.
6 Benjamin Clapp Butler, *Lake George and Lake Champlain: From Their First Discovery to 1759* (New York: G. P. Putnam & Son, 1869), p. 122.
7 Henry Wheatland, *Standard History of Essex County, Massachusetts* (Boston: C. F. Jewett and Company, 1878), p. 320; Greenslet, *The Lowells and Their Seven Worlds*, pp. 38–39.
8 Psalm 23, King James Version.
9 John James Currier, *History of Newbury, MA, 1635–1902* (Boston: Damrell & Upham, 1902), p. 235.

7. 1765–1774
1 Oxenbridge Thacher, "Draft of an Address to the King and Parliament" [1764], in *Proceedings of the Massachusetts Historical Society* 20 (1882–1883), p. 51.
2 "A Collection of Poems Written by a Young Gentleman of Harvard College & a Young Lady of Newbury, 1759–1760," Harvard University Archives, Pusey Library, Cambridge, MA.
3 John James Currier, *A History of Newburyport, Mass., 1764–1905* (privately printed, 1906), p. 43.

4   John J. Currier, *Ould Newbury: Historical and Biographical Sketches* (Boston: Damrell & Upham, 1896), p. 499; a bill for the provision provided for an evening meeting at Wolfe Tavern on September 26, 1765, includes numerous bowls of punch and toddies, supper food, then more punch and toddies, followed by breakfast.

5   Joshua Coffin, *A Sketch of the History of Newbury, Newburyport, and West Newbury* (Boston: Samuel G. Drake, 1845), p. 231.

6   Currier, *Ould Newbury,* p. 492.

7   *The Statutes,* vol. 15 (London: Eyre and Spottiswoode, 1878), pp. 1290–91.

8   Frank Moore, *Songs and Ballads of the American Revolution* (New York: D. Appleton & Co., 1856), pp. 44–47.

9   Alice Morse Earle, *Customs and Fashions in Old New England* (New York: Charles Scribner's Sons, 1893), p. 69.

10   Ferris Greenslet, *The Lowells and Their Seven Worlds* (Boston: Houghton Mifflin, 1946), p. 55.

11   Ibid.

12   Ronald N. Tagney, *The World Turned Upside Down: Essex County During America's Turbulent Years, 1763–1790* (West Newbury, MA: Essex County History, 1989), p. 52.

13   Greenslet, *The Lowells and Their Seven Worlds,* p. 52.

14   "Queries respecting the introduction, progress, and abolition of slavery in Massachusetts," Jeremy Belknap Papers, Massachusetts Historical Society, Boston.

15   Henry Wager Halleck, *Halleck's International Law,* vol. 1 (London: C. K. Paul & Co., 1878), p. 205.

16   "Queries respecting the introduction, progress, and abolition of slavery in Massachusetts," Jeremy Belknap Papers, Massachusetts Historical Society, Boston.

17   Randall M. Miller and John David Smith, *Dictionary of African-American History* (Westport, CT: Greenwood Publishing, 1997), pp. 336–37.

18   George H. Moore, *The History of Slavery in Massachusetts* (New York: D. Appleton & Co., 1866), p. 181.

19   All quotations from the case are from L. Kinvin Wroth and Hiller B. Zobel, eds., *Legal Papers of John Adams,* vol. 2 (Cambridge: Harvard University Press, 1965), pp. 64–67.

20   "Queries respecting the introduction, progress, and abolition of slavery in Massachusetts," Jeremy Belknap Papers, Massachusetts Historical Society, Boston.

21   Emily Blanck, *Tyrannicide: Forging an American Law of Slavery in Revolutionary South Carolina and Massachusetts* (Athens: University Georgia Press, 2014), p. 35.

22   Letters exchanged between Lowell and Jackson quoted in James Jackson, *Honorable Jonathan Jackson, His Wife, and Many Members of His Family: Notes and Reminiscences* (Boston: Alfred Mudge & Son, 1866), pp. 7–8.

23   Delmar Lowell, *The Historic Genealogy of the Lowells of America* (Rutland, VT: Tuttle Company, 1899), p. 753.

24   Blanck, *Tyrannicide,* p. 36.

25 James Jackson Putnam, *A Memoir of Dr. James Jackson* (Boston: Houghton Mifflin, 1905), p. 50.

26 Earle, *Customs and Fashions in Old New England*, p. 181; Andrew Smith, *Oxford Encyclopedia of Food and Drink in America* (New York: Oxford University Press, 2013), p. 424.

27 Ray Raphael and Marie Raphael, *The Spirit of 74: How the American Revolution Began* (New York: The New Press, 2015), p. 22.

28 Ibid., p 48.

29 John H. Stark, *The Loyalists of Massachusetts and the Other Side of the American Revolution* (Boston: James H. Stark, 1907), pp. 124–26.

30 Ibid.

31 "Declaration of Rights, in Congress, October 14, 1774," *The Statistician* (San Franciso: L. P. McCarty, 1879), pp. 189–91.

8. 1774–1777

1 Ferris Greenslet, *The Lowells and Their Seven Worlds* (Boston: Houghton Mifflin, 1946), p. 57.

2 Alice Morse Earle, *Customs and Fashions in Old New England* (New York: Charles Scribner's Sons, 1893) p. 183.

3 Ibid., p. 172.

4 Samuel Adams, *The Writings of Samuel Adams*, vol. 2, ed. Harry Alonzo Cushing (New York: G. P. Putnam's Sons, 1906), p. 337.

5 Donald L. Hafner, "Trials and Tribulations for Concord's Tories," October 16, 2012, cited at http://www.lincolnminutemen.org/trials-and-tribulations-for-concords-tories/.

6 Nancy Rubin Stuart, *The Muse of the Revolution: The Secret Pen of Mercy Otis Warren and the Founding of a Nation* (Boston: Beacon Press, 2008), p. 74.

7 Michael Pearson, *Those Damned Rebels* (New York: Da Capo Press, 2000), p. 82.

8 Greenslet, *The Lowells and Their Worlds*, pp. 57–58.

9 Ibid., p. 58; see also Arnold S. Lekowitz, *Benedict Arnold's Army: The 1775 American Invasion of Canada During the Revolutionary War* (New York: Savas Beatie, 2008), pp. 60–63.

10 England refused over the course of the Revolution to recognize the American privateers as anything but pirates under a law passed by Parliament called a "Pirate Act," but they did not hang any colonists for piracy. Instead, the captured privateers were sent to prisons like Mill Prison in Plymouth, England, which were so awful that hanging might have been preferable. See Jack Coggins, *Ships and Seamen of the American Revolution* (New York: Dover Publications, 2002), p. 65.

11 Nathan Miller, *The U.S. Navy: A History*, 3d ed. (Annapolis, MD: Naval Institute Press, 1997), p. 15.

12 Robert H. Patton, *Patriot Pirates: The Privateer War for Freedom and Fortune in the American Revolution* (New York: Pantheon, 2008), p. 42.

13 Ibid., p. 37.

14 Ibid., p. 135.

15 Ibid., p. xx.

16   Marc Leepson, *Flag: An American Biography* (New York: St. Martin's Press, 2007), p. 15.

17   Greenslet, *The Lowells and Their Seven Worlds*, p. 57.

18   James Jackson Putnam, *A Memoir of Dr. James Jackson* (Boston: Houghton Mifflin, 1905), p. 30.

19   Greenslet, *The Lowells and Their Seven Worlds*, p. 57.

9. 1778–1789

1   James Russell Lowell, "Review of John Gorham Palfrey's History of New England During the Stuart Dynasty," *North American Review,* January 1865, p. 188.

2   Ferris Greenslet, *The Lowells and Their Seven Worlds* (Boston: Houghton Mifflin, 1946), p. 63.

3   Ronald M. Peters, *The Massachusetts Constitution of 1780: A Social Compact* (Amherst: University of Massachusetts Press, 1978), pp. 42–43.

4   Ronald N. Tagney, *The World Turned Upside Down: Essex County During America's Turbulent Years, 1763–1790* (West Newbury, MA: Essex County History, 1989), pp. 323–30.

5   George Washington to Continental Congress, May 27, 1780, George Washington Papers, Library of Congress, Washington, D.C.

6   Richard K. Showman, Robert E. McCarthy, and Margaret Cobb, eds., *The Papers of General Nathanael Greene*, vol. 2 (Chapel Hill: University of North Carolina Press, 1980), p. 230.

7   Mercy Otis Warren, "The Genius of America Weeping the Absurd Follies of the Day," printed October 10, 1778; quoted in Nancy Rubin Stuart, *The Muse of the Revolution: The Secret Pen of Mercy Otis Warren and the Founding of a Nation* (Boston: Beacon Press, 2008), p. 136.

8   Conversation as recorded in a letter written by the Reverend Charles Lowell to Charles E. Stevens in 1856; quoted and cited in Charles Deane, *Judge Lowell and the Massachusetts Declaration of Rights* (Boston: John Wilson and Son, 1874), p. 1; see also *Proceedings of the Vermont Historical Society* (Barre, VT: Vermont Historical Society, 1866), p. 142.

9   Greenslet, *The Lowells and Their Seven Worlds*, p. 67.

10   "Proclamation of the Government and People of the Massachusetts Bay, in New England," John Lowell Papers, Houghton Library, Harvard University, Cambridge, MA.

11   Greenslet, *The Lowells and Their Seven Worlds*, p. 64.

10. 1796–1802

1   Mrs. William Lowell Putnam, *The Happiness of Our Garden* (New York: William Edwin Rudge, 1926), p. 9.

2   Anna Cabot Lowell to Eliza Susan Morton, January 6, 1797, Anna Cabot Lowell Papers (1795–1810), Massachusetts Historical Society, Boston.

3   Ibid.

4   Poem, Anna Cabot Lowell Papers.

5   Ibid.

6   The Reverend Zedekiah Sawyer to Judge Lowell, 1793. Ferris Greenslet, *The Lowells and Their Seven Worlds* (Boston: Houghton Mifflin, 1946), p. 93. Francis Cabot had spent his period of rustication living with the Reverend Sawyer.

7   Francis Cabot Lowell to John Lowell, September 21, 1795, Francis Cabot Lowell Papers (1775–1817), Massachusetts Historical Society, Boston.

8   John Lowell, Jr., to Francis Cabot Lowell, February 10, 1796, Francis Cabot Lowell Papers.

9   Greenslet, *The Lowells and Their Seven Worlds*, p. 77.

10   Ibid.

11   Anna Cabot Lowell to Eliza Susan Morton, November 1795, Anna Cabot Lowell Papers.

12   Poem, Anna Cabot Lowell Papers.

13   Anna Cabot Lowell to Eliza Susan Morton, September 1796, Anna Cabot Lowell Papers.

14   Anna Cabot Lowell to Francis Cabot Lowell, September 20, 1796, Anna Cabot Lowell Papers.

15   Anna Cabot Lowell to Francis Cabot Lowell, February 3, 1793, Anna Cabot Lowell Papers.

16   Anna Cabot Lowell to Eliza Susan Morton, October 1796 and May 1797, Anna Cabot Lowell Papers.

17   Anna Cabot Lowell to Eliza Susan Morton, May 19, 1796, Anna Cabot Lowell Papers.

18   Anna Cabot Lowell to Eliza Susan Morton, September 1796, Anna Cabot Lowell Papers.

19   Anna Cabot Lowell to Eliza Susan Morton, January 6, 1797, Anna Cabot Lowell Papers.

20   Poem titled "To Hope," Anna Cabot Lowell Papers.

21   Chaim M. Rosenberg, *The Life and Times of Francis Cabot Lowell, 1775–1857* (Lanham, MD: Rowman & Littlefield, 2011), p. 90.

22   Anna Cabot Lowell to Eliza Susan Morton, April 10, 1797, Anna Cabot Lowell Papers.

23   Anna Cabot Lowell to Eliza Susan Morton, May 1797, Anna Cabot Lowell Papers.

24   Poem, Anna Cabot Lowell Papers.

25   Journal entry, October 2, 1797, Anna Cabot Lowell Papers.

26   Anna Cabot Lowell to Eliza Susan Quincy, October 1797, Anna Cabot Lowell Papers.

27   Poem, Anna Cabot Lowell Papers.

28   Anna Cabot Lowell to Miss Ann Bromfield, James Jackson Putnam, *A Memoir of Dr. James Jackson* (Boston: Houghton Mifflin, 1905), p. 75.

29   Ibid., pp. 76–77.

30   Poem, Anna Cabot Lowell Papers.

31   Psalm 37:4, King James Version.

32   Letter from John Lowell, Jr., to Francis Cabot Lowell, dated May 12, 1802, Lowell Family Papers (1728–1878), Massachusetts Historical Society, Boston.

11. 1802–1812

1   John Lowell, Jr., to Rebecca Amory, 1789, Lowell Family Papers (1728–1878), Massachusetts Historical Society, Boston.

2   John Lowell, Jr., to Rebecca Amory, 1790, Lowell Family Papers.

3   John Lowell, Jr., to Rebecca Amory, 1791, Lowell Family Papers.

4   John Lowell, Jr., to John Lowell Sr., August 1791, Lowell Family Papers.

5   John Lowell, Jr., to Rebecca Amory, 1792, Lowell Family Papers.

6   *Report of the Trial of Jason Fairbanks on an Indictment for the Murder of Miss Elizabeth Fales* (Boston: Russell and Cutler, 1801), pp. 11–13.

7   Ibid.

8   Ibid.

9   Ibid., p. 8.

10 Ibid., pp. 21–22.

11 *Boston Gazette*, August 11, 1801.

12 *Report of the Trial of Jason Fairbanks*, p. 83.

13 Alan Rogers, *Murder and the Death Penalty in Massachusetts* (Amherst: University of Massachusetts Press, 2008), p. 67.

14 John Lowell, Jr., to Rebecca Amory Lowell, May 1816 (written after their daughter Sarah died at age five), Lowell Family Papers.

15 Ibid.

16 Jack Larkin, *The Reshaping of Everyday Life, 1790–1840* (New York: Harper-Perennial, 1989), p. 87.

17 John Lowell, Jr., to Francis Cabot Lowell, Francis Cabot Lowell Papers (1775–1817), Massachusetts Historical Society, Boston.

18 Fragments of letters written by John Lowell, Jr., Lowell Family Papers.

19 John Lowell, Jr., to Susan Gorham, 1806, Lowell Family Papers.

20 Fragment of a letter written by John Lowell, Jr., Lowell Family Papers.

21 Letter from Thomas Jefferson to Philip Mazzei, January 1, 1797; available at http://oll.libertyfund.org/quotes/463.

22 Jon Meacham, *Thomas Jefferson: The Art of Power* (New York: Random House, 2012), pp. 294–96.

23 Ibid., p. 355.

24 Thomas Jefferson, Second Inaugural Address, March 4, 1805; available at http://www.inaugural.senate.gov/swearing-in/address/address-by-thomas-jefferson-1805.

25 Ibid.

26 Ibid.

27 All titles (pamphlets) can be found in the holdings of the Massachusetts Historical Society, Boston.

28 James Jackson Putnam, *A Memoir of Dr. James Jackson* (Boston: Houghton Mifflin, 1905), p. 74.

29 Letter from Anna Cabot Lowell to Eliza Susan Quincy, October 1803, Anna Cabot Lowell Papers (1795–1810), Massachusetts Historical Society, Boston.

30 Letter from Anna Cabot Lowell to Eliza Susan Quincy, January 24, 1809, Anna Cabot Lowell Papers.

31   John Lowell, Jr., *Peace without dishonour, war without hope: Being a calm and dispassionate enquiry into the question of the Chesapeake and the necessity and expediency of war, by a Yankee Farmer* (Boston: Greenough and Stebbins, 1807), Massachusetts Historical Society, Boston.

32   Ibid.

33   Chaim Rosenberg, *The Life and Times of Francis Cabot Lowell, 1775–1857* (Lanham, MD: Rowman & Littlefield, 2011), p. 161.

34   Meacham, *Thomas Jefferson,* p. 433.

35   Ibid., p. 430.

12. 1812–1817

1   David Stephen Heidler and Jeanne T. Heidler, eds., *Encyclopedia of the War of 1812* (Annapolis, MD: Naval Press Institute, 2004), p. 173.

2   John Lowell, Jr., *Mr. Madison's war: A dispassionate inquiry into the reasons alleged by Mr. Madison for declaring an offensive and ruinous war against Great Britain: Together with some suggestions as to a peacable and constitutional mode of averting that dreadful calamity/by a New England farmer* (Boston: Russell & Cutler, 1812), Massachusetts Historical Society, Boston.

3   John Lowell, Jr., *Perpetual War, the policy of Mr. Madison: Being a Candid examination of his late message to Congress . . ./By a New England Farmer* (Boston: C. Stebbins, 1813), Massachusetts Historical Society, Boston.

4   John Lowell, Jr., *Mr. Madison's war.*

5   Ibid.

6   *Samuel Slater and Francis Cabot Lowell: The Factory System in U.S. Cotton Manufacturing,* Case Study prepared by Tom Nichols and Matthew Guilford, Harvard Business School, 2014, and quoting from David J. Jeremy, *Transatlantic Industrial Revolution: The Diffusion of Textile Technologies Between Britain and America, 1790–1830s* (Cambridge: MIT Press, 1981), pp. 6–7.

7   Nathan Appleton, *Introduction of the Power Loom and Origin of Lowell* (Lowell, MA: B. H. Penhallow, 1858), p. 15.

8   Robert Owen, *Manifesto of Robert Owen* (London: The Social Institution, 1840), pp. 18, 30, 41.

9   Letter of Hannah Jackson Lowell to Anne MacVicar Grant, undated, Francis Cabot Lowell Papers (1775–1817), Massachusetts Historical Society, Boston.

10   Alexander Hamilton, *Report of the Secretary of the Treasury of the United States on the Subject of Manufactures,* December 5, 1791 (New York: Childs & Swaine, 1791).

11   Robert Sobel, *The Entrepreneurs: Explorations Within the American Business Tradition* (Washington, D.C.: Beard Books, 2000), p. 12.

12   Thomas Jefferson, *Notes on the State of Virginia,* 1787, Query XIX (Philadelphia: H. C. Carey & I. Lea, 1825).

13   Sobel, *The Entrepreneurs,* p. 13; Caroline Ware, *The Early New England Cotton Manufacture* (Boston: Houghton Mifflin Co., 1931), p. 10.

14   "Boston MFG. Co. Reorganized," *American Wool and Cotton Reporter,* October 31, 1901.

[15] Recollection of Henry Lee in 1839, quoted in Chaim Rosenberg, *The Life and Times of Francis Cabot Lowell, 1775–1857* (Lanham, MD: Rowman & Littlefield, 2011), p. 236.

[16] Ibid.; see also Frederick W. Coburn, *History of Lowell and Its People*, vol. 1 (New York: Lewis Historical Publishing Company, 1920), p. 139.

[17] *American Wool and Cotton Reporter, for the Combined Textile Industries*, April 18, 1901, p. 486.

[18] Appleton, *Introduction to the Power Loom and Origin of Lowell*, p. 15.

[19] Ware, *The Early New England Cotton Manufacture*, p. 203.

[20] John Lowell, Jr., to Timothy Pickering, December 8, 1814, Ferris Greenslet, *The Lowells and Their Seven Worlds* (Boston: Houghton Mifflin, 1946), p. 150.

[21] Carol Bundy, *The Nature of Sacrifice: A Biography of Charles Russell Lowell* (New York: Farrar, Straus and Giroux, 2005), p. 21.

[22] John Lowell to Rebecca Amory Lowell, 1816, Lowell Family Papers (1728–1878), Massachusetts Historical Society, Boston.

[23] Robert Manning, ed., *History of the Massachusetts Horticultural Society, 1829–1878* (Boston: Rand, Avery & Co., 1880), p. 33.

[24] Letter of John Lowell, Jr., to Rebecca Amory Lowell, August 1816, Lowell Family Papers.

[25] Isaac Watts, *The Psalms of David* (London, 1719), Psalm 89:47–48.

13. 1817–1829

[1] Jeremiah 8:7, King James Version.

[2] Ferris Greenslet, *The Lowells and Their Seven Worlds* (Boston: Houghton Mifflin, 1946), p. 220.

[3] Mrs. C. H. Dall, *Reverend Charles Lowell, D.D.* (Boston: Thomas Todd, 1855), p. 8.

[4] Charles Lowell, *Sermons: Chiefly Practical* (Boston: Ticknor and Fields, 1854), p. 218.

[5] Ibid., p. 39.

[6] Greenslet, *The Lowells and Their Seven Worlds*, pp. 116–17.

[7] Alex Goldfield, *The North End: A Brief History of Boston's Oldest Neighborhood* (Charleston, SC: History Press, 2009), pp. 93–98.

[8] Lowell, *Sermons: Chiefly Practical*, pp. 330, 270, 279.

[9] Ibid., p. 280.

[10] Greenslet, *The Lowells and Their Seven Worlds*, p. 133.

[11] Psalm 23:6, King James Version.

[12] Psalm 119: 27–28, King James Version.

[13] Conrad Wright, ed., *A Stream of Light: A Short History of American Unitarianism* (Boston: Skinner House Books, 1975), pp. 1–10.

[14] Ibid., p. 20.

[15] Samuel Eliot Morison, *Three Centuries of Harvard, 1636–1936* (Cambridge: Harvard University Press, 1946), p. 245.

[16] Greenslet, *The Lowells and Their Seven Worlds*, p. 150.

[17] Lowell, *Sermons: Chiefly Practical*, p. 247.

[18] Ibid., p. 248.

19   Ibid., p. 59.

20   For Wilberforce's original wording, see Richard V. Pierard, "Little Known or Remarkable Facts About William Wilberforce and the Century of Reform," *Christian History* 53 (January 1997): 17.

21   Anna Cabot Lowell, entry dated September 1827, Anna Cabot Lowell Diaries (1818–1894), Massachusetts Historical Society, Boston.

22   Commonplace Book of Rebecca Amory Lowell, vol. 13, Rebecca Amory Lowell Papers (1794–1873), Massachusetts Historical Society, Boston.

23   Ibid.

24   John Amory Lowell and Elizabeth Cabot Putnam shared the same birthday and would celebrate fifty-one birthdays together. See Charles C. Smith, "Memoir of John Amory Lowell," *Proceedings of the Massachusetts Historical Society* 12 (1899): 127.

25   Anna Cabot Lowell, entry dated December 21, 1828, Anna Cabot Lowell Diaries.

14. 1829–1840

1   Boston *Whig*, July 3, 1846, cited in Thomas H. O'Connor, *Lords of the Loom: The Cotton Whigs and the Coming of the Civil War* (New York: Charles Scribner's Sons, 1968), p. 74.

2   William Lloyd Garrison, "Address to the Colonization Society," Park Street Church, Boston, MA, July 4, 1829 (Boston: Directors of the Old South Work, 1907).

3   Entries in journal number 15, September 1829–June 1830. Anna Cabot Lowell Diaries (1818–1894), Massachusetts Historical Society, Boston. In journal number 16, Anna wrote, quoting Samuel Johnson, "The great thing to be recorded is the state of your own mind and you should write down everything that you remember for you cannot judge at first what is good or bad; write immediately, while the impression is fresh, for it will not be the same a week afterward."

4   John Lowell, Jr., quoted in Edward Everett, *Memoir of Mr. John Lowell, Jun.* (Boston: Charles C. Little and J. Brown, 1840), p. 30, Massachusetts Historical Society, Boston.

5   Ibid., p. 66.

6   Ibid., pp. 66–68; Ferris Greenslet, *The Lowells and Their Seven Worlds* (Boston: Houghton Mifflin, 1946) pp. 183–84.

7   See *The Voice of Industry* at http://www.industrialrevolution.org/the-life-of -the-mind.html.

8   "The Lowell Factory Girl," quoted in David A. Zonderman, *Aspirations and Anxieties: New England Workers and the Mechanized Factory System, 1815– 1850* (New York: Oxford University Press, 1991), p. 237.

9   Six-line song sung during the 1836 strike, quoted in Judith A. Ranta, *Women and Children of the Mills* (Westport, CT: Greenwood Publishing Group, 1999), p. 236.

10   Carol Bundy, *The Nature of Sacrifice: A Biography of Charles Russell Lowell* (New York: Farrar, Straus and Giroux, 2005), p. 38.

11   Joan Waugh, *Unsentimental Reformer: The Life of Josephine Shaw Lowell* (Cambridge: Harvard University Press, 1998), p. 66.

[12] Charles Lowell, *Sermons: Chiefly Practical* (Boston: Ticknor and Fields, 1854), p. 176.

[13] Ibid., p. 175.

[14] Chaim Rosenberg, *The Life and Times of Francis Cabot Lowell, 1775–1857* (Lanham, MD: Rowman & Littlefield, 2011), p. 138.

[15] Ibid., p. 139.

[16] Henry Wadsworth Longfellow, *Hyperion*, vol. 2 (New York: Samuel Colman, 1839), p. 211. In 1843, Longfellow married Frances ("Fanny") Appleton, daughter of Nathan Appleton, former partner of Francis Cabot Lowell. As a wedding gift, Nathan bought Craigie House and gave it to Longfellow.

15. 1842

[1] Notes of a meeting of the Essex County Anti-Slavery Society, February 8, 1842, resolution made by Garrison, available at http://www.theliberatorfiles.com /dissolution-of-the-union/.

[2] Horace Elisha Scudder, *James Russell Lowell: A Biography*, vol. 1 (Boston: Houghton Mifflin, 1901), p. 207.

[3] *Boston Morning Post*, August 12, 1834. See also Jon Gjerde, *Catholicism and the Shaping of Nineteenth-Century America* (New York: Cambridge University Press 2011), pp. 185–86.

[4] Martin Duberman, *James Russell Lowell* (Boston: Houghton Mifflin, 1966), p. 13.

[5] Isaiah 55:12, King James Version.

[6] James Russell Lowell, *Conversations on Some of the Old Poets* (Cambridge: John Owen, 1845), dedication page.

[7] James Russell Lowell, "Cambridge Thirty Years Ago," *The Writings of James Russell Lowell* (Boston: Houghton Mifflin, 1864), p. 54.

[8] Scudder, *James Russell Lowell*, p. 19.

[9] Psalm 71:20, King James Version.

[10] Duberman, *James Russell Lowell*, p. 23.

[11] Ibid., p. 17.

[12] Van Wyck Brooks, *The Flowering of New England* (New York: Random House, 1941), p. 314.

[13] Duberman, *James Russell Lowell*, p. 170.

[14] James Russell Lowell to G. B. Loring, August 24, 1840, *Letters of James Russell Lowell*, vol. 1, ed. Charles Eliot Norton (New York: Harper & Brothers, 1894), p. 60.

[15] James Russell Lowell to G. B. Loring, December 2, 1839, *Letters of James Russell Lowell*, vol. 1, p. 51.

[16] James Russell Lowell, "Irene," *The Complete Poetical Works of James Russell Lowell*, vol. 1 (Boston: Houghton Mifflin, 1896), p. 4.

[17] James Russell Lowell, "My Love," *The Complete Poetical Works of James Russell Lowell*, p. 6.

[18] James Russell Lowell to G. B. Loring, May 17, 1840, *Letters of James Russell Lowell*, vol. 1, p. 59.

[19] James Russell Lowell, "Allegra," *The Complete Poetical Works of James Russell Lowell*, p. 10.

20   James Russell Lowell to G. B. Loring, August 1840, *The Poems of Maria Lowell*, ed. Hope Jillson Vernon (Providence, RI: Brown University, 1936).

21   James Russell Lowell to C. F. Briggs, Feb. 18, 1846, James Russell Lowell Additional Papers 1840–1846, Houghton Library, Harvard University, Cambridge, MA.

22   Maria White to James Russell Lowell, November/December 1840, in *The Poems of Maria Lowell*, p. 97.

23   Maria White to cousin Levi Thaxter, *The Poems of Maria Lowell*, p. 16.

24   James Russell Lowell to G. B. Loring, March 18, 1841, *Letters of James Russell Lowell*, vol. 1, p. 62.

25   Luke 6:38, King James Version.

26   Charles Sumner, *Charles Sumner: His Complete Works*, with Introduction by Hon. George Frisbie Hoar (Boston: Lee and Shepard, 1900), vol. 2, p. 233.

27   Nat Turner, a slave from Virginia, led a rebellion of seventy slaves against their owners in August 1831. Between fifty and sixty whites were killed before the rebellion was suppressed. Fifty-six slaves accused of being involved in the rebellion were executed and hundreds of blacks were attacked and killed by mobs. Nat Turner was captured and hanged. Legislation was passed across the South prohibiting education of free blacks and slaves, and limiting their rights of assembly. See Stephen B. Oates, *The Fires of Jubilee: Nat Turner's Fierce Rebellion* (New York: HarperPerennial, 2014).

28   Quotation from the newspaper *Whig*, published in Richmond, Virginia, quoted in Thomas H. O'Connor, "Cotton Whigs in Kansas," *Kansas Historical Quarterly* 26:35.

29   Ibid.

30   Ibid., p. 38; see also Irving H. Bartlett, *Wendell Phillips, Brahmin Radical* (Boston: Beacon Press, 1961), p. 35.

31   James Russell Lowell to G. B. Loring, May 11, 1842, *Letters of James Russell Lowell*, vol. 1, p. 67.

32   John Lowell, *Laudable character of a woman: A sermon, preached at Newbury, March 26, 1758, Occasioned by the death of Mrs. Hannah Kent, relict of the late Col. Richard Kent* (Boston: Green and Russell, 1758), p. 24. Massachusetts Historical Society, Boston.

33   Wetmore's minutes of the trial, in the case of *Caesar Hendricks v. Richard Greenleaf*, Essex Inferior Court, October 1973; cited in L. Kinvin Wroth and Hiller B. Zobel, eds., *Legal Papers of John Adams*, vol. 2 (Cambridge: Harvard University Press, 1965), p. 65.

34   Ferris Greenslet, *The Lowells and Their Seven Worlds* (Boston: Houghton Mifflin, 1946), pp. 149–50.

35   Charles Lowell, *Sermons: Chiefly Practical* (Boston: Ticknor and Fields, 1854), p. 254.

36   James Russell Lowell to G. B. Loring, January 2, 1841, *Letters of James Russell Lowell*, vol. 1, p. 61.

37   Ibid.

16. 1842–1850

[1]   Ferris Greenslet, *The Lowells and Their Seven Worlds* (Boston: Houghton Mifflin, 1946), p. 38.

[2]   James Russell Lowell, "Irene" *The Complete Poetical Works of James Russell Lowell* (Boston: Houghton Mifflin, 1896), p. 43.

[3]   James Russell Lowell to Charles F. Briggs, March 6, 1844, *Letters of James Russell Lowell*, vol. 1, ed. Charles Eliot Norton (New York: Harper & Brothers, 1894), p. 76.

[4]   The Reverend Charles Lowell to James Russell Lowell, May 1844, James Russell Lowell Additional Papers 1840–1846, Houghton Library, Harvard University, Cambridge, MA.

[5]   James Russell Lowell to G. B. Loring, May 11, 1842, *Letters of James Russell Lowell*, vol. 1, p. 67.

[6]   Martin Duberman, *James Russell Lowell* (Boston: Houghton Mifflin, 1966), pp. 73, 408 n. 10.

[7]   James Russell Lowell to Charles F. Briggs, September 1853, *The Poems of Maria Lowell*, ed. Hope Jillson Vernon (Providence, RI: Brown University, 1936), p. 37.

[8]   Duberman, *James Russell Lowell*, pp. 72, 408 n. 8.

[9]   Matthew 19:6, King James Version.

[10] James Russell Lowell to Robert Carter, January 14, 1845, *The Poems of Maria Lowell*, p. 25.

[11] Ibid.

[12] Maria Lowell to Rebecca Lowell, January 30, 1845, *The Poems of Maria Lowell*, p. 104.

[13] James Russell Lowell, *A Fable for Critics*, *The Complete Poetical Works of James Russell Lowell* (Boston: Houghton Mifflin, 1896), p. 116.

[14] Letter of Frederika Bremer, Swedish writer, quoted in Horace Elisha Scudder, *James Russell Lowell: A Biography*, vol. 1 (Boston: Houghton Mifflin, 1901), p. 298.

[15] See Alex Beam, *Gracefully Insane: The Rise and Fall of America's Premier Mental Hospital* (New York: Public Affairs, 2001).

[16] Proverbs 27:8, King James Version.

[17] Ferris Greenslet, *James Russell Lowell: His Life and Work* (Boston: Houghton Mifflin, 1905), p. 64.

[18] James Russell Lowell, "The Present Crisis," *The Complete Poetical Works of James Russell Lowell* (Boston: Houghton Mifflin, 1896), p. 67.

[19] Ibid. Martin Luther King frequently quoted from "The Present Crisis" in his speeches and orations. See *The Papers of Martin Luther King, Jr.*, vol. 1, ed. by Clayborne Carson (Berkeley: University of California Press, 1992), p. 417 n. 2; see also *A Testament of Hope: The Essential Writings and Speeches of Martin Luther King, Jr.*, ed. James Washington (San Francisco: Harper & Row, 1986), pp. 52, 141, 207, 243–44, 277, 507. The words of the poem were set to music in 1890 by Thomas J. Williams; the hymn was titled "Once to Every Man and Nation." And see Greenslet, *James Russell Lowell*, pp. 79–80.

[20] James Russell Lowell to Emma Parker, January 1, 1846, quoted in Duberman, *James Russell Lowell*, p. 89.

21   James Russell Lowell to Edward M. Davis, April 1846, Duberman, *James Russell Lowell*, p. 72.

22   James Russell Lowell to Edward M. Davis, April 16, 1846, *Letters of James Russell Lowell*, vol. 1, p. 111.

23   James Russell Lowell to Charles F. Briggs, February 18, 1846, *Complete Works of James Russell Lowell*, vol. 12 (Boston: Houghton Mifflin, 1901), p. 185.

24   Maria Lowell, "The Morning-Glory," *The Poems of Maria Lowell*, p. 53.

25   James Russell Lowell to Sydney Gay, June 16, 1846, *Complete Works of James Russell Lowell*, vol. 12, p. 200.

26   Scudder, *James Russell Lowell*, p. 188.

27   James Russell Lowell to Charles F. Briggs, August 8, 1845, *Letters of James Russell Lowell*, vol. 1, p. 93.

28   C. David Heymann, *American Aristocracy: The Lives and Times of James Russell, Amy, and Robert Lowell*, (New York: Dodd Mead, 1980), p. 56.

29   Scudder, *James Russell Lowell*, p. 237.

30   James Russell Lowell, "She Came and Went," *The Complete Poetical Works of James Russell Lowell*, p. 89.

31   Duberman, *James Russell Lowell*, p. 90.

32   Isaiah 16:20, King James Version.

33   Maria Lowell, "The Morning Glory," *The Poems of Maria Lowell*, p. 53.

34   James Russell Lowell, *The Biglow Papers*, *The Complete Poetical Works of James Russell Lowell*, pp. 181–82.

35   Duberman, *James Russell Lowell*, p. 105.

36   Van Wyck Brooks, *The Flowering of New England* (New York: Random House, 1941), p. 319.

37   James Russell Lowell to Elizabeth Wormeley Latimer, August 1, 1853, quoted in Elizabeth Wormeley Latimer, *Europe in Africa in the Nineteenth Century* (Chicago: A. C. McClurg, 1895), p. 370.

38   Maria Lowell to James Russell Lowell, August 3, 1848, *The Poems of Maria Lowell*, p. 116.

39   James Russell Lowell, "The First Snowfall," *The Complete Poetical Works of James Russell Lowell*, p. 292.

40   James Russell Lowell to Robert Carter, September 1847, *The Poems of Maria Lowell*, p. 32.

41   James Russell Lowell, *The Complete Poetical Works of James Russell Lowell*, p. 140 (Po), p. 144 (Lowell).

42   Brooks, *The Flowering of New England*, p. 317.

43   Duberman, *James Russell Lowell*, p. 116.

44   James Russell Lowell to Sydney Gay, February 2, 1850, *The Poems of Maria Lowell*, p. 34.

45   James Russell Lowell, "The Darkened Mind," *The Complete Poetical Works of James Russell Lowell*, p. 319.

17. 1850–1853

1   Charles Lowell, *Sermons: Chiefly Practical* (Boston: Ticknor and Fields, 1854), p. 247.

2 Lewis Tappan, *The Fugitive Slave Bill* (New York: American and Foreign Anti-Slavery Society, 1850), pp. 34–35.

3 Herman Vandenburg Ames, *State Documents on Federal Relations: The States and the United States* (Clark, NJ: Lawbook Exchange, Ltd., 2006), p. 242.

4 "No Union with Slaveholders!" *The Liberator*, October 18, 1850, p. 2.

5 Wendell Phillips Garrison and Francis Jackson Garrison, *William Lloyd Garrison, 1805–1879: The Story of His Life Told by His Children*, vol. 3, (New York: Century, 1885), p. 303.

6 Dorothy Porter Vesley and Constance Porter Uzelac, eds., *William Copper Nell, Nineteenth-Century African American Abolitionist, Historian, Integrationist: Selected Writings from 1832–1874* (Baltimore: Black Classic Press, 2002), p. 24.

7 "Hear Reverend Henry Ward Beecher!" *The Liberator*, October 11, 1850, p. 2.

8 Gary Collison, "Anti-Slavery, Blacks, and the Boston Elite: Notes on the Reverend Charles Lowell and the West Church," *The New England Quarterly* 61, no. 3 (1988): 422.

9 Carol Bundy, *The Nature of Sacrifice: A Biography of Charles Russell Lowell* (New York: Farrar, Straus and Giroux, 2005), p. 65.

10 *The Liberator*, October 18, 1850, quoted in Irving H. Bartlett, *Wendell Phillips: Brahmin Radical* (Boston: Beacon Press, 1961), p. 148.

11 James Russell Lowell to Sidney Gay, November 1850, *Letters of James Russell Lowell*, vol. 1, ed. Charles Eliot Norton (New York: Harper & Brothers, 1894), p. 188.

12 Psalm 85:10, King James Version.

13 Collison, "Anti-Slavery, Blacks, and the Boston Elite," p. 423, quoting from *The Liberator*, October 18, 1850; an introductory note states that the prayer, printed from a stenographic transcript, is "substantially as follows."

14 Harold Schwartz, "Fugitive Slave Days in Boston," *The New England Quarterly* 27, no. 2 (1954): 191.

15 Ibid., p. 192.

16 Stephen Puleo, *A City So Grand: The Rise of an American Metropolis, Boston 1850–1900* (Boston: Beacon Press, 2011), p. 7.

17 Ibid., p. 16.

18 "Collison, "Anti-Slavery, Blacks, and the Boston Elite," p. 425, quoting Charles Lowell to "My dear brethren," June 11, 1854, a copy of which is in the Theodore Parker Papers, Massachusetts Historical Society, Boston.

19 Charles Lowell, *Sermons: Chiefly Practical*, p. 247.

20 See Thomas O'Connor, *Lords of the Loom: The Cotton Whigs and the Coming of the Civil War* (New York: Charles Scribner's Sons, 1968), p. 184 nn. 23, 25; Emerson quote is from Edward Waldo Emerson and Waldo Emerson Forbes, eds., *Journals of Ralph Waldo Emerson*, 10 vols. (Boston: Houghton Mifflin, 1909–1914), vol. 8, p. 363; Parker quote is from Theodore Parker, *Additional Speeches, Addresses, and Occasional Sermons*, vol. 1 (Boston: Little, Brown, 1855), p. 89; Phillips quote is from Wendell Phillips, *Speeches, Lectures, and Letters*, vol. 2 (Boston: James Redpath, 1863), p. 65; and Quincy quote is from Garrison and Garrison, *William Lloyd Garrison, 1805–1879*, vol. 3, p. 328.

21 Newspaper quote from Puleo, *A City So Grand*, p. 18; Massachusetts senate
    quote is also from *A City So Grand*, p. 30.

22 James Russell Lowell to Sydney Gay, March 17, 1850, *Letters of James Russell
    Lowell*, vol. 1, p. 175.

23 James Russell Lowell, "At Sea," *Fireside Travels* (Boston: Houghton Mifflin,
    1890), "shoal of fish," p. 160; "sails," p. 113; "sunrise," p. 114; "naked sun," p. 115.

24 Horace Elisha Scudder, *James Russell Lowell: A Biography*, vol. 1 (Boston:
    Houghton Mifflin, 1901), p. 311.

25 James Russell Lowell, "At Sea," *Fireside Travels*, p. 165.

26 James Russell Lowell to Sydney Gay, April 20, 1852, *Letters of James Russell
    Lowell*, vol. 1, p. 190.

27 James Russell Lowell, "Leaves from My Journal," *Fireside Travels* (Boston:
    Houghton Mifflin, 1904), vol. 2, p. 147.

28 James Russell Lowell to Mary Lowell Putnam, Martin Duberman, *James Rus-
    sell Lowell* (Boston: Houghton Mifflin, 1966), p. 126.

29 John Milton, "To the Nightingale," *The Poetical Works of John Milton* (London:
    George Routledge and Co., 1857), p. 483.

30 James Russell Lowell to the Reverend Charles Lowell, March 1852, Scudder,
    James Russell Lowell, vol. 1, p. 337.

31 Maria Lowell, "The Grave of Keats," *The Poems of Maria Lowell*, ed. Hope Jilli-
    son Vernon (Providence, RI: Brown University, 1936), p. 58.

32 Maria Lowell to Sarah Shaw, July 3, 1852, *The Poems of Maria Lowell*, p. 149.

33 James Russell Lowell to Mary Lowell Putnam, Duberman, *James Russell Lowell*,
    pp. 128, 418 n. 17.

34 James Russell Lowell to Edmund Quincy, June 7, 1854, *The Poems of Maria
    Lowell*, p. 37.

35 Nathaniel Hawthorne, "The Sister Years," *Twice-Told Tales* (Boston: Ticknor and
    Fields, 1851), p. 84.

36 James Russell Lowell to C. F. Briggs, October 6, 1853, *Letters of James Russell
    Lowell*, vol. 1, pp. 203–4.

37 Scudder, *James Russell Lowell*, vol. 1, p. 358.

38 Henry Longfellow, "The Two Angels," *The Poetical Works of Longfellow* (Lon-
    don: Griffith and Farran, 1890), p. 317.

39 Matthew 5:4, King James Version.

40 Ferris Greenslet, *The Lowells and Their Seven Worlds* (Boston: Houghton Miff-
    lin, 1946), p. 258.

41 Duberman, *James Russell Lowell*, p. 143.

42 Maria Lowell, "Sonnet," *Poems of Maria Lowell*, p. 62.

43 James Russell Lowell, "The Dead House," *The Complete Poetical Works of
    James Russell Lowell* (Boston: Houghton Mifflin, 1896), p. 310.

18. 1853–1861

1 *Elisabeth Rebecca Sprague: A Tribute* (Boston: privately printed, 1905), pp. xxi–xxii.

2 James Russell Lowell to Charles F. Briggs, February 8, 28, 1854, James Russell
   Lowell Papers, Houghton Library, Harvard University, Cambridge, MA.

3   James Russell Lowell to nephew Charles Russell Lowell, June 11, 1849, James Russell Lowell Papers.

4   Ibid.

5   James M. McPherson, *Battle Cry of Freedom: The Civil War Era* (New York: Oxford University Press, 2003), pp. 119–20; Stephen Puleo, *A City So Grand: The Rise of an American Metropolis, Boston 1850–1900* (Boston: Beacon Press, 2011), pp. 33–34.

6   Carol Bundy, *The Nature of Sacrifice: A Biography of Charles Russell Lowell* (New York: Farrar, Straus and Giroux, 2005), p. 88.

7   Amos A. Lawrence to Giles Richards, June 1, 1854, Thomas H. O'Connor, *Lords of the Loom: The Cotton Whigs and the Coming of the Civil War* (New York: Charles Scribner's Sons, 1968), p. 98.

8   Directors of the New England Emigrant Aid Company, *History of the New England Emigrant Aid Company* (Boston: Press of J. Wilson and Son, 1862), p. 4.

9   James Russell Lowell to Edmund Quincy, February 25, 1855, Martin Duberman, *James Russell Lowell* (Boston: Houghton Mifflin, 1966), p. 139.

10 Edward Everett Hale, "James Russell Lowell and His Friends," *The Outlook* 39 (1898): 47; Duberman, *James Russell Lowell*, p. 140.

11 Journal of Henry Wadsworth Longfellow, January 31, 1855, Henry Wadsworth Longfellow Papers, Houghton Library, Harvard University, Cambridge, MA.

12 James Russell Lowell to Charles Eliot Norton, July 14, 1859, Duberman, *James Russell Lowell*, p. 157.

13 Journal of Annie Fields, July 30, 1874, Annie Fields Papers (1847–1912), Massachusetts Historical Society, Boston; quoted in Duberman, *James Russell Lowell*, p. 157.

14 Thomas H. O'Connor, "Cotton Whigs in Kansas," *Kansas Historical Quarterly* XXVI, no. 1 (Spring 1960), 51.

15 Ibid., p. 50.

16 John M. Blum, ed., *The National Experience: A History of the United States* (New York: Harcourt, Brace & World, 1963), p. 309.

17 David S. Reynolds, *John Brown, Abolitionist: The Man Who Killed Slavery, Sparked the Civil War, and Seeded Civil Rights* (New York: Random House, 2005), p. 104.

18 Amos A. Lawrence to Charles Robinson, March 31, 1857, Thomas H. O'Connor, "Cotton Whigs in Kansas," p. 54.

19 *The Crime Against Kansas. Speech of Honorable Charles Sumner, of Massachusetts. In the Senate of the United States, May 19, 1856* (New York: Greeley & McElrath, 1856).

20 Kermit Hall, James W. Ely, Jr., and Joel B. Grossman, eds., *The Oxford Companion to the Supreme Court of the United States* (New York: Oxford University Press, 2005), p. 888.

21 James Russell Lowell, "The Election in November," *The Complete Writings of James Russell Lowell*, vol. 6 (Boston: Houghton Mifflin, 1904), p. 27.

22 Amos A. Lawrence to Charles Robinson, October 19, 1857, O'Connor, *Lords of the Loom*, p. 125.

23 Henry Longfellow to Charles Sumner, August 12, 1848, Charles Sumner Correspondence, 1829–1874, Houghton Library, Harvard University, Cambridge, MA.

24 James Russell Lowell, "Columbus," *The Complete Poetical Works of James Russell Lowell* (Boston: Houghton Mifflin, 1896) p. 56.

25 Senator James H. Hammond, "On the Admission of Kansas," Speech delivered before the United States Senate, March 4, 1858, *Selections of Letters and Speeches of the Hon. James H. Hammond* (John F. Trow & Co., 1866), p. 317.

26 Cited in *John Brown's Raid*, by Christopher Hamner, available at http://teachinghistory.org/history-content/beyond-the-textbook/25478.

27 Ferris Greenslet, *The Lowells and Their Seven Worlds* (Boston: Houghton Mifflin, 1946), p. 270.

28 James Russell Lowell, "The Election in November," *The Complete Writings of James Russell Lowell*, vol. 6 (Boston: Houghton Mifflin, 1904), pp. 28–29.

29 Wendell Phillips, "Mobs and Education," *Speeches, Lectures, and Letters*, vol. 1 (Boston: Lee and Shepard, 1894), p. 325.

30 Duberman, *James Russell Lowell*, p. 198.

31 *Proceedings in the West Church on the Occasion of the Decease of Charles Lowell, D.D.* (Boston: Walker, Wise, and Company, 1861), p. 44.

32 Reverend Charles Russell Lowell to James Russell Lowell, February 22, 1860, James Russell Lowell Additional Papers 1840–1846, Houghton Library Harvard University, Cambridge, MA.

33 *Proceedings in the West Church on the Occasion of the Decease of Charles Lowell, D.D.*, p. 37.

34 James Russell Lowell, "The Shepherd of King Admetus," *The Complete Poetical Works of James Russell Lowell*, p. 44.

35 James Russell Lowell to C. F. Briggs, March 11, 1861, *Letters of James Russell Lowell*, vol. 1, ed. Charles Eliot Norton (New York: Harper & Brothers, 1894), p. 310.

36 *Selections from the Diaries of William Appleton, 1786–1862*, ed. Susan M. Loring, (Boston: privately printed, 1922), p. 237.

37 James Russell Lowell to John Lothrop Motley, March 27, 1862, James Russell Lowell Additional Papers 1840–1846.

19. 1861–1864

1 Elizabeth Cabot Putnam, comp., *Memoirs of the War of '61* (Boston: Geo. H. Ellis Co., 1920), pp. 50–51.

2 William Lowell Putnam to Mary Putnam, October 1861, Carol Bundy, *The Nature of Sacrifice: A Biography of Charles Russell Lowell* (New York: Farrar, Straus and Giroux, 2005), p. 197; Richard F. Miller, *Harvard's Civil War: A History of the Twentieth Massachusetts Volunteer Infantry* (Hanover, NH: University Press of New England, 2005), p. 28.

3 Letter from Charles Lowell to his mother, Anna Cabot Jackson Lowell, April 15, 1861, Edward W. Emerson, *Life and Letters of Charles Russell Lowell* (Boston: Houghton Mifflin, 1907), p. 197.

4 Henry Wadsworth Longfellow, "Paul Revere's Ride," www.theatlantic.com/magazine/archive/1861/01/paul-revere-s-ride/308349/.

5   See http://www.massmoments.org/moment.cfm?mid=26.

6   Thomas H. O'Connor, *Lords of the Loom: The Cotton Whigs and the Coming of the Civil War* (New York: Charles Scribner's Sons, 1968), p. 160.

7   Stephen Puleo, *A City So Grand: The Rise of an American Metropolis, Boston 1856–1900* (Boston: Beacon Press 2011), p. 131, quoting George Templeton Strong, an American lawyer who kept an extensive diary during the Civil War.

8   Memoir of George W. Brown, at http://perspectives.jhu.edu/2011/04/pratt-street-riots-a-first-hand-account/.

9   Letter of Charles Lowell to his mother, Anna Cabot Jackson Lowell, May 5, 1861, Emerson, *Life and Letters of Charles Russell Lowell*, pp. 206–7; see also Bundy, *The Nature of Sacrifice*, p. 170.

10 Charles Russell Lowell to Charles Sumner, April 23, 1861, Emerson, *Life and Letters of Charles Russell Lowell*, pp. 201–2.

11 Miller, *Harvard's Civil War*, p. 28.

12 Putnam, comp., *Memoirs of the War of '61*, p. 45.

13 Bundy, *The Nature of Sacrifice*, p. 193.

14 Putnam, comp., *Memoirs of the War of '61*, p. 52.

15 John 14:27, King James Version.

16 Miller, *Harvard's Civil War*, p. 82.

17 William Shakespeare, Sonnet 18.

18 Mary Lowell Putnam, *William Lowell Putnam* (Cambridge: Riverside Press, 1863), Massachusetts Historical Society, Boston; Putnam, comp., *Memoirs of the War of '61*, p. 52.

19 Ephesians 6:13, King James Version.

20 Charles Russell Lowell to James Jackson Lowell, February 1862, quoted in Bundy, *The Nature of Sacrifice*, p. 207.

21 Miller, *Harvard's Civil War*, p. 127.

22 Putnam, comp. *Memoirs of the War of '61*, p. 46.

23 Miller, *Harvard's Civil War*, p. 151.

24 Putnam, comp., *Memoirs of the War of '61*, pp. 46–47; Bundy, *The Nature of Sacrifice*, pp. 208–9; Miller, *Harvard's Civil War*, p. 152.

25 Charles Russell Lowell to Anna Cabot Jackson Lowell, July 27, 1863, Emerson, *Life and Letters of Charles Russell Lowell*, p. 223.

26 Thomas Wentworth Higginson, ed., *Harvard Memorial Biographies*, vol. 2 (Cambridge: Sever and Francis, 1866), p. 171.

27 Martin Duberman, *James Russell Lowell* (Boston: Houghton Mifflin, 1966), p. 213.

28 Ralph Waldo Emerson, "The Boston Hymn," in *The Cry for Justice: An Anthology of Social Protest*, ed. Upton Sinclair (Philadelphia: John C. Winston Co., 1915), p. 235.

29 Putnam, comp., *Memoirs of the War of '61*, p. 54.

30 Ibid.

31 Ibid.

32 Letter of James Russell Lowell to Sarah Shaw, April 6, 1863, *Letters of James Russell Lowell*, vol. 1, ed. Charles Eliot Norton (New York: Harper & Brothers, 1894), p. 327.

33 Putnam, comp., *Memoirs of the War of '61,* pp. 30–31.

34 Robert Gould Shaw to his wife, Annie Shaw, June 1, 1863, at http://54th-mass .org/tag/march-through-boston/.

35 Putnam, comp., *Memoirs of the War of '61,* p. 56.

36 Charles Russell Lowell to Josephine Shaw, July 28, 1863, Bundy, *The Nature of Sacrifice,* p. 313.

37 Charles Russell Lowell to Josephine Shaw, August 2, 1863, Emerson, *Life and Letters of Charles Russell Lowell,* pp. 289–90.

38 Letter of Charles Russell Lowell to Josephine Shaw Lowell, October 1864, Emerson, *Life and Letters of Charles Russell Lowell,* pp. 357–58.

39 Charles Russell Lowell to Josephine Shaw Lowell, October 15, 1864, Emerson, *Life and Letters of Charles Russell Lowell,* p. 360; Charles Russell Lowell to Anna Cabot Jackson Lowell, Emerson, *Life and Letters of Charles Russell Lowell,* October 17, 1864, p. 364.

40 Caspar Crowninshield to Mammy, October 21, 1864, Crowninshield-Magnus Papers (1834–1965), Massachusetts Historical Society, Boston; quoted in Bundy, *The Nature of Sacrifice,* p. 469.

41 Bundy, *The Nature of Sacrifice,* p. 471.

42 Oscar DeWolf to Josephine Shaw Lowell, October 21, 1864, James Russell Lowell Papers (1842–1924), Massachusetts Historical Society, Boston.

43 Bundy, *The Nature of Sacrifice,* p. 472.

44 Oscar DeWolf to Josephine Shaw Lowell, October 21, 1864, James Russell Lowell Papers; quoted in Bundy, *The Nature of Sacrifice,* p. 473.

45 Ferris Greenslet *The Lowells and Their Seven Worlds* (Boston: Houghton Mifflin, 1946), p. 297.

46 Charles Russell Lowell to Josephine Shaw Lowell, July 24, 1863, Emerson, *Life and Letters of Charles Russell Lowell,* p. 282.

47 Emerson, *Life and Letters of Charles Russell Lowell,* p. 68.

48 George Putnam, *An Address Spoken in the College Chapel, Cambridge, October 28, 1864, at the Funeral of Brig.-Gen. Charles Russell Lowell, Who Fell at the Battle of Cedar Creek, October 19, 1864* (Cambridge: Welch Bigelow, 1864), YA Pamphlet Collection, Library of Congress, Washington, D.C.

49 Bundy, *The Nature of Sacrifice,* p. 11.

50 James Russell Lowell, "Ode Recited at the Harvard Commemoration," July 21, 1865, *The Complete Poetical Works of James Russell Lowell* (Boston: Houghton Mifflin, 1896), p. 343.

20. June 9, 1888

1 Henry A. Yeomans, *Abbott Lawrence Lowell* (Cambridge: Harvard University Press, 1948), p. 22. This comes from Ecclesiastes 9:10, King James Version: "Whatsoever thy hand findeth to do, do it with thy might . . ."

2 Percival Lowell, *Noto: An Unexplored Corner of Japan* (Boston: Houghton Mifflin, 1895), p. 9.

3 Percival Lowell to Katharine Lowell, December 1888, A. Lawrence Lowell, *Biography of Percival Lowell* (New York: Macmillan, 1935), p. 31.

4   Percival Lowell to Elizabeth Lowell, August 25 (no year given), Letters to Elizabeth Lowell Putnam (Mrs. William Lowell Putnam) and William Lowell Putnam 1876–1916, Houghton Library, Harvard University, Cambridge, MA.

5   Yeomans, *Abbot Lawrence Lowell*, p. 30.

6   Diary entry dated September 16, 1848, Diaries of Katharine B. Lawrence Lowell (1847–1852), Lamb Family Papers, Massachusetts Historical Society, Boston.

7   Diary entries dated October 15 and 31, 1851, Diaries of Katharine B. Lawrence Lowell.

8   Mrs. William Lowell Putnam, *The Happiness of Our Garden* (New York: William Edmund Rudge, 1926), p. 9.

9   S. Foster Damon, *Amy Lowell: A Chronicle with Extracts from Her Correspondence* (Boston: Houghton Mifflin, 1935), p. 36.

10 "Augustus Lowell is a hard man but he is absolutely honest." This was overheard by Augustus Lowell in a Boston railroad station and frequently invoked by him, as quoted in Percival Lowell, "Augustus Lowell," *Proceedings of the American Academy of Arts and Sciences* 37 (1902): 653.

21. 1891–1897

1   Katharine Bowlker, *Women's Municipal League of Boston, A Campaign of Education by Means of a Traveling Exhibit* (Boston: T. W. Ripley, 1910), p. 16, Sterling Memorial Library Yale University, New Haven, CT.

2   A. Lawrence Lowell, *Biography of Percival Lowell* (New York: Macmillan, 1935), p. 4.

3   Jacob Abbott, *Rollo on the Atlantic* (Boston: DeWolfe, Fiske & Co., 1858), p. 11.

4   Edgar Allan Poe, "The Raven," www.poestories.com/read/raven.

5   A. Lawrence Lowell, *Biography of Percival Lowell*, p. 49.

6   S. Foster Damon, *Amy Lowell: A Chronicle with Extracts from Her Correspondence* (Boston: Houghton Mifflin, 1935), p. 38.

7   Ibid., p. 109.

8   Ibid., p. 109.

9   Henry A. Yeomans, *Abbott Lawrence Lowell* (Cambridge: Harvard University Press, 1948), p. 44.

10 A. Lawrence Lowell to Barrett Wendell, January 23, 1879; February 4, 1879; June 4, 1879, Wendell Family Papers, circa 1620–1921, Houghton Library, Harvard University, Cambridge: MA.

11 Yeomans, *Abbott Lawrence Lowell*, p. 48.

12 Percival Lowell, "Comets," article for Boston Society of the Arts, March 10, 1910.

13 David Strauss, *Percival Lowell: The Culture and Science of a Boston Brahmin* (Cambridge: Harvard University Press, 2001), p. 5.

14 William Graves Hoyt, *Lowell and Mars* (Tucson: University of Arizona Press, 1976), p. 7.

15 Percival Lowell to Augustus Lowell, December 10, 1895, A. Lawrence Lowell, *Biography of Percival Lowell*, p. 93.

16 Percival Lowell, *Mars and Its Canals* (New York: Macmillan, 1906), p. 8.

17   Hoyt, *Lowell and Mars*, p. 7.

18   C. A. Young, "Is Mars Inhabited?" *Boston Herald*, October 18, 1896; cited in Hoyt, *Lowell and Mars*, p. 94.

19   Percival Lowell, *Mars* (Boston: Houghton Mifflin, 1895), p. 201.

20   Ibid., p. 212.

21   Strauss, *Percival Lowell*, pp. 9, 14–15.

22   Katharine Lowell to Percival Lowell, August 1894, Strauss, *Percival Lowell*, p. 15.

23   Percival Lowell, *Mars*, p. 74.

24   Hoyt, *Lowell and Mars*, p. 90.

25   Paper by Percival Lowell, published May 26, 1894, in the Boston newspaper *Commonwealth*; cited in Hoyt, *Lowell and Mars*, p. 57.

26   Percival Lowell to Elizabeth Lowell Putnam, 1896, Letters to Elizabeth Lowell Putnam (Mrs. William Lowell Putnam) and William Lowell Putnam 1876–1916, Houghton Library, Harvard University, Cambridge, MA.

27   Percival Lowell, *Mars*, p. 9.

28   Robert Richardson, *William James: In the Maelstrom of American Modernism* (Boston: Houghton Mifflin, 2006), p. 119.

22. 1897–1900

1   Elizabeth Putnam Lowell, "A Glimpse of Amy's Childhood by Her Sister," Papers of Mrs. William Lowell Putnam, 1887–1935, Schlesinger Library, Radcliffe Institute, Harvard University Cambridge, MA.

2   S. Foster Damon, *Amy Lowell: A Chronicle with Extracts from Her Correspondence* (Boston: Houghton Mifflin, 1935), p. 89.

3   John Keats, "Faery Song" 1 (1818), www.Keats-poems.com/faery-songs.

4   Paper books, colored with pencils; Amy Lowell Papers, Houghton Library, Harvard University, Cambridge, MA.

5   Ferris Greenslett, *The Lowells and Their Seven Worlds* (Boston: Houghton Mifflin, 1946), p. 229.

6   Damon, *Amy Lowell*, p. 56.

7   Ibid., p. 48. The story was printed in *Life* in 1894, under the title, "A Short Way Out of It."

8   Percival Lowell to Elizabeth Lowell Putnam, December 1876/77, Letters to Elizabeth Lowell Putnam (Mrs. William Lowell Putnam) and William Lowell Putnam 1876–1916, Houghton Library, Harvard University, Cambridge MA.

9   Damon, *Amy Lowell*, p. 119.

10   Amy Lowell to Augustus Lowell, December 26, 1897, Damon, *Amy Lowell*, p. 122.

11   Ibid.

12   Amy Lowell to Augustus Lowell, January 2, 1898, Damon, *Amy Lowell*, p. 124.

13   Amy Lowell to Anna Lowell, wife of Lawrence, January 14, 1898, Damon, *Amy Lowell*, p. 127.

14   Amy Lowell to Winifred Bryher, July 28, 1919, Damon, *Amy Lowell*, p. 129.

15   Damon, *Amy Lowell*, p. 132.

16   Amy Lowell to Augustus Lowell, March 15, 1898, Damon, *Amy Lowell*, p. 136.

[17] Amy Lowell to Augustus Lowell, December 26, 1897, Damon, *Amy Lowell,* p. 122.

23. 1901–1913

[1] From an early manuscript of Lowell's *Mars,* quoted in Robert Crossely, *Imagining Mars: A Literary History* (Middletown, CT: Wesleyan University Press, 2011), p. 74.

[2] William Graves Hoyt, *Lowell and Mars* (Tucson: University of Arizona Press, 1976), p. 28.

[3] Louise Leonard to Percival Lowell, William Lowell Putnam, *The Explorers of Mars Hill: A Centennial History of Lowell Observatory, 1894–1994* (West Kennebunk, ME: Phoenix Press, 1994), p. 72.

[4] Percival Lowell has been proved correct, at least in terms of his insistence that conditions had existed on Mars that could have supported life. Recent discoveries by NASA scientists demonstrate that water does exist on Mars, and that the conditions of the planet would support life, or would have supported life at some time. See http://www.nytimes.com/2015/09/29/science/space/mars-life-liquid-water .html; http://www.vice.com/read/men-are-from-mars-so-are-women-maybe-says -nasa-928.

[5] Percival Lowell, "Great Discoveries and Their Reception," lecture given August 1916, quoted in Hoyt, *Lowell and Mars,* p. 23.

[6] Percival Lowell, "Commemoration Day Address," given May 30, 1903, at the Flagstaff observatory, quoted in Hoyt, *Lowell and Mars,* p. 21.

[7] Percival Lowell, "Great Discoveries and Their Reception," quoted in Hoyt, *Lowell and Mars,* p. 21.

[8] Hoyt, *Lowell and Mars,* p. 20.

[9] Percival Lowell, *Mars and Its Canals* (New York: Macmillan, 1906), p. 5.

[10] Ibid., p. viii.

[11] Ibid., p. 384.

[12] Ibid., p. 383.

[13] Louise Leonard, *Percival Lowell: An Afterglow* (Boston: Gorham Press, 1921), p. 25.

[14] Ibid., pp. 25–26.

[15] *New York Times,* August 30, 1907.

[16] *Philadelphia Press,* December 1906; *New York Herald,* December 30, 1906; *New York Times,* November 13, 1907; all newspapers quoted in Hoyt, *Lowell and Mars,* p. 204.

[17] C. N. Chadburne to Percival Lowell, April 27, 1907; H. Menke to Percival Lowell, May 1, 1907; both letters quoted in Hoyt, *Lowell and Mars,* p. 208.

[18] *Wall Street Journal,* December 28, 1907; quoted in Hoyt, *Lowell and Mars,* p. 13.

[19] William Wallace Campbell to George E. Hale, May 11, 1908, David Strauss, *Percival Lowell: The Culture and Science of a Boston Brahmin* (Cambridge: Harvard University Press, 2001), p. 222.

[20] Katharine Bowlker, "Address of the President," *An Account of the Women's Municipal League of Boston* (Boston: T. W. Ripley Co., Southgate Press, 1909), p. 3.

[21] Ibid., pp. 2–3.

22 Sonya Michel and Robyn Rosen, "Elizabeth Lowell Putnam and the American Welfare State," *Gender and History* 3, no. 3 (1992): 369.
23 William Lowell Putnam, *The Explorers of Mars Hill*, pp. 82–84.
24 Ibid., pp. 71–72.
25 Ibid., p. 85.
26 Percival Lowell, Diary (manuscript), entry dated October 3 (1904), Houghton Library, Harvard University, Cambridge, MA.
27 William Lowell Putnam, *The Explorers of Mars Hill*, p. 84 n. 12.
28 A. Lawrence Lowell, *Percival Lowell: A Biography* (New York: Macmillan, 1935), p. 151.
29 A. Lawrence Lowell, Inaugural Address 1909, Harvard University Archives, Pusey Library, Cambridge, MA; printed in *Science*, October 15, 1909, p. 497–505.
30 Ibid.
31 Speech of A. Lawrence Lowell given in 1910, Henry A. Yeomans, *Abbott Lawrence Lowell* (Cambridge: Harvard University Press, 1948), p. 169.
32 Ibid.
33 A. Lawrence Lowell, "Irish Agitation in America," *The Forum* 4 (1887): 396–407.
34 Nathaniel Ward, *The Simple Cobler of Aggawam in America* (London: Stephen Bowtell, 1647), p. 6.

24. 1913–1917

1 Amy Lowell to Eunice Tietjens, June 5, 1923, Jean Gould, *Amy: The World of Amy Lowell and the Imagist Movement* (New York: Dodd, Mead, 1975), p. 148.
2 Louis Untermeyer, "—and Other Poems," *Chicago Evening Post*, February 14, 1913.
3 F. S. Flint, "Imagisme," and Ezra Pound, "A Few Don'ts by an Imagiste," *Poetry*, March 1913, pp. 198–206.
4 Jean Gould, *Amy*, p. 118.
5 Ibid., p. 132.
6 Thomas Hardy, "The Going of the Battery," *Poems of the Past and Present* (Harper & Brothers, 1902), p. 12.
7 Amy Lowell, "A Letter from London," *Little Review*, October 1914; quoted in S. Foster Damon, *Amy Lowell: A Chronicle with Extracts from Her Correspondence* (Boston: Houghton Mifflin, 1935), p. 242.
8 Ibid., p. 243.
9 Gould, *Amy*, p. 139.
10 D. H. Lawrence to Amy Lowell, November 18, 1914, Damon, *Amy Lowell*, p. 277. The letter goes on to criticize many of Amy's poems in *Sword Blades and Poppy Seed*: "I was quite cross with you for writing about bohemian glass and stalks of flame, when the thing is so ugly and bitter to the soul."
11 Amy Lowell, "Bombardment," *Men, Women and Ghosts* (New York: Macmillan, 1916), p. 228.
12 Amy Lowell, "Tribute to Frost," March 5, 1925, Damon, *Amy Lowell*, p. 289.
13 Amy Lowell, "North of Boston," *New Republic*, February 20, 1915, pp. 81–82.

[14] Amy Lowell, "Tribute to Frost," Damon, *Amy Lowell*, p. 289.

[15] Amy Lowell, "Spring Day," *Men, Women* and *Ghosts*, p. 330.

[16] Gould, *Amy*, p. 174; Damon, *Amy Lowell*, p. 292; Melissa Bradshaw, *Amy Lowell, Diva Poet* (Burlington, VT: Ashgate, 2011), pp. 28–29, citing Margaret Widdemer, "The Legend of Amy Lowell," *Texas Quarterly* 2 (1963): 193–200.

[17] Amy Lowell, "Poetry and Polemics," a speech given before the MacDowell Club, February 22, 1916; quoted in Damon, *Amy Lowell*, p. 338.

[18] Amy Lowell, "Grotesque," *Pictures of the Floating World* (New York: Macmillan, 1919), p. 84.

[19] Sandra M. Gilbert and Susan Gubar, *No Man's Land: The Place of the Woman Writer in the Twentieth Century*, vol. 3, (New Haven: Yale University Press, 1994), p. 65.

[20] Amy Lowell "Poetry and Polemics," Damon, *Amy Lowell*, p. 339.

[21] Amy Lowell, "Absence," *Sword Blades and Poppy Seed* (Boston: Houghton Mifflin, 1914), p. 85.

[22] Amy Lowell, "Aubade," Ibid., p. 239.

[23] Amy Lowell, "Stravinsky's Three Pieces 'Grotesques,' for String Quartet," *Men, Women and Ghosts*, p. 342.

[24] Gould, *Amy*, p. 93.

[25] Percival Lowell, *The Solar System: Six Lectures Delivered at Massachusetts Institute of Technology in December, 1902* (Boston: Houghton Mifflin, 1903), p. 17.

[26] Percival Lowell, *Memoir on a Trans-Neptunian Planet* (Lynn, MA: P. Nichols, 1915), p. 1.

[27] Percival Lowell to Carl Lampland, December 1, 1910, William Graves Hoyt, *Lowell and Mars* (Tucson: University of Arizona Press, 1976), p. 271.

[28] Telegram from Percival Lowell to Carl Lampland, March 13, 1911, Hoyt, *Lowell and Mars*, p. 271.

[29] Louise Leonard to Carl Lampland, March 22, 1911, Hoyt, *Lowell and Mars*, p. 271.

[30] Clyde Tombaugh, "The Discovery of Pluto: Some Generally Unknown Aspects of the Story," *Mercury: The Journal of the Astronomical Society of the Pacific* 15 (1986): 15; cited in David Strauss, *Percival Lowell: The Culture and Science of a Boston Brahmin* (Cambridge: Harvard University Press, 2001), p. 317 n. 1.

[31] Louise Leonard to Vesto Slipher, November 8, 1912, Hoyt, *Lowell and Mars*, p. 273.

[32] Percival Lowell, *Memoir on a Trans-Neptunian Planet*, p. 104.

[33] Percival Lowell, "Great Discoveries and Their Reception," lecture given August 1916; quoted in Hoyt, *Lowell and Mars*, p. 300.

[34] Katharine Bowlker, *Women's Municipal League of Boston: A Campaign of Education by Means of a Traveling Exhibit* (Boston: T. W. Ripley, The Southgate Press, 1910), p. 6.

[35] Mrs. William Lowell Putnam, *The Happiness of Our Garden* (New York: William Edmund Rudge, 1926), dedication page.

[36] Mrs. William Lowell Putnam, *Committee on Infant Social Service of the Women's Municipal League of Boston, Prenatal Work* (Boston: Women's Municipal League of Boston, 1910), p. 1.

37   Mrs. William Lowell Putnam to Dr. Wadsworth of the Obstetrical Society of Boston, October 18, 1911; cited in Marika Seigel, *The Rhetoric of Pregnancy* (Chicago: University of Chicago Press, 2013), p. 54.

38   Mrs. William Lowell Putnam, "A Successful Pay Prenatal Clinic," in *The Modern Hospital*, vol. 10 (New York: McGraw-Hill, 1918), p. 10.

39   Mrs. William Lowell Putnam, *An Experiment in Preventive Work with Mothers & Babies, Prenatal and Postnatal* (Boston: Women's Municipal League of Boston, 1910), p. 1.

40   Katharine Bowlker, "Address of the President," *An Account of the Women's Municipal League of Boston, As Given at the First Public Meeting, January 20, 1909* (Boston: T. W. Ripley, Co., Southgate Press, 1909), p. 6.

41   Mrs. William Putnam, *The Happiness of Our Garden*, p. 8.

42   A. Lawrence Lowell to Barrett Wendell, May 13, 1916, Letters to Elizabeth Lowell Putnam (Mrs. William Lowell Putnam) and William Lowell Putnam, 1876–1916, Houghton Library, Harvard University, Cambridge, MA.

43   A. Lawrence Lowell, *At War with Academic Traditions in America* (Cambridge: Harvard University Press, 1934), p. 35.

44   Ferris Greenslet, *The Lowells and Their Seven Worlds* (Boston: Houghton Mifflin, 1946), p. 323.

45   *The Women's Municipal League of Boston Bulletin*, February 1917, p. 28.

25. 1917–1919

1   Melissa Bradshaw, *Amy Lowell, Diva Poet* (Burlington, VT: Ashgate 2011), p. 52.

2   Fanny Butcher, *Many Lives—One Love* (New York: Harper & Row, 1972), p. 96.

3   Ibid.

4   Ezra Pound to Alice Corbin Henderson, May 5, 1916, *The Letters of Ezra Pound to Alice Corbin Henderson*, ed. Ira B. Nadel (Austin: University of Texas Press, 1993), p. 138.

5   Ezra Pound to William Carlos Williams, September 1920, *The Selected Letters of Ezra Pound, 1907–1941*, ed. D. D. Paige (New York: New Directions, 1971), p. 157.

6   Ezra Pound to Alice Corbin Henderson, March 1917, *The Letters of Ezra Pound to Alice Corbin Henderson*, p. 162.

7   Ezra Pound to Margaret C. Anderson, August 1917, *The Selected Letters of Ezra Pound*, p. 114.

8   Ezra Pound to Margaret C. Anderson, January 1918, *The Selected Letters of Ezra Pound*, p. 129.

9   Ezra Pound to Edgar Jepson, May 1918, *The Selected Letters of Ezra Pound*, p. 136.

10   Amy Lowell to Harriet Monroe, September 15, 1914, Damon, *Amy Lowell: A Chronicle with Extracts from Her Correspondence* (Boston: Houghton Mifflin, 1935), pp. 237–38.

11   Damon, *Amy Lowell*, p. 208.

12   Amy Lowell, *Some Imagist Poets* (Boston: Houghton Mifflin, 1915), p. xiv.

13   Damon, *Amy Lowell*, p. 435 n. 2.

14 Herbert Hoover, "Herbert Hoover on Food Conservation," printed at the request of the Women's Municipal League of Boston in *The Christian Register*, June 28, 1917, p. 614.

15 Ibid.

16 Ibid.

17 Amy Lowell, "Modern Poetry: Its Differences, Its Aims, Its Achievements," Damon, *Amy Lowell*, p. 440.

18 Typed poem, Amy Lowell Photographs and Additional Materials, 1758–1970, Houghton Library, Harvard University, Cambridge, MA.

19 Diana Souhami, introduction to Gertrude Stein, *Three Lives & Tender Buttons* (New York: Signet, 2003), p. xiii.

20 Amy Lowell to Donald Evans, June 7, 1918, Damon, *Amy Lowell*, pp. 458–59.

21 Donald Evans to Amy Lowell, June 18, 1918, Damon, *Amy Lowell*, pp. 460–61.

22 Donald Evans, *Ironica* (New York: Nicholas L. Brown, 1919), pp. 43, 50.

23 Jean Gould, *Amy: The World of Amy Lowell and the Imagist Movement* (New York: Dodd, Mead, 1975), p. 138.

24 Ibid., p. 201.

25 Amy Lowell, "Madonna of the Evening Flowers," *Pictures of the Floating World* (New York: Macmillan, 1919), p. 45.

26 Gould, *Amy*, p. 247.

27 Amy Lowell, *Tendencies in Modern American Poetry* (New York: Macmillan, 1917), p. v.

28 Damon, *Amy Lowell*, p. 341.

29 Amy Lowell, "Guns as Keys," *Seven Arts*, August 1917; quoted in Damon, *Amy Lowell*, p. 419.

30 *Reedy's Mirror*, vol. 27 (1918), p. 695, listing advertisement for *Can Grande's Castle* that cites the *New York Sun* review.

31 Amy Lowell, "Can Grande's Castle," *Can Grande's Castle* (New York: The Macmillan Company, 1918), p. 194.

32 Richard Slotkin, *Lost Battalions* (New York: Henry Holt, 2005), pp. 416–17.

26. 1919–1922

1 Henry A. Yeomans, *Abbott Lawrence Lowell* (Cambridge: Harvard University Press, 1948), p. 317.

2 "Lowell Replies to Kuno Meyer," *New York Times*, April 29, 1915.

3 Katharine Bowlker, "Address of the President," *An Account of the Women's Municipal League of Boston* (Boston: T. W. Ripley Co., Southgate Press, 1909), p. 7.

4 Mrs. William Lowell Putnam, "Suffragism and the Sex Problem," in *Anti-Suffrage Essays by Massachusetts Women*, ed. Ernest Bernbaum (Boston: Forum Publications, 1916), p. 140.

5 Muriel Caswall, "President Lowell's Sister Tells Why She's in Politics," *Boston Sunday Post*, undated, scrapbook item, Papers of Mrs. William Lowell Putnam 1887–1935, Schlesinger Library, Radcliffe Institute, Harvard University, Cambridge, MA.

6 *Acts and Resolves of Massachusetts, 1887*, p. 1009, ch. 436, enacted June 16, 1887.

Notes

7   A. Lawrence Lowell, *At War with Academic Traditions in America* (Cambridge: Harvard University Press, 1934), p. 35.

8   "Lowell Emphasizes Post-War Problems in Address," *Stanford Daily,* February 20, 1919.

9   The rest had to make their way in the world with a dark stain on their academic records. When Joe Lumbard, one of the expelled students, applied for admission to Brown, the nature of his expulsion was shared with Otis Randall, the dean at the school. Randall wrote to Greenough, thanking him for the information and informing him that "it goes without saying we will inform Mr. Lumbard that we do not care to consider his application for admission to Brown. . . . How frequently we uncover messes of this sort, and how disagreeable it is to deal with such matters!" See William Wright, *Harvard's Secret Court* (New York: St. Martin's Press, 2005), p. 177.

10 Wright, *Harvard's Secret Court,* p. 144.

11 A. Lawrence Lowell to Sidney L. Gulick, August 28, 1918, Marcia Graham Synnott, *The Half-Opened Door: Discrimination and Admissions at Harvard, Yale, and Princeton* (Westport, CT: Greenwood Press, 1976), p. 35.

12 A. Lawrence Lowell, "The Inaugural Address of the President of Harvard University," *Science,* October 15, 1909, p. 503.

13 Amy Lowell, "Poetry and Polemics," S. Foster Damon, *Amy Lowell: A Chronicle with Extracts from Her Correspondence* (Boston: Houghton Mifflin, 1935), p. 339.

14 "Abbott Lawrence Lowell," Harvard University, Faculty of Arts and Sciences, 1943, Harvard Archives, Pusey Library, Cambridge, MA.

15 A. Lawrence Lowell to William Ernest Hocking, May 19, 1922, Susanne Klingenstein, *Enlarging America: The Cultural Work of Jewish Literary Scholars, 1930–1990* (Syracuse, NY: Syracuse University Press, 1998), p. 43.

16 A. Lawrence Lowell to James Ford Rhodes, January 16, 1923, Yeomans, *Abbott Lawrence Lowell,* pp. 176–77.

17 Amy Lowell, "In Excelsis," *What's O'Clock* (Boston: Houghton Mifflin, 1925), p. 54.

18 Amy Lowell to Grace Parker, May 25, 1918, Damon, *Amy Lowell,* pp. 451–52. Theodore ("Teddy") Amussen later became editor in chief of Henry Holt.

19 Amy Lowell, "Madonna of the Evening Flowers," *Pictures of the Floating World* (New York: Macmillan, 1919), p. 45.

20 Jean Gould, *Amy: The World of Amy Lowell and the Imagist Movement* (New York: Dodd, Mead, 1975), p. 282.

21 "Miss Amy Lowell to Speak October 18," *Harvard Crimson,* October 12, 1920.

22 Malcolm Vaughan to Amy Lowell, undated, Amy Lowell Collection, Houghton Library, Harvard University, Cambridge, MA.

23 Amy Lowell, "Lilacs," *What's O'Clock,* p. 74.

24 Damon, *Amy Lowell,* p. 524.

25 Jean Gould, *Amy,* p. 304.

26 Harriet Monroe, *Poets and Their Art* (New York: Macmillan, 1926), p. 78.

27 Amy Lowell to Florence Ascough, May 27, 1922, Damon, *Amy Lowell,* p. 604.

28 Gould, *Amy,* p. 295.

29 Elizabeth Lowell Putnam, "Prohibition Speech," p. 2, scrapbook item, Papers of Mrs. William Lowell Putnam.

30 Undated newspaper clipping of an article by Murial Caswall, scrapbook item, Papers of Mrs. William Lowell Putnam.

31 Amy Lowell, *Legends* (Boston: Houghton Mifflin, 1921), pp. v–vi.

32 Dan Bessie, *Rare Birds: An American Family* (ebook, Untreed Reads, 2012).

33 Amy Lowell, "Appuldurcombe Park," *Pictures of the Floating World*, p. 201.

34 Amy Lowell to Henry H. Bellaman (of Columbia, South Carolina), April 15, 1922, Carl Rollyson, *Amy Lowell Anew* (Lanham, MD: Rowman & Littlefield, 2013), p. 157.

35 Robert Frost, "Salute to Amy Lowell," *Christian Science Monitor,* May 16, 1925.

36 All quotations taken from Amy Lowell, "Lilacs," *What's O'Clock*, pp. 68–74.

Afterword

1 S. Foster Damon, *Amy Lowell: A Chronicle with Extracts from Her Correspondence* (Boston: Houghton Mifflin, 1935), p. 602.

2 Amy Lowell to Fred Holland Day, February 11, 1922, Damon, *Amy Lowell,* p. 677.

3 Jean Gould, *Amy: The World of Amy Lowell and the Imagist Movement* (New York: Dodd, Mead, 1975), p. 236.

4 Henry A. Yeomans, *Abbott Lawrence Lowell* (Cambridge: Harvard University Press, 1948), p. 51.

5 A. Lawrence Lowell, Inaugural Address of 1909, Harvard University Archives, Pusey Library, Cambridge, MA; printed in *Science,* October 15, 1909, pp. 499–500.

Selected Bibliography

Appleton, Nathan, *Introduction of the Power Loom and Origin of Lowell.* Lowell, MA: B. H. Penhallow, 1858.

Bartlett, Irving H., *Wendell Phillips: Brahmin Radical.* Boston: Beacon Press, 1961.

Blanck, Emily, *Tyrannicide: Forging an American Law of Slavery in Revolutionary South Carolina and Massachusetts.* Athens: University of Georgia Press, 2014.

Boorstin, Daniel, *The Americans: The Colonial Experience.* New York: Vintage Books, 1958.

Bradshaw, Melissa, and Adrienne Munich, editors, *Amy Lowell: American Modern.* New Brunswick, NJ: Rutgers University Press, 2004.

Bremer, Frances J., *John Winthrop: America's Forgotten Founding Father.* New York: Oxford University Press, 2003.

———, *The Puritan Experiment: New England Society from Bradford to Edwards.* Hanover, NH: University Press of New England, 1995.

Brooks, Van Wyck, *The Flowering of New England, 1815-1865.* New York: E. P. Dutton, 1941.

Brown, Charles Raymond, *The Northern Confederacy: According to the Plans of the Essex Junto, 1796-1814.* Princeton, NJ: Princeton University Press, 1915.

Bundy, Carol, *The Nature of Sacrifice: Charles Russell Lowell, Jr., 1834-1864.* New York: Farrar, Straus and Giroux, 2005.

Bunting, Bainbridge, *Harvard Architectural History.* Cambridge, MA: The Belknap Press of Harvard University Press, 1985.

Coffin, Joshua, *The History of Ancient Newbury.* Boston: 1845.

Currier, John J., *Ould Newbury: Historical and Biographical Sketches.* Boston: Damrell and Upham, 1896.

———, *History of Newburyport, Mass.* Newburyport, MA: 1906.

Dalzell, Robert F., Jr., *Enterprising Elite: The Boston Associates and the World They Made.* Cambridge, MA: Harvard University Press, 1987.

Damon, S. Foster, *Amy Lowell.* Boston: Houghton Mifflin, 1935.

Duberman, Martin, *James Russell Lowell.* Boston: Houghton Mifflin, 1966.

Earle, Alice Morse, *Customs and Fashions in Old New England.* New York: Charles Scribner's Sons, 1893.

Emerson, Edward W., *Life and Letters of Charles Russell Lowell.* Boston: Houghton Mifflin, 1907.

Foletta, Marshall, *Coming to Terms with Democracy: Federalist Intellectuals and the Shaping of an American Culture.* Charlottesville: University Press of Virginia, 2001.

Gould, Jean, *Amy: The World of Amy Lowell and the Imagist Movement*. New York: Dodd, Mead, 1975.

Greenslet, Ferris, *The Lowells and Their Seven Worlds*. Boston: Houghton Mifflin, 1946.

Gregory, Horace, *Amy Lowell: Portrait of the Poet in her Time*. New York: Thomas Nelson & Sons, 1958.

Healey, E. Claire and Keith Cushman, *The Letters of D. H. Lawrence & Amy Lowell, 1914-1925*. Santa Barbara, CA: Black Sparrow Press, 1985.

Heymann, C. David, *American Aristocracy: The Lives and Times of James Russell, Amy, and Robert Lowell*. New York: Dodd, Mead, 1980.

Higginson, Thomas Wentworth, *Memorial Biographies*. Cambridge, MA: Sever and Francis, 1866.

Hilen, Andrew, editor, *The Letters of Henry Wadsworth Longfellow, Volume 1*. Cambridge, MA: The Belknap Press of Harvard University Press, 1966.

Howard, Leon, *Victorian Knight-Errant: A Study of the Early Literary Career of James Russell Lowell*. Berkeley: University of California Press, 1952.

Hoyt, William Graves, *Lowell and Mars*. Tucson: The University of Arizona Press, 1996.

Humphrey, Zephine, *Book of New England*. New York: Howell, Soskin, 1947.

Jackson, James, *Honorable Jonathan Jackson, His Wife, and Many Members of His Family: Notes and Reminiscences*. Boston: Alfred Mudge & Son, 1866.

Josselyn, John, *An Account of Two Voyages to New-England, Made During the Years 1638, 1663*. Boston: Riverside Press, 1865.

Lowell, A. Lawrence Lowell, *Biography of Percival Lowell*. New York: Macmillan, 1935.

Lowell, Amy, *Ballads for Sale*. Boston: Houghton Mifflin, 1927.

———, *Can Grande's Castle*. New York: Macmillan, 1918.

———, *A Critical Fable*. Boston: Houghton Mifflin, 1922.

———, *A Dome of Many-Coloured Glass*. Boston: Houghton Mifflin, 1912.

———, *East Wind*, edited by Ada Dwyer Russell. Boston: Houghton Mifflin, 1926.

———, *Legend*. New York: Macmillan, 1921.

———, *Men, Women, and Ghosts*. New York: Macmillan, 1916.

———, *Pictures of the Floating World*. New York: Macmillan, 1919.

———, *Six French Poets*. New York: Macmillan, 1917.

———, *Sword Blades and Poppy Seed*. New York: Macmillan, 1914.

———, *Tendencies in Modern American Poetry*. New York: Macmillan, 1917.

———, *What's O'Clock*, edited by Ada Dwyer Russell. Boston: Houghton Mifflin, 1925.

———, editor, *Some Imagist Poets: An Anthology*. Boston: Houghton Mifflin, 1915.

Lowell, Reverend Charles, *Sermons, Chiefly Practical*. Boston: Ticknor & Fields, 1854.

Lowell, Delmar, *The Historic Genealogy of the Lowells of America*. Rutland, VT: Tuttle, 1899.

Lowell, James Russell, *The Anti-Slavery Papers*. Boston: Houghton Mifflin, 1902.

———, *The Biglow Papers, Second Series*. Boston: James R. Osgood, 1873.

———, *Fireside Travels*. Boston: Houghton Mifflin, 1890.

——, *Literary Essays*. Boston: Houghton Mifflin, 1890.

——, *Lowell's Poetical Works*. Boston: Houghton Mifflin, 1890.

——, *Political Essays*. Boston: Houghton Mifflin, 1904.

Lowell, Percival, *Choson*. Boston: Ticknor & Company, 1885.

——, *Occult Japan*. Boston: Houghton Mifflin, 1895.

——, *Mars*. Boston: Houghton Mifflin, 1895.

——, *Mars, Abode of Life*. New York: Macmillan, 1908.

——, *Mars and its Canals*. New York: Macmillan, 1906.

——, *Memoir of a Trans-Neptunian Planet*. Lynn, MA: Thos. P. Nichols & Son, 1915.

Marsden, George M., *Jonathan Edwards, A Life*. New Haven, CT: Yale University Press, 2003.

Meacham, Jon, *Thomas Jefferson, The Art of Power*. New York: Random House, 2012.

Miller, Richard F., *Harvard's Civil War: A History of the Twentieth Massachusetts Volunteer Infantry*. Hanover, NH: University Press of New England, 2005.

Moore, George H., *Notes on the History of Slavery in Massachusetts*. New York: D. Appleton, 1866.

Morison, Samuel Eliot, *Three Centuries of Harvard 1636–1936*. Cambridge, MA: Harvard University Press, 1946.

Norton, Charles Eliot, editor, *Letters of James Russell Lowell, Vol. I*. New York: Harper and Brothers, 1894.

O'Connor, Thomas H., *Lords of the Loom: The Cotton Whigs and the Coming of the Civil War*. New York: Charles Scribner's Sons, 1968.

Patton, Robert H., *Patriot Pirates*. New York: Random House, 2008.

Petrie, Donald, *The Prize Game*. Annapolis, MD: Naval Institute Press, 1999.

Puleo, Stephen, *A City So Grand: The Rise of an American Metropolis, Boston 1850–1900*. Boston: Beacon Press, 2010.

Putnam, James Jackson, *A Memoir of Dr. James Jackson*. Boston: Houghton Mifflin, 1905.

Putnam, William Lowell, *The Explorers of Mars Hill*. West Kennebunk, ME: Phoenix Publishing (for Lowell Observatory), 1994.

——, *Percival Lowell's Big Red Car*. Jefferson, NC: McFarland & Company, 2002.

——, *A Yankee Image*. West Kennebunk, ME: Phoenix Publishing (for Lowell Observatory), 1991.

Rollyson, Carl, *Amy Lowell Among Her Contemporaries*. New York: ASJA Press, 2009.

Rosenberg, Chaim M., *The Life and Times of Francis Cabot Lowell*. Lanham, MD: Rowman & Littlefield, 2011.

Scudder, Horace, *James Russell Lowell*. Boston: Houghton Mifflin, 1901.

Stark, John H., *The Loyalists of Massachusetts and the Other Side of the American Revolution*. Boston: J. H. Stark, 1907.

Stout, Harry S., *The New England Soul: Preaching and Religious Culture in Colonial New England*. New York: Oxford University Press, 1986.

Strauss, David, *Percival Lowell*. Cambridge, MA: Harvard University Press, 2001.

Tagney, Ronald N., *The World Turned Upside Down*. West Newbury, MA: Essex County History, 1989.

Vernon, Hope Jillson, *The Poems of Maria Lowell*. Providence, RI: Brown University, 1936.

Ware, Caroline, *The Early New England Cotton Manufacture*: Boston: Houghton Mifflin, 1931.

Weeden, William B., *Economic and Social History of New England 1620–1789*. Gansevoort, NY: Corner House Publishers, 1978.

Weidensaul, Scott, *The First Frontier*. Boston: Houghton Mifflin Harcourt, 2012.

Winthrop, Robert C., *Life and Letters of John Winthrop, Vol. 2*. Boston: Little, Brown, 1869.

Wright, Louis B., *The Cultural Life of the American Colonies*. 1957; reprint New York: Dover, 2002.

Wright, William, *Harvard's Secret Court*. New York: St. Martin's Press, 2005.

Yeomans, Henry A., *Abbott Lawrence Lowell*. Cambridge, MA: Harvard University Press 1948.

Index

Roundheads, 34–35
Royalists (English), 34
Royal Navy, 124–25, 131
Royal Province of Massachusetts Bay, 38
rum, 41, 67, 80
running of goods, illegal, 72
Russel, Cabot Jackson, 227–29, 233
Russel, William, 228
Russell, Ada Dwyer, 277–83, 295, 301, 306–9, 311, 316–17, 319–22, 327
  daughter and family of, 316–17
  fulfills Amy Lowell's last wishes, 1–2, 328
  theater career, 277–78
Russell, Francis (brother of Warren Dutton Russell), 226, 233
Russell, Thomas, 98
Russell, Warren Dutton (grandson of Elizabeth Cutts Lowell), 226, 233
rustication, 169
Rymkus, B., 298

Salem, Massachusetts, 87
Sanborn, Frank, 210, 227, 232
Sandburg, Carl, 300, 321
Sarter, Caesar, 76
sassafras, 13
Sassoon, Siegfried, 316, 319
Savage, James, 233
Schiaparelli, Giovanni Virginio, 250–51, 252
Schmitt, George, 220, 221
science, 48
Scotland, 15
Scott, Dred, 208
scrutoire (writing desk), 16
sea trade
  British, 70
  hazards of, 135
  New England prospering with, 43–44
  profit from, 99–100, 104
sea voyaging, difficulty of, in the 1600s, 16–22

secession from the Union
  contemplated by New England, 131, 136, 165
  by southern states, 211
Second Massachusetts Cavalry, 231
Second Massachusetts Volunteer Infantry, 219
Sevenels estate, 1, 237, 242–44, 256, 264, 280–81, 303, 305–6, 327, 328
  dogs of, 305
Seven Years' War, 58–61, 66
Sewall, Samuel, 44
sex and marriage, Puritans' views on, 21
Shaller, Elizabeth (1675–1761), ix
Shattuck, Goodman, 57
Shaw, Francis "Frank," 214, 227, 228, 230
Shaw, Josephine "Effie," 228, 230, 231
Shaw, Robert, 227, 228–30, 233
Shaw, Sarah, 197, 214, 227
Shepherd, Arthur, 285
shipbuilding, 71
Silliman, Benjamin, 155
Simpkins, Captain, 229
Sims, Thomas, 193
Sixth Massachusetts Volunteer Infantry, 216–18
Slatter, Hope H., 187
slave hunters, 188–90, 193
slavery
  abolished by Emancipation Proclamation, 227
  abolished in Massachusetts, 93
  Dred Scott decision, 208
  expansion of, 153, 188–89, 203
  Lowell family's ambivalent relation to, 162
  movement against, 73–76, 151, 172
  New England secession contemplated, in response to, 165–66
slaves, in New England, 44, 76
slave states, 189
slave traders, 187
Slipher, Earl C., 266n